Shadowline™ im ®

www.ShadowlineOnline.com

Edited and Book Designed by

Jim Valentino
Publisher

Cover Illustration by

Mike and Laura Allred
from a sketch by Jim Valentino

Cover Design and Graphics by

Tim Daniel

Bios proofread by
Kristen K. Simon

Special thanks to
Marc Lombardi

for image:

Eric Stephenson
publisher

Todd Martinez
sales & licsnsing

Sarah deLaine
pr & marketing

Branwyn Bigglestone
accounts manager

Emily Miller
adminstrative assistant

Jamie Parreno
marketing assistant

Kevin Yuen
digital rights

Tyler Shainline
production manager

Drew Gill
art director

Jonathan Chan
senior production artist

Monica Garcia
Vincent Kukua
Jana Cook
production artists

image is:

Robert Kirkman
chief operating officer

Erik Larsen
chief financial officer

Todd McFarlane
president

Marc Silvestri
chief executive officer

Jim Valentino
vice-president

www.imagecomics.com

FRACTURED FABLES
ISBN: 978-1-60706-496-1

AGES 12+

Published by Image Comics, Inc. Office of publication: 2134 Allston Way, Second Floor, Berkeley, California 94704.
Copyright © 2012 JIM VALENTINO. All rights reserved. FRACTURED FABLES™ is a Trademark of JIM
VALENTINO. All stories and character likenesses are ™ and © their respective creators. All rights reserved, used by
permission. Image Comics® and its logos are registered Trademarks of Image Comics, Inc. Shadowline and its logos are ™ and
© 2012 Jim Valentino. No part of this publication may be reproduced or transmitted, in any form or by any means (except for
short excerpts for review purposes) without the express written permission of Mr. Valentino or copyright holders. All names,
characters, events and locales in this publication are entirely fictional. Any resemblance to actual persons (living or dead),
events or places, without satiric intent, is coincidental. International rights representative: Christine Meyer
(christine@floystudio.com).   Printed in SOUTH KOREA
Second printing January 2012

Table of Contents

The Silly Statue (Alice In Wonderland)   9
Written and Lettered by Dara Naraghi
Illustrated by Grant Bond

Fee Fi Fo Fum   12
Written and Illustrated by Ben Templesmith

Little Red Riding Hood   16
Written by Bryan Talbot
Illustrated by Camilla d'Errico
Colored by Edison Yan Lettered by Ed Brisson

The Toad Prince (The Frog Prince)   21
Written and Illustrated by Terry Moore

Mary Had A Little Spam   24
Written by Kristen K. Simon,
Penciled by Jim Valentino
Inked by Aaron Valentino Colored by Paul John Little

Row, Row, Row   26
Written and Illustrated by Shannon Wheeler

The Secret Princess Society   30
Written by Marie Cruz,
Illustrated by Whilce Portacio

Trouble At the North Pole (Santa Claus) 38
Written and Illustrated by Shane White

Rumplestiltskin 41
Written and Illustrated by Doug TenNapel

There Was An Old Giant… 49
Written and Illustrated by Bill Alger

On Top of Spaghetti 55
Written and Illustrated by Bill Morrison
Colored and Lettered by Serban Cristescu

Starlight, Starbright 58
Written by Phil Hester
Penciled by Mike Laughead
Inked, Colored and Lettered by Keaton Kohl

Little Miss Muffet 60
Written and Illustrated by Royden Lepp

The House That Jack Built 67
Written by Neil Kleid
Illustrated by Fernando Pinto

The Fox and the Cat 73
Written by Nikki Dy-Liacco
Illustrated by May Ann Licudine

Pippi Van Wrinkles 81
Written by Len Strazewski
Ilustrated by Paul Fricke
Colored by Paul and Mary Fricke

The Real Princess (The Princess and the Pea) 88
Written and lettered by Alexander Grecian
Illustrated by Christian Ward

Pie Eating Contest (Tortoise and the Hare) 93
Written and Lettered by Joshua Williamson
Illustrated by Vicente Navarrete

The Strange Feast 98
Written and Illustrated by Jill Thompson

Three Blind Mice 100
Written and Illustrated by Scott Morse

The People vs. Hansel and Gretel 106
Written and Illustrated by Jeremy R. Scott

Snoring Beauty 109
Written by Kristen K. Simon
Illustrated by Seth Damoose
Lettered by Ed Dukeshire Colored by Paul John Little

The Little Mermaid 113
Written by Peter David
Illustrated by Juan Ferreyra Lettered by Johnny Lowe

The Ugly Duckling 121
Written and Illustrated by Brian Haberlin

Spanking Robots (Pinocchio) 125
Written by Laini Taylor
Illustrated by Jim Di Bartolo

Little Matchstick Girl 129
Written and Illustrated by Joel Valentino

Raponsel 135
Written by Derek McCulloch
Illustrated by Anthony Peruzzo

Troll Bridge (Three Billy Goats Gruff) 141
Written and Illustrated by Larry Marder

Hey Diddle, Diddle 145
Written and Illustrated by Ted McKeever

Cinderella 148
Written by Nick Spencer
Illustrated by Rodin Esquejo Lettered by Thomas Mauer

Illustration 155
By Michael Allred, Colors by Laura Allred

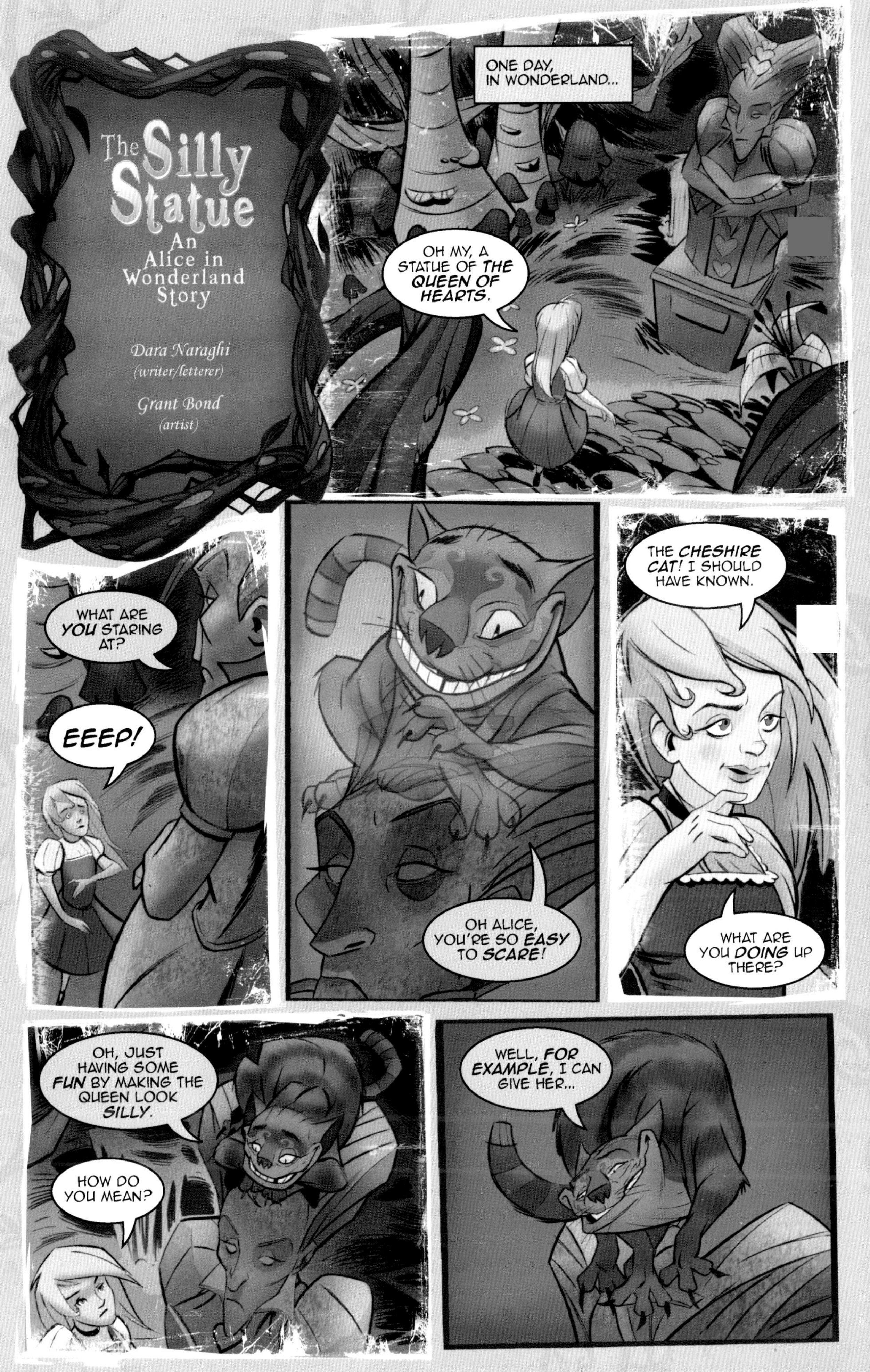
The Silly Statue
An Alice in Wonderland Story
Dara Naraghi
(writer/letterer)
Grant Bond
(artist)
ONE DAY, IN WONDERLAND...
OH MY, A STATUE OF THE QUEEN OF HEARTS.
WHAT ARE YOU STARING AT?
EEEP!
OH ALICE, YOU'RE SO EASY TO SCARE!
THE CHESHIRE CAT! I SHOULD HAVE KNOWN.
WHAT ARE YOU DOING UP THERE?
OH, JUST HAVING SOME FUN BY MAKING THE QUEEN LOOK SILLY.
HOW DO YOU MEAN?
WELL, FOR EXAMPLE, I CAN GIVE HER...

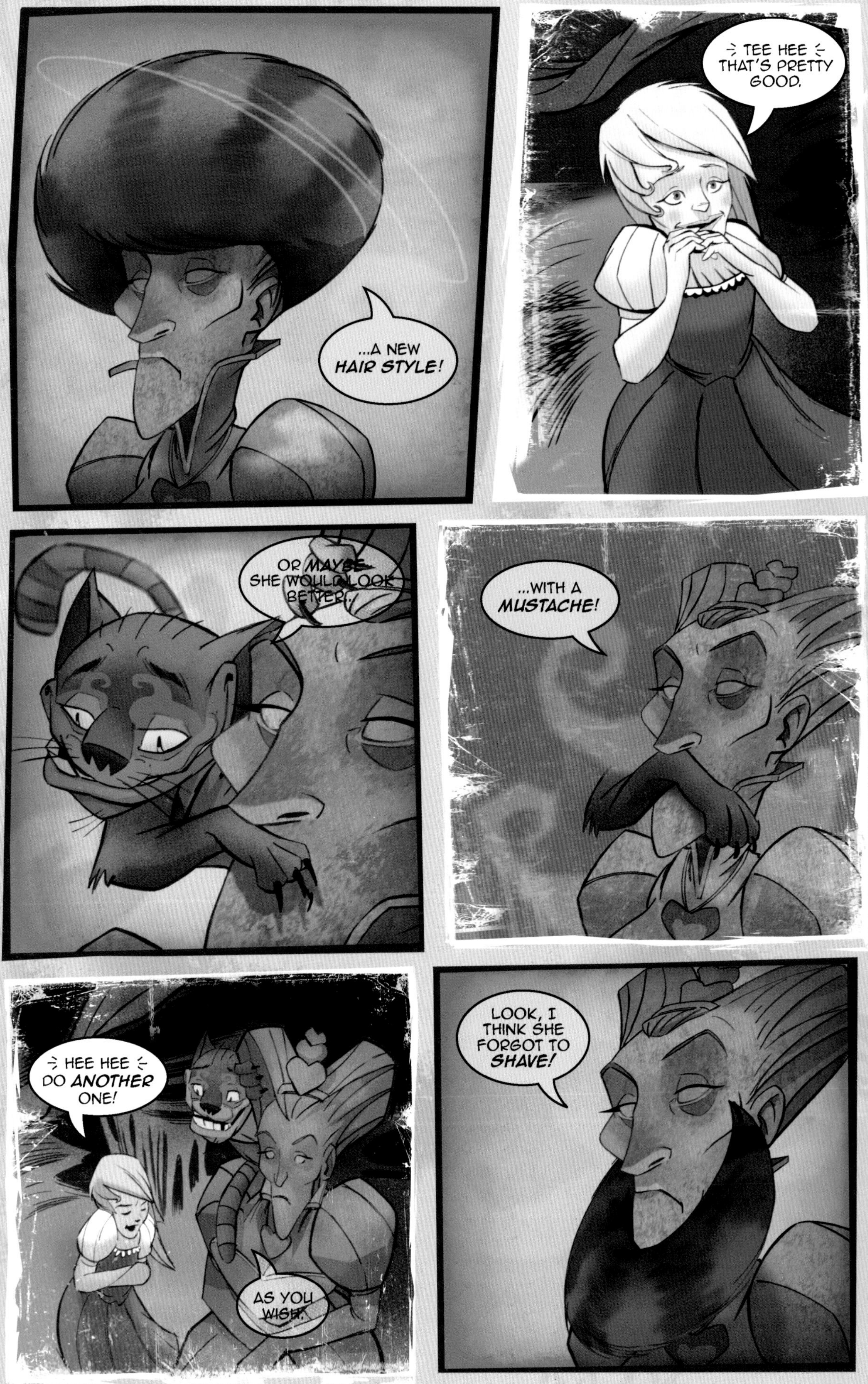
...A NEW HAIR STYLE!
TEE HEE THAT'S PRETTY GOOD.
OR MAYBE SHE WOULD LOOK BETTER...
...WITH A MUSTACHE!
HEE HEE DO ANOTHER ONE!
AS YOU WISH.
LOOK, I THINK SHE FORGOT TO SHAVE!

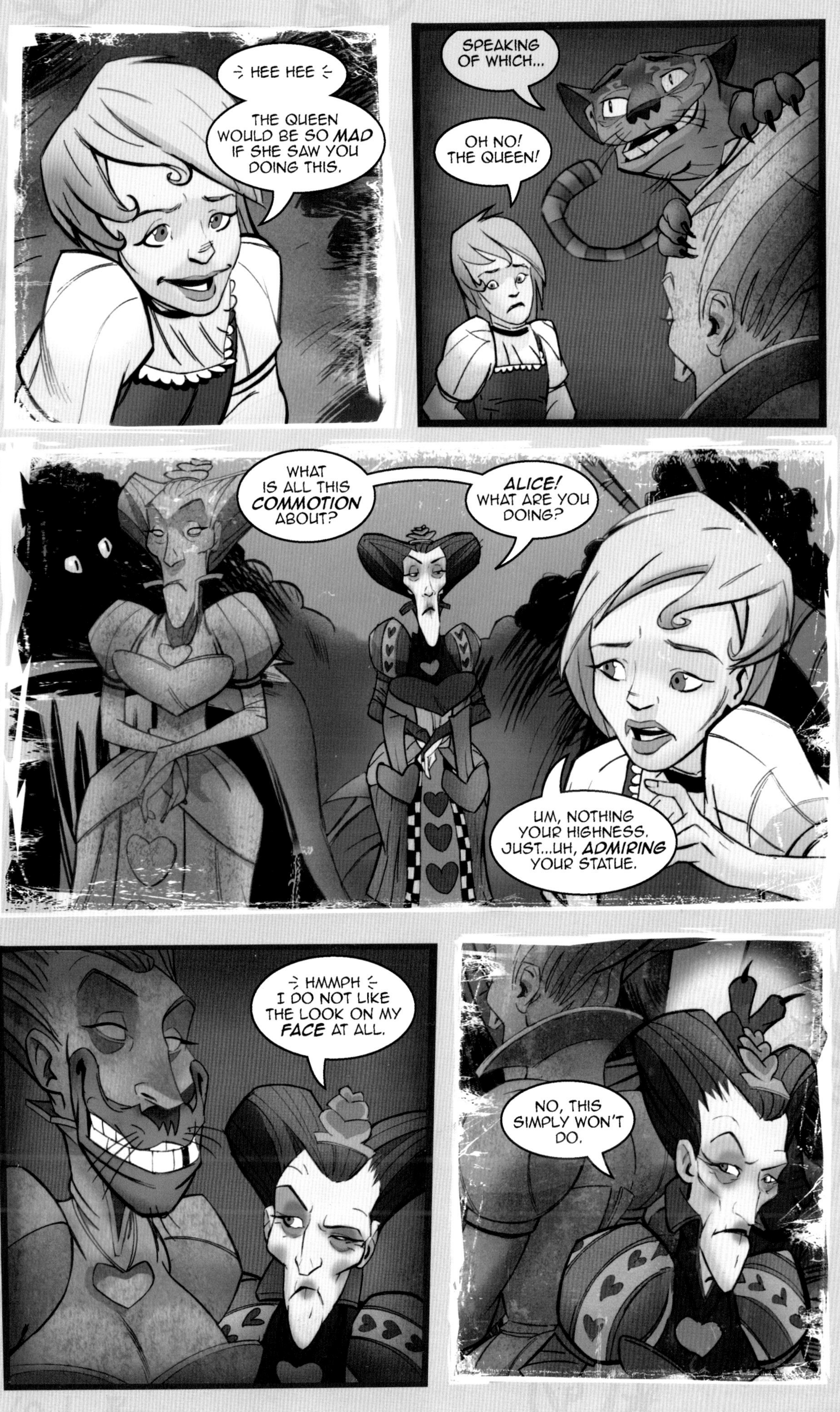

HEE HEE
THE QUEEN WOULD BE SO MAD IF SHE SAW YOU DOING THIS.
SPEAKING OF WHICH...
OH NO! THE QUEEN!
WHAT IS ALL THIS COMMOTION ABOUT?
ALICE! WHAT ARE YOU DOING?
UM, NOTHING YOUR HIGHNESS. JUST...UH, ADMIRING YOUR STATUE.
HMMPH I DO NOT LIKE THE LOOK ON MY FACE AT ALL.
NO, THIS SIMPLY WON'T DO.

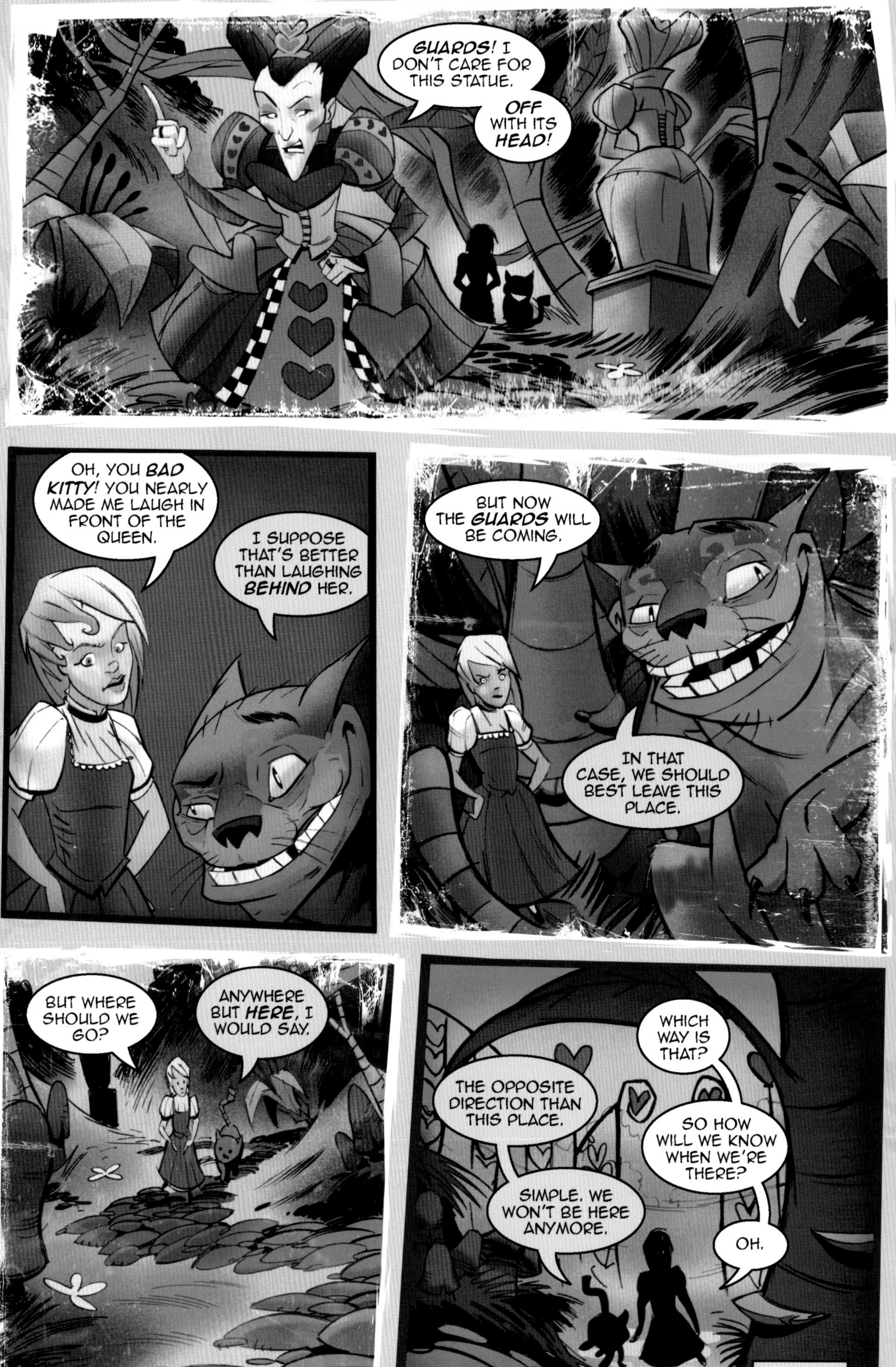
GUARDS! I DON'T CARE FOR THIS STATUE.
OFF WITH ITS HEAD!
OH, YOU BAD KITTY! YOU NEARLY MADE ME LAUGH IN FRONT OF THE QUEEN.
I SUPPOSE THAT'S BETTER THAN LAUGHING BEHIND HER.
BUT NOW THE GUARDS WILL BE COMING.
IN THAT CASE, WE SHOULD BEST LEAVE THIS PLACE.
BUT WHERE SHOULD WE GO?
ANYWHERE BUT HERE, I WOULD SAY.
WHICH WAY IS THAT?
THE OPPOSITE DIRECTION THAN THIS PLACE.
SO HOW WILL WE KNOW WHEN WE'RE THERE?
SIMPLE. WE WON'T BE HERE ANYMORE.
OH.
THE END.

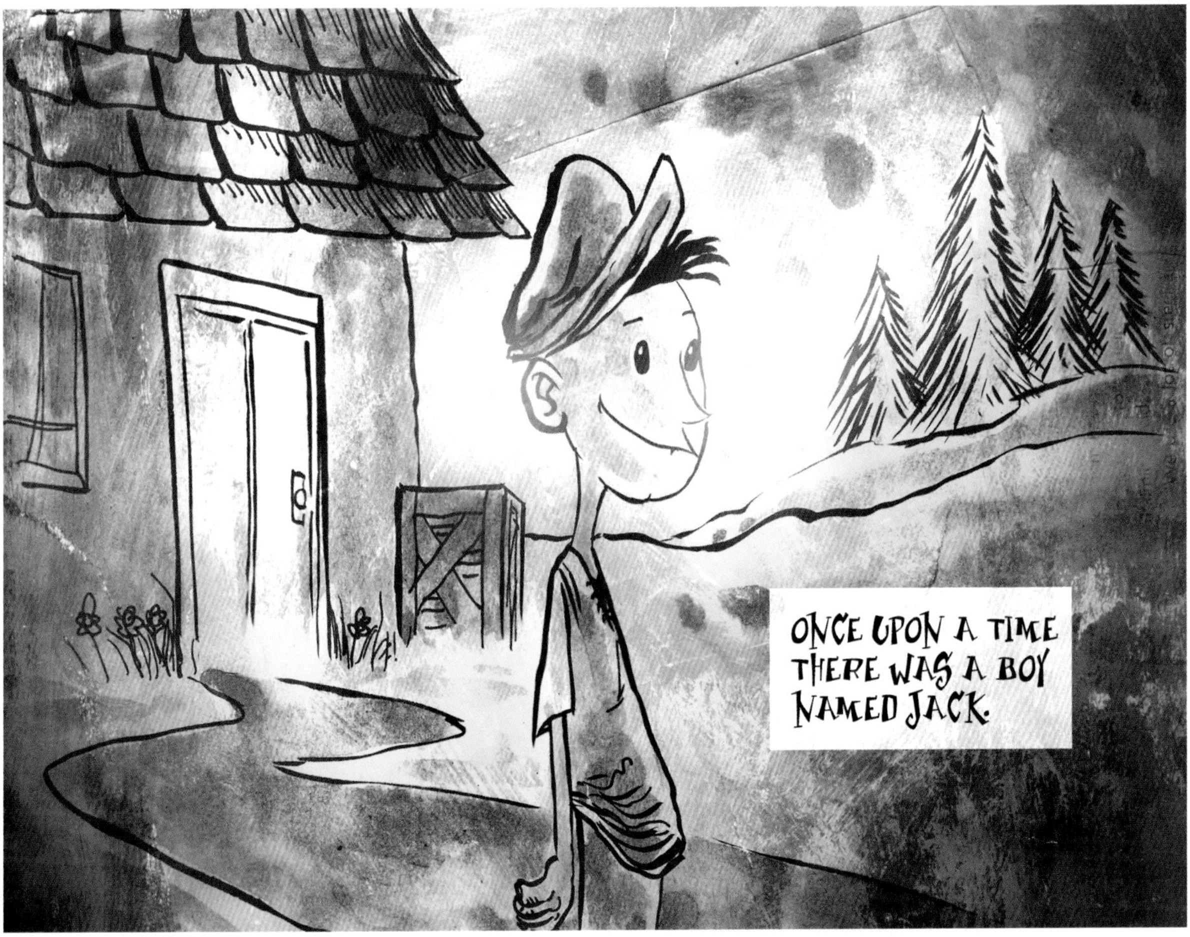
ONCE UPON A TIME THERE WAS A BOY NAMED JACK.

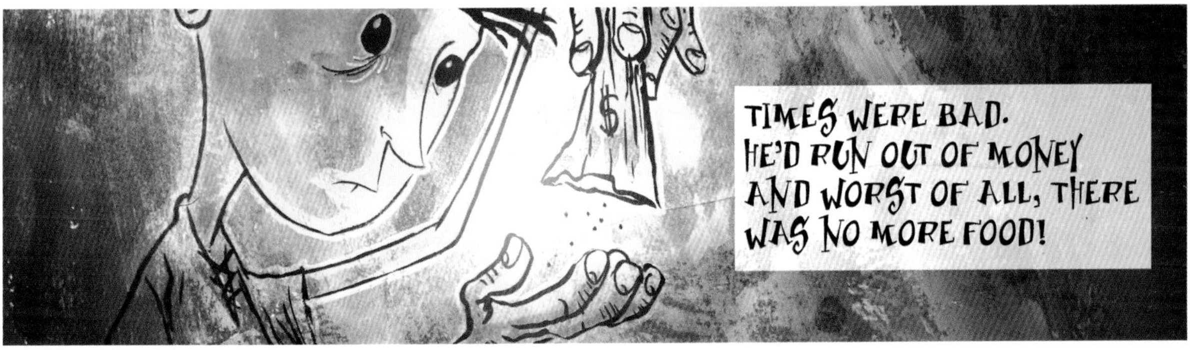
TIMES WERE BAD. HE'D RUN OUT OF MONEY AND WORST OF ALL, THERE WAS NO MORE FOOD!

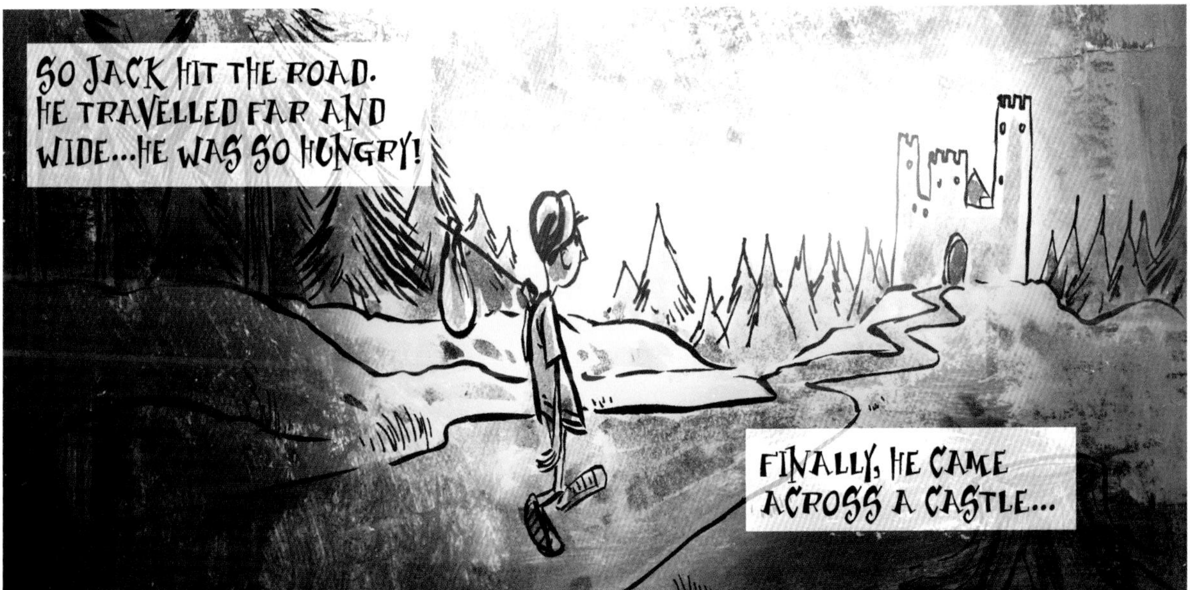
SO JACK HIT THE ROAD. HE TRAVELLED FAR AND WIDE...HE WAS SO HUNGRY!
FINALLY, HE CAME ACROSS A CASTLE...

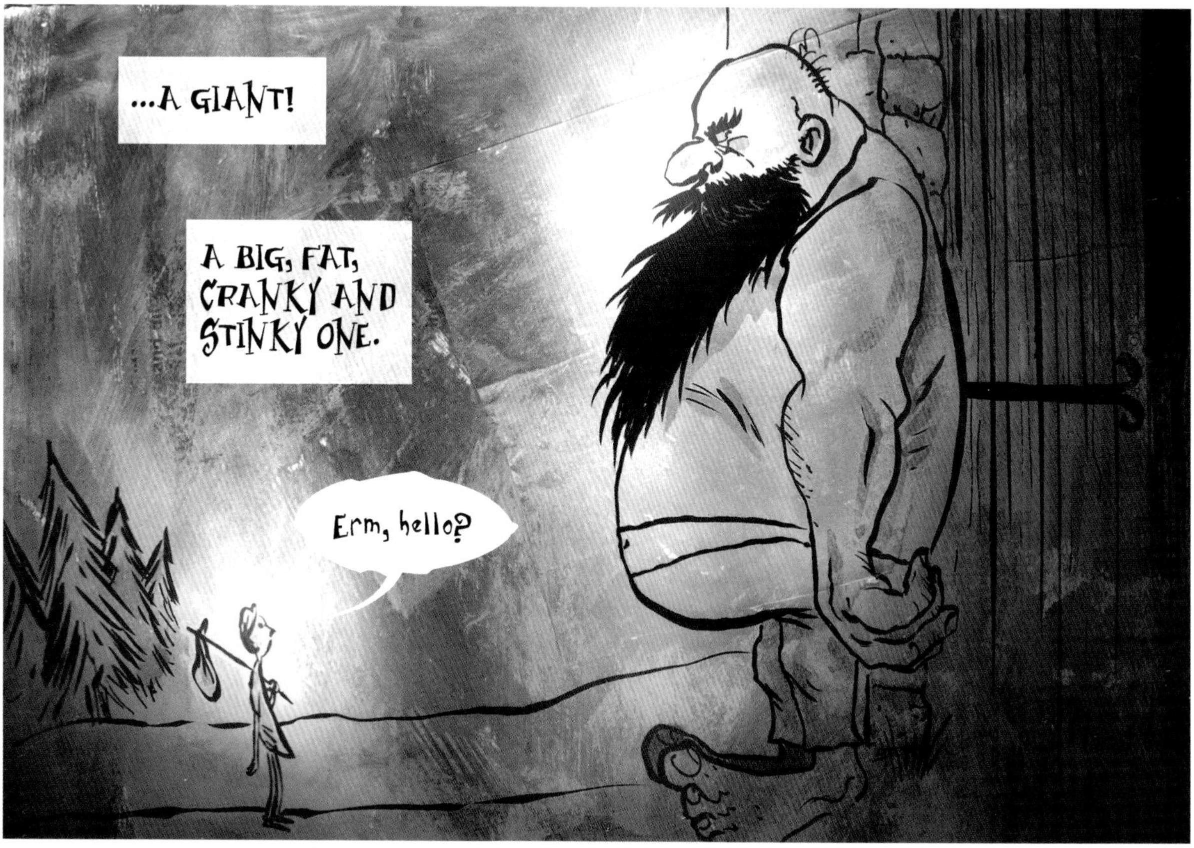
...A GIANT!
A BIG, FAT, CRANKY AND STINKY ONE.
Erm, hello?

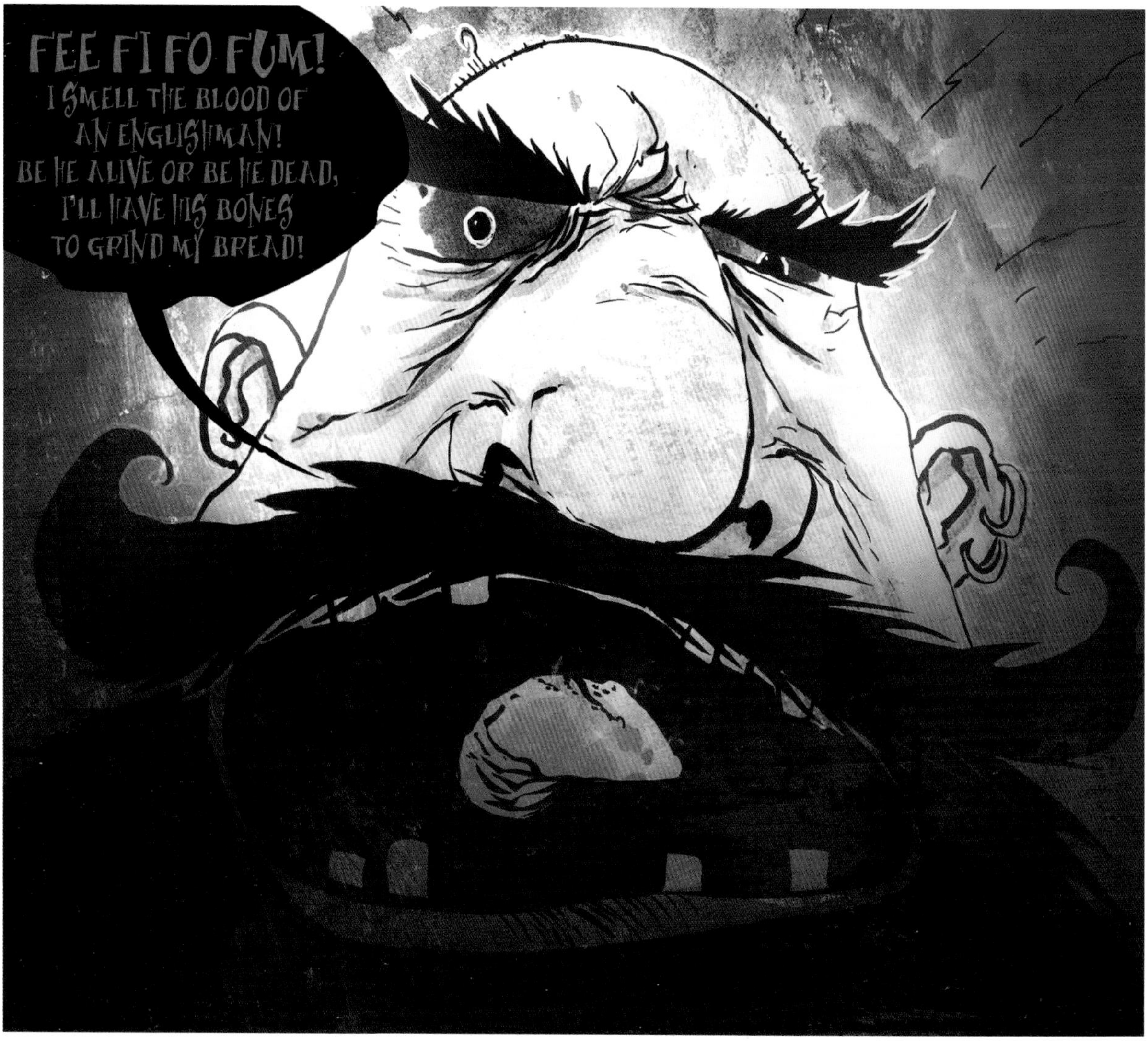
FEE FI FO FUM!
I SMELL THE BLOOD OF AN ENGLISHMAN!
BE HE ALIVE OR BE HE DEAD,
I'LL HAVE HIS BONES TO GRIND MY BREAD!

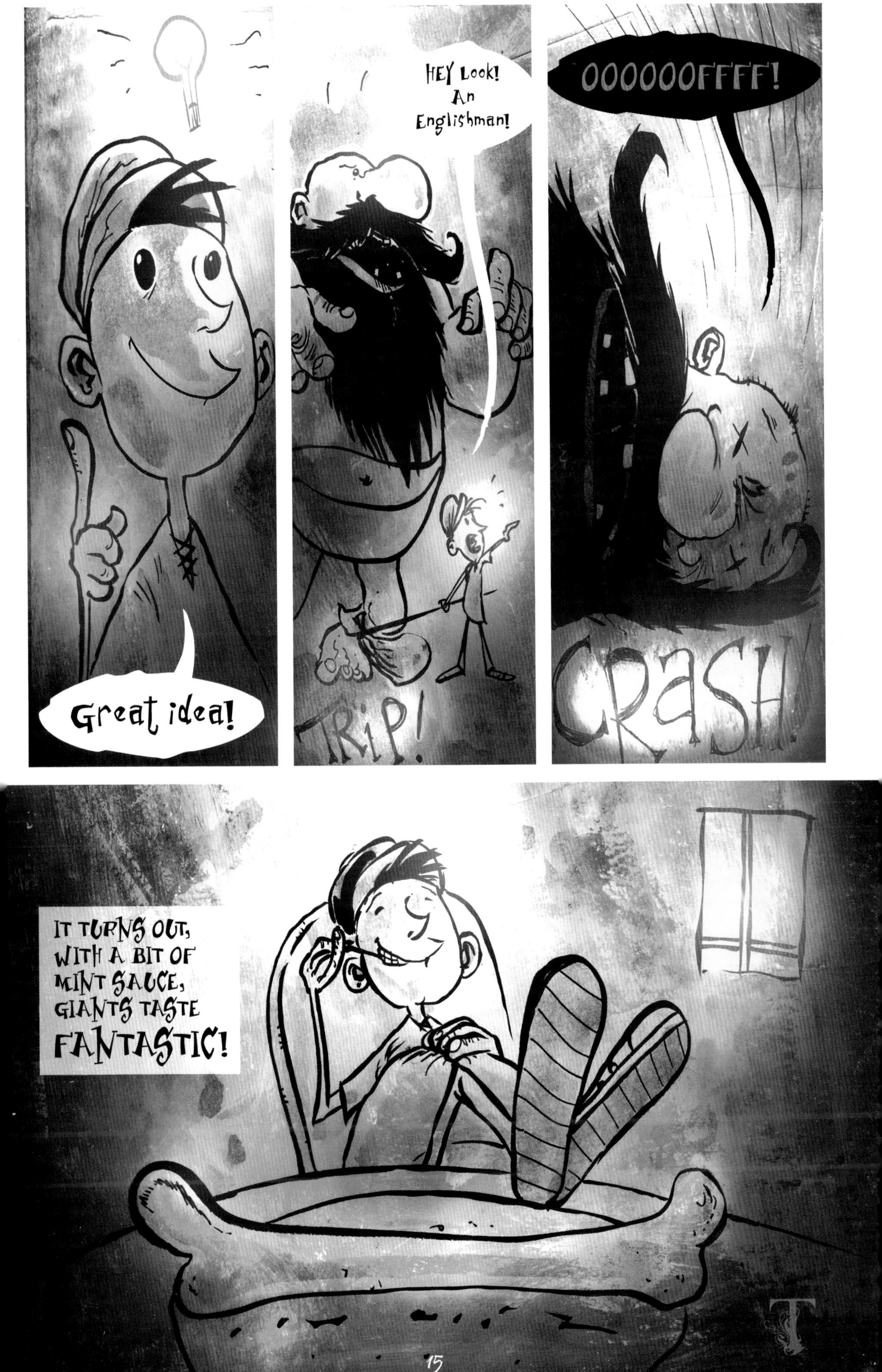
Great idea!
HEY Look! An Englishman!
TRIP!
OOOOOOFFFF!
CRASH!
IT TURNS OUT, WITH A BIT OF MINT SAUCE, GIANTS TASTE FANTASTIC!

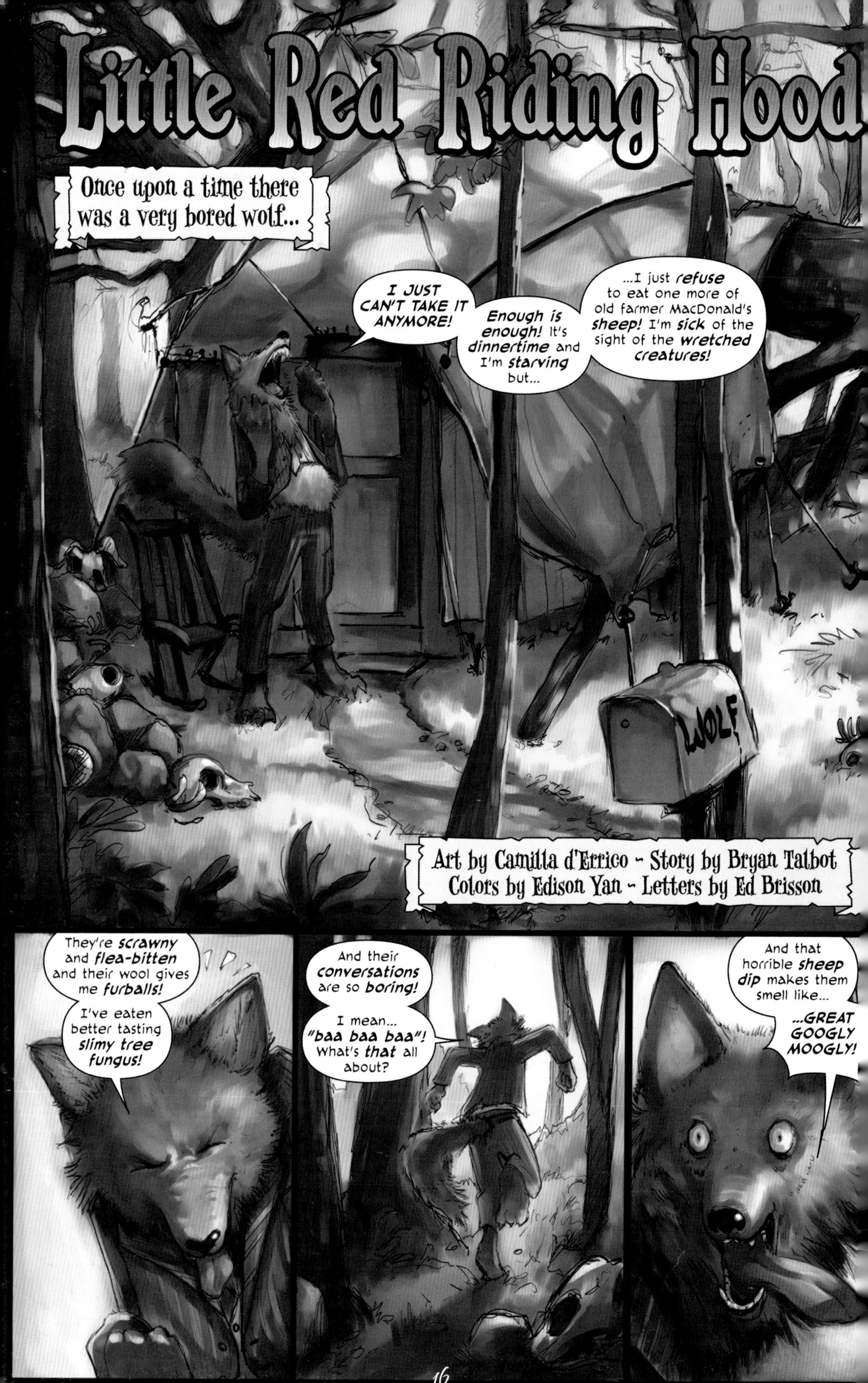
Little Red Riding Hood
Once upon a time there was a very bored wolf...
I JUST CAN'T TAKE IT ANYMORE!
Enough is enough! It's dinnertime and I'm starving but...
...I just refuse to eat one more of old farmer MacDonald's sheep! I'm sick of the sight of the wretched creatures!
WOLF
Art by Camilla d'Errico - Story by Bryan Talbot
Colors by Edison Yan - Letters by Ed Brisson
They're scrawny and flea-bitten and their wool gives me furballs!
I've eaten better tasting slimy tree fungus!
And their conversations are so boring!
I mean... "baa baa baa"! What's that all about?
And that horrible sheep dip makes them smell like...
...GREAT GOOGLY MOOGLY!

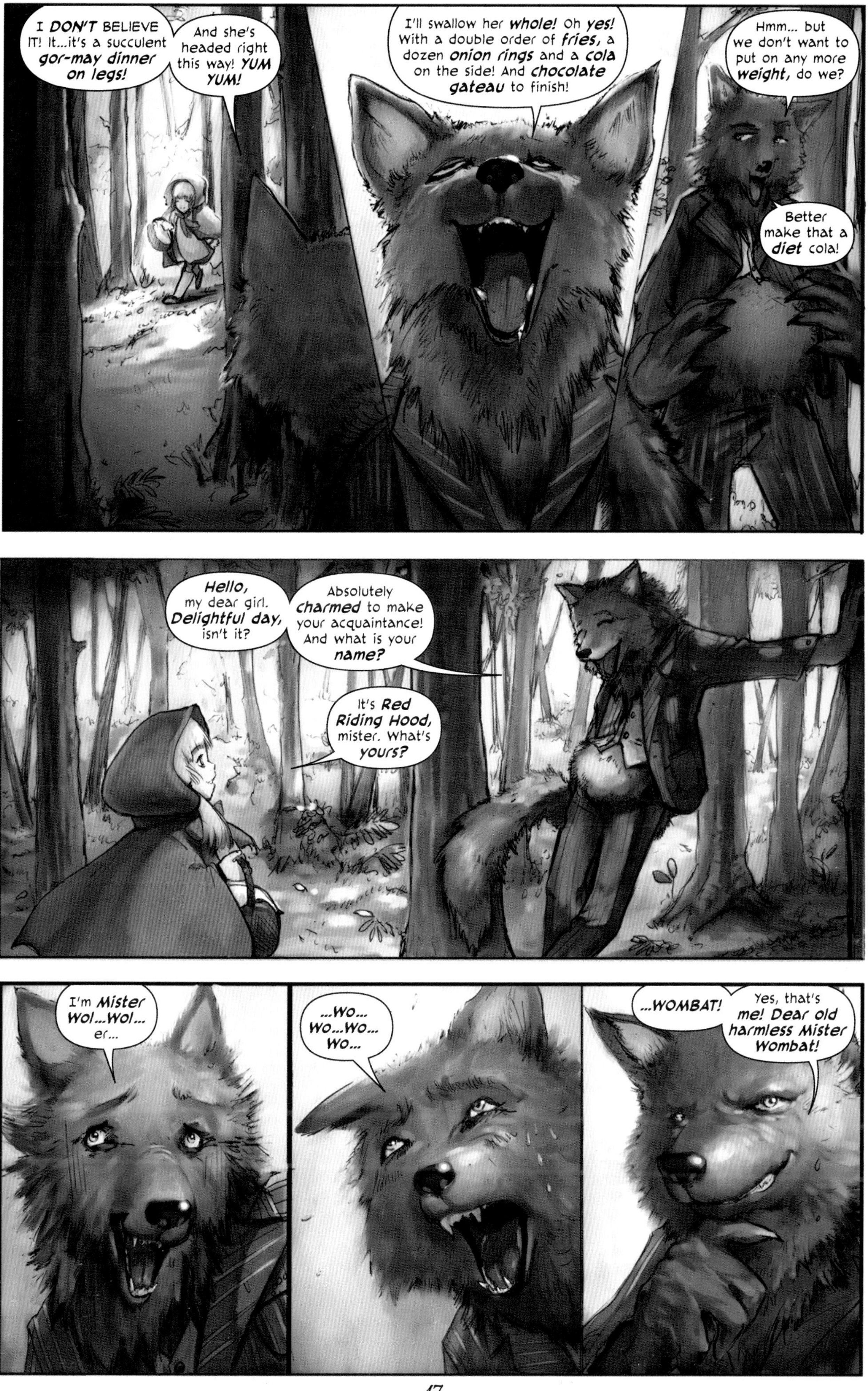
I DON'T BELIEVE IT! It...it's a succulent gor-may dinner on legs!
And she's headed right this way! YUM YUM!
I'll swallow her whole! Oh yes! With a double order of fries, a dozen onion rings and a cola on the side! And chocolate gateau to finish!
Hmm... but we don't want to put on any more weight, do we?
Better make that a diet cola!
Hello, my dear girl. Delightful day, isn't it?
Absolutely charmed to make your acquaintance! And what is your name?
It's Red Riding Hood, mister. What's yours?
I'm Mister Wol...Wol... er...
...Wo... Wo...Wo... Wo...
...WOMBAT!
Yes, that's me! Dear old harmless Mister Wombat!

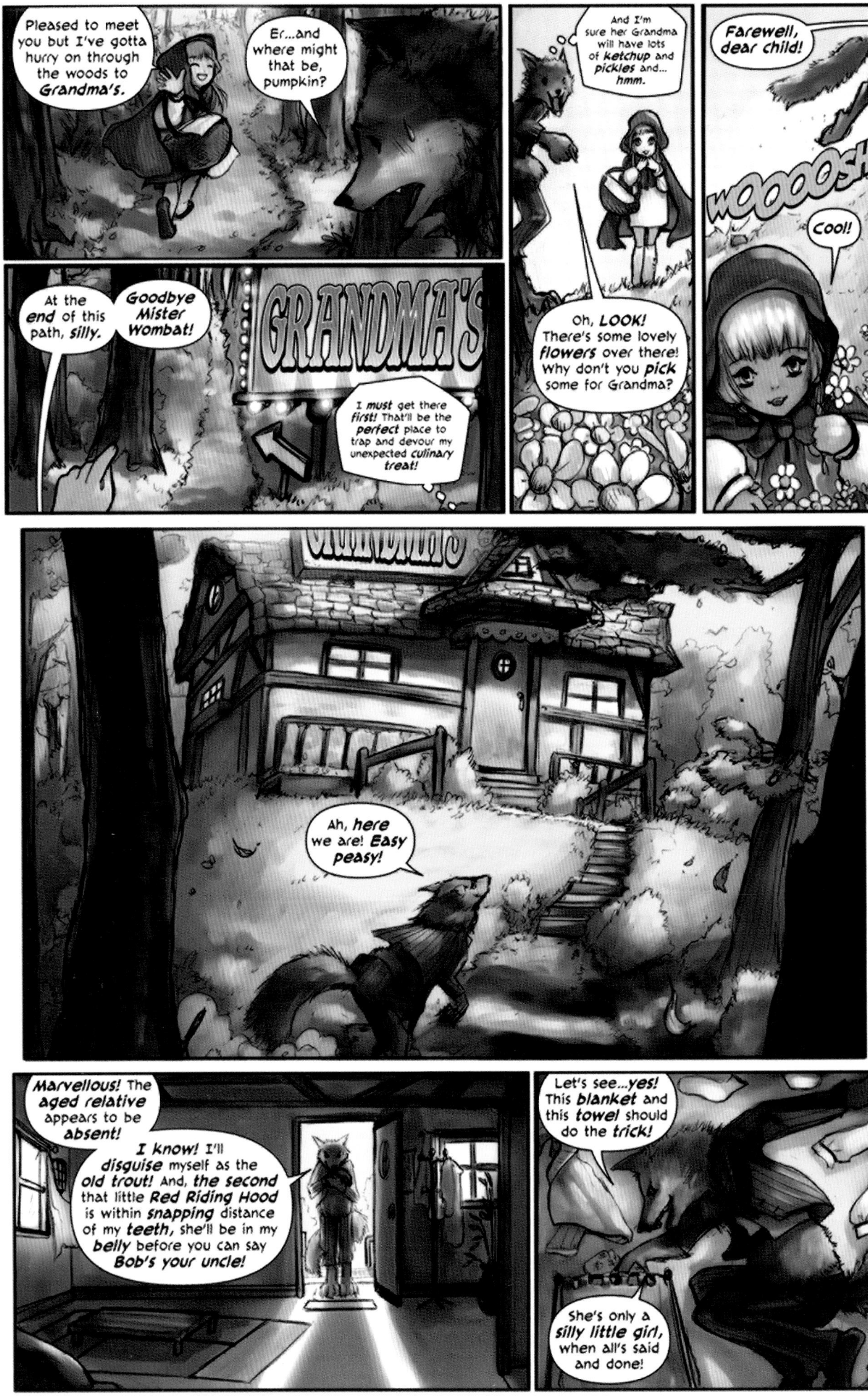
Pleased to meet you but I've gotta hurry on through the woods to Grandma's.
Er...and where might that be, pumpkin?
And I'm sure her Grandma will have lots of ketchup and pickles and... hmm.
Farewell, dear child!
WOOOOSH
Cool!
At the end of this path, silly.
Goodbye Mister Wombat!
GRANDMA'S
I must get there first! That'll be the perfect place to trap and devour my unexpected culinary treat!
Oh, LOOK! There's some lovely flowers over there! Why don't you pick some for Grandma?
Ah, here we are! Easy peasy!
Marvellous! The aged relative appears to be absent!
I know! I'll disguise myself as the old trout! And, the second that little Red Riding Hood is within snapping distance of my teeth, she'll be in my belly before you can say Bob's your uncle!
Let's see...yes! This blanket and this towel should do the trick!
She's only a silly little girl, when all's said and done!

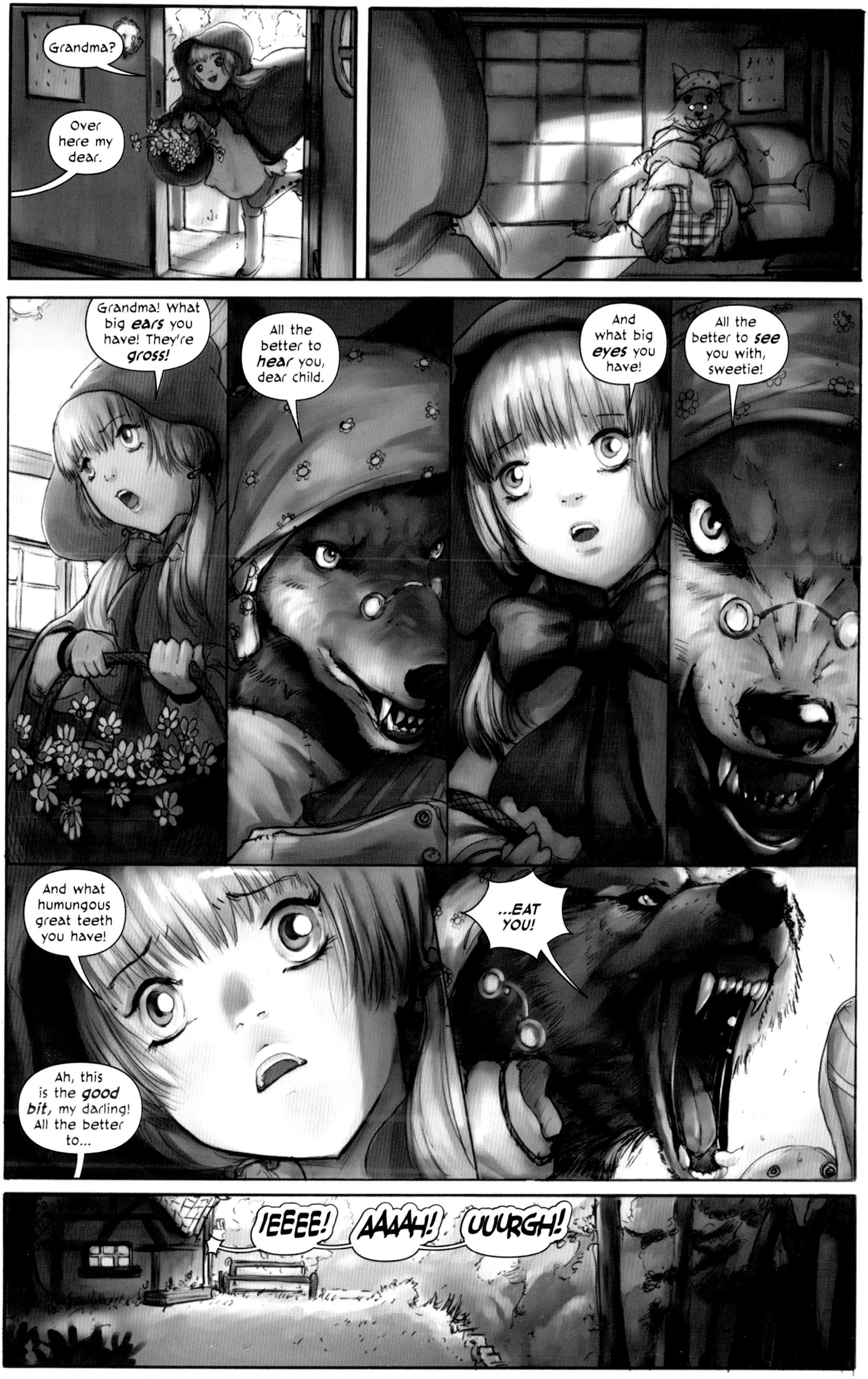
Grandma?
Over here my dear.
Grandma! What big ears you have! They're gross!
All the better to hear you, dear child.
And what big eyes you have!
All the better to see you with, sweetie!
And what humungous great teeth you have!
Ah, this is the good bit, my darling! All the better to...
...EAT YOU!
IEEEE! AAAAH! UUURGH!

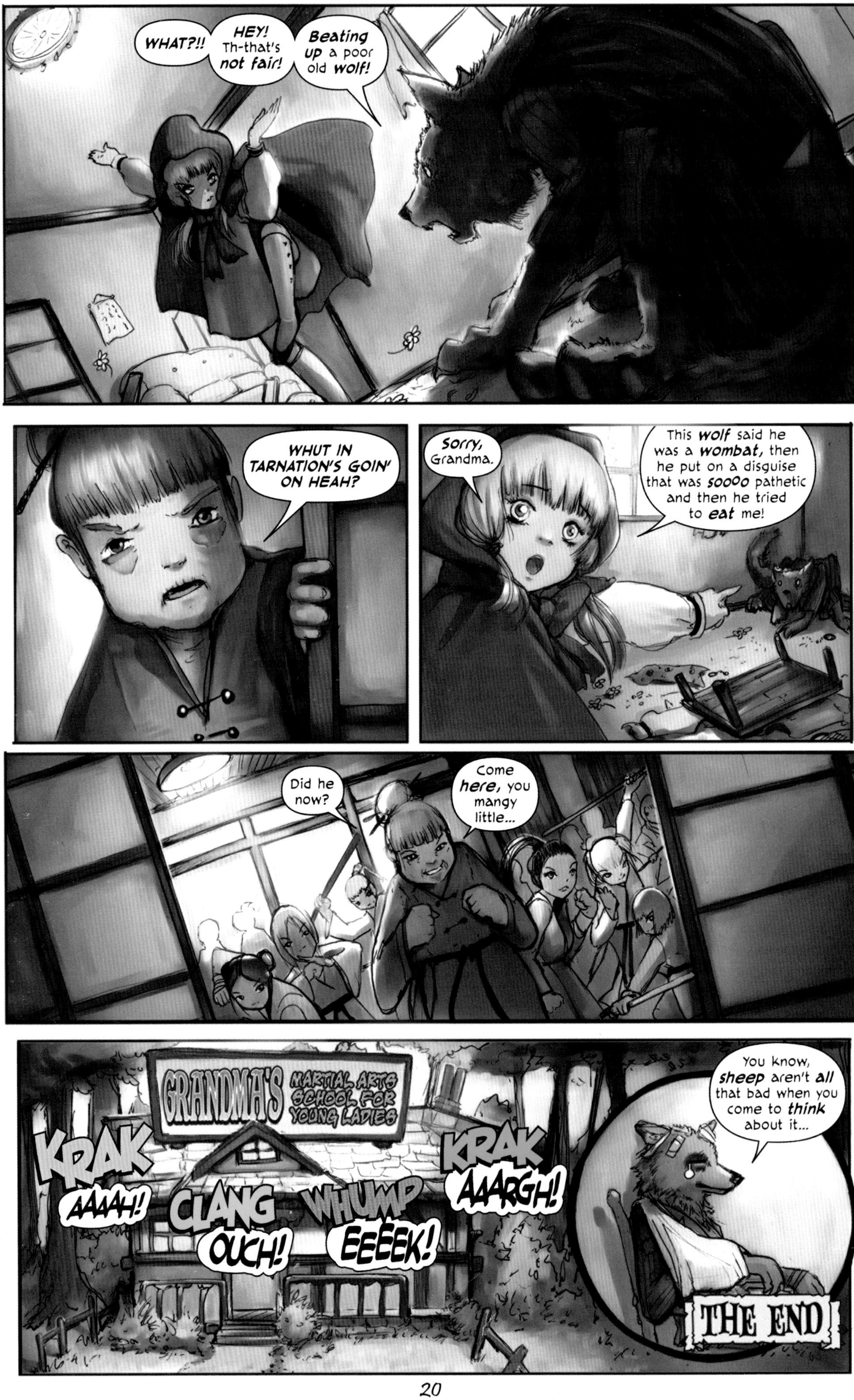
WHAT?!!
HEY! Th-that's not fair!
Beating up a poor old wolf!
WHUT IN TARNATION'S GOIN' ON HEAH?
Sorry, Grandma.
This wolf said he was a wombat, then he put on a disguise that was soooo pathetic and then he tried to eat me!
Did he now?
Come here, you mangy little...
GRANDMA'S MARTIAL ARTS SCHOOL FOR YOUNG LADIES
KRAK
AAAAH!
CLANG
OUCH!
WHUMP
EEEEK!
KRAK
AAARGH!
You know, sheep aren't all that bad when you come to think about it...
THE END

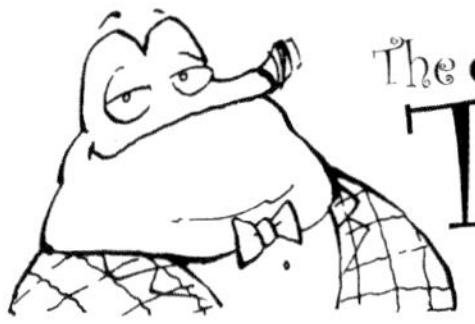

The TOAD PRINCE

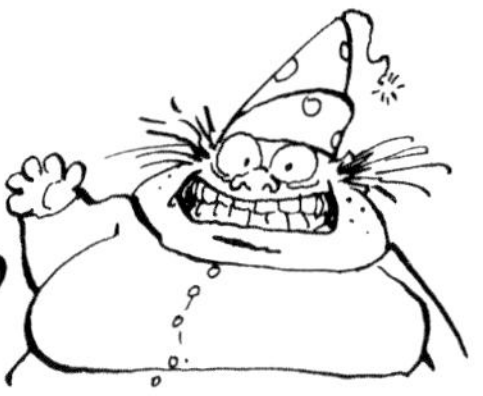

by Terry Moore

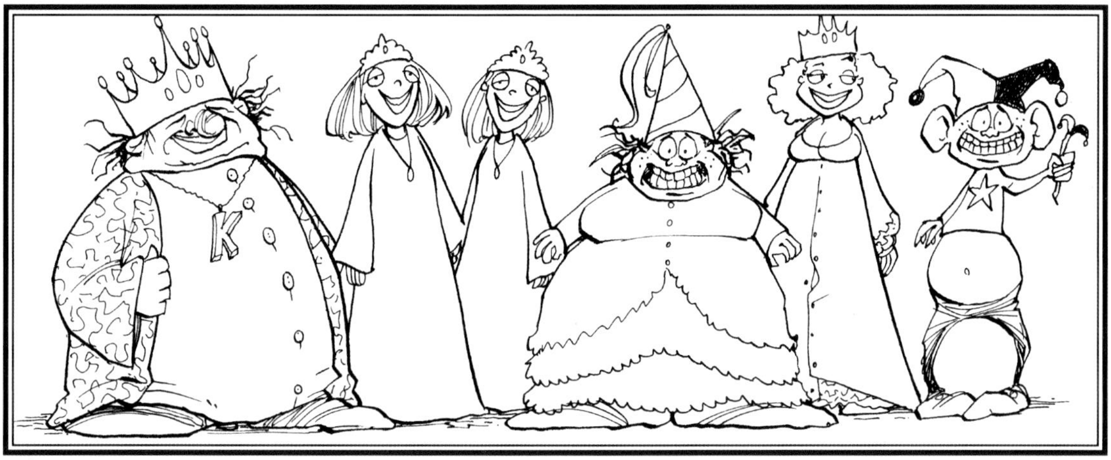

There once was a king with two beautiful daughters, and another one named Gertie. For some reason, Gertie didn't look like the rest of the family, instead bearing a strong resemblance to Skippy, the court jester. All the same, the good king loved his three daughters equally, because he had a kind heart and weak eyes.

One day, Gertie was standing by a well near the castle stables, texting a friend, when a loud noise startled her so that she dropped her phone. Plop! Plop! Crash! Splash! went the phone, down the well, into the muddy water where all the mosquitoes lived. Oh, the princess was mad! She cried. She wailed. She even said a bad word that no nice girl should ever say unless she catches her husband making a fool of himself with a tart half his age.

Gertie was seriously considering diving down the well after her phone when, all of a sudden, a voice said, "You have a potty mouth. But those legs... HarrrUMBah!"

When the princess turned there was... a fat little toad in a plaid suit, smoking a cigar and looking at her the way a moose looks at a Mini Cooper. You know the look I'm talking about.

Gertie sniffed and turned back to the well. "Go away, toad. I have a terrible problem and you can't help me."

The toad puffed on his cigar. "Dropped your phone down the well, didn't ya? Wish you could get it back, don't ya? I dare say none of the king's stable boys will go down that well for you. But I would... for a price."

"You've got a deal!" said the princess, grabbing the toad by his shorts.

"Wait! Don't you want to hear the price?" he squealed.

"Whatever! Just do it!" said the princess, and she heaved the toad into the well.

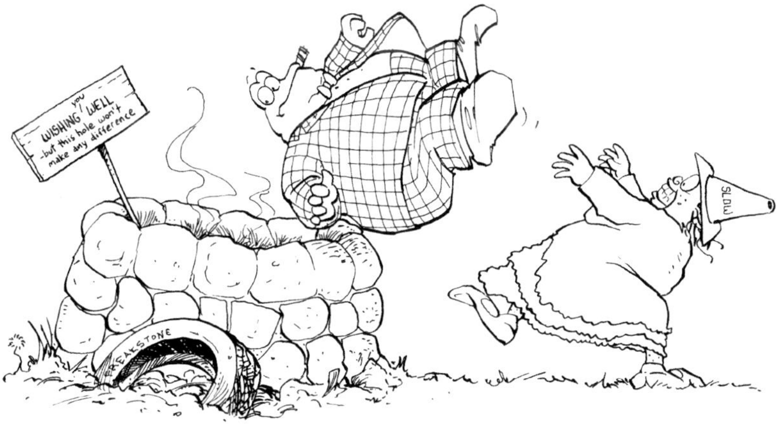
WISHING you WELL
-but this hole won't make any difference

mary had a little spam

story-kristen k. simon pencils-jim valentino inks-aaron valentino colors-paul john little

MARY HAD A LITTLE SPAM
HER EXCITEMENT WAS QUITE LOW

IT DIDN'T REALLY
TASTE THAT GREAT

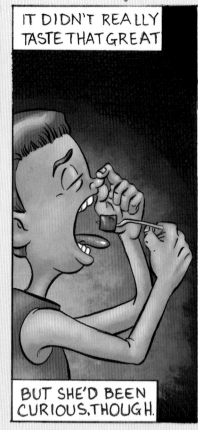

BUT SHE'D BEEN
CURIOUS, THOUGH.

SHE FRIED IT IN
A PAN ONE DAY

WHICH TASTED PRETTY COOL. BUT
IT MADE HER BROTHERS LAUGH AT HER...

... AND TREAT HER O, SO CRUEL.

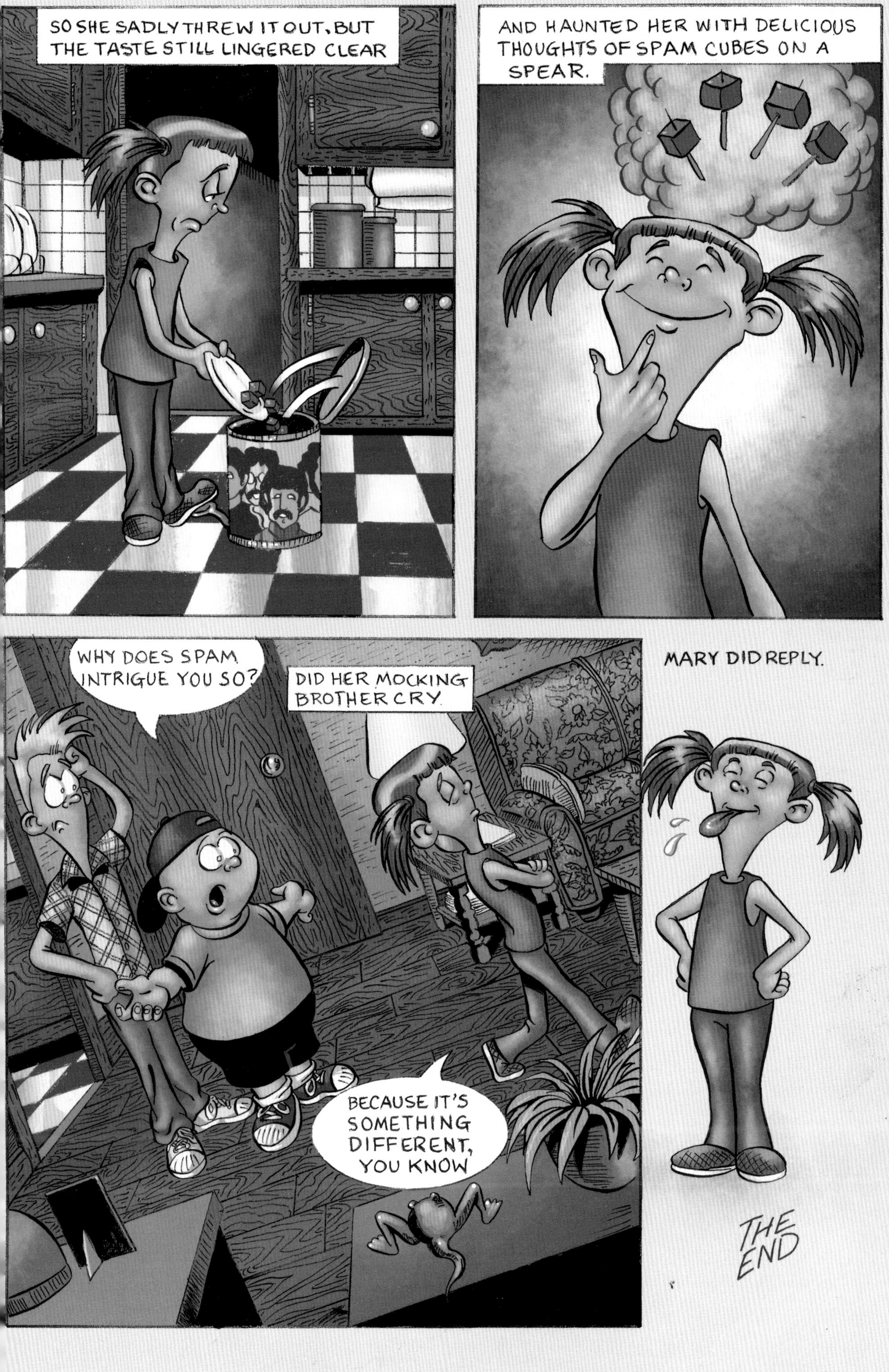
SO SHE SADLY THREW IT OUT, BUT THE TASTE STILL LINGERED CLEAR
AND HAUNTED HER WITH DELICIOUS THOUGHTS OF SPAM CUBES ON A SPEAR.
WHY DOES SPAM INTRIGUE YOU SO?
DID HER MOCKING BROTHER CRY.
MARY DID REPLY.
BECAUSE IT'S SOMETHING DIFFERENT, YOU KNOW
THE END

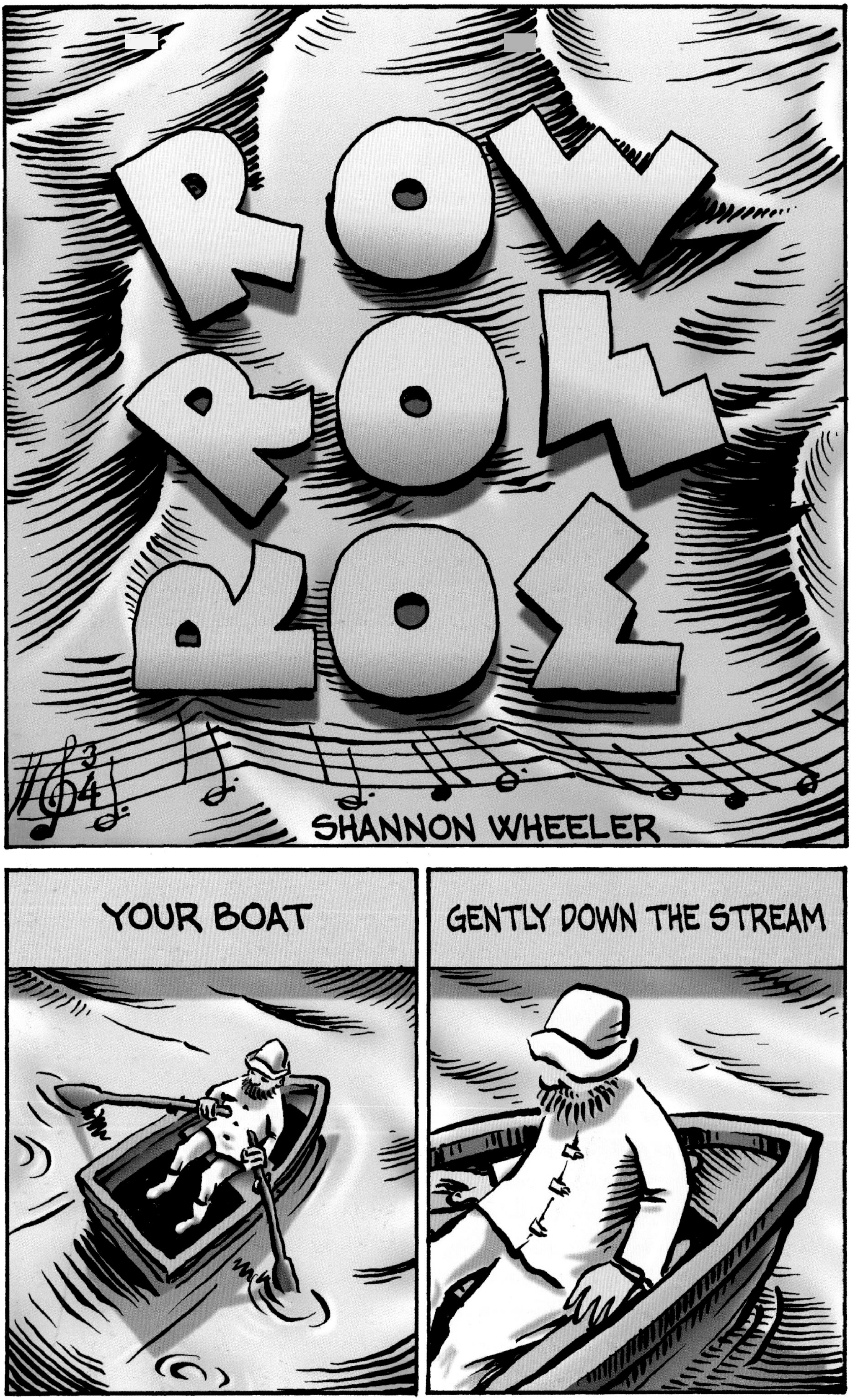
ROW ROW ROW
SHANNON WHEELER
YOUR BOAT
GENTLY DOWN THE STREAM

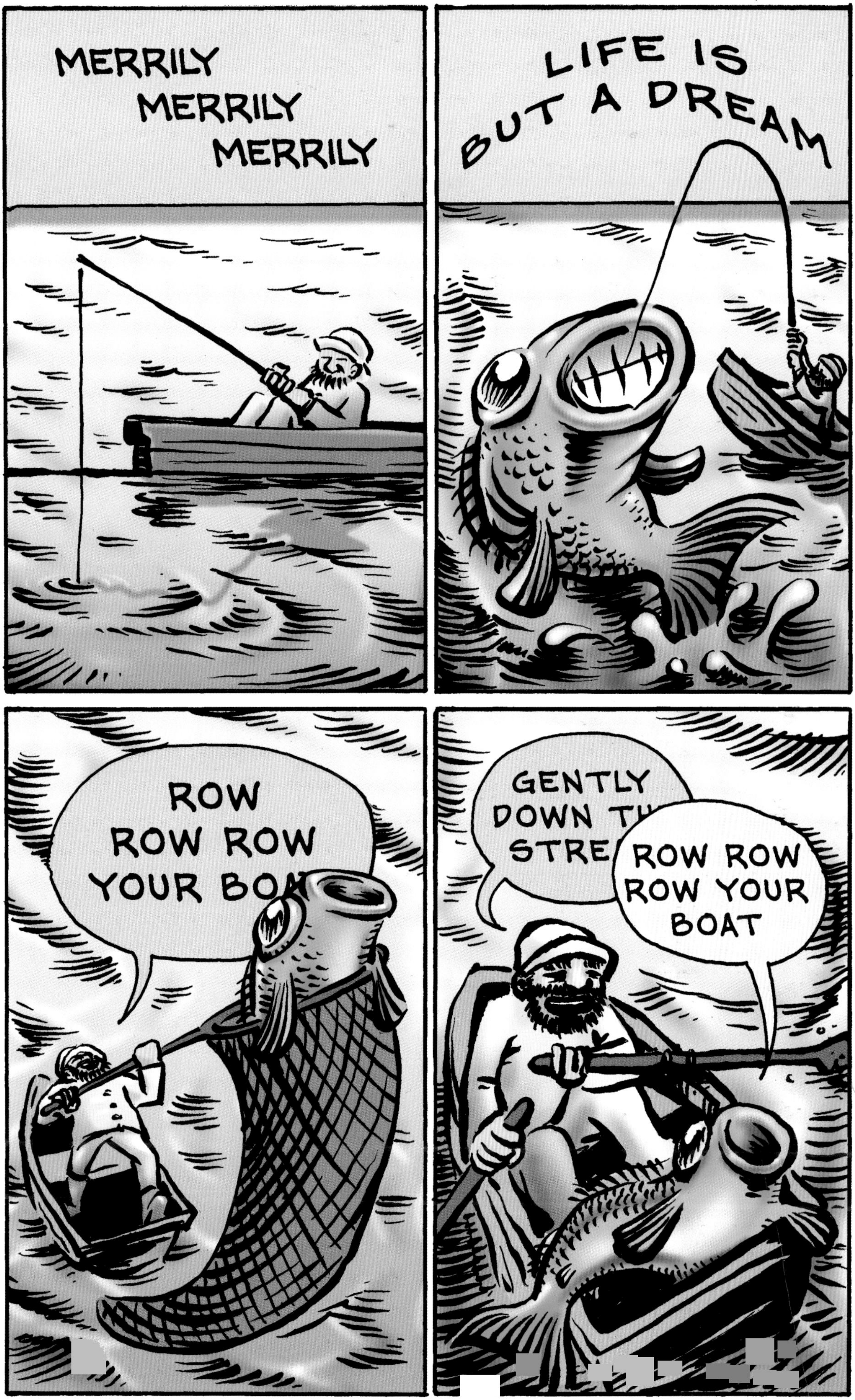
MERRILY
MERRILY
MERRILY
LIFE IS BUT A DREAM
ROW ROW ROW YOUR BO
GENTLY DOWN TH STRE
ROW ROW ROW YOUR BOAT

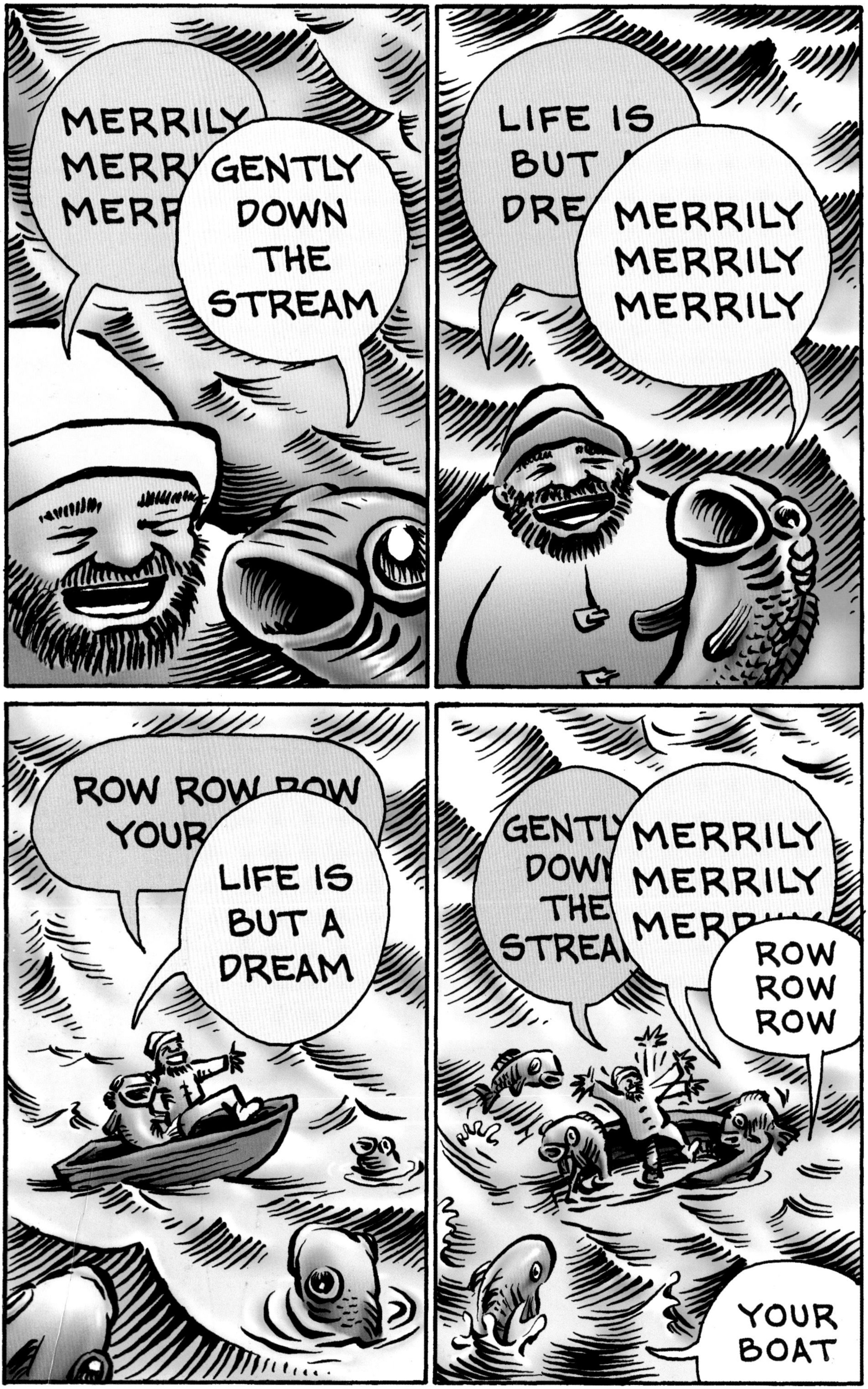
MERRILY MERR MERR
GENTLY DOWN THE STREAM
LIFE IS BUT DRE
MERRILY MERRILY MERRILY
ROW ROW YOUR
LIFE IS BUT A DREAM
GENTL DOW THE STREA
MERRILY MERRILY MERR
ROW ROW ROW
YOUR BOAT

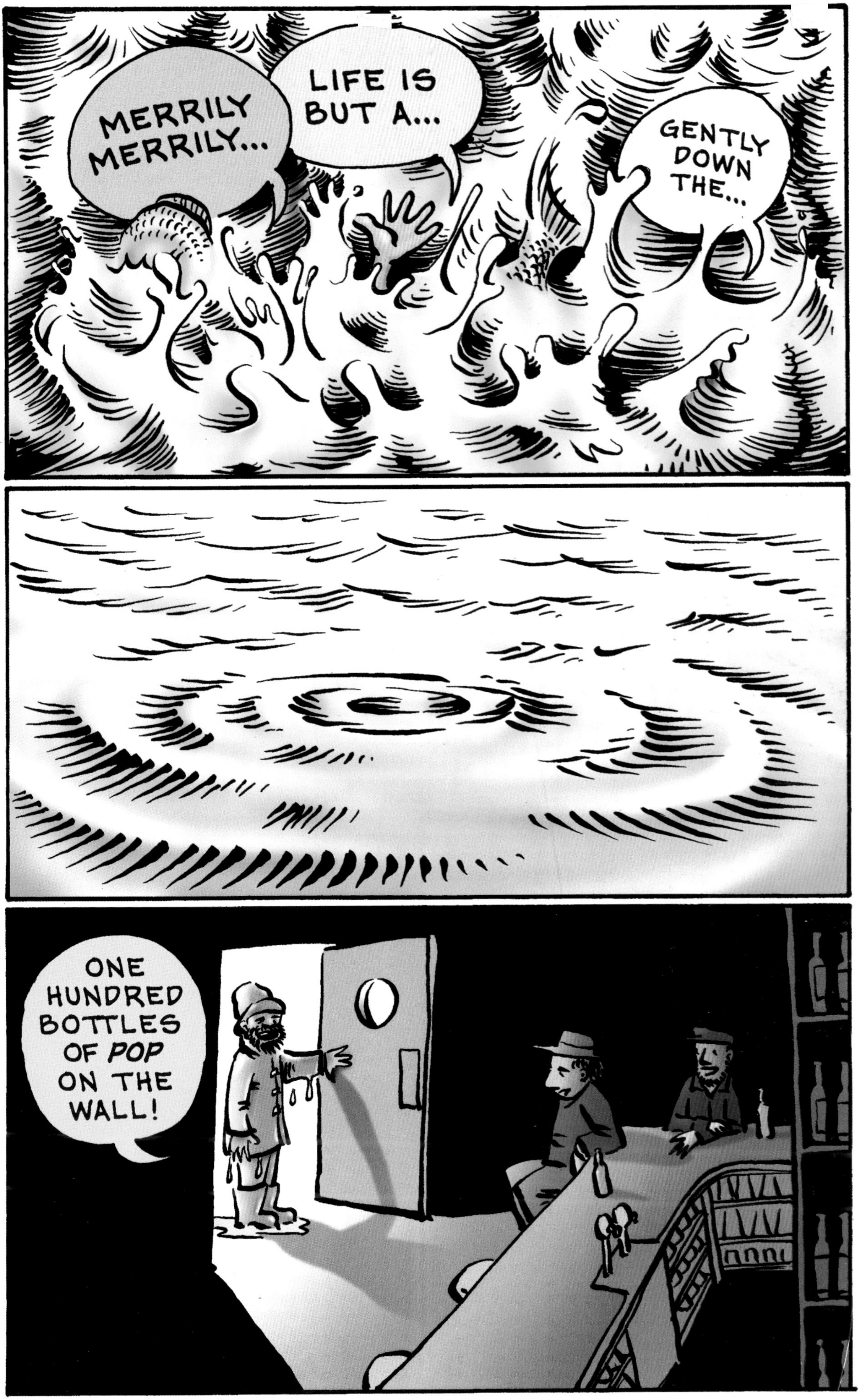
MERRILY MERRILY...
LIFE IS BUT A...
GENTLY DOWN THE...
ONE HUNDRED BOTTLES OF *POP* ON THE WALL!

THE SECRET PRINCESS SOCIETY

Marie Cruz - writer Whilce Portacio - art

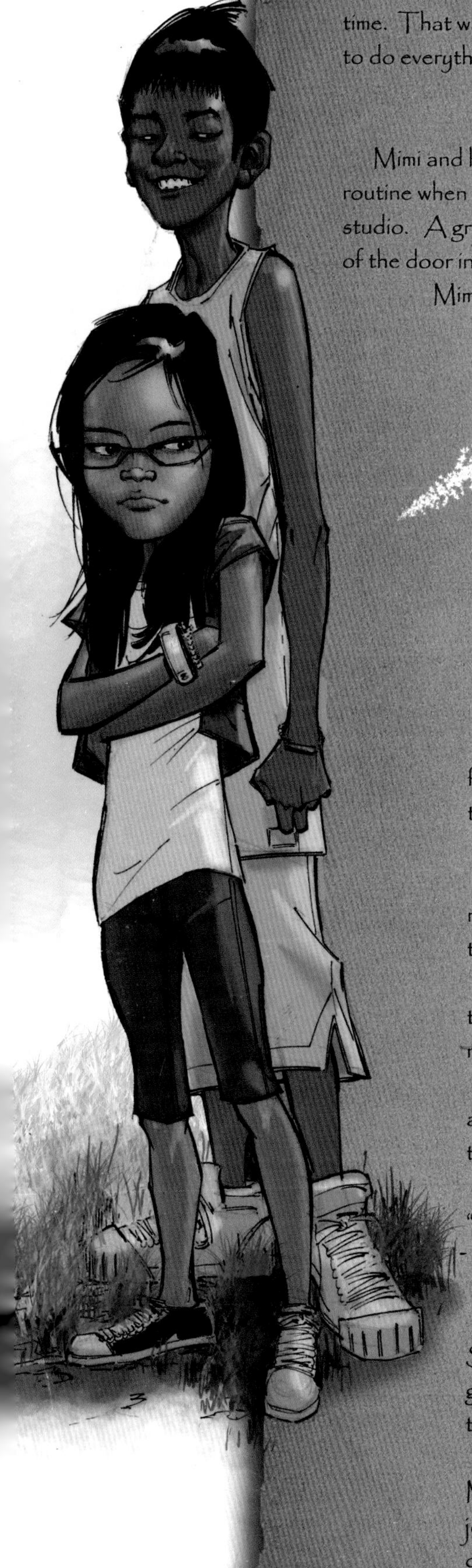

Going to Lionhead Dance Camp was a dream come true for Mimi. She would be truly happy if she didn't have her little sister to look after. Mimi had been worried that Meg would be following her around the whole time. That was because Meg thought her big sister was cool and wanted to do everything she did.

But not this time.

Mimi and her cousin, Justin, had just finished rehearsing their tap dance routine when the ballroom dance group let out on the other side of the studio. A group of giggling girls in their billowing practice skirts spilled out of the door in a swirl of color.

Mimi nudged Justin and said, "Here come the Princesses."

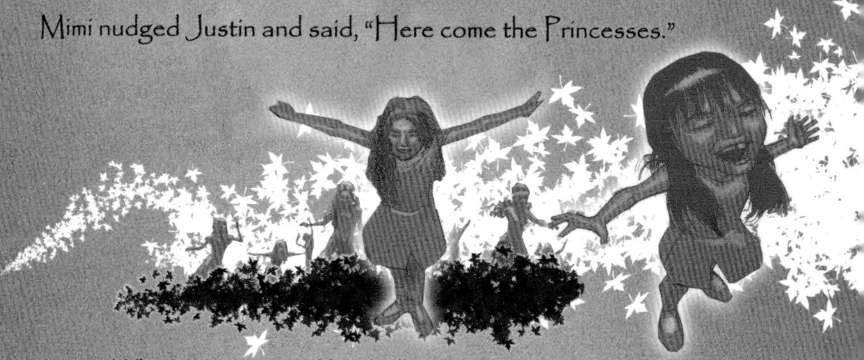

When Meg started her ballroom dance class, she had been thrilled to find out that they would be performing the Waltz of the Twelve Dancing Princesses.

Her new friends were just as excited so they banded together to form the Secret Princess Society. Justin thought it was silly. Mimi thought it was cute even though her sister didn't invite her to join.

Meg and her friends whispered and giggled so much they didn't notice Mimi and Justin coming toward them. Just as they came up to the group, Meg whispered, "Don't worry, I won't tell my sister."

Mimi couldn't believe what she just heard because her little sister told her everything. That was just how she was. So Mimi couldn't resist teasing her sister and asked, "Tell me what, Meg?"

Meg, bouncing with excitement, looked from her friends to Mimi and back again. "Oh, Mimi, guess what?" asked Meg, already forgetting her promise, "We're going to have a sleepover!"

It was Mimi's turn to look surprised. She thought, Oh, so it was "Mimi" now instead of "Ate". She missed hearing Meg use the Filipino word for big sister.

"There's no such a thing as a sleepover at camp."

"Oh, yes there is! It's going to be in Jenna's room and only Secret Princesses are allowed! Oops, sorry," said Meg. The other girls smiled at her but said nothing. Then they all skipped back into the studio behind them with Meg in tow.

Mimi tried not to feel bad. She thought she would feel glad that Meg had friends. But the truth was she felt sad and maybe a little jealous. She thought that Meg would always be there. Mimi wondered if her sister still looked up to her.

Mimi stared at Meg's empty bed and wondered if her little sister was having fun. She had wanted to tell Meg not to go but she couldn't come up with a good reason to make her stay.

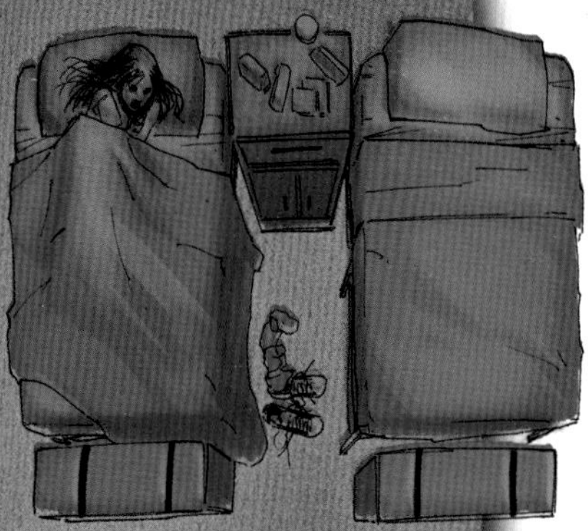

Her parents made her promise to keep an eye on her little sister, to keep her close when they didn't have dance class. Mimi hoped she wasn't breaking her promise.

After all, Meg's sleepover was just on the other side of the building.

Between the pillow and her cheek was the silver medallion her grandmother had given her before leaving for camp.

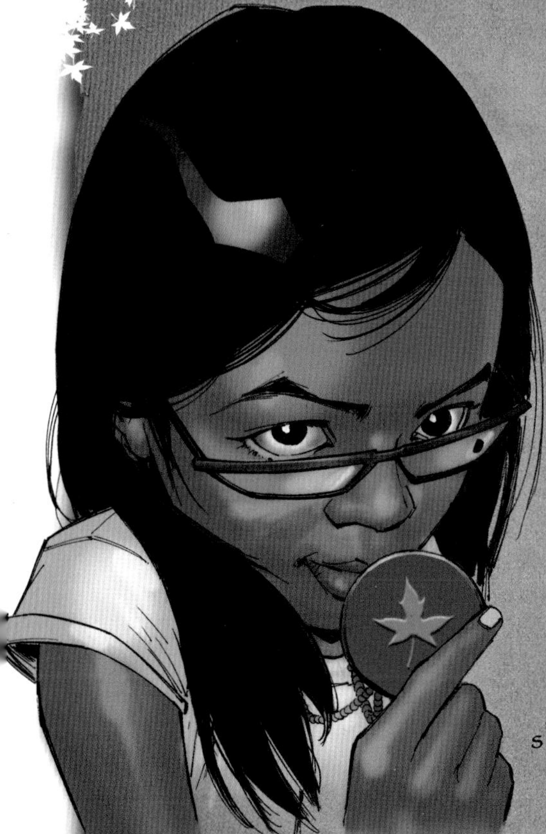

Justin and Meg each had one too, but they didn't like wearing necklaces.

Mimi brought the pendant close to her face so she could see the pretty flower design on the front.

Her grandmother said it was a special pendant that would protect her from harm. She turned the pendant over to see the reflection of the moon on its polished surface.

Mimi suddenly heard a thump and a giggle outside her window.

She thought she imagined it until she heard another giggle. She crept to the window to investigate.

Out on the lawn were Meg and her friends walking toward the forest. They each carried a lighted candle that looked like little stars dancing on the grass as they walked.

What were they doing outside?

Mimi tried to push the window open but it was stuck. She wanted to bang on the window to get their attention, to let them know that she caught them sneaking out. But they were too far away. She had to go after them. After putting on a robe, she ran to Justin's room to wake him.

Mimi and Justin found the side door unlocked. They slipped out into the chilly night. Mimi ran toward the glow of candle light with Justin close behind her. The medallion bounced on her chest as she ran.

In the distance, Mimi saw the twelve Secret Princesses entering the forest one by one. Each girl plucked a flower from a low bush with glossy green leaves. Mimi had gone hiking with Justin on this trail many times but never noticed the bush there before.

The flowers were so white they seemed to glow like the moon. Meg, in her sparkling recital dress, was the last to pick a flower. She tucked it behind her ear as the girls in front of her did. Then Meg stepped into the forest just as Mimi and Justin caught up with them.

"Meg! Hey, Meg!" Mimi couldn't believe that Meg would ignore her but she did. Meg continued to follow the girl in front of her. Mimi walked along-side her sister but Meg didn't seem to notice her. She tried to talk to each of the girls in line but they paid no attention to her.

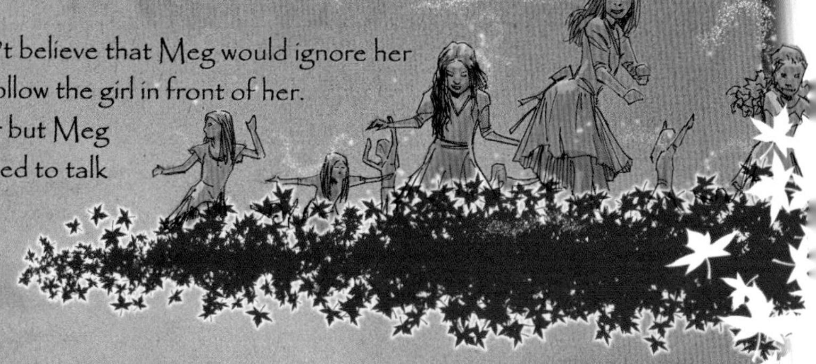

Mimi turned around and saw Justin pluck a flower from the bush. She watched in fascination as he held the flower in front of him and began to walk in the same direction as Meg and her friends.

The flowers looked like tiny stars against its dark green leaves. Its perfume enveloped her, inviting her to come closer. Mimi had seen the flower before! It was the same flower on her medallion.

She plucked one.

A path appeared before her. It led to a large tree. Thin branches snaked down into the ground around it. Surrounding the base of the tree were small green mounds that made the hairs on Mimi's arms stand on end and the medallion felt like a piece of ice on her chest.

Meg and her friends chanted "tabi tabi po" in their high sing-song voices as they walked along the path that wove between the mounds toward the tree. The massive trunk had a cleft as tall and wide as a door. One by one, the princesses stepped into the opening in the tree. "Come on," whispered Mimi, holding the flower in front of her.

She fell in step behind Meg.

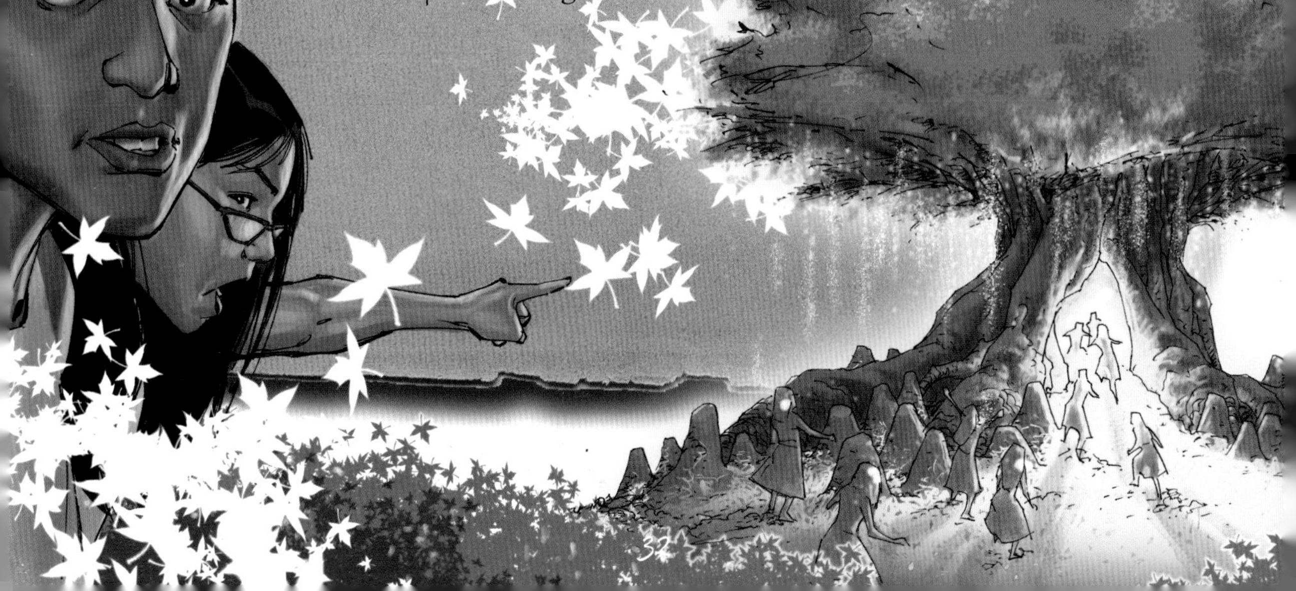

Justin and Mimi followed Meg into the tree.

The walls were covered with white scaly fungus. A tunnel spiraled downward and opened into a carpeted hallway lined with marble columns and portraits of kings and queens.

At the end of the hall stood twelve young (handsome?) princes with their hands out-stretched toward Meg and her friends (they really seemed like princesses now!).

The couples turned and paraded into a grand ballroom lit with hundreds of candles. They followed the last couple, imitating their walk and posture.

On each side of the room were rows of golden tables with silver plates of fruit and glasses filled with honey colored liquid.

At the end of the room was a long banquet table with platters of roasted meat and cheeses and at its center sat a big man dressed like a king.

He beckoned to the couples with a smile on his long horse-like face.

Mimi and Justin jumped behind the first table as they entered.

"What are we going to do?" whispered Mimi, sneaking a peek at the dance floor.

The princes and their princesses paraded before this king. They bowed and curtsied then twirled onto the dance floor. Music played and the twelve couples twirled across the polished floor.

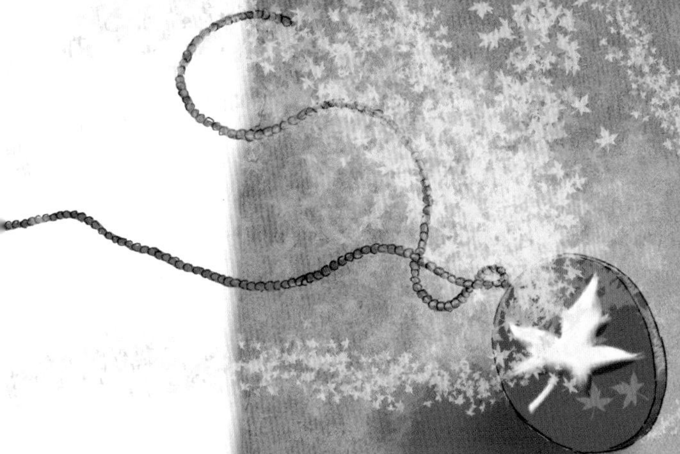

"Watch and see what happens, I guess," said Justin, staring at the plate of fruit on the table. He reached out to take one but Mimi smacked his hand away.

The not-so-handsome princes were clumsy dancers. They stepped on dresses and toes but the princesses didn't seem to notice. There was something strange about their faces too. Eyes and noses seemed to slide out of place and back again.

The dance ended.

The princes led their partners to the banquet table. Mimi wanted to get a closer look.

She tried to sneak over to the next table when she tripped and fell. Her medallion snapped off its chain and rolled onto the dance floor. She scrambled over to it as fast as she could and snatched it up. Mimi polished the pendant on her robe and opened her hand to have a look at it before dropping it into her pocket.

Mimi stared into the medallion in confusion.

She saw herself reflected there but something was wrong.

The room did not look the same. The reflection didn't show candles, golden tables or silver plates of fruit.

Instead of candles she saw sticks covered with something bright and writhing. The tables and chairs were raw stumps of wood. When she tilted the medallion, she saw wooden cages sus pended on ropes above each set of rough wooden tables and chairs.

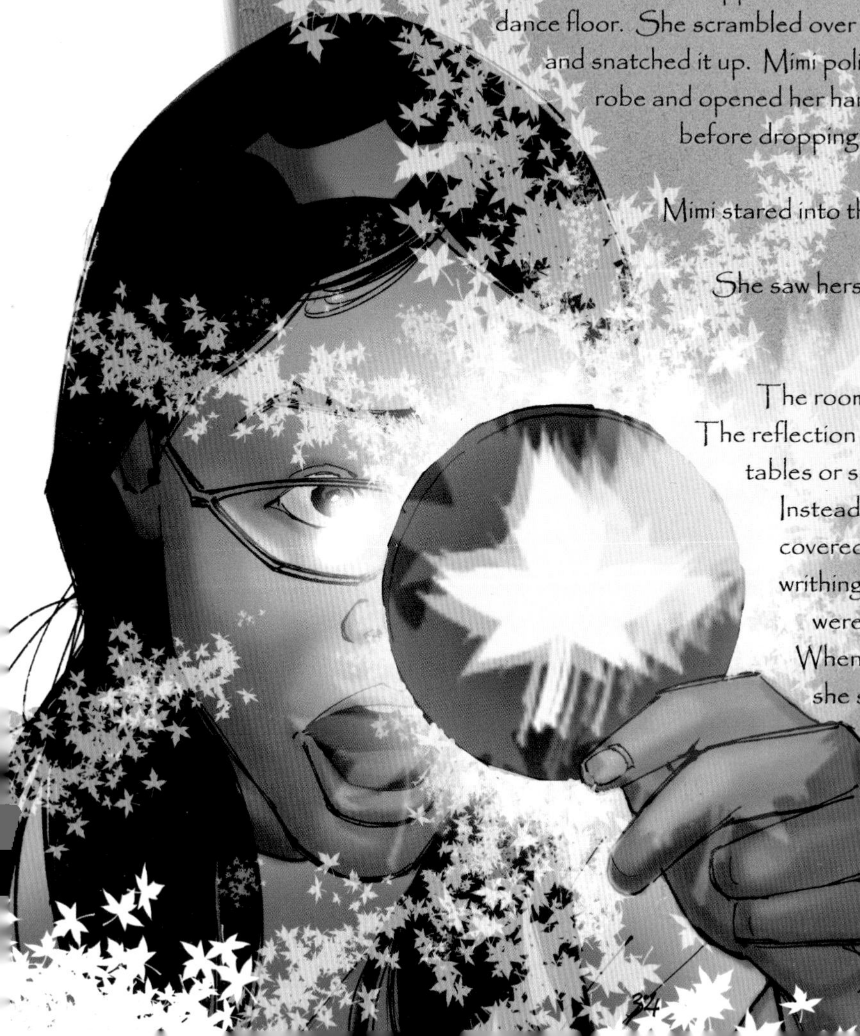

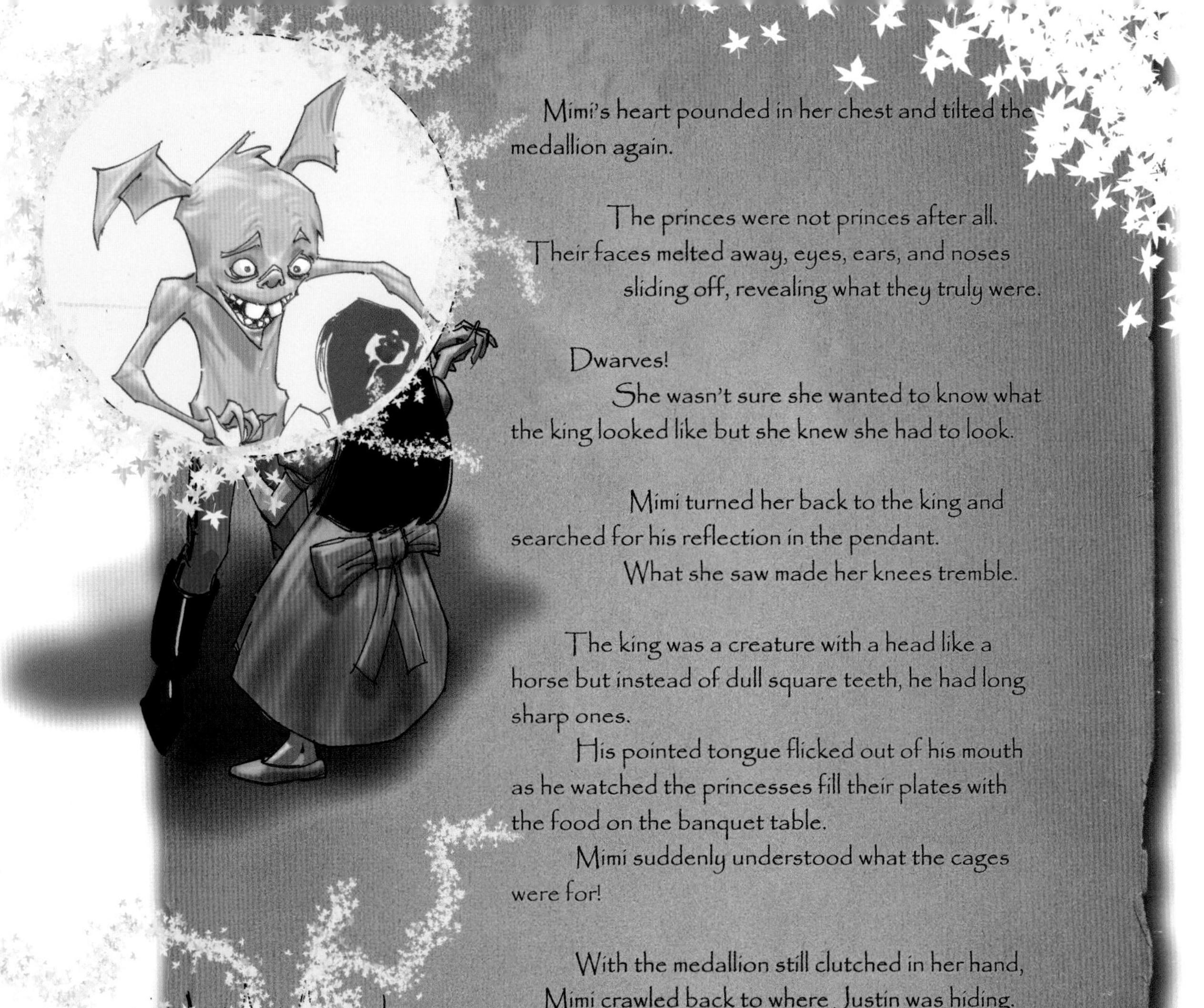

Mimi's heart pounded in her chest and tilted the medallion again.

The princes were not princes after all. Their faces melted away, eyes, ears, and noses sliding off, revealing what they truly were.

Dwarves!

She wasn't sure she wanted to know what the king looked like but she knew she had to look.

Mimi turned her back to the king and searched for his reflection in the pendant.

What she saw made her knees tremble.

The king was a creature with a head like a horse but instead of dull square teeth, he had long sharp ones.

His pointed tongue flicked out of his mouth as he watched the princesses fill their plates with the food on the banquet table.

Mimi suddenly understood what the cages were for!

With the medallion still clutched in her hand, Mimi crawled back to where Justin was hiding.

"This whole place is just a mirage! I think that monster is going to trap Meg and the others.

We have to find a way to break this spell and get them out of here," said Mimi.

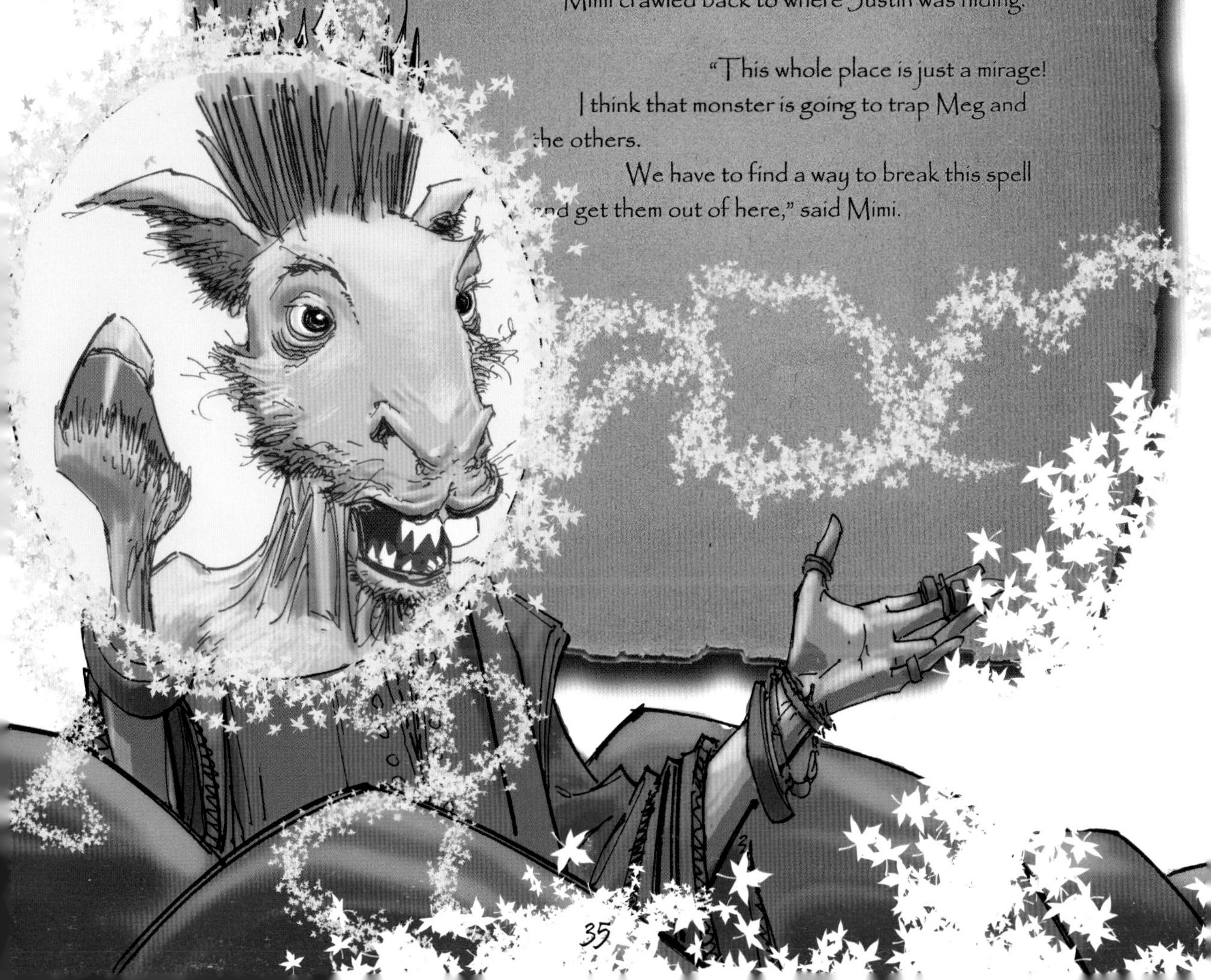

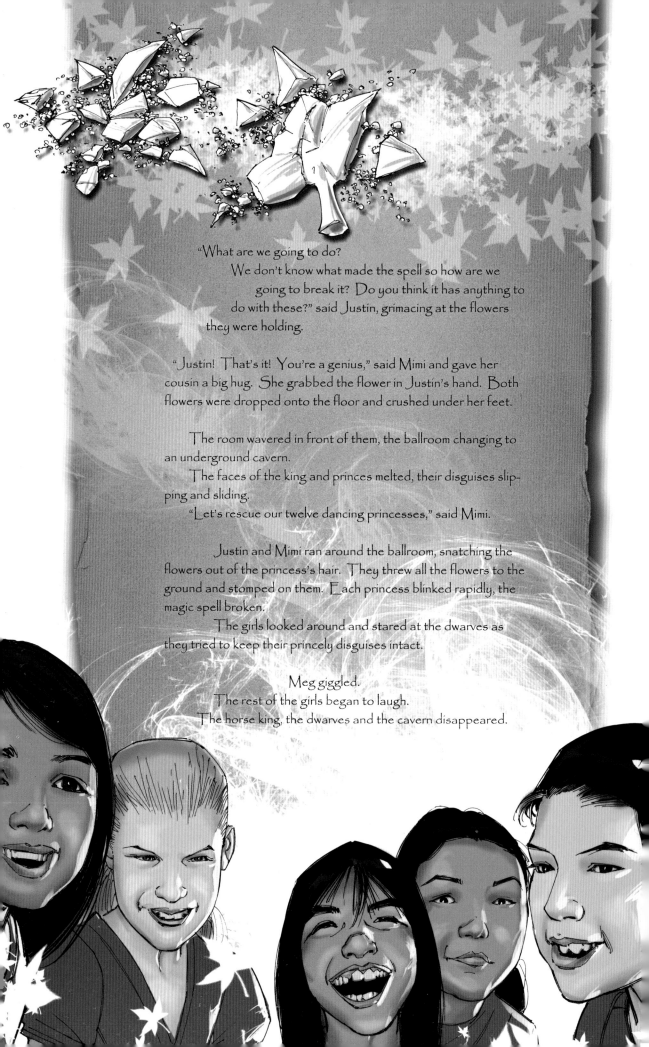

"What are we going to do?
We don't know what made the spell so how are we
going to break it? Do you think it has anything to
do with these?" said Justin, grimacing at the flowers
they were holding.

"Justin! That's it! You're a genius," said Mimi and gave her
cousin a big hug. She grabbed the flower in Justin's hand. Both
flowers were dropped onto the floor and crushed under her feet.

The room wavered in front of them, the ballroom changing to
an underground cavern.
The faces of the king and princes melted, their disguises slip-
ping and sliding.
"Let's rescue our twelve dancing princesses," said Mimi.

Justin and Mimi ran around the ballroom, snatching the
flowers out of the princess's hair. They threw all the flowers to the
ground and stomped on them. Each princess blinked rapidly, the
magic spell broken.
The girls looked around and stared at the dwarves as
they tried to keep their princely disguises intact.

Meg giggled.
The rest of the girls began to laugh.
The horse king, the dwarves and the cavern disappeared.

They all stood on the lawn just outside their dormitory. The moon was still high and bright in the sky.

Meg hugged her big sister and cried, "Ate!"

Back in their room, Mimi still couldn't sleep. She wondered if the forest held other secrets and imagined what they might be.

Meg, on the other hand, was tucked in her bed, fast asleep, wearing her own medallion.

Mimi was happy to have her little sister there with her.

After what happened tonight, she knew that Meg would probably stick to her like glue for the rest of dance camp and would want to do everything her "Ate" did.

And Mimi didn't mind this one single bit.

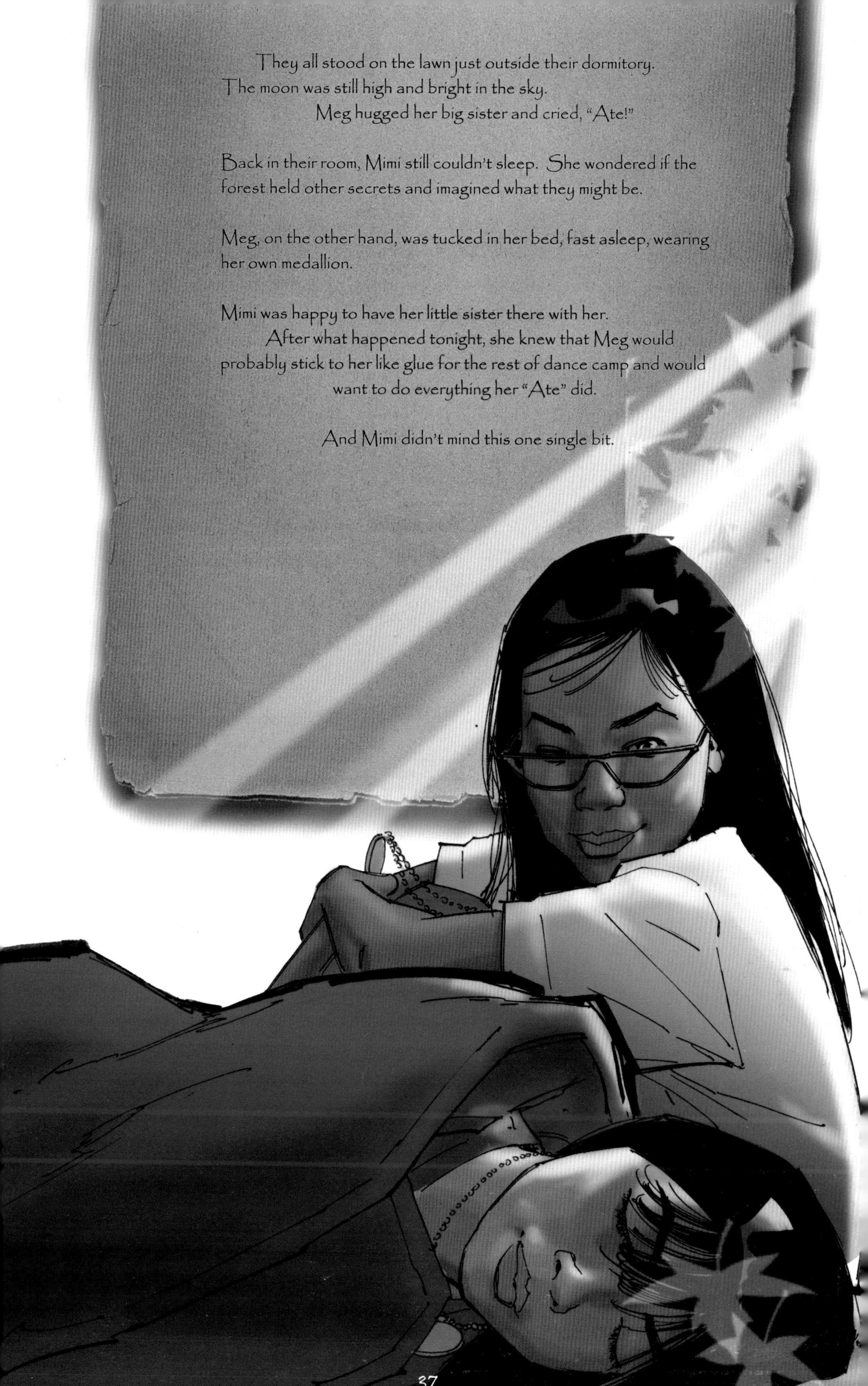

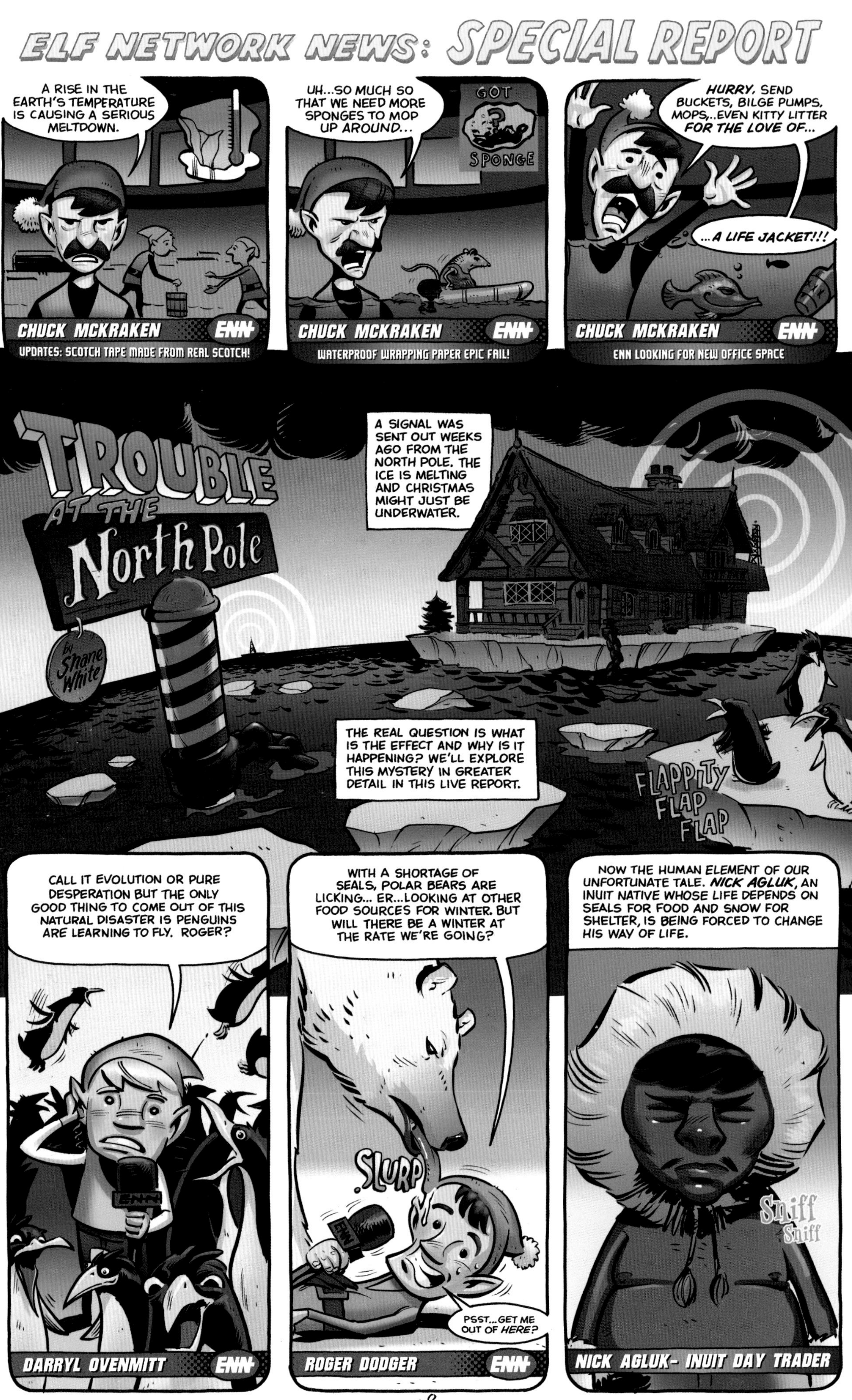
ELF NETWORK NEWS: SPECIAL REPORT
A RISE IN THE EARTH'S TEMPERATURE IS CAUSING A SERIOUS MELTDOWN.
CHUCK MCKRAKEN
ENN
UPDATES: SCOTCH TAPE MADE FROM REAL SCOTCH!
UH...SO MUCH SO THAT WE NEED MORE SPONGES TO MOP UP AROUND...
GOT ? SPONGE
CHUCK MCKRAKEN
ENN
WATERPROOF WRAPPING PAPER EPIC FAIL!
HURRY, SEND BUCKETS, BILGE PUMPS, MOPS,..EVEN KITTY LITTER FOR THE LOVE OF...
...A LIFE JACKET!!!
CHUCK MCKRAKEN
ENN
ENN LOOKING FOR NEW OFFICE SPACE
TROUBLE AT THE North Pole
by Shane White
A SIGNAL WAS SENT OUT WEEKS AGO FROM THE NORTH POLE. THE ICE IS MELTING AND CHRISTMAS MIGHT JUST BE UNDERWATER.
THE REAL QUESTION IS WHAT IS THE EFFECT AND WHY IS IT HAPPENING? WE'LL EXPLORE THIS MYSTERY IN GREATER DETAIL IN THIS LIVE REPORT.
FLAPPITY FLAP FLAP
CALL IT EVOLUTION OR PURE DESPERATION BUT THE ONLY GOOD THING TO COME OUT OF THIS NATURAL DISASTER IS PENGUINS ARE LEARNING TO FLY. ROGER?
ENN
DARRYL OVENMITT
ENN
WITH A SHORTAGE OF SEALS, POLAR BEARS ARE LICKING... ER...LOOKING AT OTHER FOOD SOURCES FOR WINTER. BUT WILL THERE BE A WINTER AT THE RATE WE'RE GOING?
SLURP
ENN
PSST...GET ME OUT OF HERE?
ROGER DODGER
ENN
NOW THE HUMAN ELEMENT OF OUR UNFORTUNATE TALE. NICK AGLUK, AN INUIT NATIVE WHOSE LIFE DEPENDS ON SEALS FOR FOOD AND SNOW FOR SHELTER, IS BEING FORCED TO CHANGE HIS WAY OF LIFE.
Sniff Sniff
NICK AGLUK- INUIT DAY TRADER

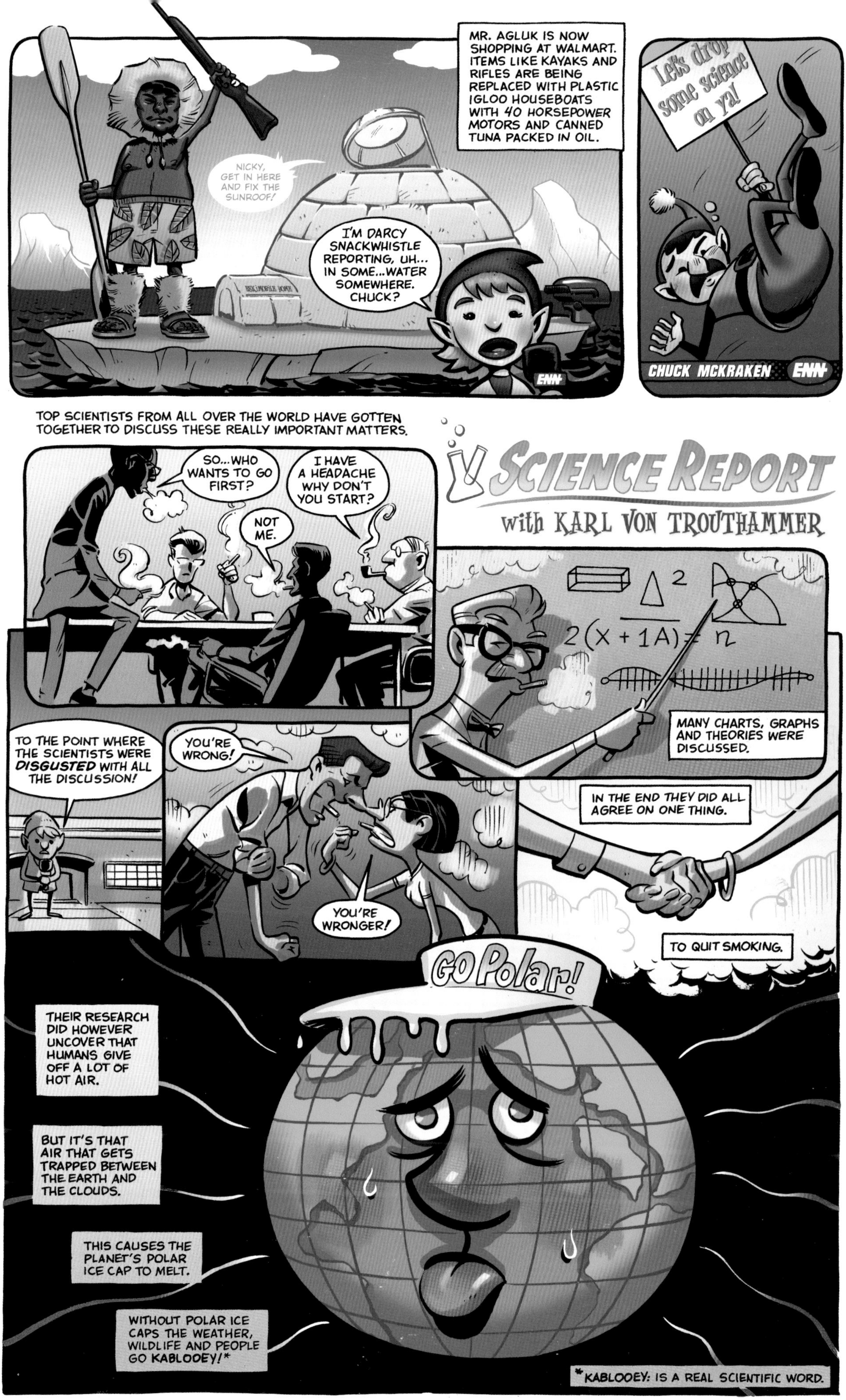
MR. AGLUK IS NOW SHOPPING AT WALMART. ITEMS LIKE KAYAKS AND RIFLES ARE BEING REPLACED WITH PLASTIC IGLOO HOUSEBOATS WITH 40 HORSEPOWER MOTORS AND CANNED TUNA PACKED IN OIL.
NICKY, GET IN HERE AND FIX THE SUNROOF!
I'M DARCY SNACKWHISTLE REPORTING, UH... IN SOME...WATER SOMEWHERE. CHUCK?
ENN
Let's drop some science on ya!
CHUCK MCKRAKEN
ENN
TOP SCIENTISTS FROM ALL OVER THE WORLD HAVE GOTTEN TOGETHER TO DISCUSS THESE REALLY IMPORTANT MATTERS.
SCIENCE REPORT
with KARL VON TROUTHAMMER
SO...WHO WANTS TO GO FIRST?
I HAVE A HEADACHE WHY DON'T YOU START?
NOT ME.
2(X + 1A) = n
MANY CHARTS, GRAPHS AND THEORIES WERE DISCUSSED.
TO THE POINT WHERE THE SCIENTISTS WERE DISGUSTED WITH ALL THE DISCUSSION!
YOU'RE WRONG!
YOU'RE WRONGER!
IN THE END THEY DID ALL AGREE ON ONE THING.
TO QUIT SMOKING.
GO Polar!
THEIR RESEARCH DID HOWEVER UNCOVER THAT HUMANS GIVE OFF A LOT OF HOT AIR.
BUT IT'S THAT AIR THAT GETS TRAPPED BETWEEN THE EARTH AND THE CLOUDS.
THIS CAUSES THE PLANET'S POLAR ICE CAP TO MELT.
WITHOUT POLAR ICE CAPS THE WEATHER, WILDLIFE AND PEOPLE GO KABLOOEY!*
*KABLOOEY: IS A REAL SCIENTIFIC WORD.

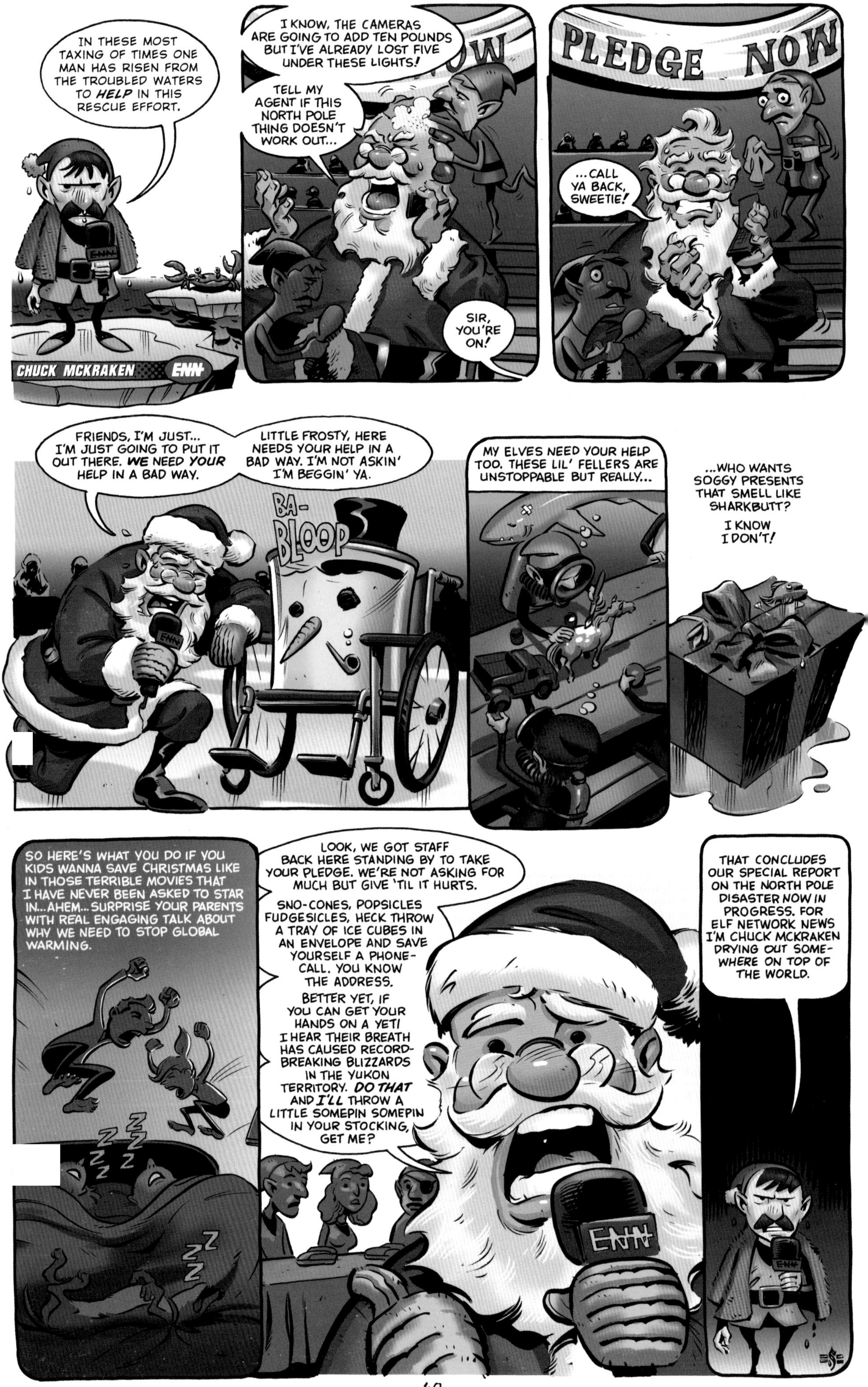

IN THESE MOST TAXING OF TIMES ONE MAN HAS RISEN FROM THE TROUBLED WATERS TO HELP IN THIS RESCUE EFFORT.
CHUCK MCKRAKEN
ENN
I KNOW, THE CAMERAS ARE GOING TO ADD TEN POUNDS BUT I'VE ALREADY LOST FIVE UNDER THESE LIGHTS!
TELL MY AGENT IF THIS NORTH POLE THING DOESN'T WORK OUT...
SIR, YOU'RE ON!
PLEDGE NOW
...CALL YA BACK, SWEETIE!
FRIENDS, I'M JUST... I'M JUST GOING TO PUT IT OUT THERE. WE NEED YOUR HELP IN A BAD WAY.
LITTLE FROSTY, HERE NEEDS YOUR HELP IN A BAD WAY. I'M NOT ASKIN' I'M BEGGIN' YA.
BA-BLOOP
MY ELVES NEED YOUR HELP TOO. THESE LIL' FELLERS ARE UNSTOPPABLE BUT REALLY...
...WHO WANTS SOGGY PRESENTS THAT SMELL LIKE SHARKBUTT?
I KNOW I DON'T!
SO HERE'S WHAT YOU DO IF YOU KIDS WANNA SAVE CHRISTMAS LIKE IN THOSE TERRIBLE MOVIES THAT I HAVE NEVER BEEN ASKED TO STAR IN...AHEM...SURPRISE YOUR PARENTS WITH REAL ENGAGING TALK ABOUT WHY WE NEED TO STOP GLOBAL WARMING.
LOOK, WE GOT STAFF BACK HERE STANDING BY TO TAKE YOUR PLEDGE. WE'RE NOT ASKING FOR MUCH BUT GIVE 'TIL IT HURTS.
SNO-CONES, POPSICLES FUDGESICLES, HECK THROW A TRAY OF ICE CUBES IN AN ENVELOPE AND SAVE YOURSELF A PHONE-CALL. YOU KNOW THE ADDRESS.
BETTER YET, IF YOU CAN GET YOUR HANDS ON A YETI I HEAR THEIR BREATH HAS CAUSED RECORD-BREAKING BLIZZARDS IN THE YUKON TERRITORY. DO THAT AND I'LL THROW A LITTLE SOMEPIN SOMEPIN IN YOUR STOCKING, GET ME?
ENN
THAT CONCLUDES OUR SPECIAL REPORT ON THE NORTH POLE DISASTER NOW IN PROGRESS. FOR ELF NETWORK NEWS I'M CHUCK MCKRAKEN DRYING OUT SOME-WHERE ON TOP OF THE WORLD.

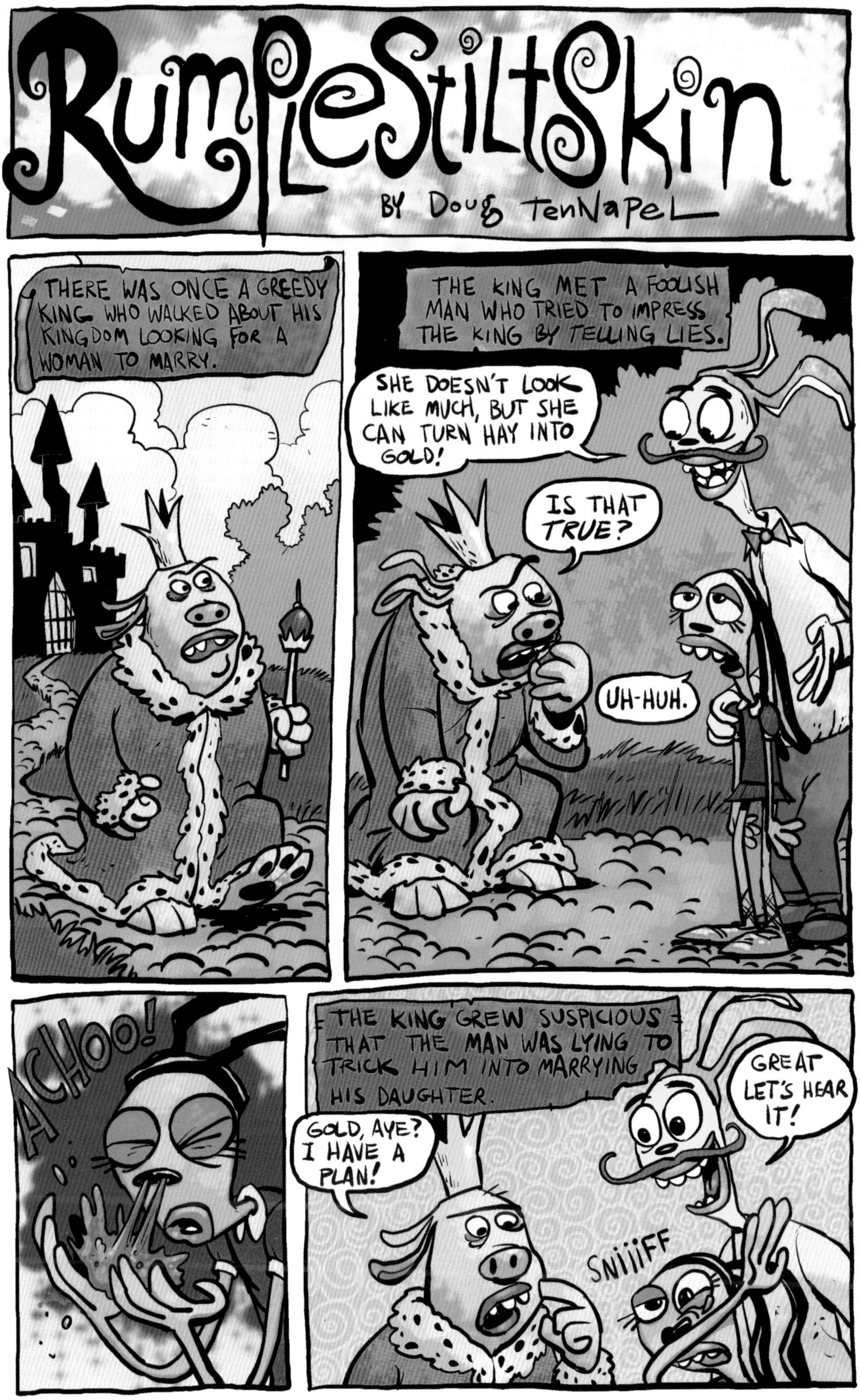
RUMPLESTILTSKIN
BY DOUG TENNAPEL
THERE WAS ONCE A GREEDY KING WHO WALKED ABOUT HIS KINGDOM LOOKING FOR A WOMAN TO MARRY.
THE KING MET A FOOLISH MAN WHO TRIED TO IMPRESS THE KING BY TELLING LIES.
SHE DOESN'T LOOK LIKE MUCH, BUT SHE CAN TURN HAY INTO GOLD!
IS THAT TRUE?
UH-HUH.
ACHOO!
THE KING GREW SUSPICIOUS THAT THE MAN WAS LYING TO TRICK HIM INTO MARRYING HIS DAUGHTER.
GOLD, AYE? I HAVE A PLAN!
GREAT LET'S HEAR IT!
SNIIIFF

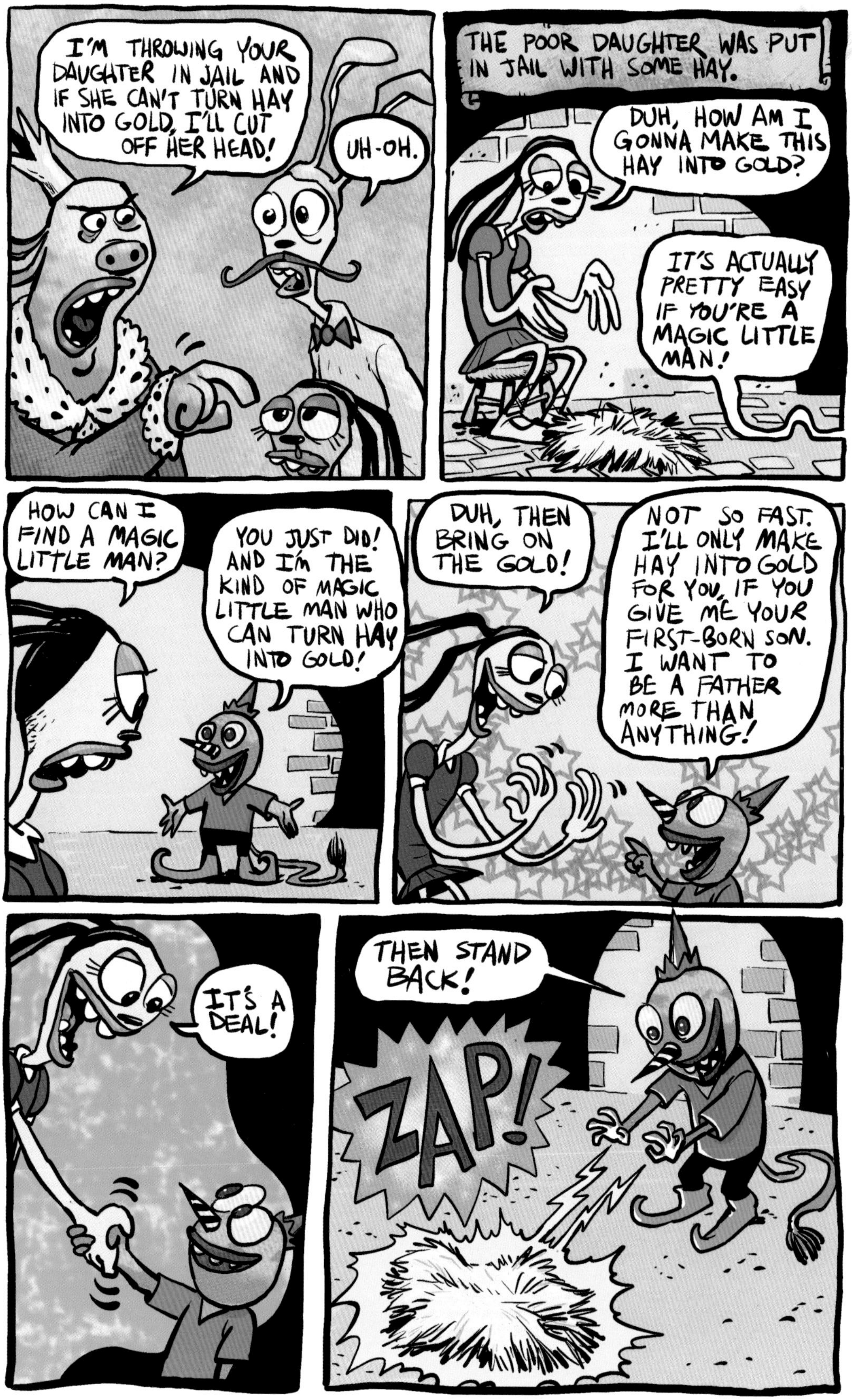
I'M THROWING YOUR DAUGHTER IN JAIL AND IF SHE CAN'T TURN HAY INTO GOLD, I'LL CUT OFF HER HEAD!
UH-OH.
THE POOR DAUGHTER WAS PUT IN JAIL WITH SOME HAY.
DUH, HOW AM I GONNA MAKE THIS HAY INTO GOLD?
IT'S ACTUALLY PRETTY EASY IF YOU'RE A MAGIC LITTLE MAN!
HOW CAN I FIND A MAGIC LITTLE MAN?
YOU JUST DID! AND I'M THE KIND OF MAGIC LITTLE MAN WHO CAN TURN HAY INTO GOLD!
DUH, THEN BRING ON THE GOLD!
NOT SO FAST. I'LL ONLY MAKE HAY INTO GOLD FOR YOU, IF YOU GIVE ME YOUR FIRST-BORN SON. I WANT TO BE A FATHER MORE THAN ANYTHING!
IT'S A DEAL!
THEN STAND BACK!
ZAP!

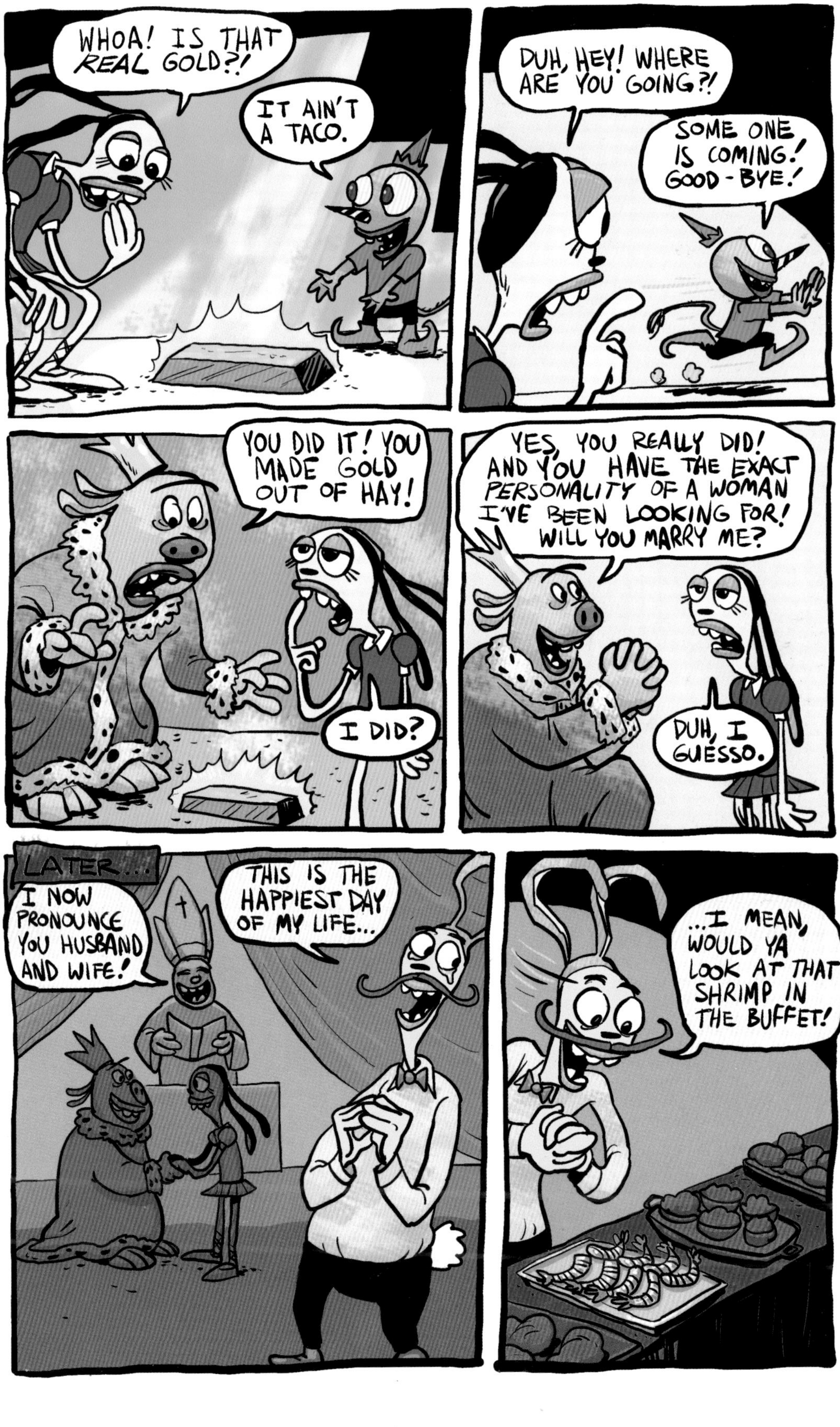
WHOA! IS THAT REAL GOLD?!
IT AIN'T A TACO.
DUH, HEY! WHERE ARE YOU GOING?!
SOME ONE IS COMING! GOOD-BYE!
YOU DID IT! YOU MADE GOLD OUT OF HAY!
I DID?
YES, YOU REALLY DID! AND YOU HAVE THE EXACT PERSONALITY OF A WOMAN I'VE BEEN LOOKING FOR! WILL YOU MARRY ME?
DUH, I GUESSO.
LATER...
I NOW PRONOUNCE YOU HUSBAND AND WIFE!
THIS IS THE HAPPIEST DAY OF MY LIFE...
...I MEAN, WOULD YA LOOK AT THAT SHRIMP IN THE BUFFET!

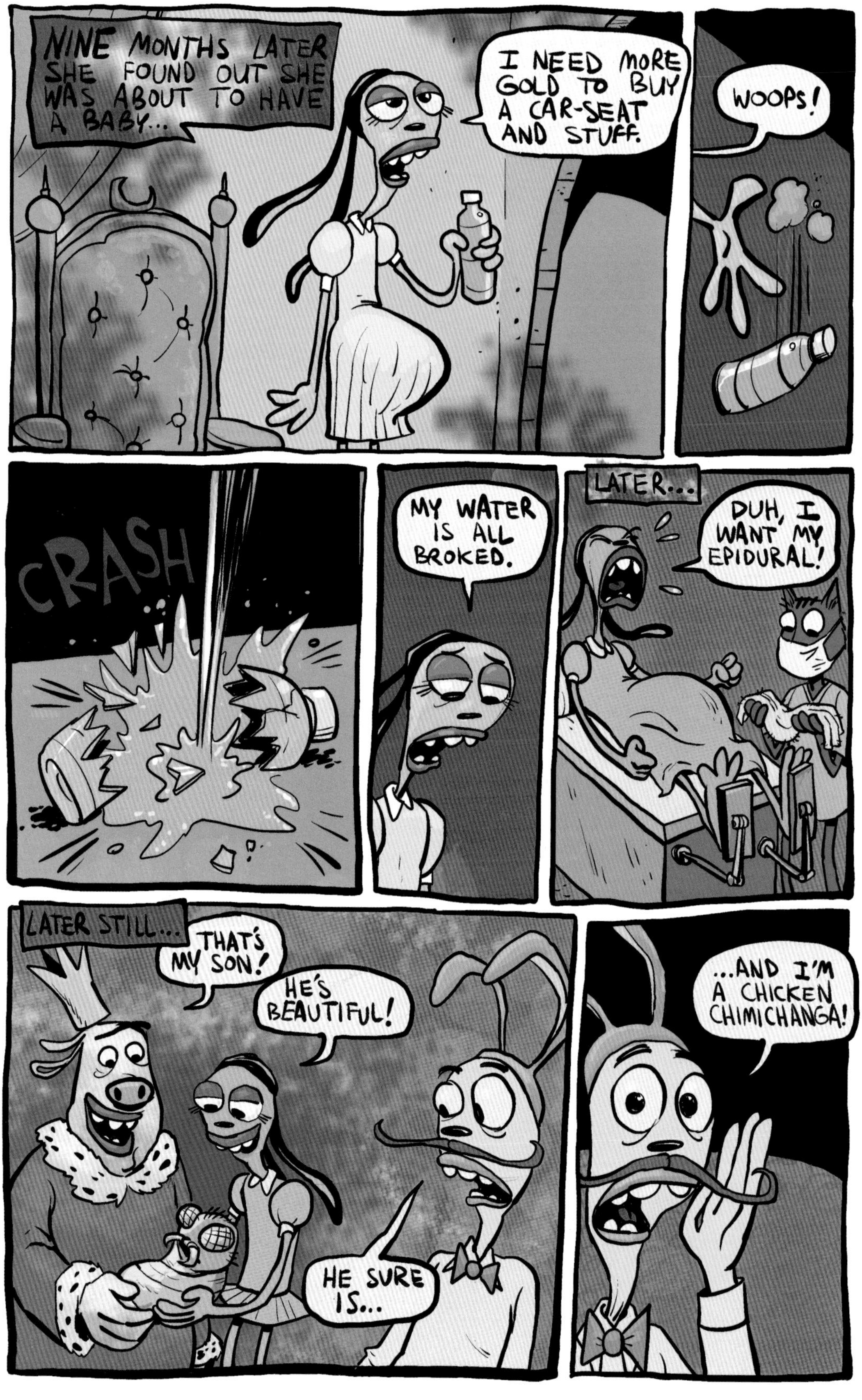

NINE MONTHS LATER SHE FOUND OUT SHE WAS ABOUT TO HAVE A BABY...
I NEED MORE GOLD TO BUY A CAR-SEAT AND STUFF.
WOOPS!
CRASH
MY WATER IS ALL BROKED.
LATER...
DUH, I WANT MY EPIDURAL!
LATER STILL...
THAT'S MY SON!
HE'S BEAUTIFUL!
HE SURE IS...
...AND I'M A CHICKEN CHIMICHANGA!

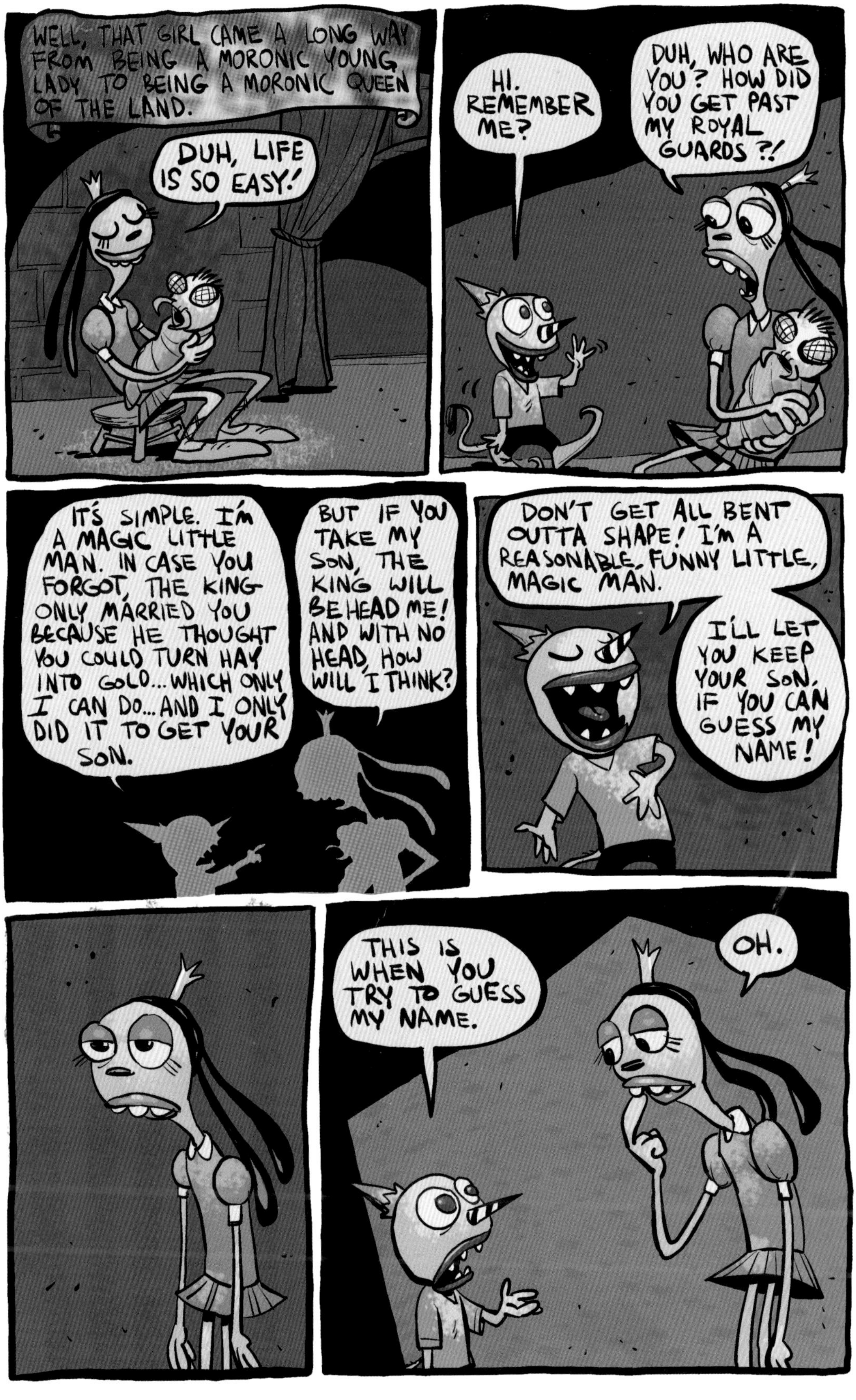
WELL, THAT GIRL CAME A LONG WAY FROM BEING A MORONIC YOUNG LADY TO BEING A MORONIC QUEEN OF THE LAND.
DUH, LIFE IS SO EASY!
HI. REMEMBER ME?
DUH, WHO ARE YOU? HOW DID YOU GET PAST MY ROYAL GUARDS?!
IT'S SIMPLE. I'M A MAGIC LITTLE MAN. IN CASE YOU FORGOT, THE KING ONLY MARRIED YOU BECAUSE HE THOUGHT YOU COULD TURN HAY INTO GOLD... WHICH ONLY I CAN DO... AND I ONLY DID IT TO GET YOUR SON.
BUT IF YOU TAKE MY SON, THE KING WILL BEHEAD ME! AND WITH NO HEAD, HOW WILL I THINK?
DON'T GET ALL BENT OUTTA SHAPE! I'M A REASONABLE, FUNNY LITTLE, MAGIC MAN.
I'LL LET YOU KEEP YOUR SON, IF YOU CAN GUESS MY NAME!
THIS IS WHEN YOU TRY TO GUESS MY NAME.
OH.

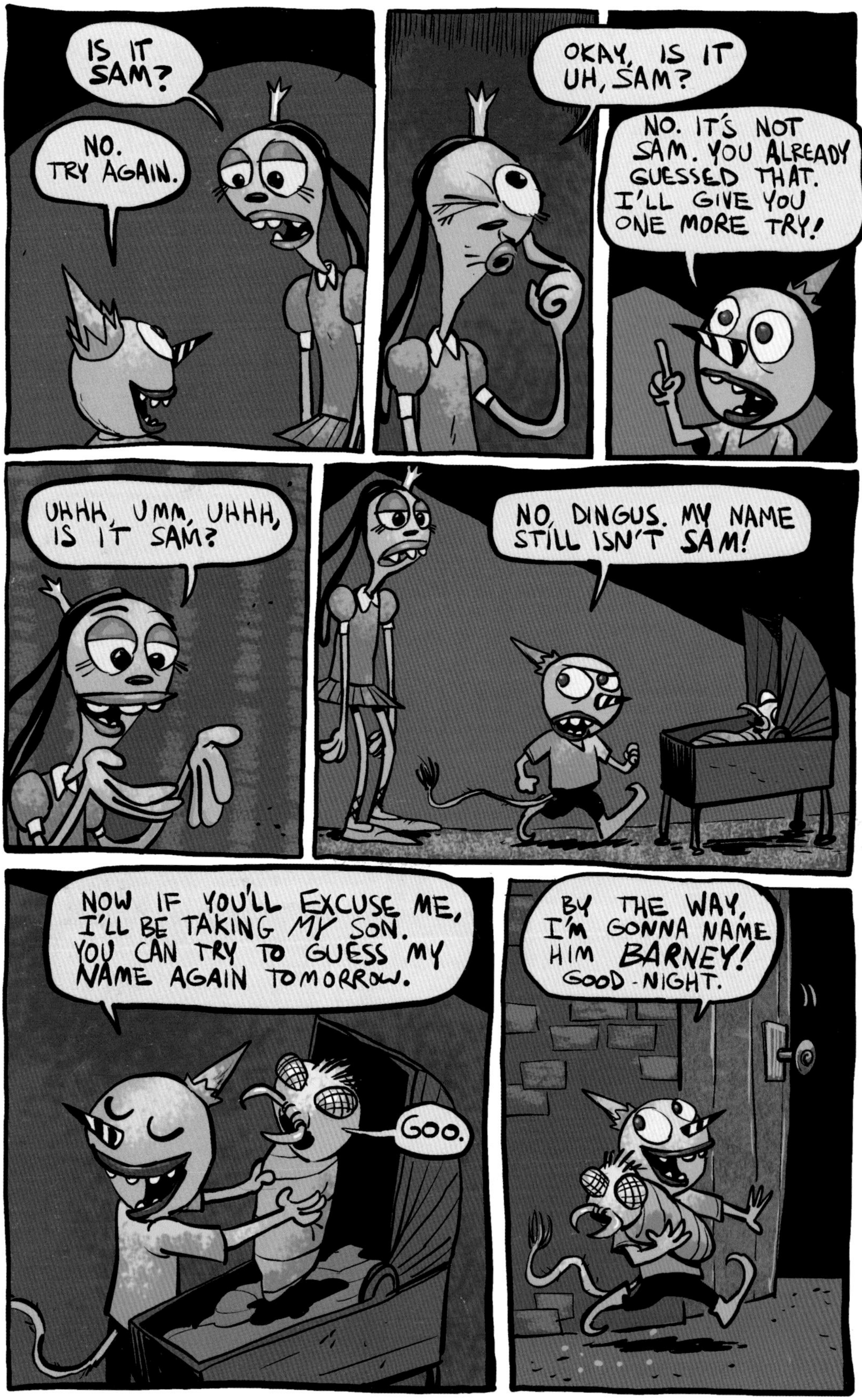
IS IT SAM?
NO. TRY AGAIN.
OKAY, IS IT UH, SAM?
NO. IT'S NOT SAM. YOU ALREADY GUESSED THAT. I'LL GIVE YOU ONE MORE TRY!
UHHH, UMM, UHHH, IS IT SAM?
NO, DINGUS. MY NAME STILL ISN'T SAM!
NOW IF YOU'LL EXCUSE ME, I'LL BE TAKING MY SON. YOU CAN TRY TO GUESS MY NAME AGAIN TOMORROW.
GOO.
BY THE WAY, I'M GONNA NAME HIM BARNEY! GOOD-NIGHT.

OH, BOO-HOO! HE CAN'T DO THIS...

...HE CAN'T NAME HIM BARNEY!

THE NEXT DAY, THE LITTLE MAGIC MAN LEARNED HOW HARD IT IS TO TAKE CARE OF A BABY.

HOW AM I SUPPOSED TO FIGURE OUT ALL OF THESE STUPID CAR-SEAT STRAPS?!

GOO!

THAT NIGHT HE CAME BACK TO THE GIRL, HOPING SHE WOULD GUESS HIS NAME!

OKAY, IF YOU CAN GUESS MY NAME, YOU CAN HAVE YOUR BRAT-- I MEAN, YOUR SON BACK.

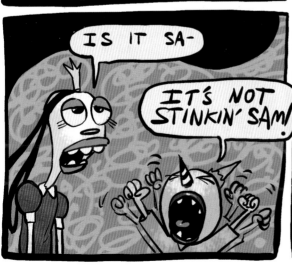

IS IT SA-

IT'S NOT STINKIN' SAM!

IT RHYMES WITH SHMUMPLESTILTSKIN!

OHHH!

47

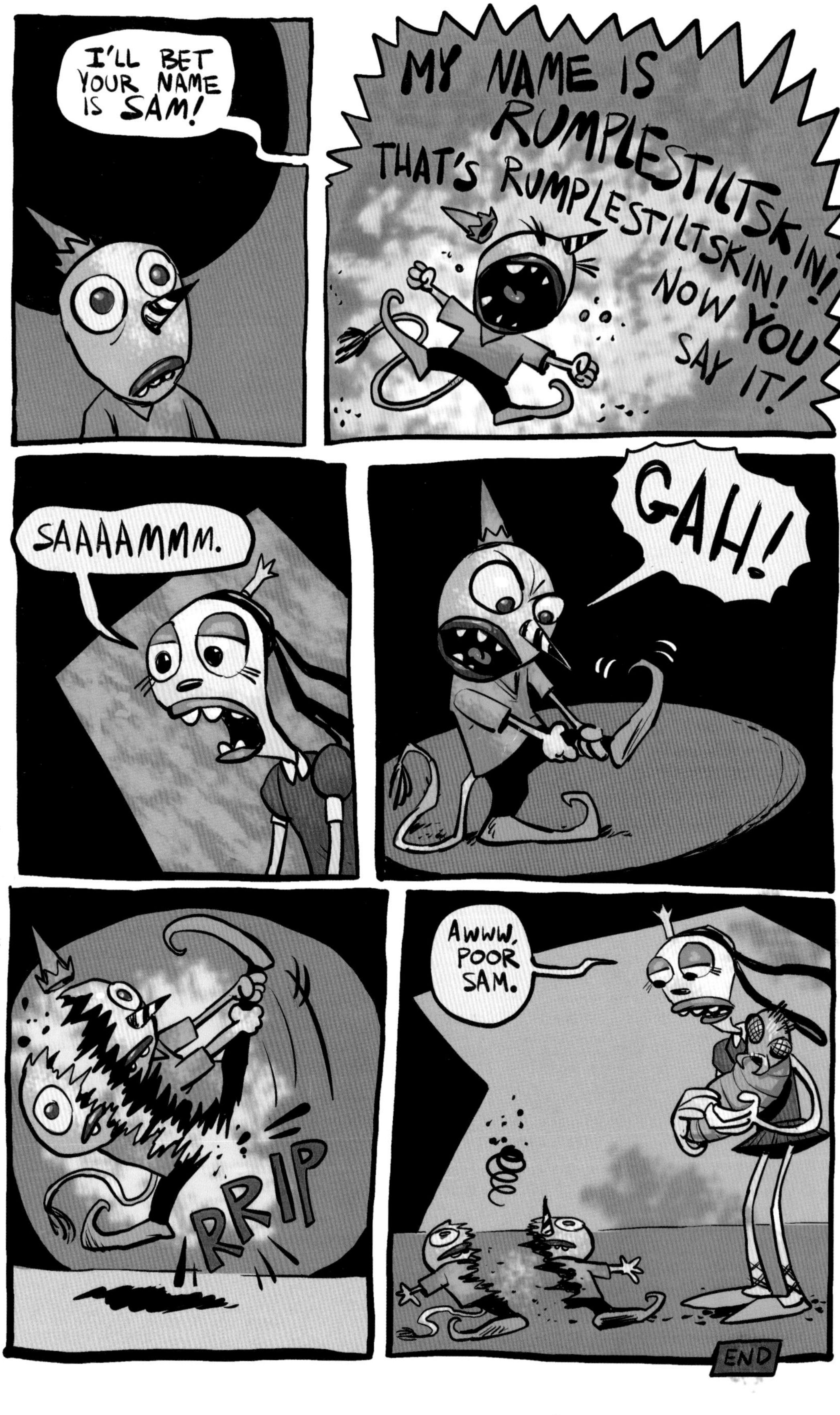
I'LL BET YOUR NAME IS SAM!
MY NAME IS RUMPLESTILTSKIN! THAT'S RUMPLESTILTSKIN! NOW YOU SAY IT!
SAAAAMMM.
GAH!
RRIP
AWWW, POOR SAM.
END

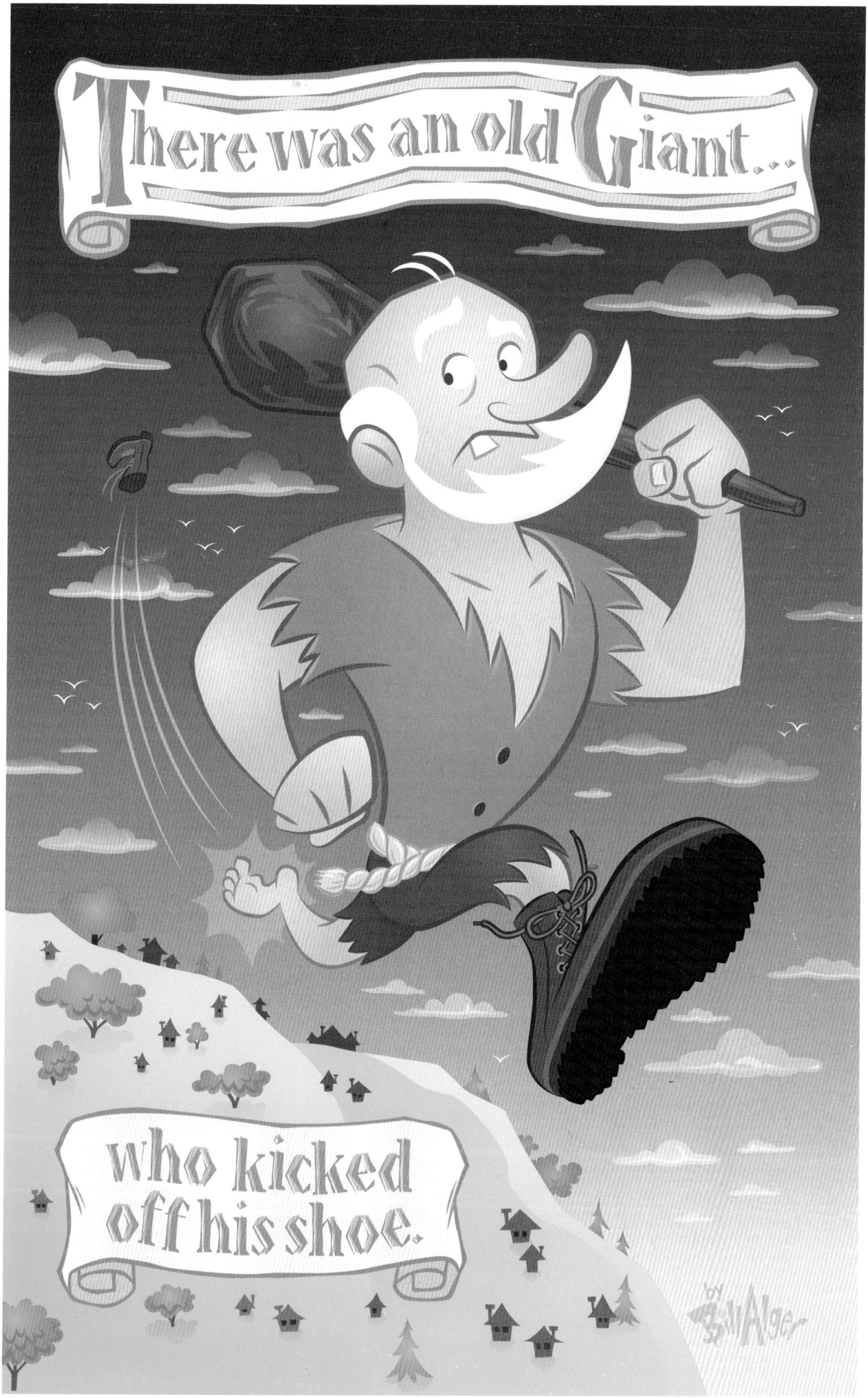
There was an old Giant...
who kicked off his shoe.
by Bill Alger

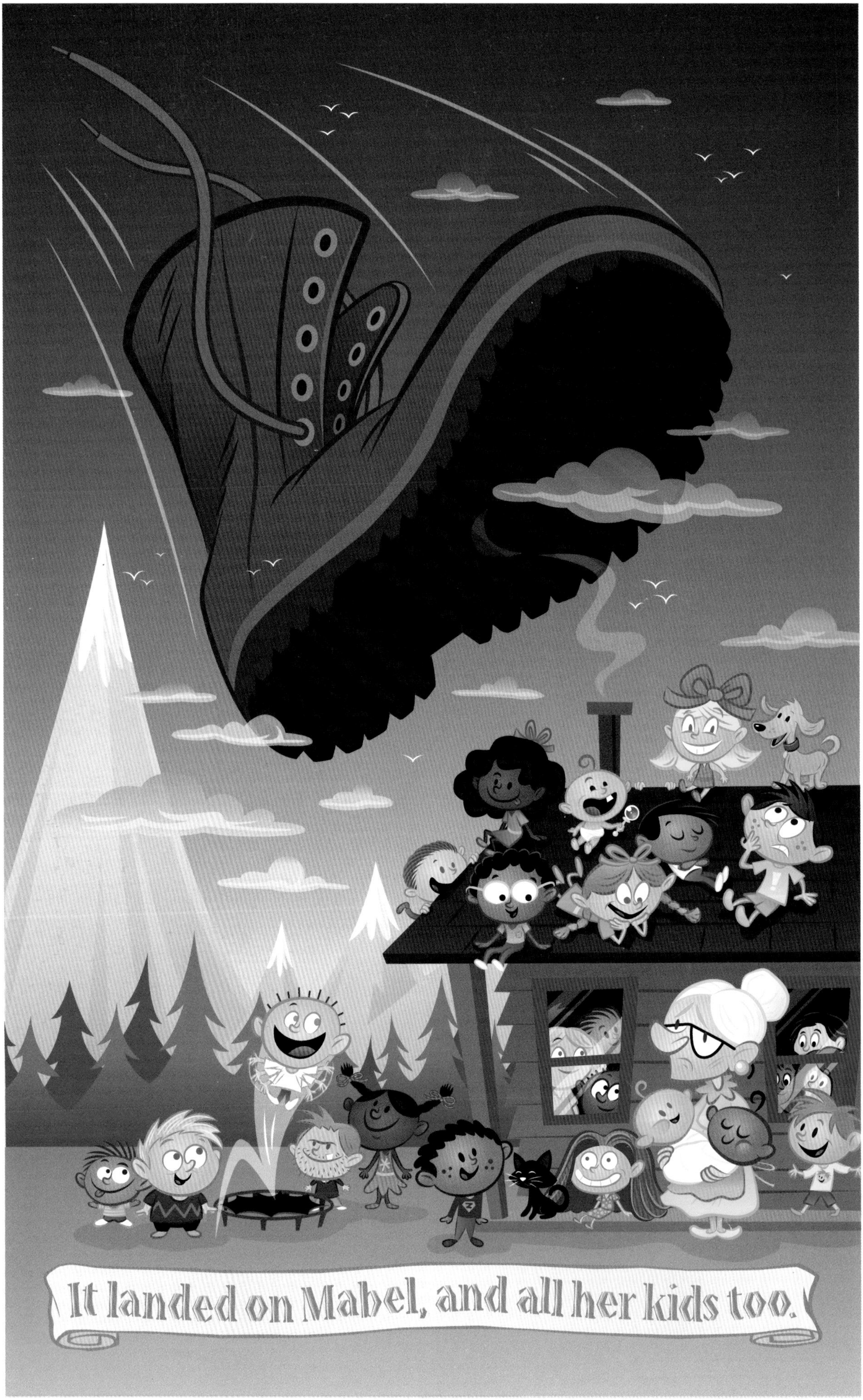
It landed on Mabel, and all her kids too.

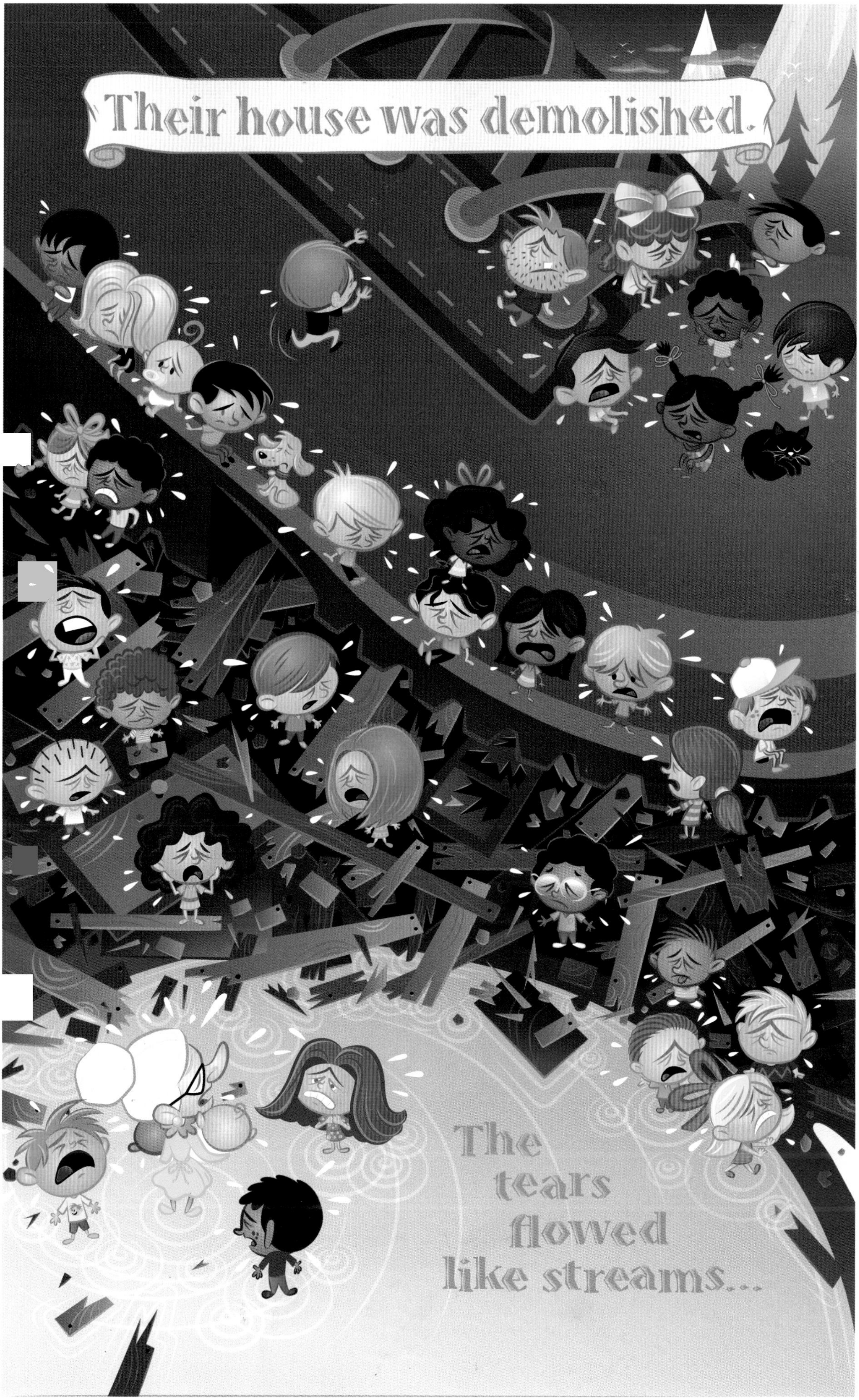
Their house was demolished.
The tears flowed like streams...

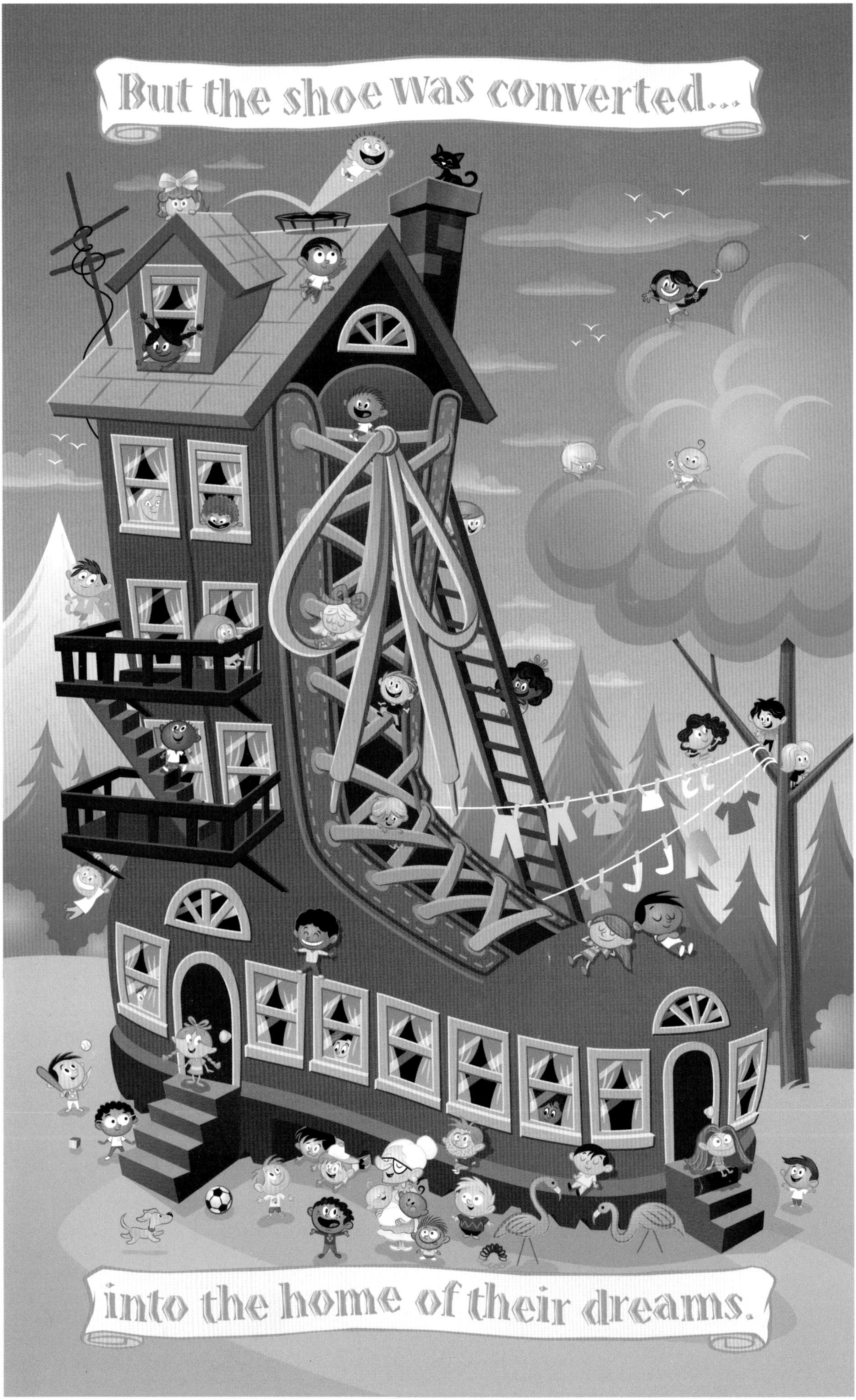
But the shoe was converted...
into the home of their dreams.

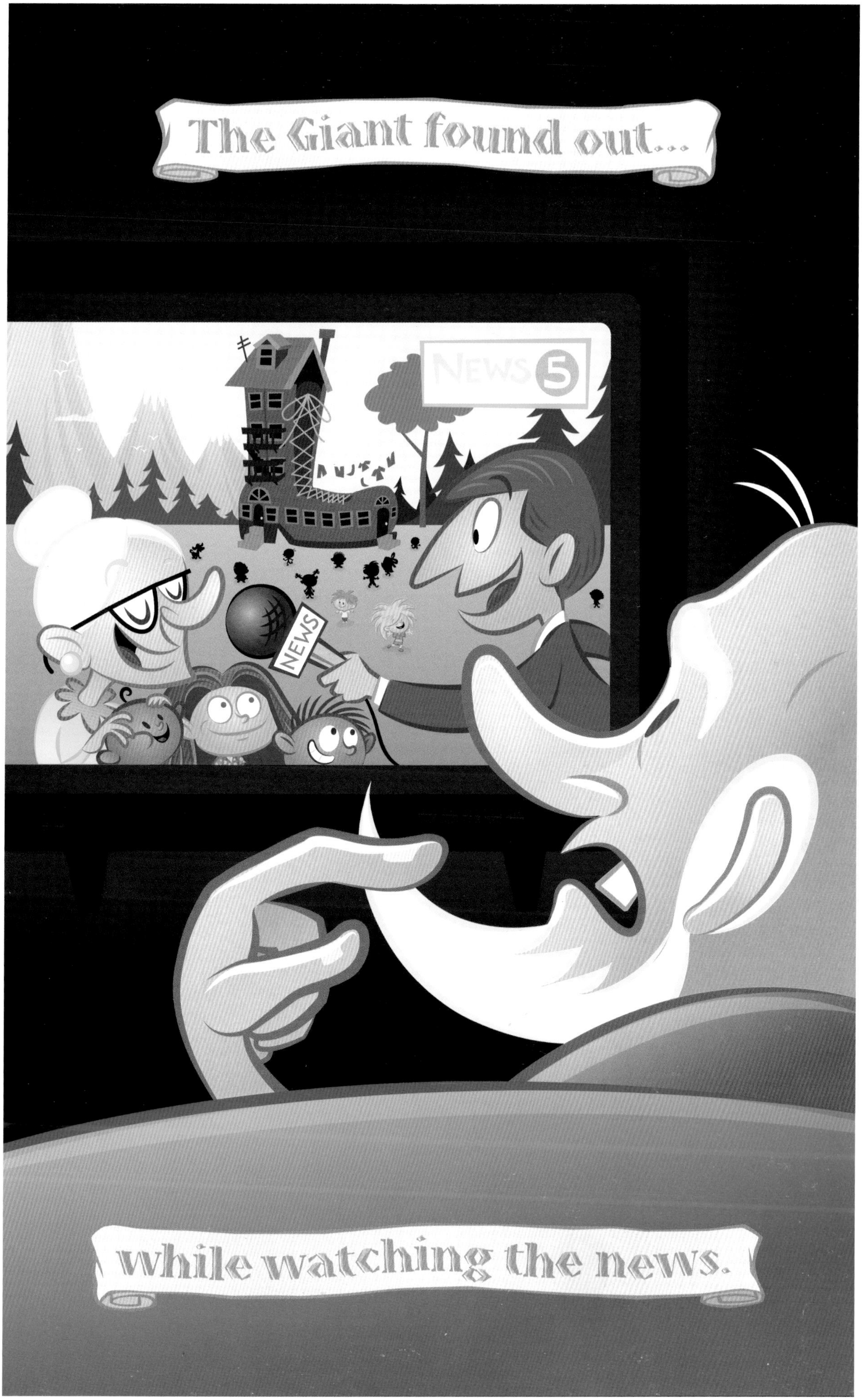
The Giant found out...
NEWS 5
NEWS
while watching the news.

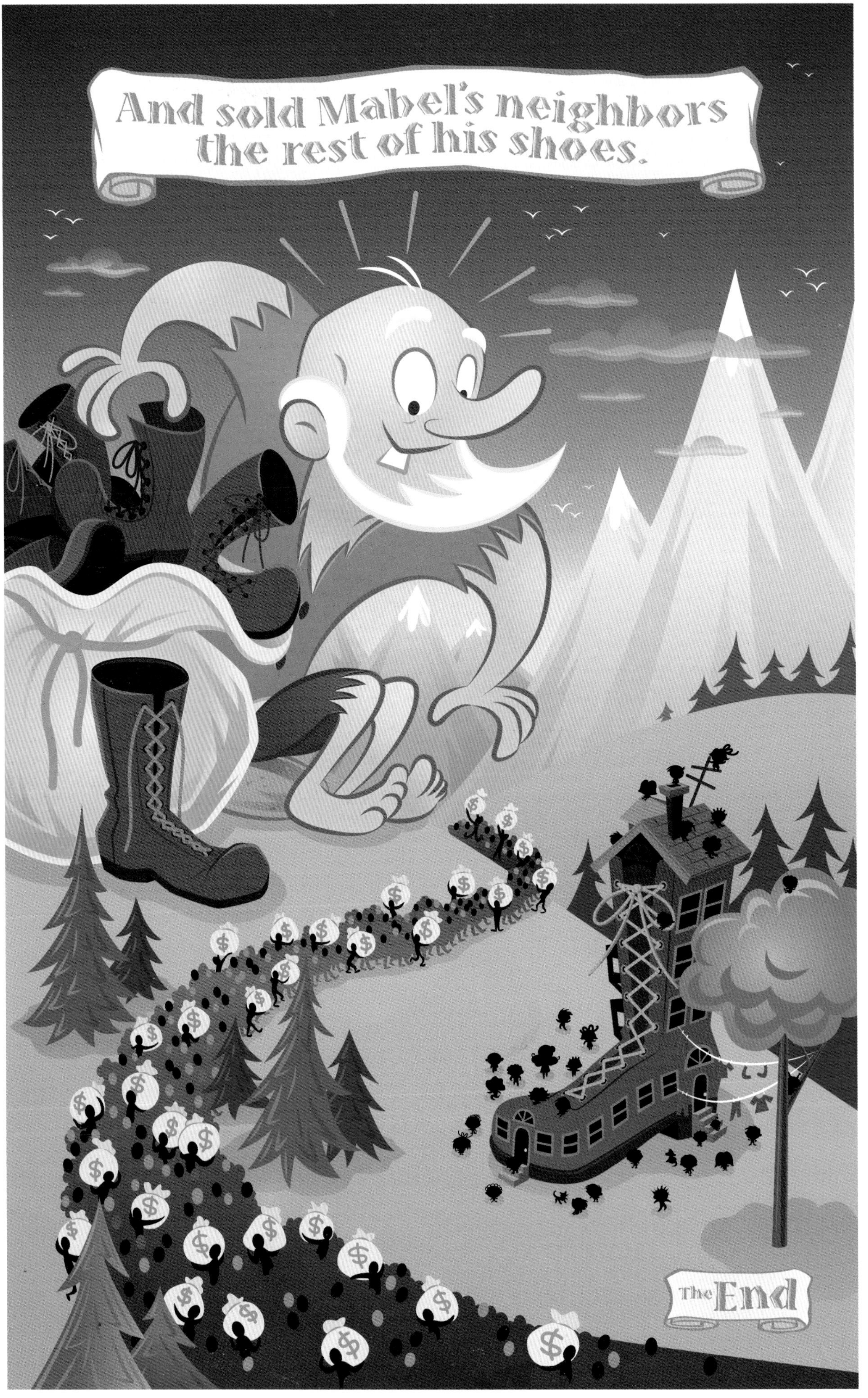
And sold Mabel's neighbors
the rest of his shoes.
The End

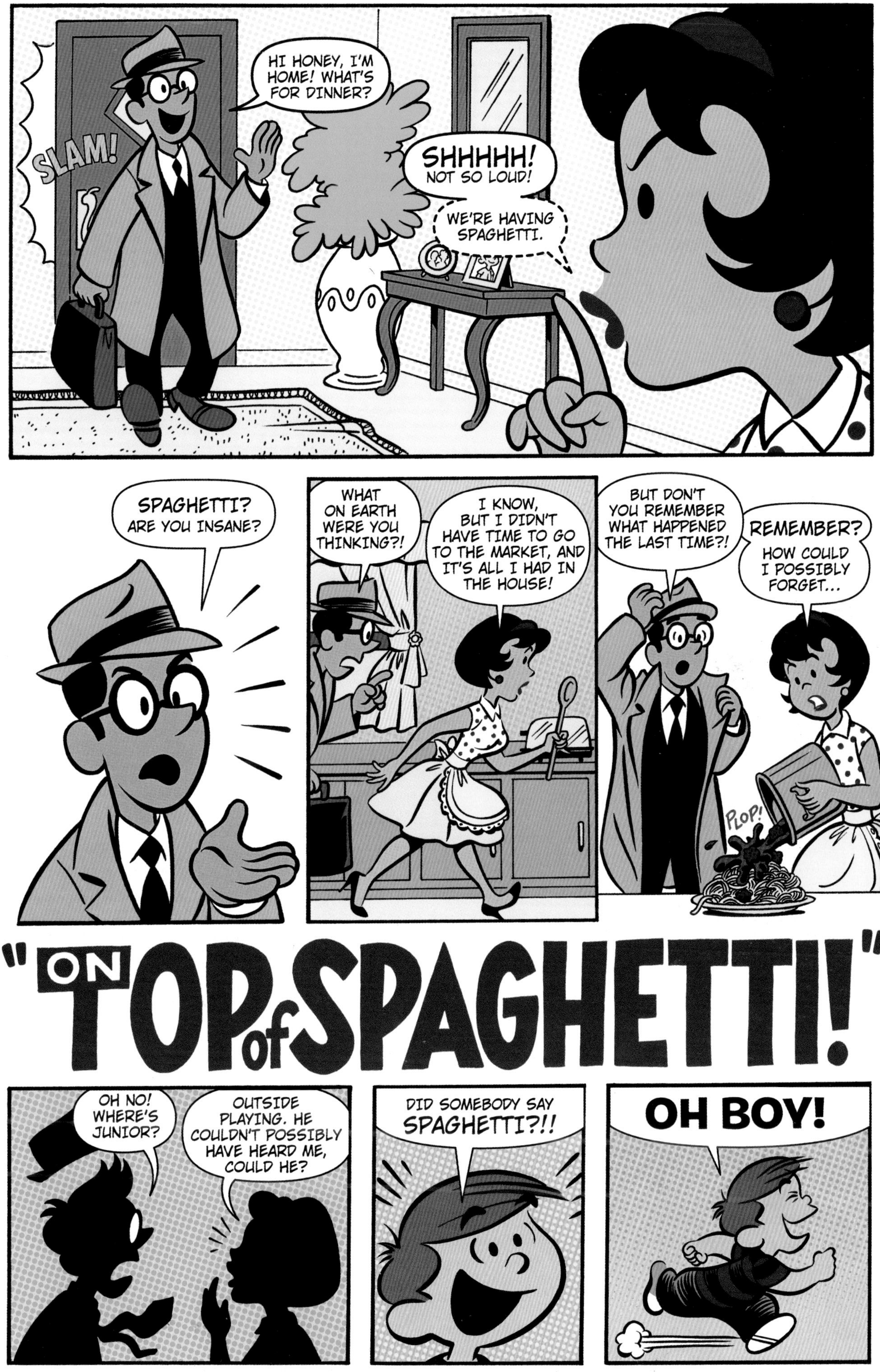
SLAM!
HI HONEY, I'M HOME! WHAT'S FOR DINNER?
SHHHHH! NOT SO LOUD!
WE'RE HAVING SPAGHETTI.
SPAGHETTI? ARE YOU INSANE?
WHAT ON EARTH WERE YOU THINKING?!
I KNOW, BUT I DIDN'T HAVE TIME TO GO TO THE MARKET, AND IT'S ALL I HAD IN THE HOUSE!
BUT DON'T YOU REMEMBER WHAT HAPPENED THE LAST TIME?!
REMEMBER? HOW COULD I POSSIBLY FORGET...
PLOP!
"ON TOP of SPAGHETTI!"
OH NO! WHERE'S JUNIOR?
OUTSIDE PLAYING. HE COULDN'T POSSIBLY HAVE HEARD ME, COULD HE?
DID SOMEBODY SAY SPAGHETTI?!!
OH BOY!

STORY & ART: BILL "MAMA-MIA" MORRISON • COLORS AND LETTERS: SERBAN "CARBONARA" CRISTESCU

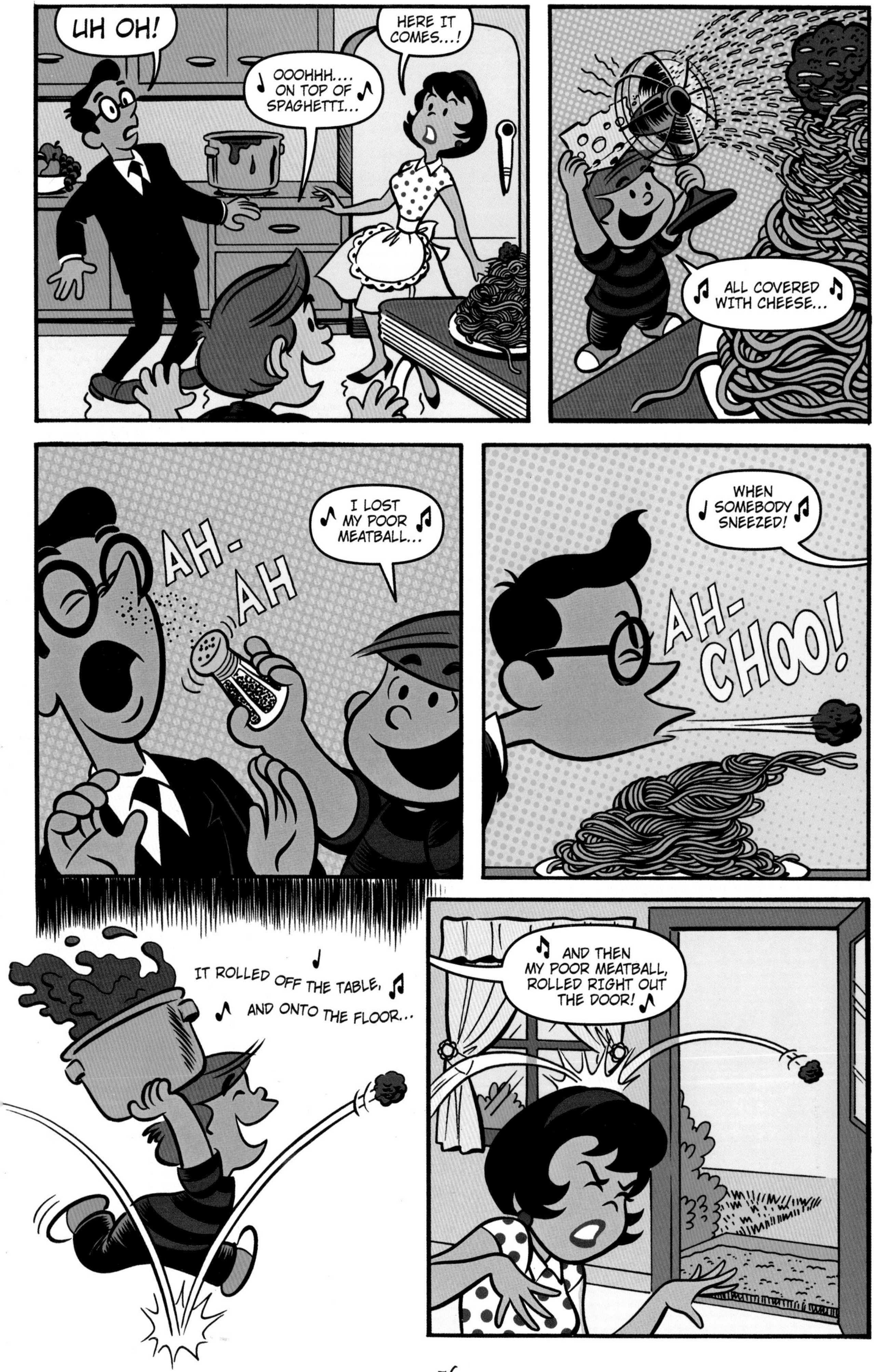
UH OH!
OOOHHH.... ON TOP OF SPAGHETTI...
HERE IT COMES...!
ALL COVERED WITH CHEESE...
AH-AH
I LOST MY POOR MEATBALL...
WHEN SOMEBODY SNEEZED!
AH-CHOO!
IT ROLLED OFF THE TABLE, AND ONTO THE FLOOR...
AND THEN MY POOR MEATBALL, ROLLED RIGHT OUT THE DOOR!

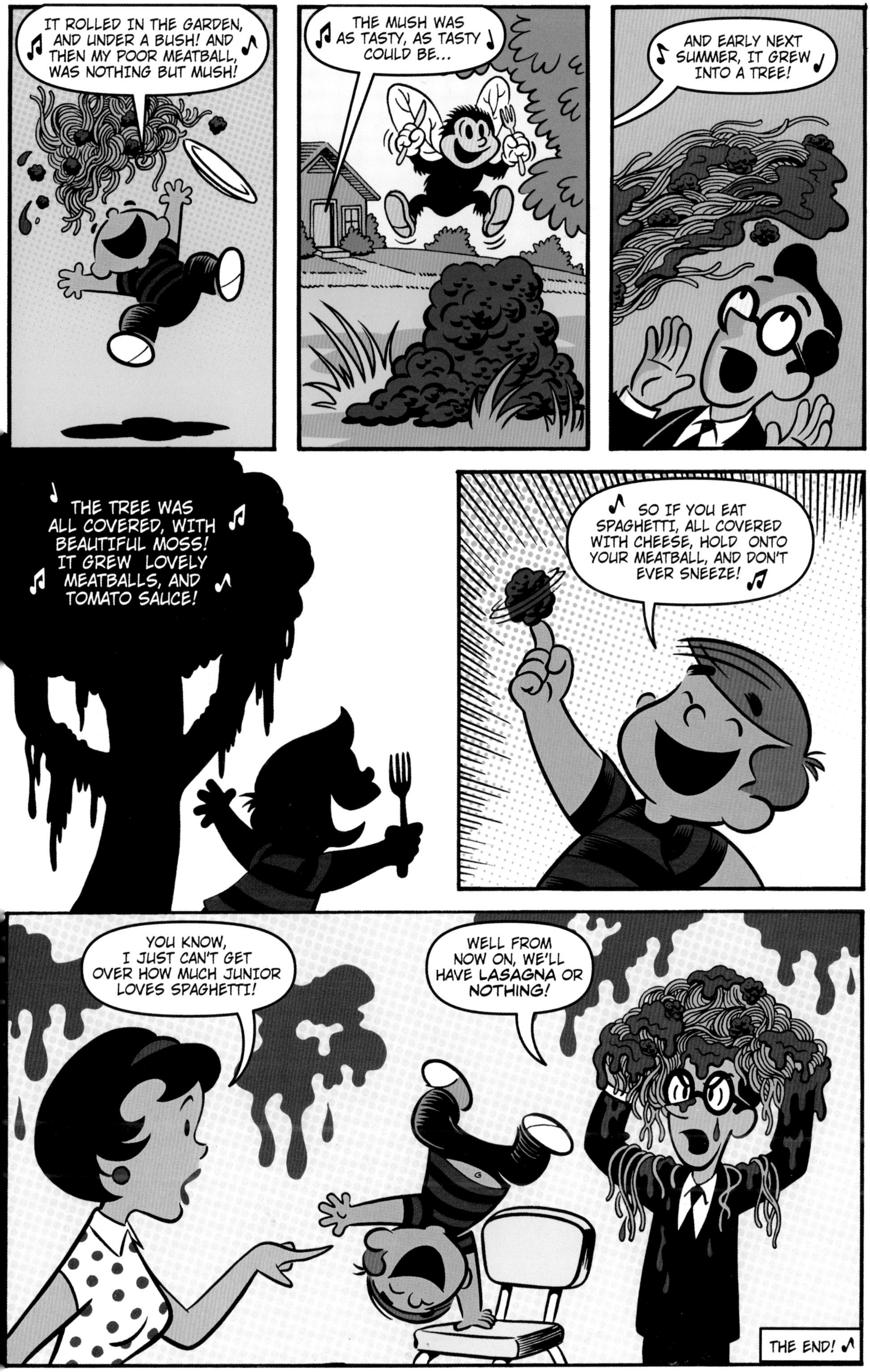
IT ROLLED IN THE GARDEN, AND UNDER A BUSH! AND THEN MY POOR MEATBALL, WAS NOTHING BUT MUSH!
THE MUSH WAS AS TASTY, AS TASTY COULD BE...
AND EARLY NEXT SUMMER, IT GREW INTO A TREE!
THE TREE WAS ALL COVERED, WITH BEAUTIFUL MOSS! IT GREW LOVELY MEATBALLS, AND TOMATO SAUCE!
SO IF YOU EAT SPAGHETTI, ALL COVERED WITH CHEESE, HOLD ONTO YOUR MEATBALL, AND DON'T EVER SNEEZE!
YOU KNOW, I JUST CAN'T GET OVER HOW MUCH JUNIOR LOVES SPAGHETTI!
WELL FROM NOW ON, WE'LL HAVE LASAGNA OR NOTHING!
THE END!

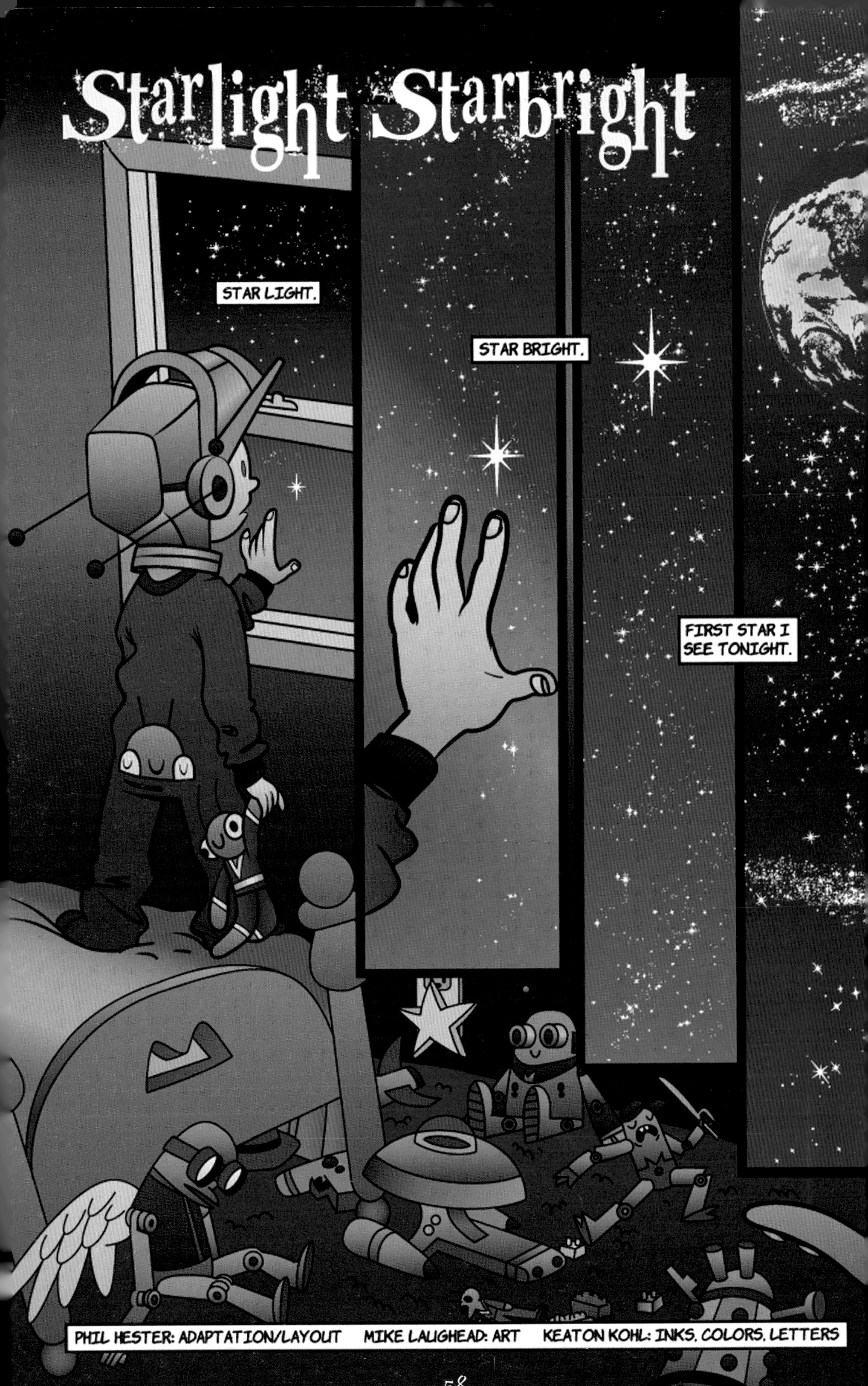
Starlight Starbright
STAR LIGHT.
STAR BRIGHT.
FIRST STAR I SEE TONIGHT.
PHIL HESTER: ADAPTATION/LAYOUT MIKE LAIGHEAD: ART KEATON KOHL: INKS, COLORS, LETTERS

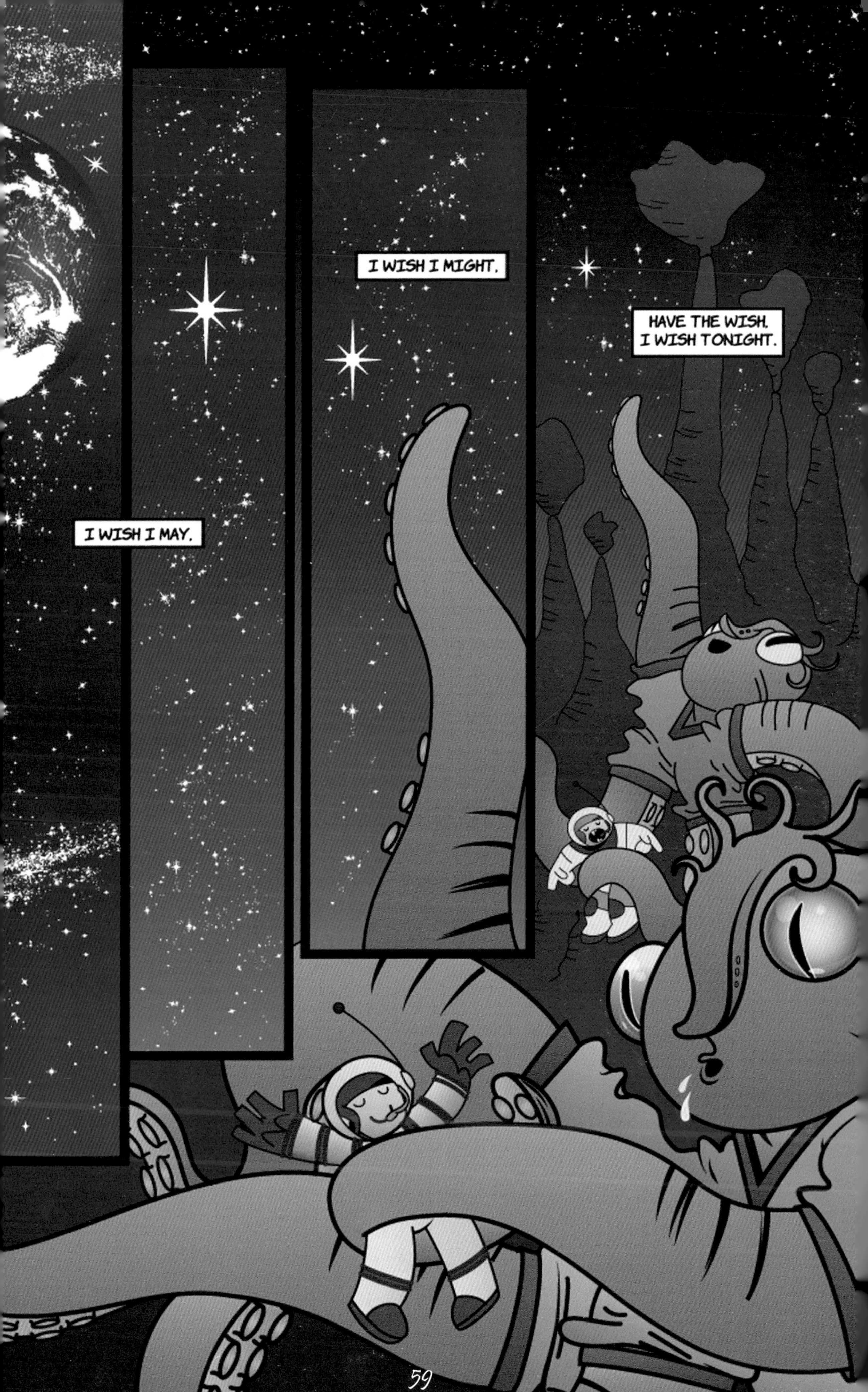
I WISH I MAY.
I WISH I MIGHT.
HAVE THE WISH.
I WISH TONIGHT.

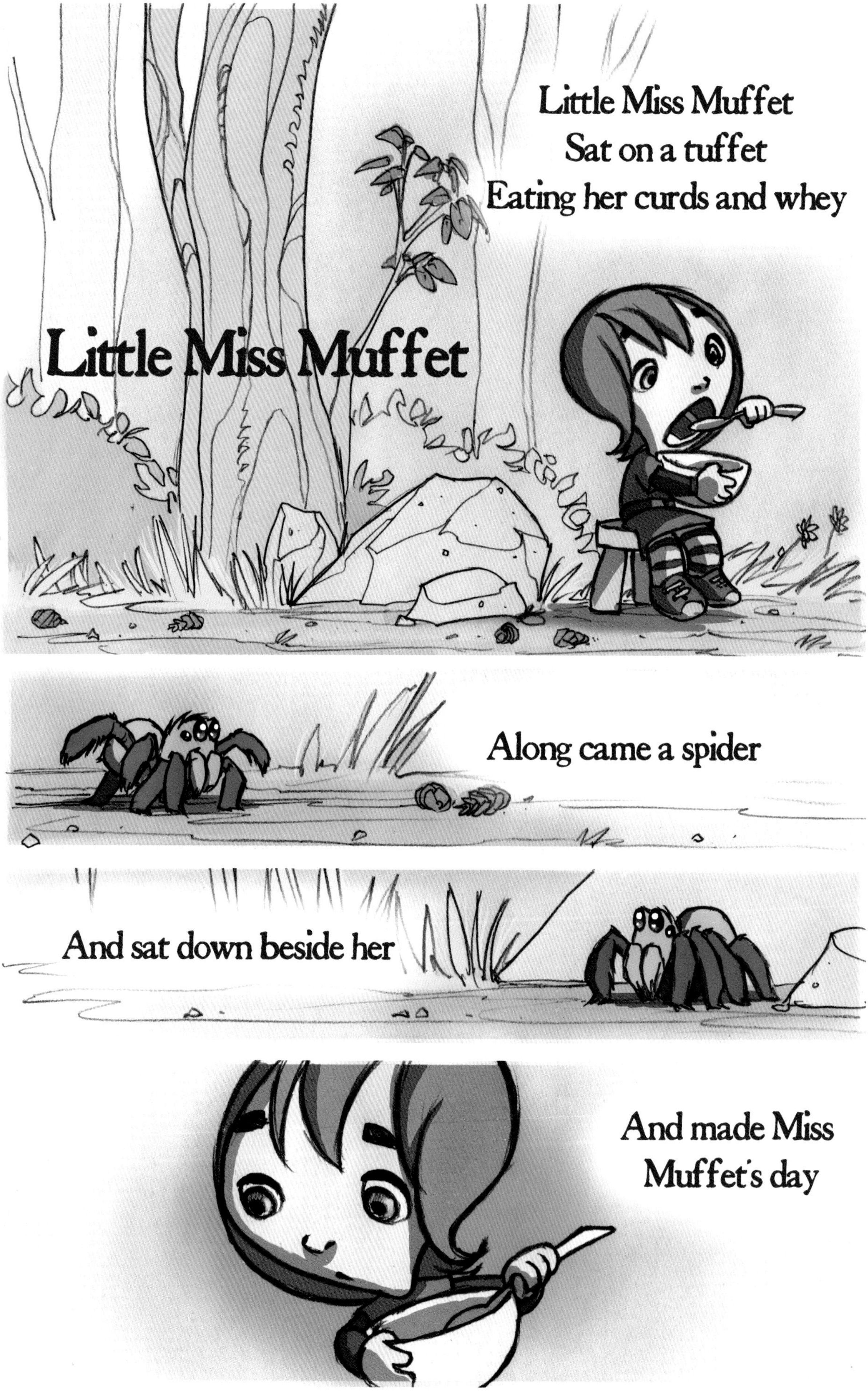
Little Miss Muffet
Sat on a tuffet
Eating her curds and whey
Little Miss Muffet
Along came a spider
And sat down beside her
And made Miss Muffet's day

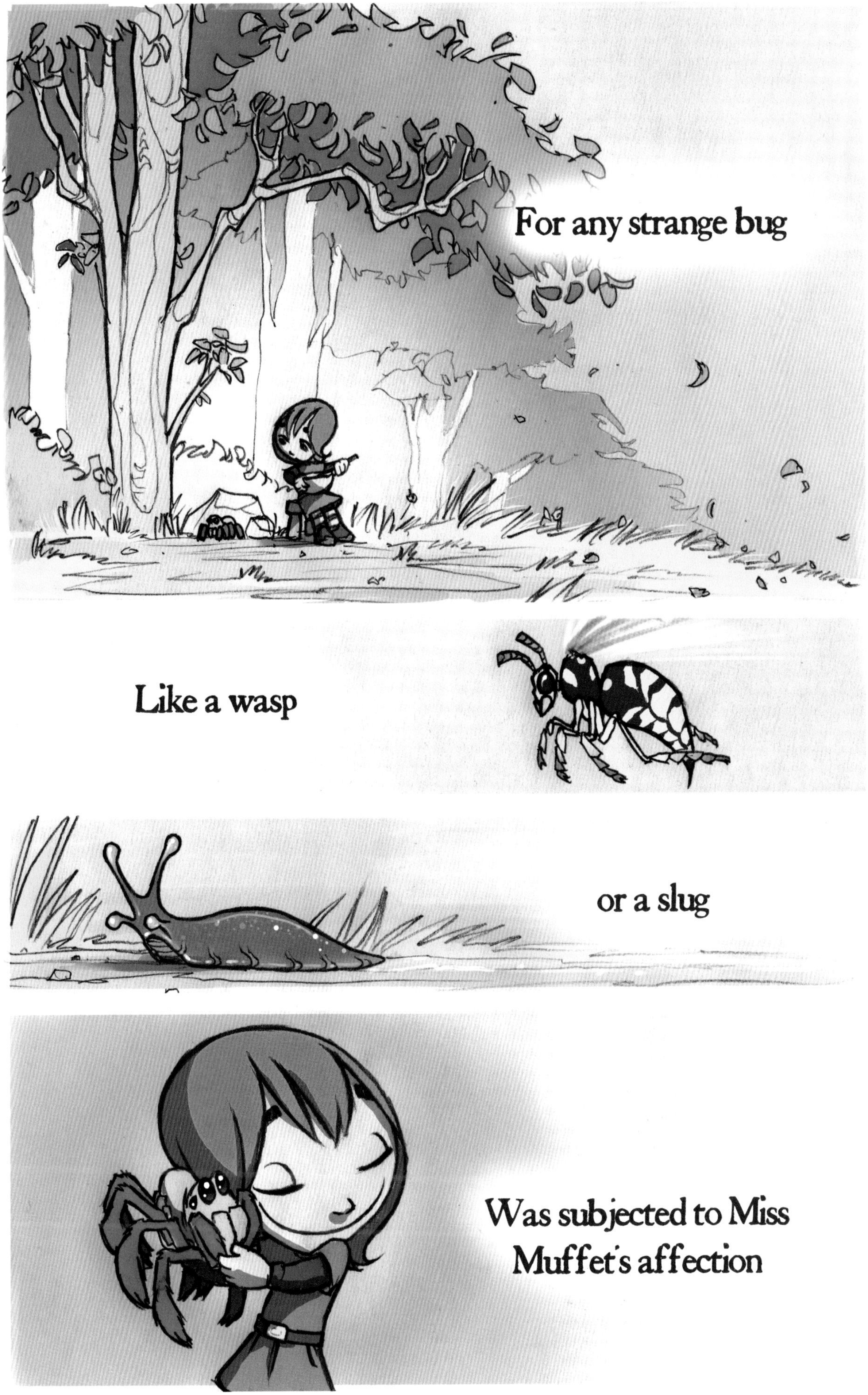
For any strange bug
Like a wasp
or a slug
Was subjected to Miss Muffet's affection

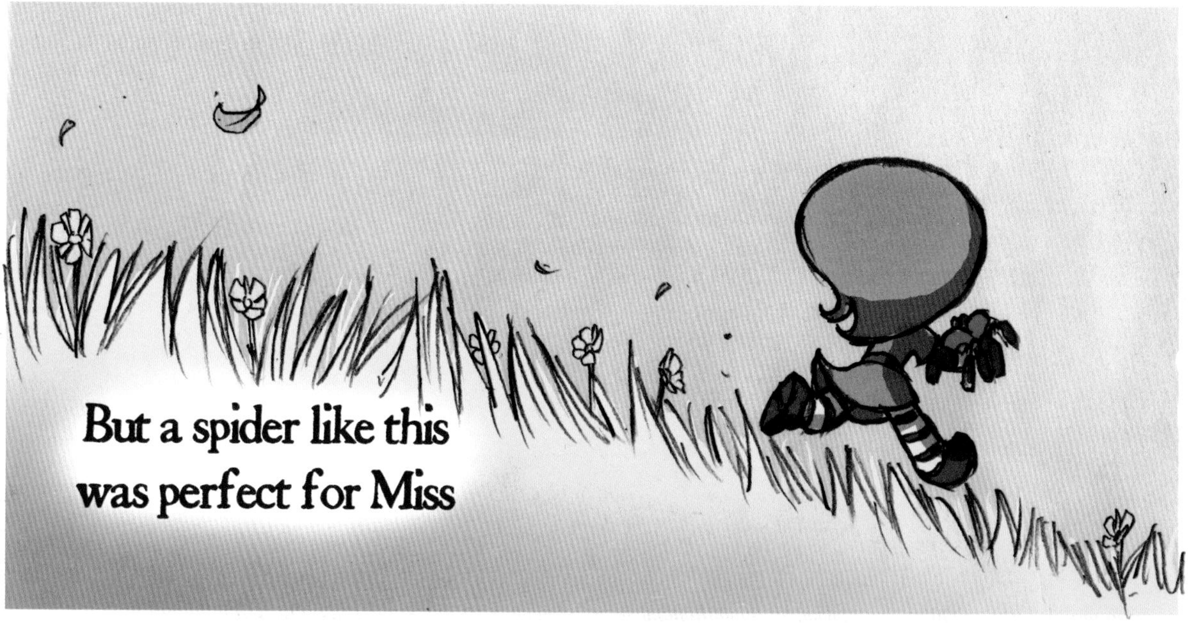
But a spider like this
was perfect for Miss

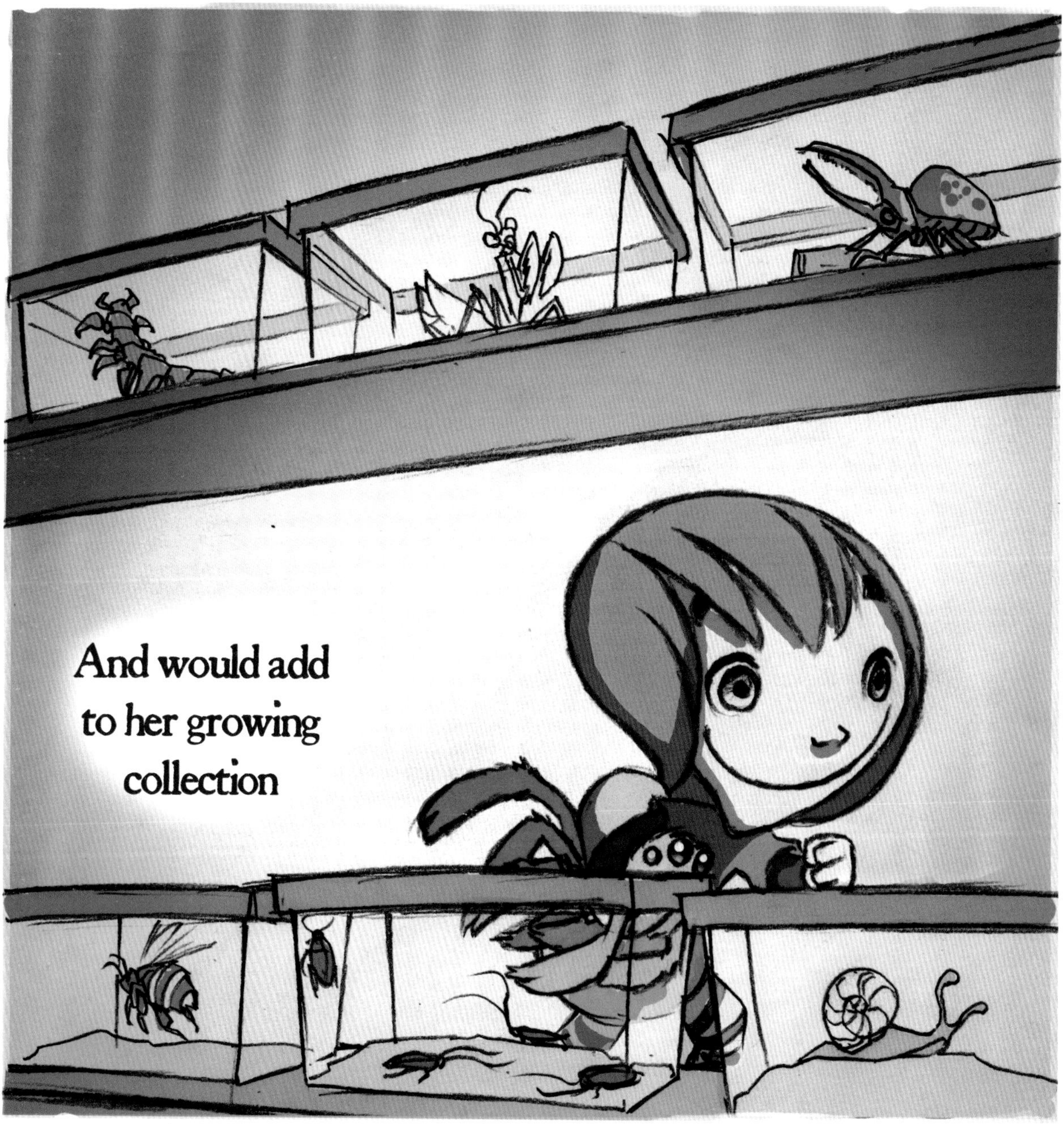
And would add
to her growing
collection

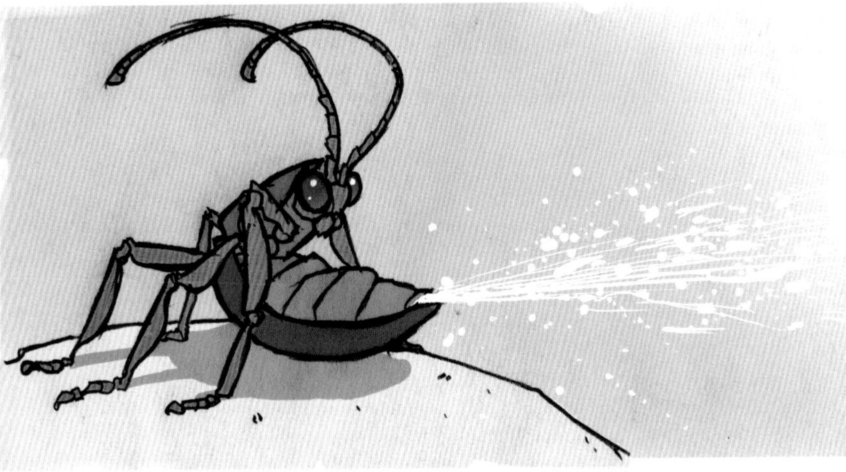

Beetles that
spray

And Mantids
that pray

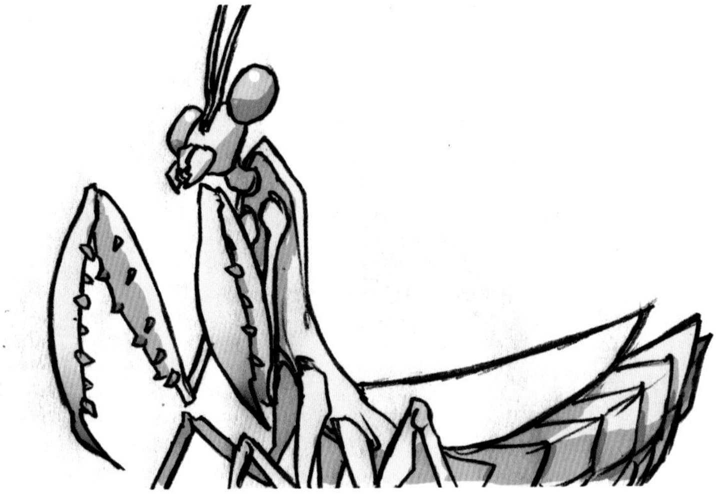

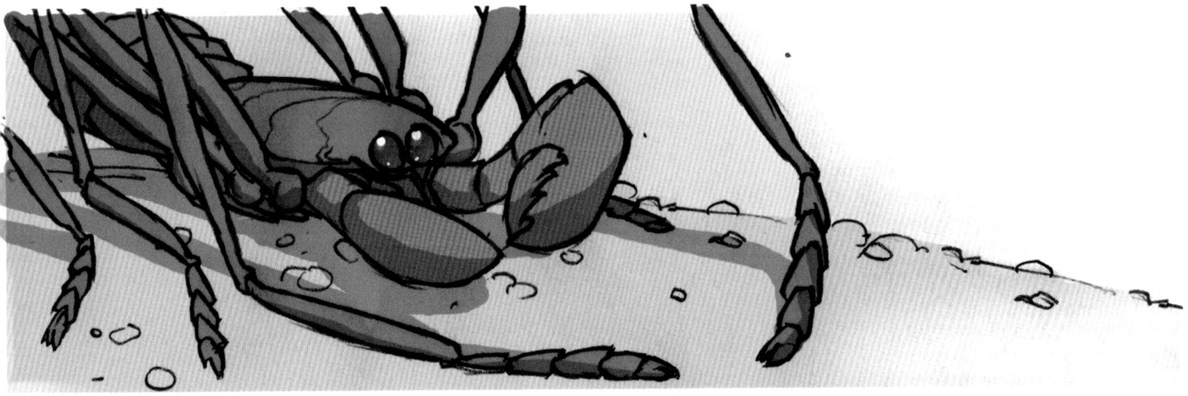

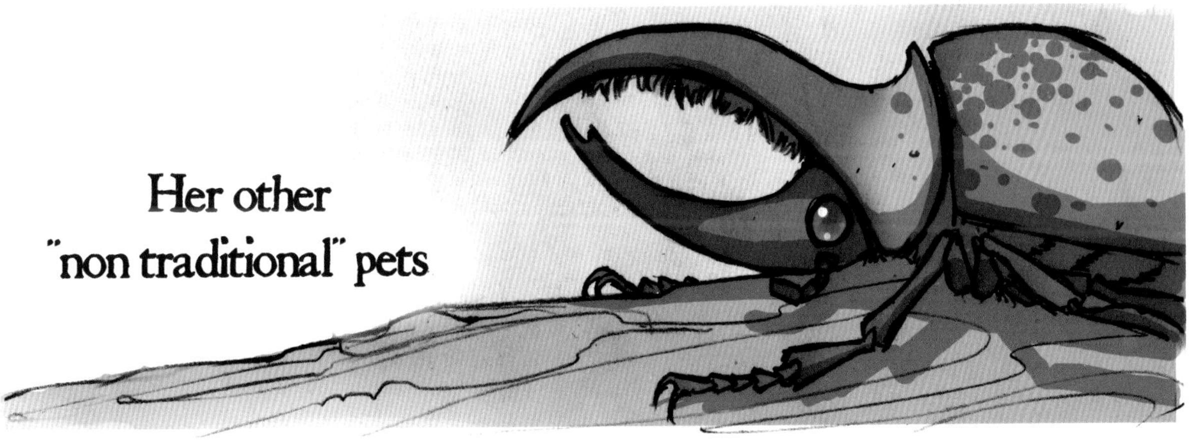
Her other
"non traditional" pets

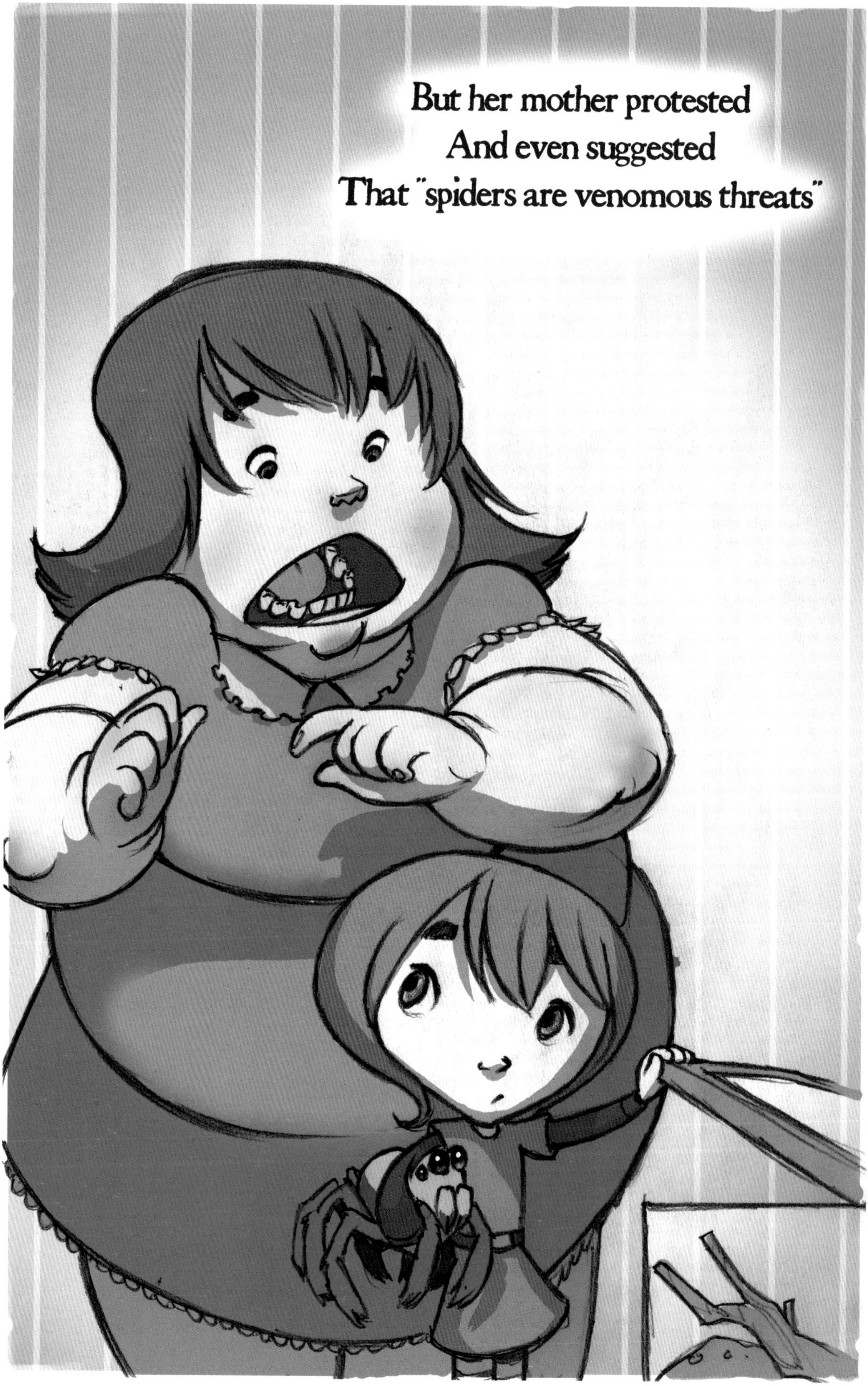
But her mother protested
And even suggested
That "spiders are venomous threats"

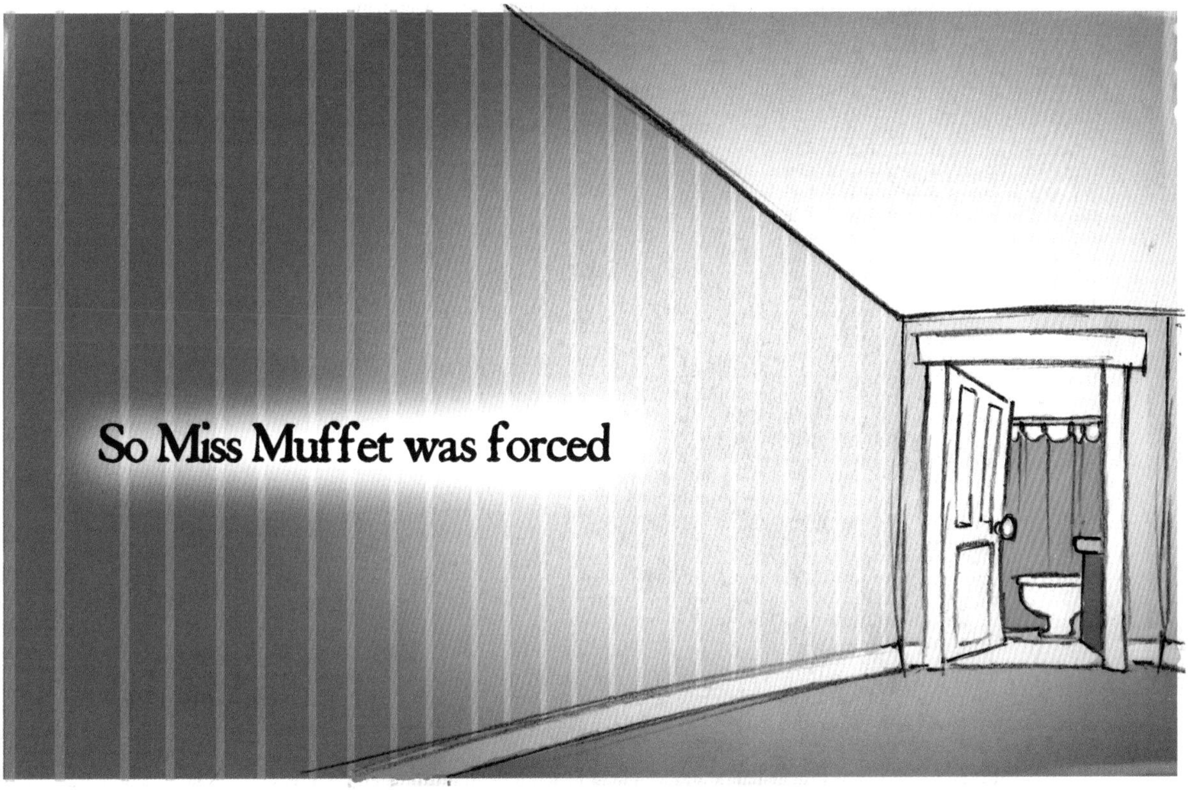
So Miss Muffet was forced

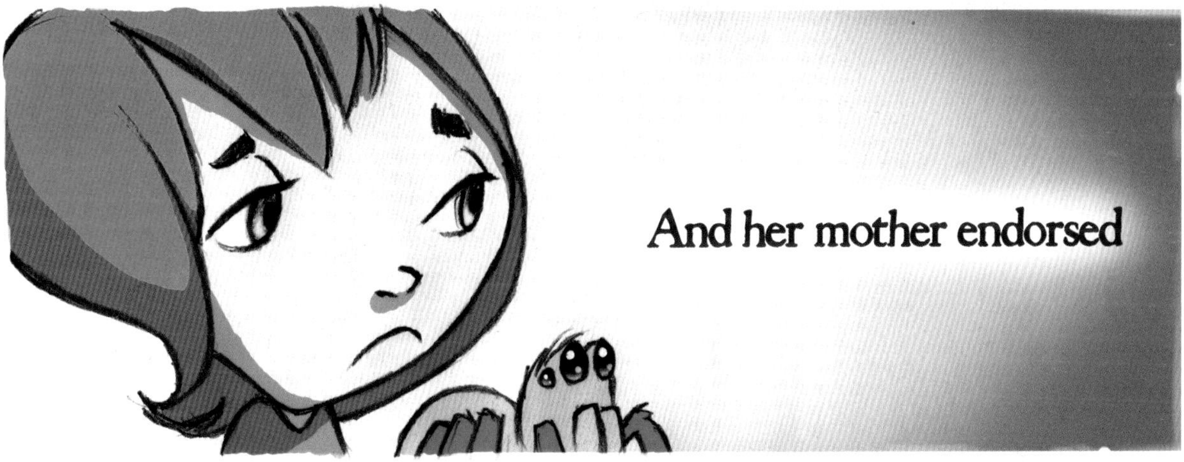
And her mother endorsed

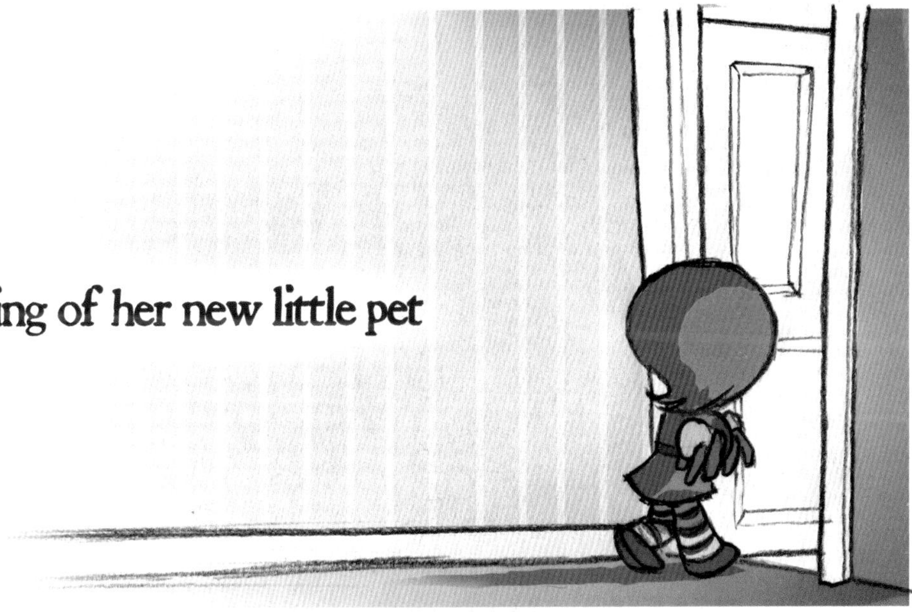
The flushing of her new little pet

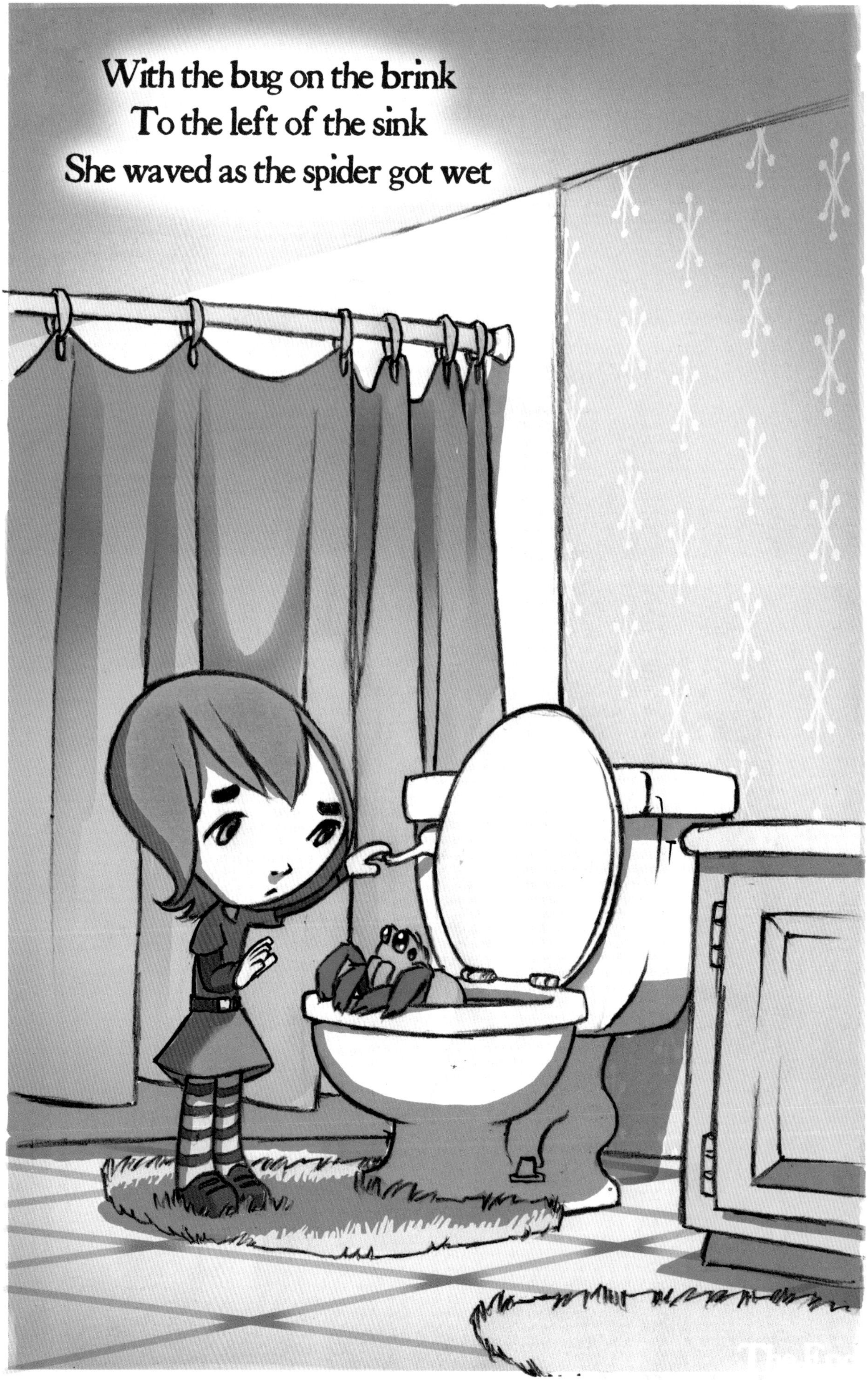
With the bug on the brink
To the left of the sink
She waved as the spider got wet

This is...

the house that jack built

Loosely adapted by **Neil Kleid** and **Fernando Pinto**

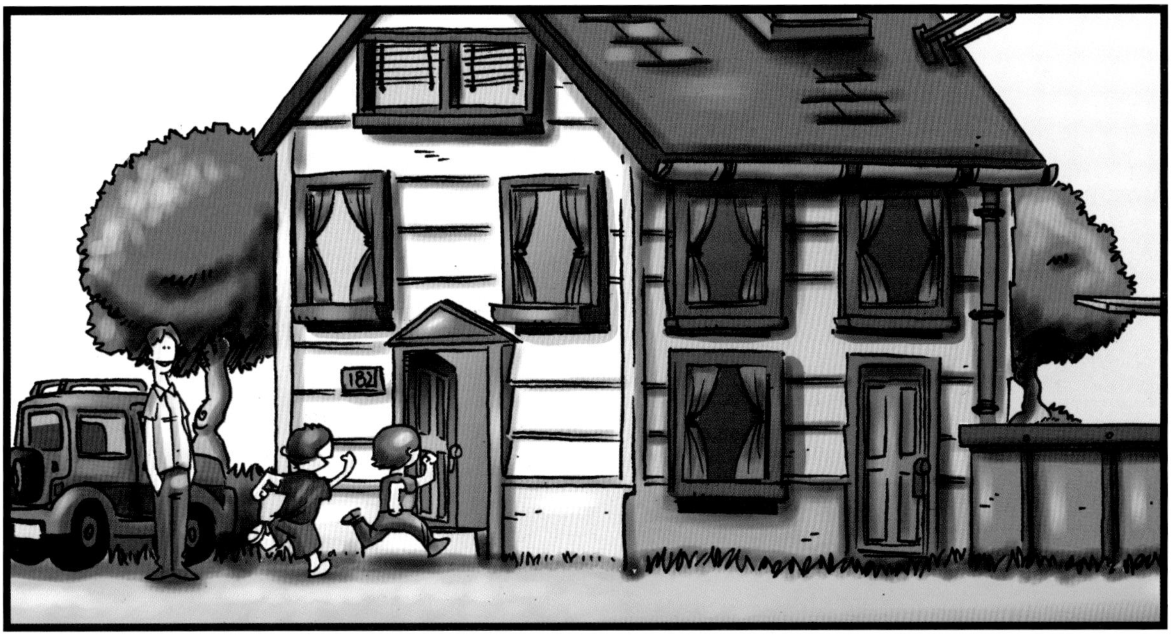

This is the house that Jack built.

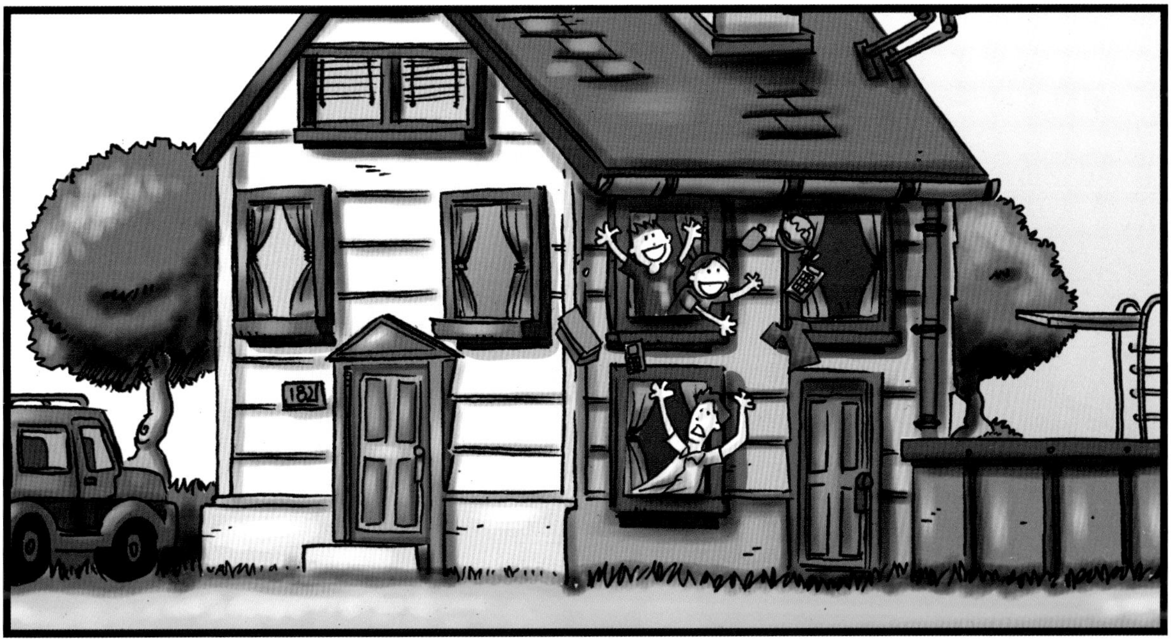

These are the boys
That live in the house that Jack built.

These are the toys
Thrown by the boys
That live in the house that Jack built.

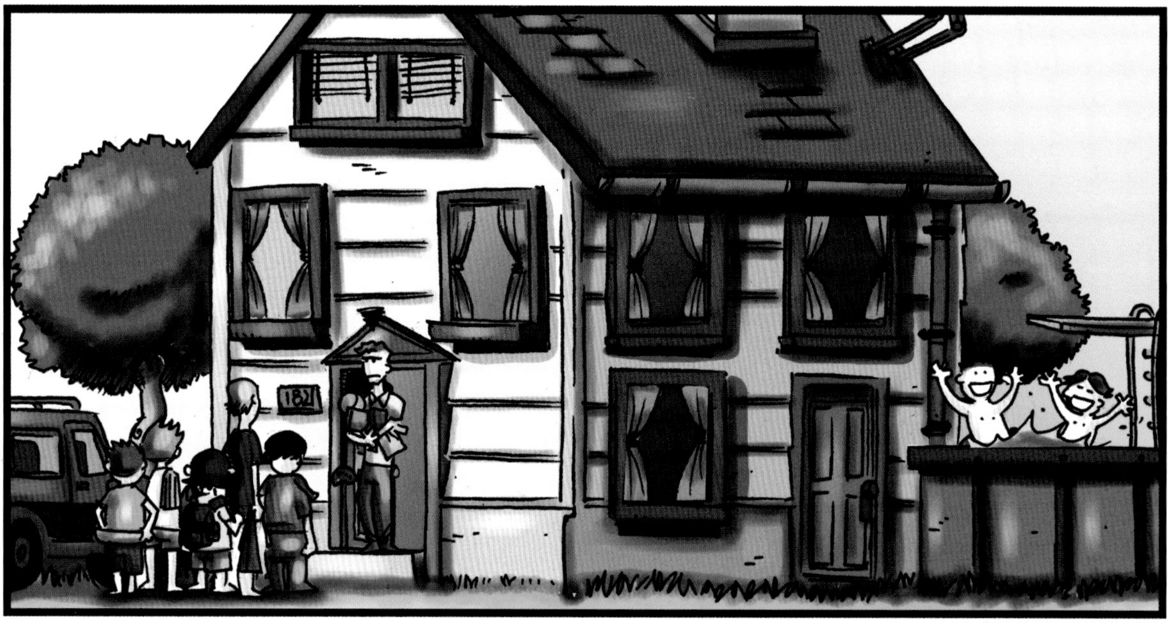

These are the neighbor kids
Who bring more toys
Just like the ones
Thrown by the boys
That live in the house that Jack built.

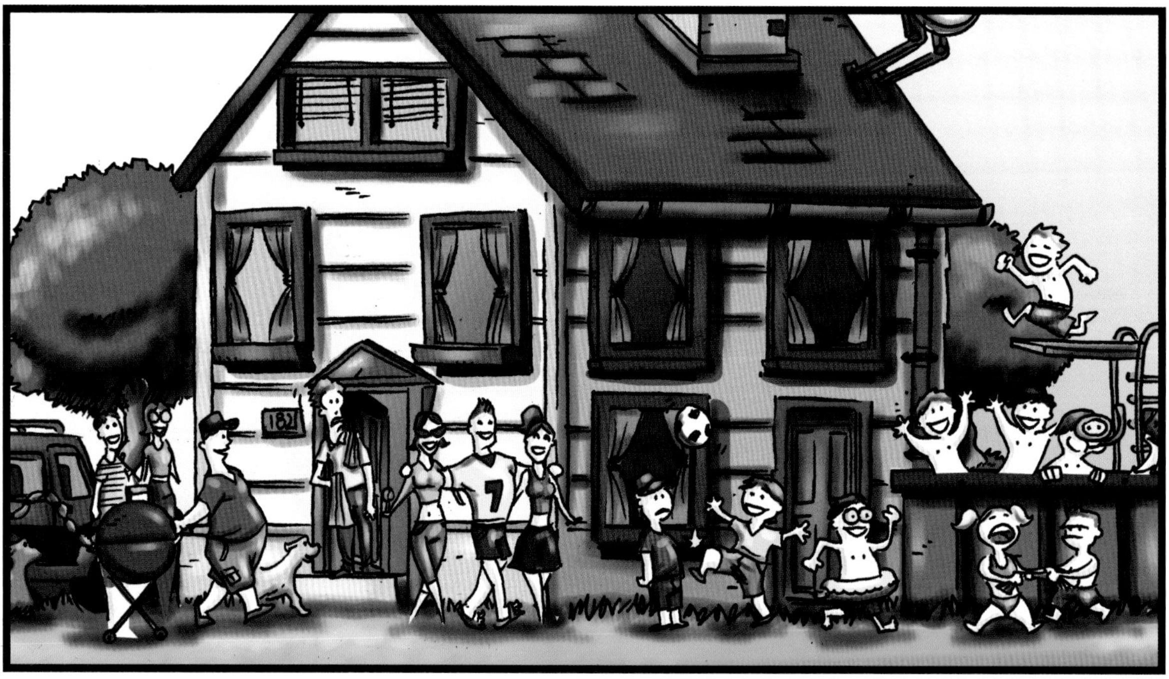

These are the parents
That raised the kids
Who tossed their toys
Just like the boys
That live in the house that Jack built.

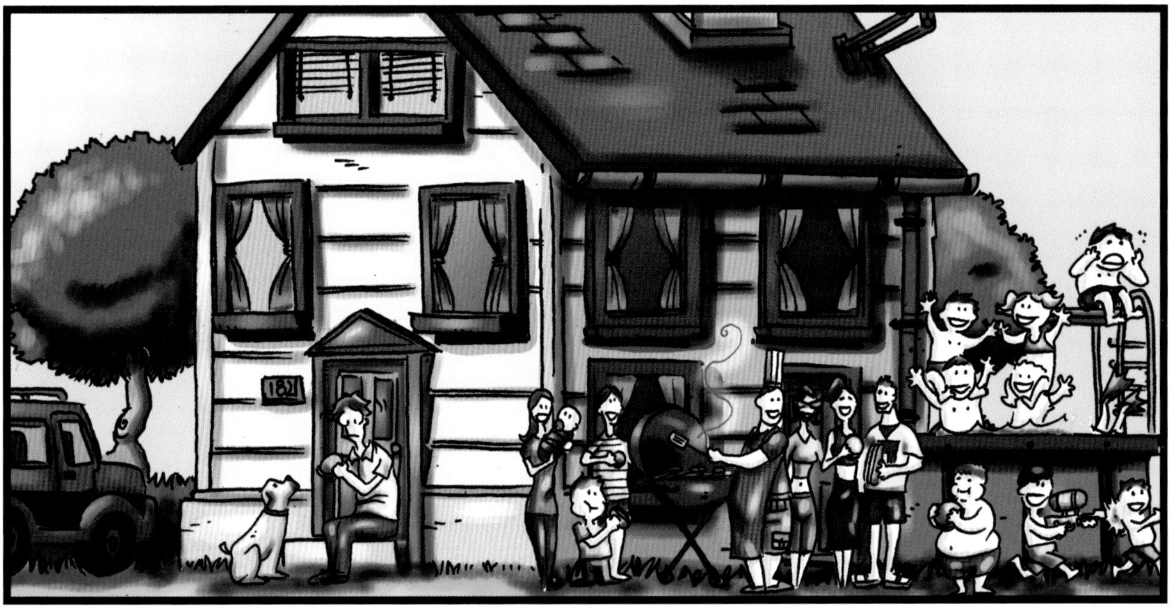
1821

This is the grill (gas, not coal!)
Owned by the neighbors
That raised the kids
Who threw their toys
Just like the boys
That live in the house that Jack built.

Dinner's served! And eaten whole,
Cooked by the grill (gas, not coal)
Owned by the neighbors
That raised the kids
Who threw their toys
Just like the boys
That live in the house that Jack built.

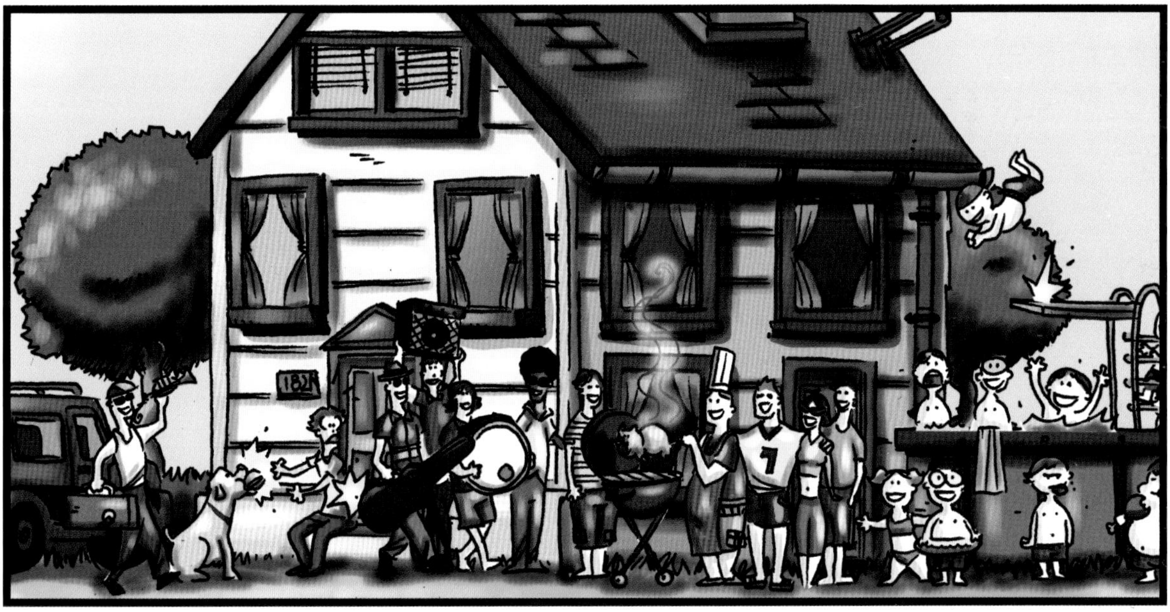
1821

These high school kids
Will rock n' roll
For a few hamburgers
Cooked well and whole
By the grill that's gas
And still not coal

Owned by the neighbors
That raised the kids
Who threw their toys
Just like the boys
That live in the house that Jack built.

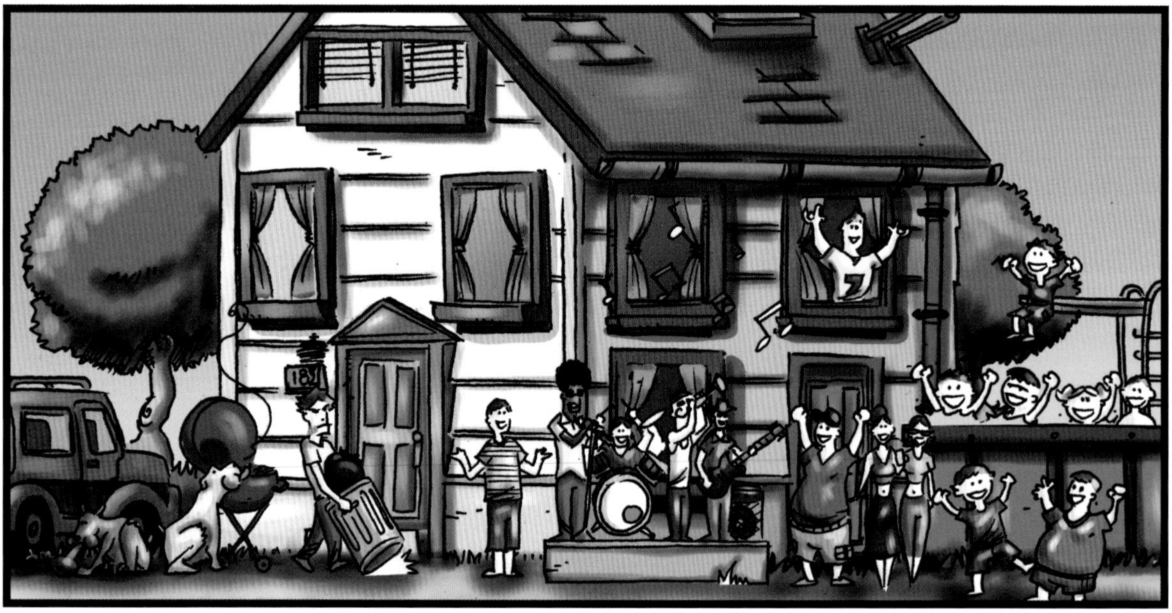
182

These are guitars
Played full blast
By high school kids
Who rocked n' rolled
After eating burgers from the grill
Owned by the neighbors
That raised the kids
Who threw their toys
Just like the boys
That live in the house that Jack built.

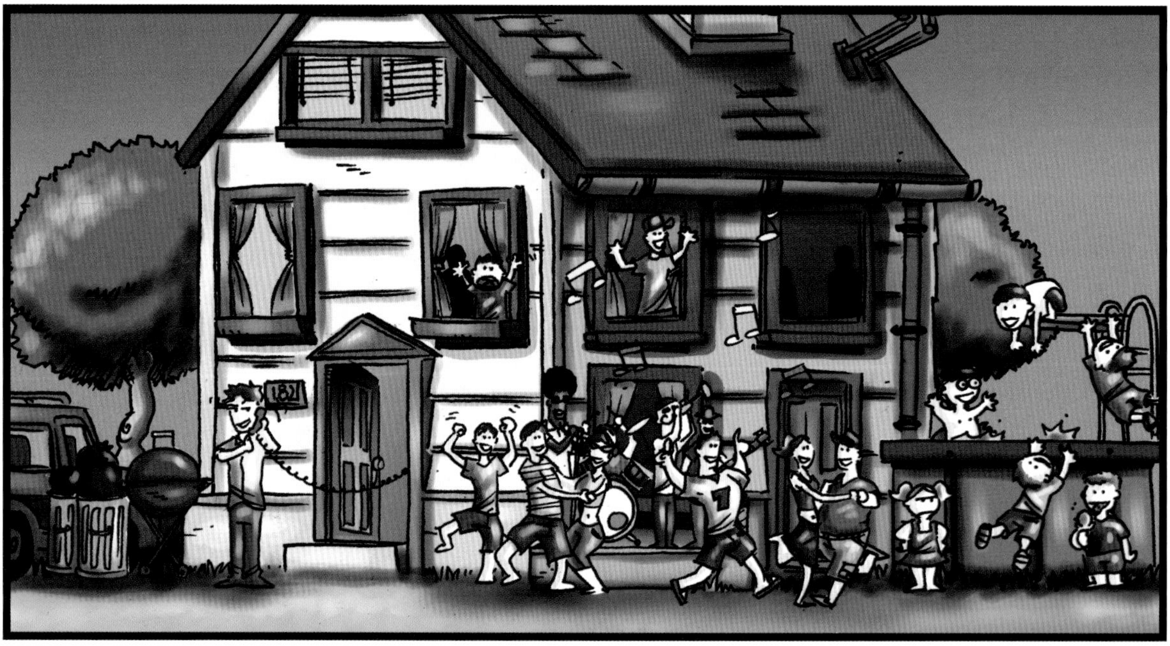
182

The party's loud
And growing fast
Thanks to music
Played full blast
By high school kids
That rocked the block
And ate the food
Cooked on the grill
Owned by the neighbors
That raised the kids
Who —oh, the toys!
Just like the boys
That live in the house that Jack built

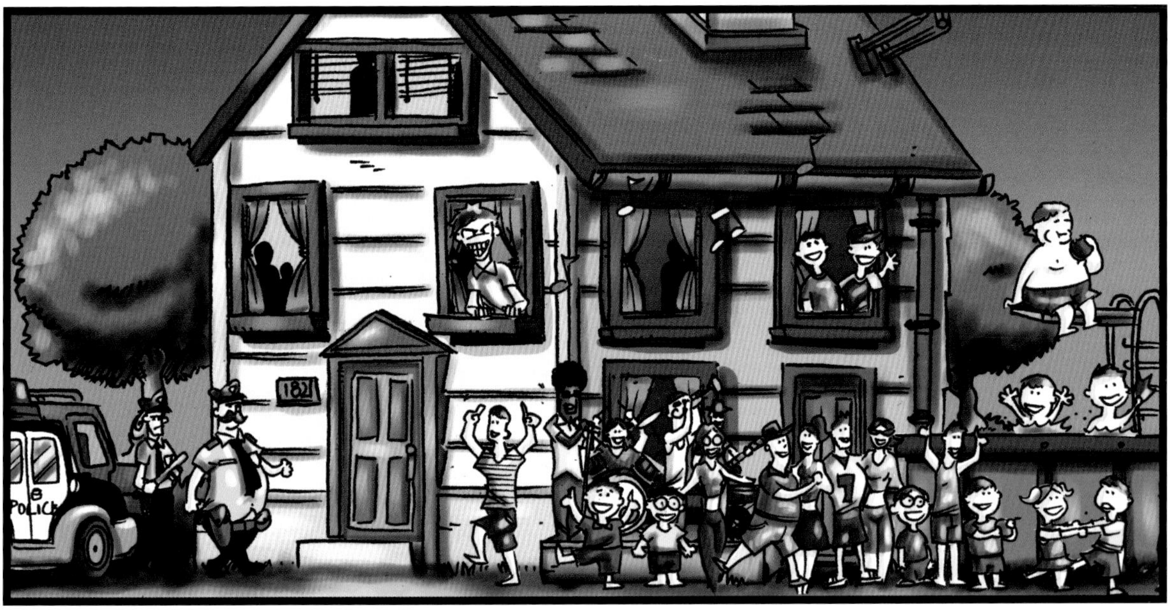
1821

Someone called the cops at last
To stop the noise and stop it fast!
And music, loud and played full blast
By high school kids
That rocked the block
And ate the food
Cooked on the grill
Owned by the neighbors
That raised the kids
Who threw their toys
Just like the boys
That live in the house that Jack built.

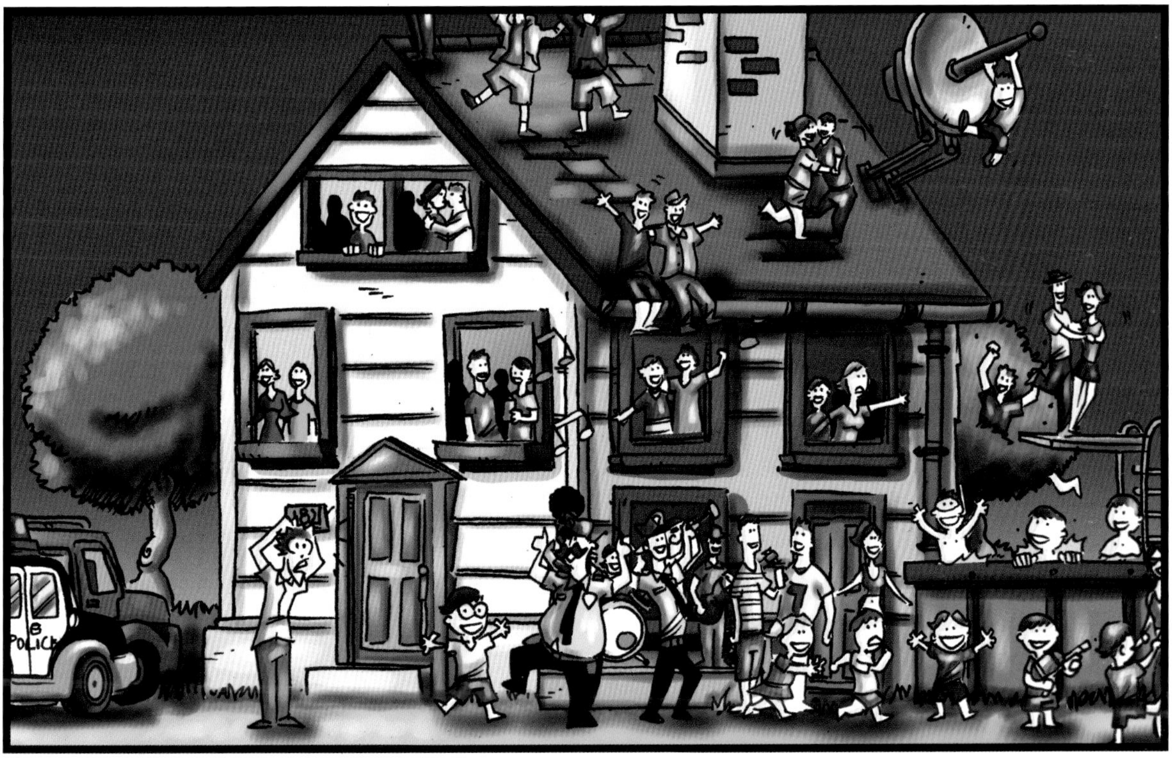

Here's our story's final cast
Cops joining in to make it last
This crazy party's quite a blast
With rock and roll that's loud and fast
Played by kids that rocked the block
And ate the food
Cooked on the grill
Owned by the neighbors
That raised the kids
Who threw their toys
Just like the boys
That live in the house that Jack built.

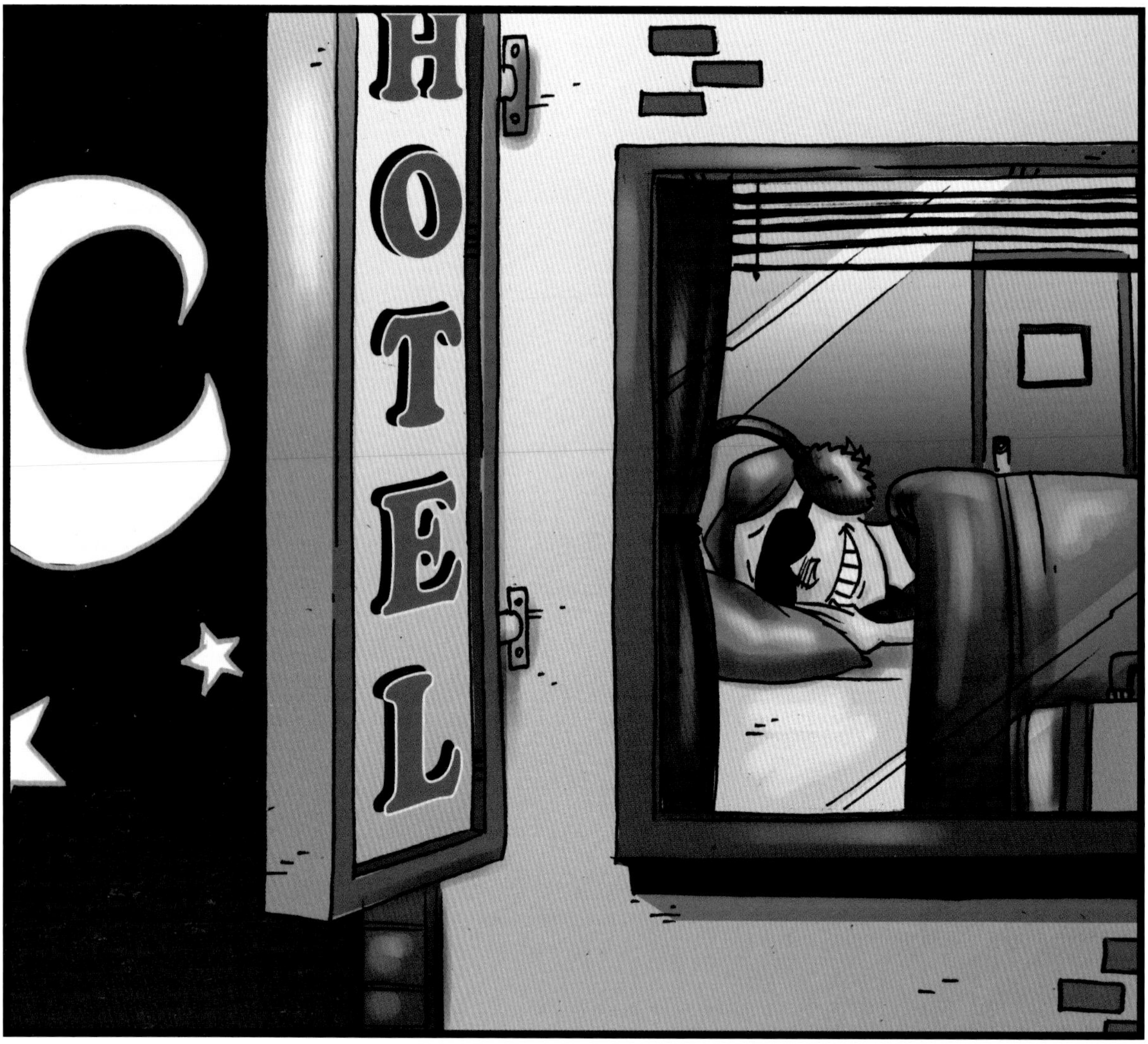
HOTEL

This is the hotel room
Quiet and cheap
Where poor old Jack
Can get some sleep
Far from the party
Going full blast
And rock and roll
That's loud and fast
By high school kids
That rock the block
And eat the food
Cooked on a grill
Owned by the neighbors
Who raised some kids
That threw their toys
Just like those boys

But here there's not
A bit of noise

Like the noise at the
house that Jack built.

THE FOX and THE CAT

RE-WRITTEN BY: NIKKI DY-LIACCO
DRAWN BY: MAY ANN LICUDINE

THE CAT ALWAYS WANTED TO MEET MR. FOX. SHE HEARD SO MUCH ABOUT HIM...

MR FOX IS THE MOST INTELLIGENT OF US ALL!

DID YOU SEE HIS LATEST GADGET?

HE HAS THE BEST-LOOKING CLOTHES!

HE IS THE COOLEST FOX IN ALL THE WOODS!

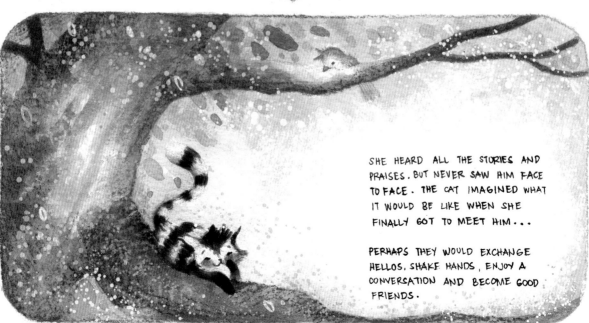

SHE HEARD ALL THE STORIES AND PRAISES. BUT NEVER SAW HIM FACE TO FACE. THE CAT IMAGINED WHAT IT WOULD BE LIKE WHEN SHE FINALLY GOT TO MEET HIM...

PERHAPS THEY WOULD EXCHANGE HELLOS, SHAKE HANDS, ENJOY A CONVERSATION AND BECOME GOOD FRIENDS.

THEN IT FINALLY HAPPENED ONE DAY THAT THE CAT MET MR. FOX.

HELLO, MY DEAR MR. FOX. I'VE HEARD SO MUCH ABOUT YOU! HOW ARE YOU TODAY?

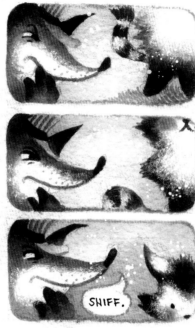

SHIFF.

OH, YOU POOR BEARD LICKER, YOU SPOTTED FOOL, YOU HUNGRY MOUSE HUNTER. WHAT WERE YOU THINKING?

YOU HAVE SOME NERVE ASKING ME HOW I AM! WHAT DO YOU KNOW? HOW MANY TRICKS DO YOU UNDERSTAND?

IF YOU MUST KNOW.. I UNDERSTAND BUT ONE.

WHAT KIND OF A TRICK IS IT?

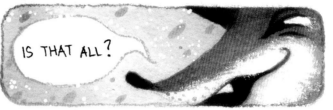

WELL, WHEN THE DOGS ARE CHASING ME, I CAN JUMP MYSELF INTO A TREE AND SAVE MYSELF.

IS THAT ALL?

HAHA!

I HAVE A SACKFUL OF TRICKS AND I'VE MASTERED ALL ONE HUNDRED AND ONE OF THEM!

LET ME PULL OUT 15 COLORFUL BALLS!

WOW.

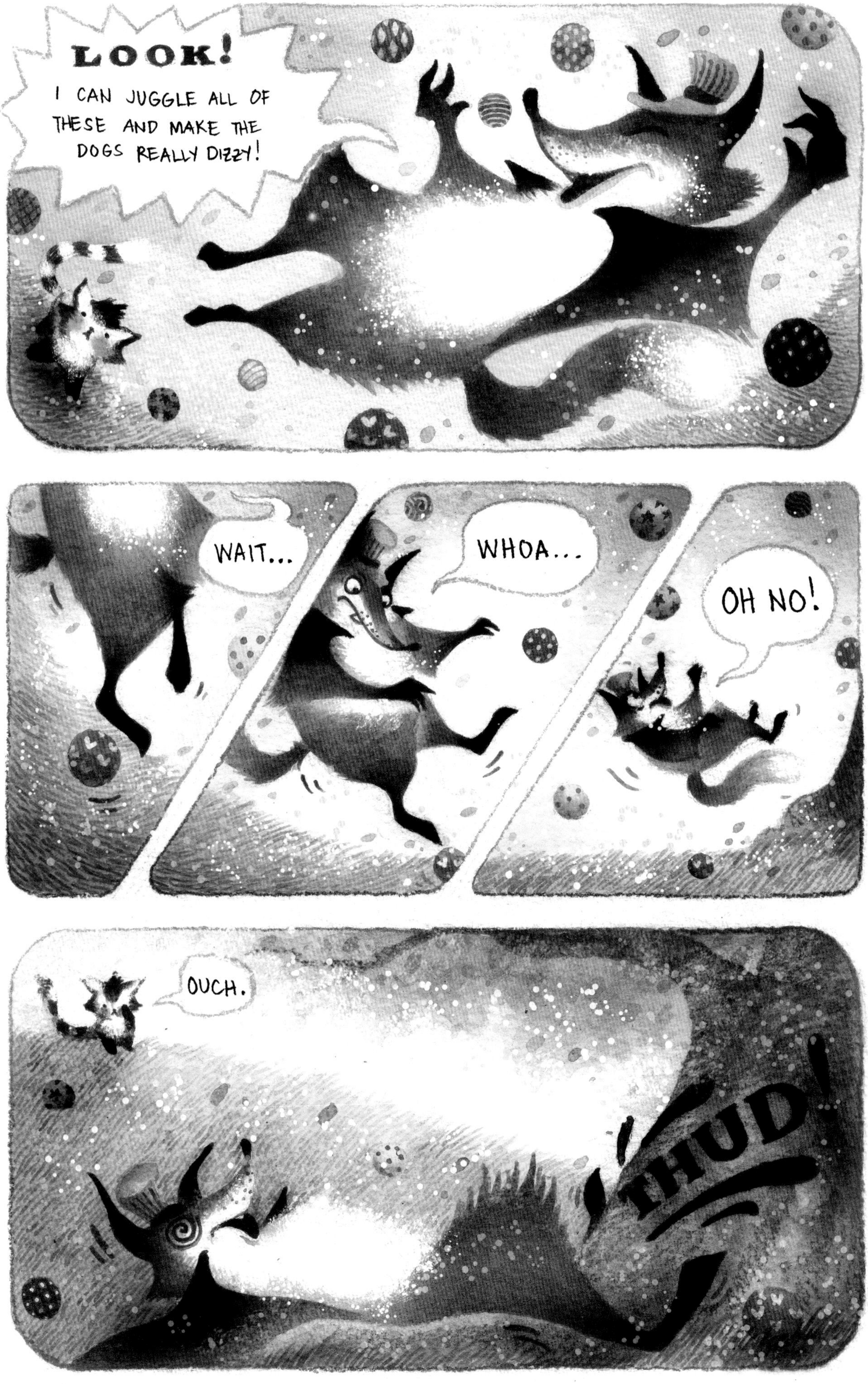
LOOK!
I CAN JUGGLE ALL OF THESE AND MAKE THE DOGS REALLY DIZZY!
WAIT...
WHOA...
OH NO!
OUCH.
THUD!

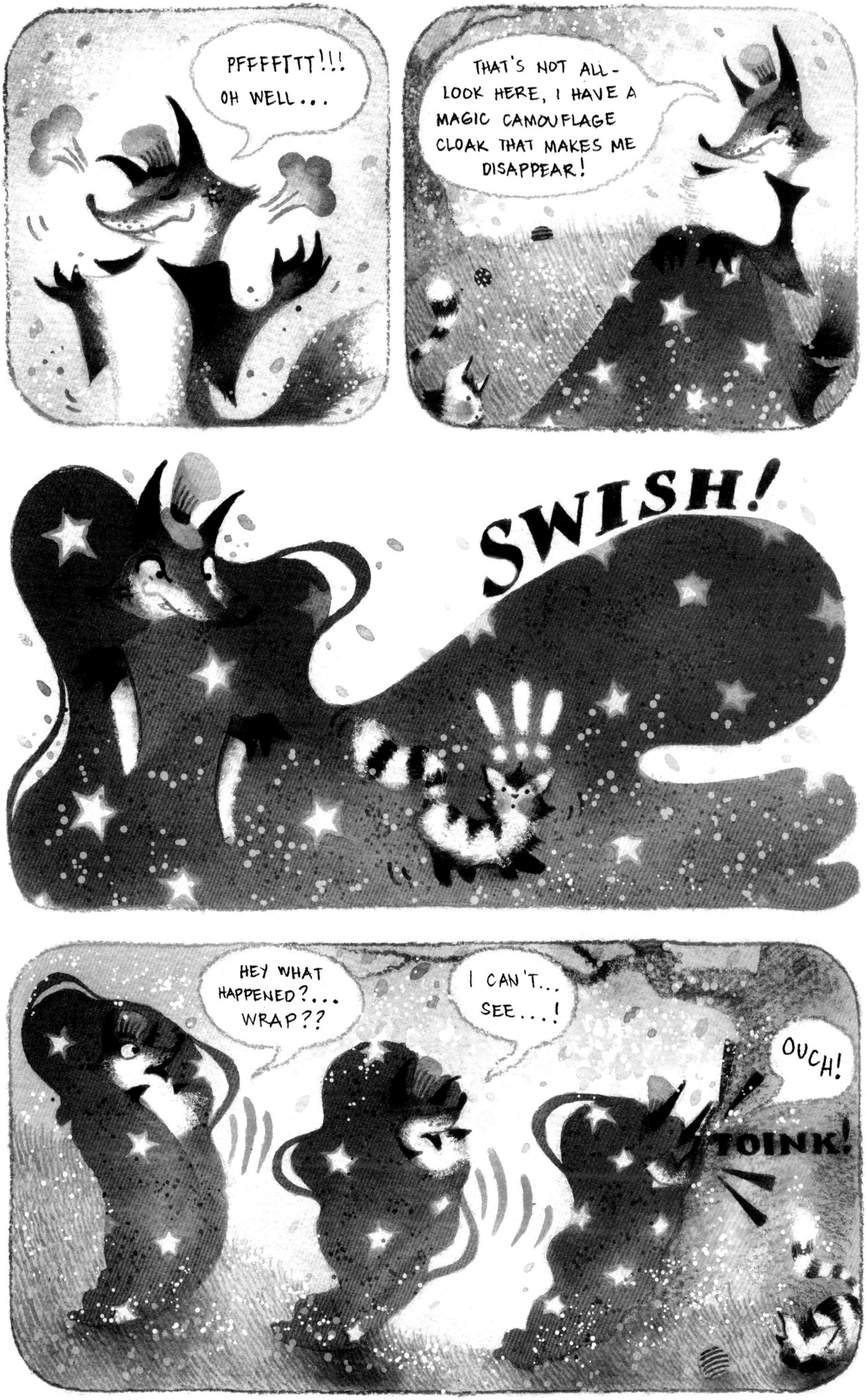
PFFFFTTT!!!
OH WELL...
THAT'S NOT ALL- LOOK HERE, I HAVE A MAGIC CAMOUFLAGE CLOAK THAT MAKES ME DISAPPEAR!
SWISH!
HEY WHAT HAPPENED?... WRAP??
I CAN'T... SEE...!
OUCH!
TOINK!

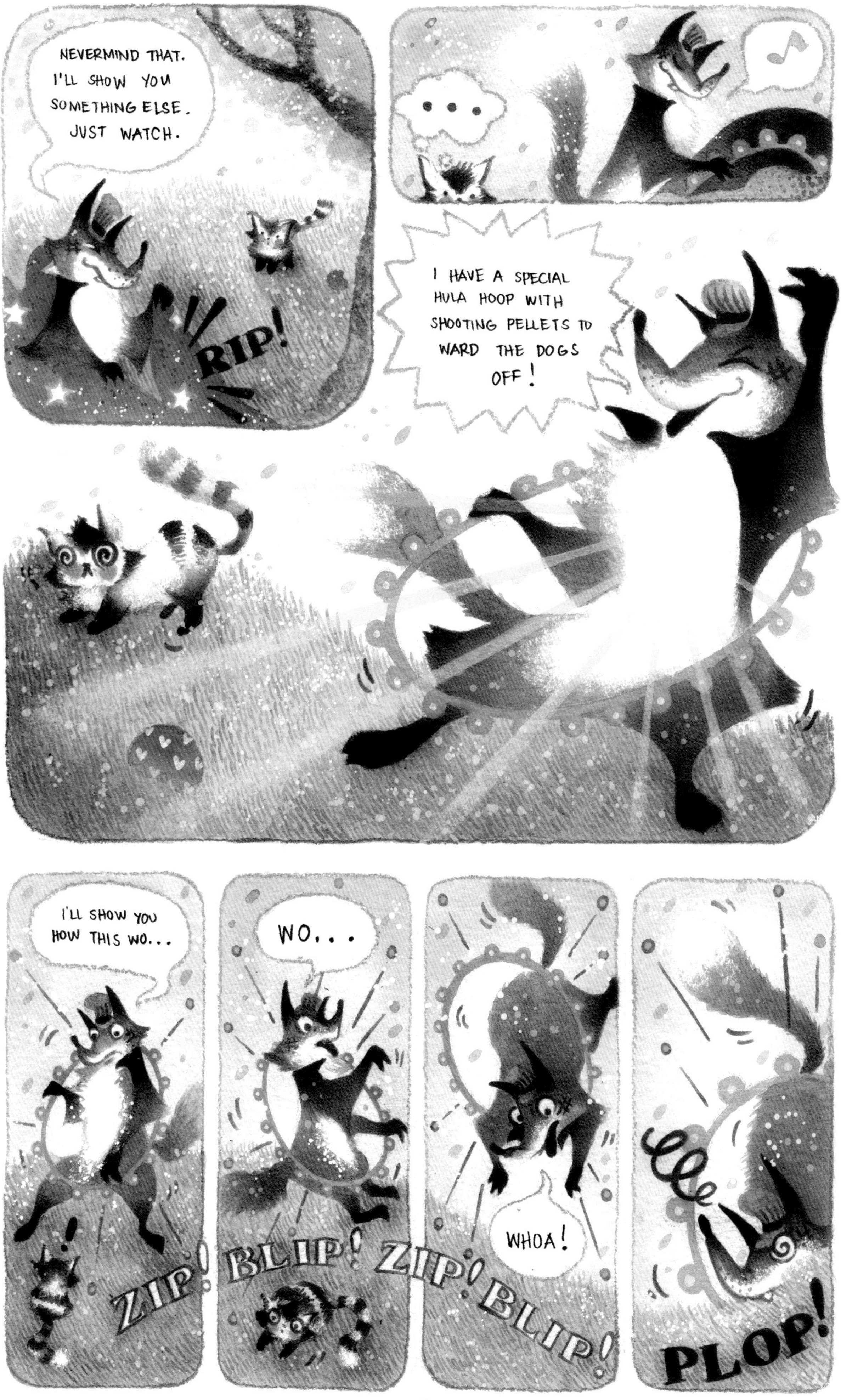
NEVERMIND THAT. I'LL SHOW YOU SOMETHING ELSE. JUST WATCH.
RIP!
...
I HAVE A SPECIAL HULA HOOP WITH SHOOTING PELLETS TO WARD THE DOGS OFF!
I'LL SHOW YOU HOW THIS WO...
WO...
ZIP!
BLIP!
ZIP!
BLIP!
WHOA!
PLOP!

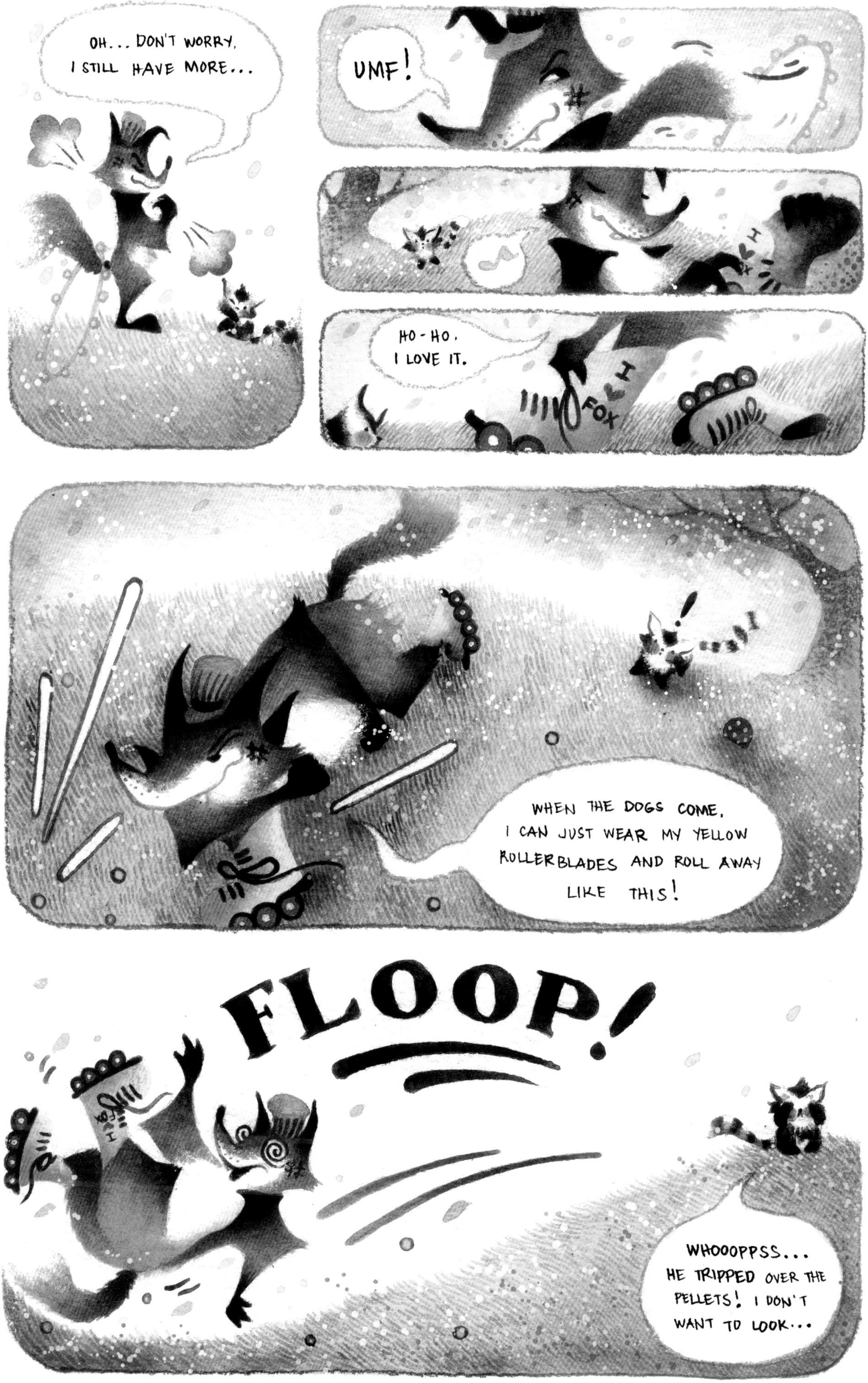
OH... DON'T WORRY, I STILL HAVE MORE...
UMF!
HO-HO. I LOVE IT.
I ♥ FOX
WHEN THE DOGS COME, I CAN JUST WEAR MY YELLOW ROLLERBLADES AND ROLL AWAY LIKE THIS!
FLOOP!
WHOOOPPSS... HE TRIPPED OVER THE PELLETS! I DON'T WANT TO LOOK...

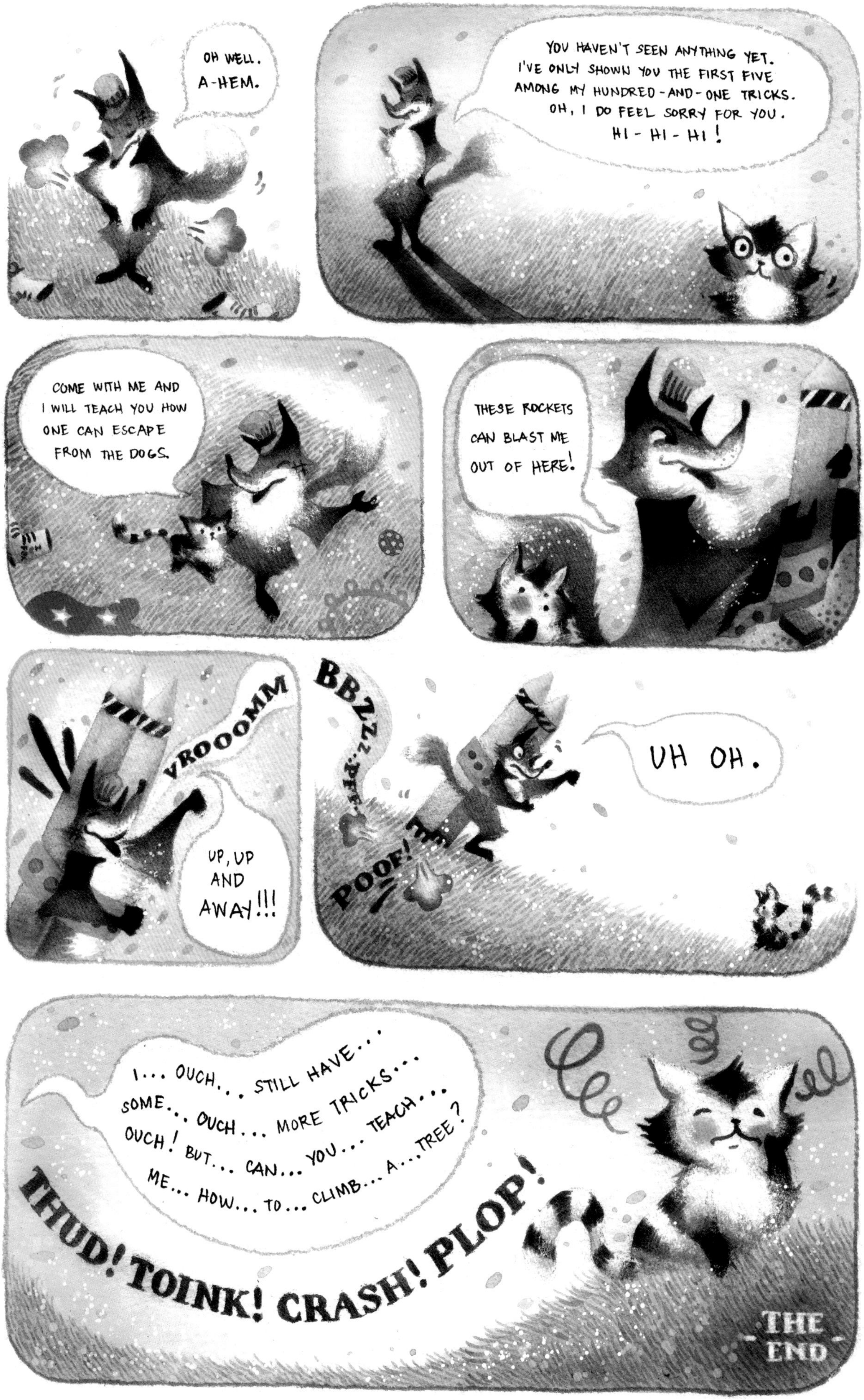
OH WELL. A-HEM.
YOU HAVEN'T SEEN ANYTHING YET. I'VE ONLY SHOWN YOU THE FIRST FIVE AMONG MY HUNDRED-AND-ONE TRICKS. OH, I DO FEEL SORRY FOR YOU. HI-HI-HI!
COME WITH ME AND I WILL TEACH YOU HOW ONE CAN ESCAPE FROM THE DOGS.
THESE ROCKETS CAN BLAST ME OUT OF HERE!
VROOOOMM
UP, UP AND AWAY!!!
BBZZZ..PFF..
POOF!
UH OH.
I... OUCH... STILL HAVE... SOME... OUCH... MORE TRICKS... OUCH! BUT... CAN... YOU... TEACH... ME... HOW... TO... CLIMB... A... TREE?
THUD! TOINK! CRASH! PLOP!
THE END

Pippi Van Wrinkles

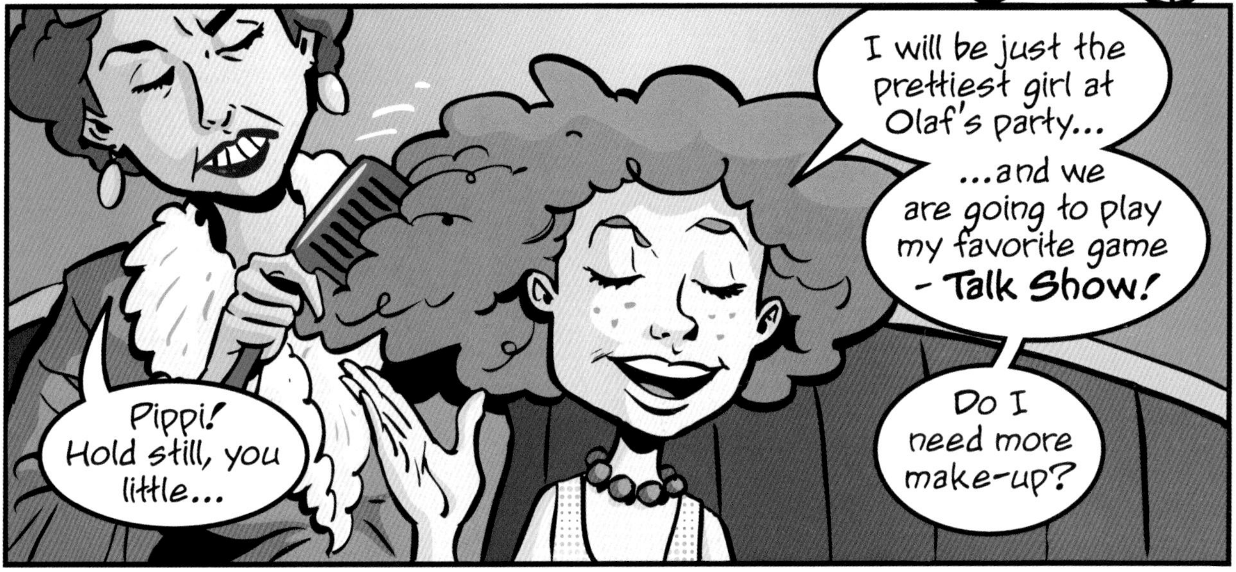
I will be just the prettiest girl at Olaf's party...
...and we are going to play my favorite game - **Talk Show!**
Pippi! Hold still, you little...
Do I need more make-up?

Once upon a time there was a kingdom called Minny-soda which was known for its many lakes and its cute-as-a-button families! And there lived a little girl named **Pippi Van Wrinkles!**

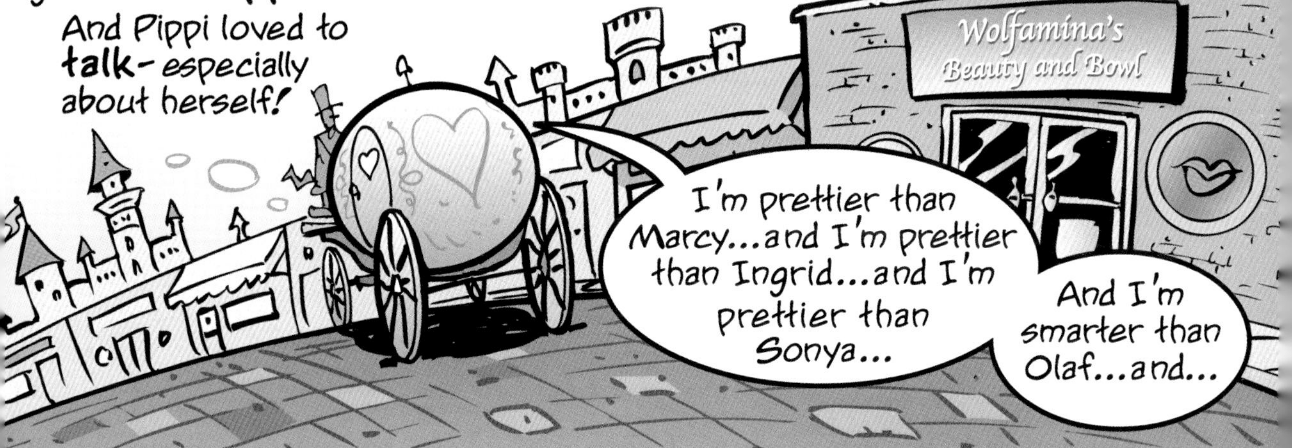
And Pippi loved to **talk**- especially about herself!
Wolfamina's Beauty and Bowl
I'm prettier than Marcy...and I'm prettier than Ingrid...and I'm prettier than Sonya...
And I'm smarter than Olaf...and...

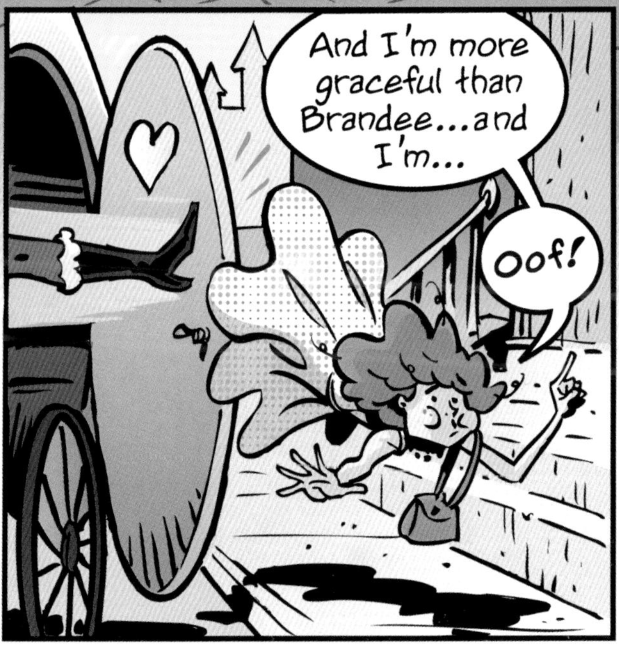
And I'm more graceful than Brandee...and I'm...
Oof!

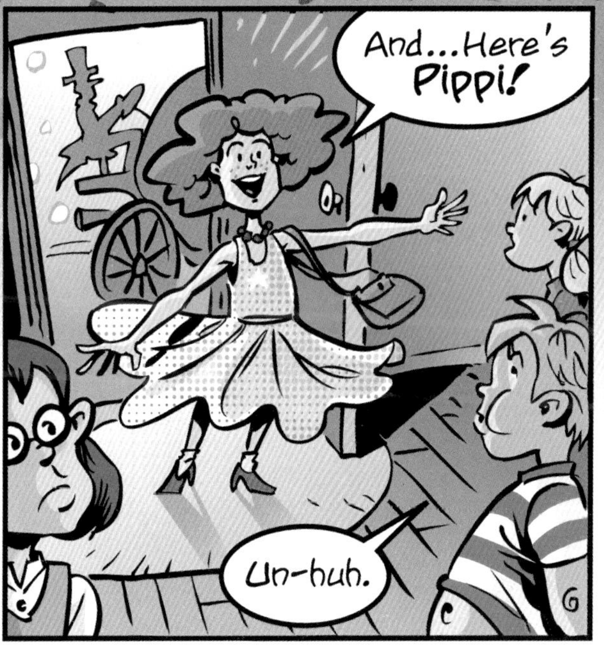
And...Here's **Pippi!**
Un-huh.

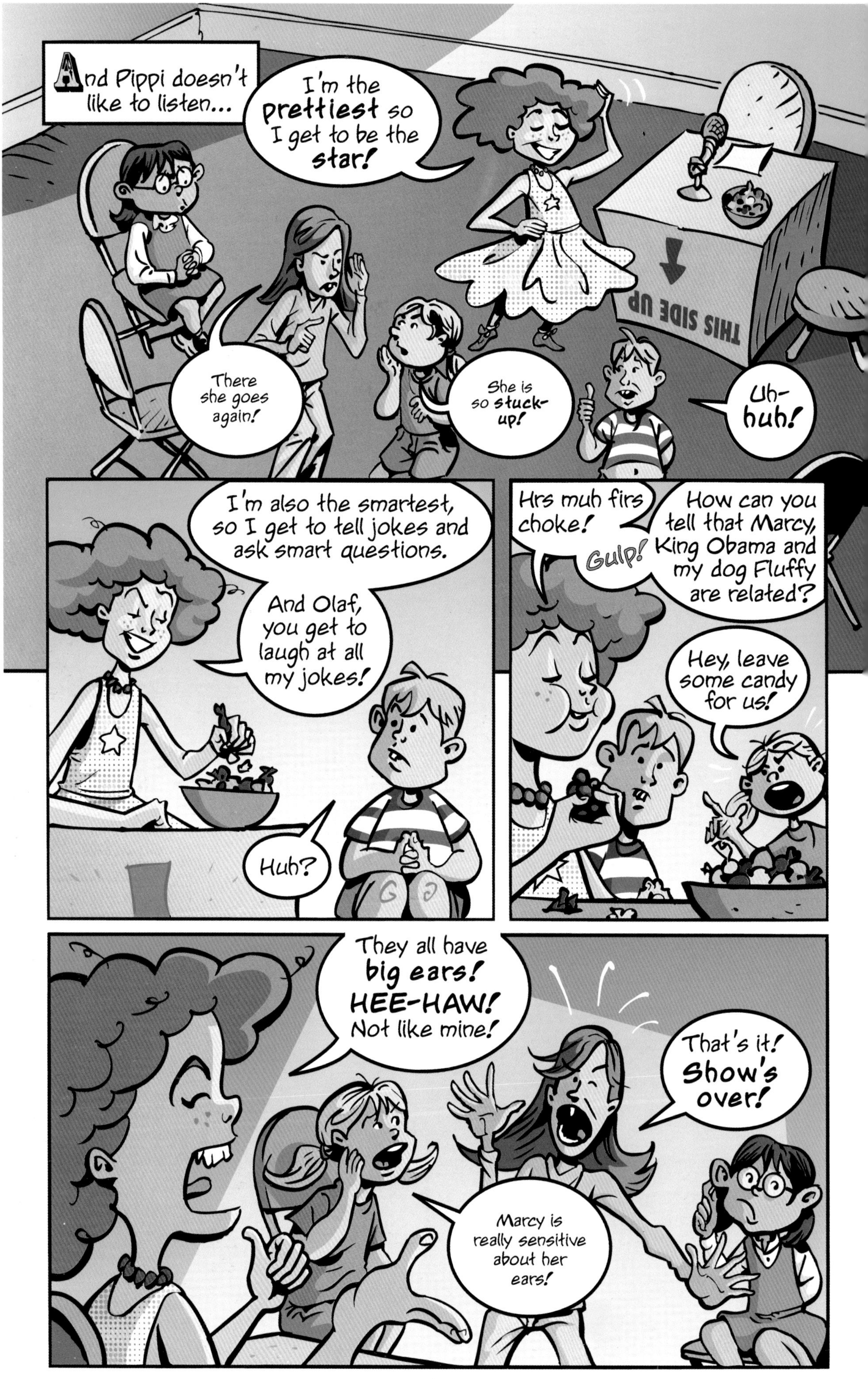
And Pippi doesn't like to listen...
I'm the prettiest so I get to be the star!
There she goes again!
She is so stuck-up!
Uh-huh!
I'm also the smartest, so I get to tell jokes and ask smart questions.
And Olaf, you get to laugh at all my jokes!
Huh?
Hrs muh firs choke!
Gulp!
How can you tell that Marcy, King Obama and my dog Fluffy are related?
Hey, leave some candy for us!
They all have big ears! HEE-HAW! Not like mine!
That's it! Show's over!
Marcy is really sensitive about her ears!
THIS SIDE UP

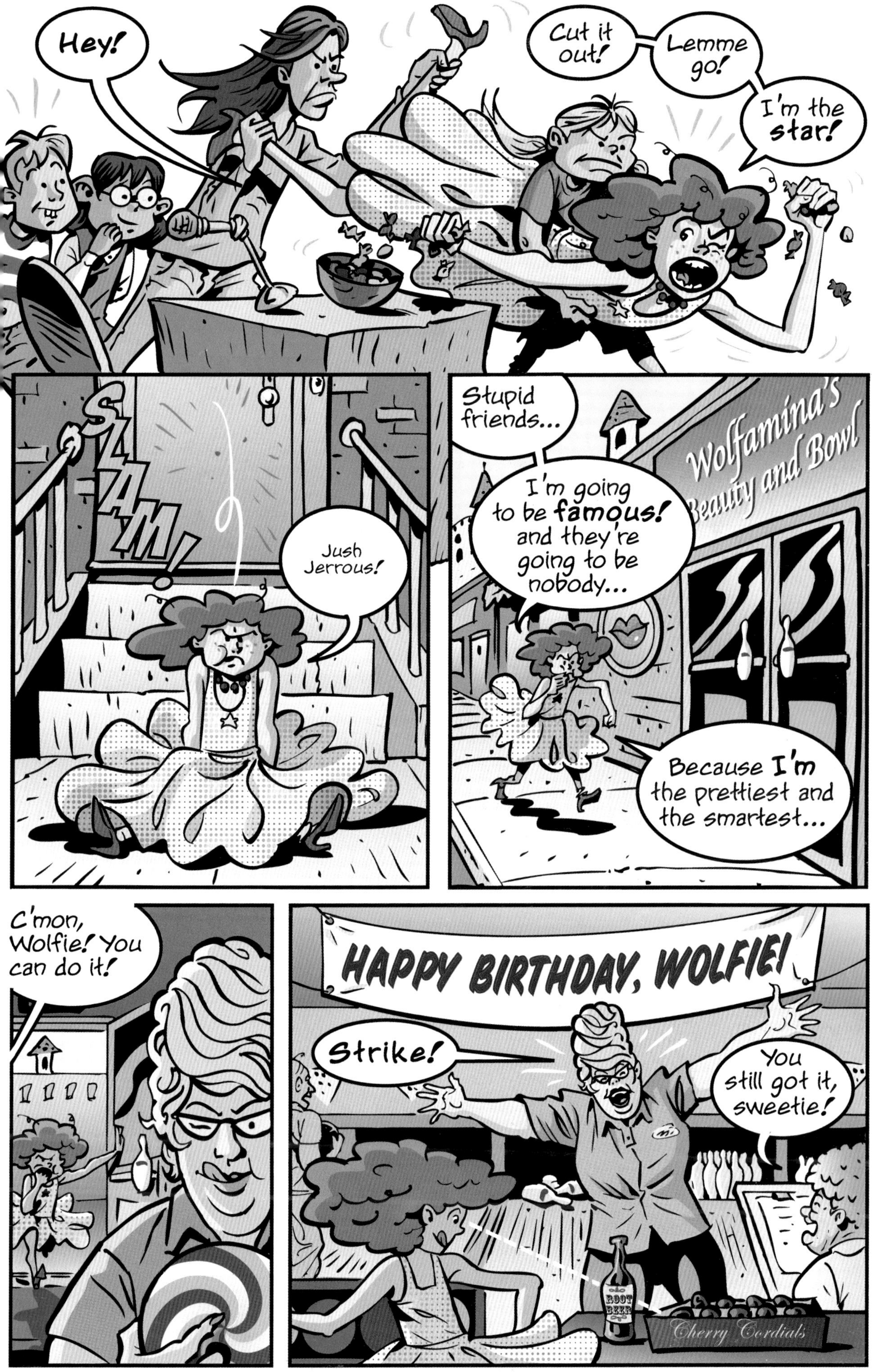
Hey!
Cut it out!
Lemme go!
I'm the star!
SLAM!
Jush Jerrous!
Stupid friends...
Wolfamina's Beauty and Bowl
I'm going to be famous! and they're going to be nobody...
Because I'm the prettiest and the smartest...
C'mon, Wolfie! You can do it!
HAPPY BIRTHDAY, WOLFIE!
Strike!
You still got it, sweetie!
ROOT BEER
Cherry Cordials

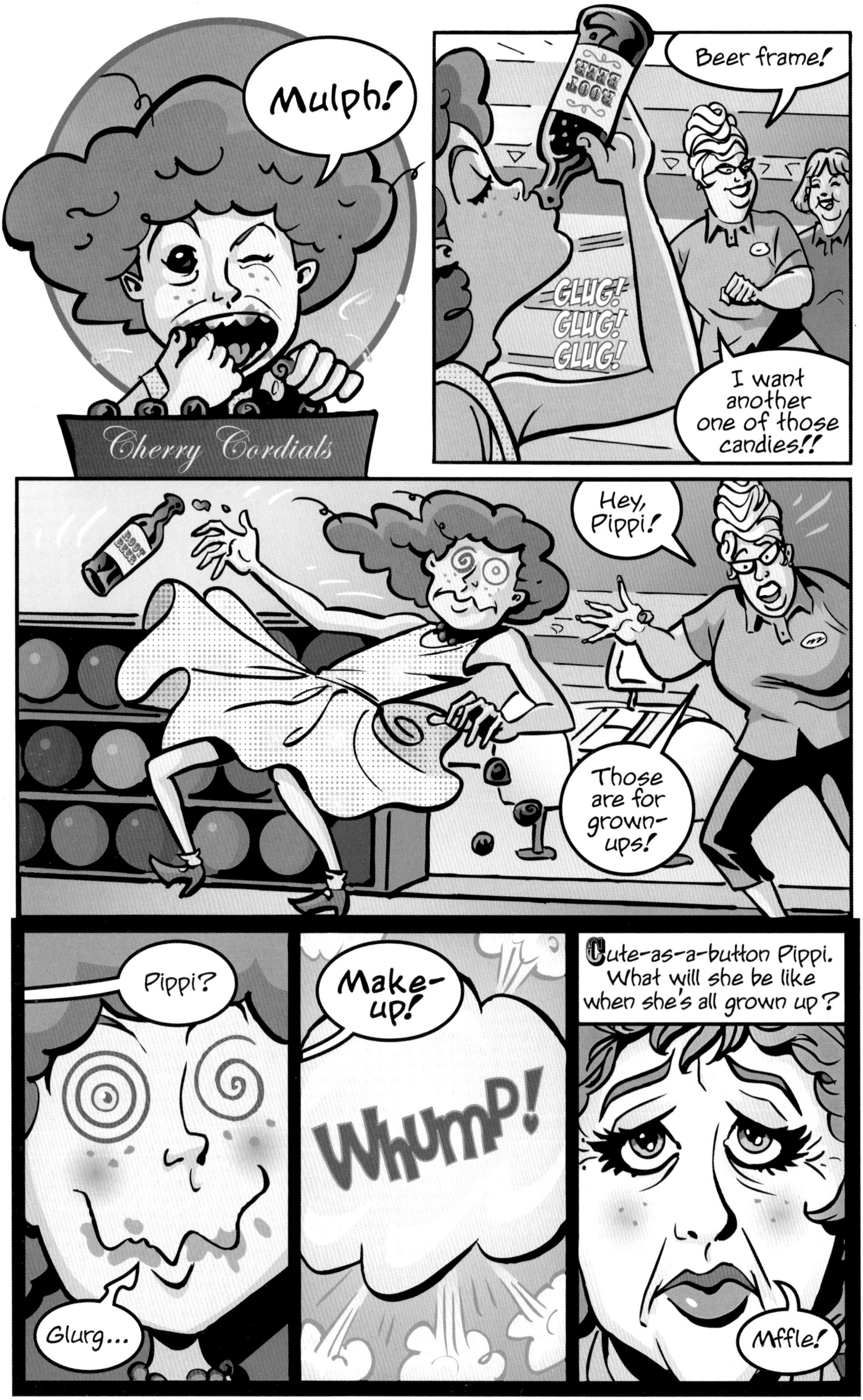
Mulph!
Cherry Cordials
Beer frame!
ROOT BEER
GLUG! GLUG! GLUG!
I want another one of those candies!!
Hey, Pippi!
ROOT BEER
Those are for grown-ups!
Pippi?
Glurg...
Make-up!
WHUMP!
Cute-as-a-button Pippi. What will she be like when she's all grown up?
Mffle!

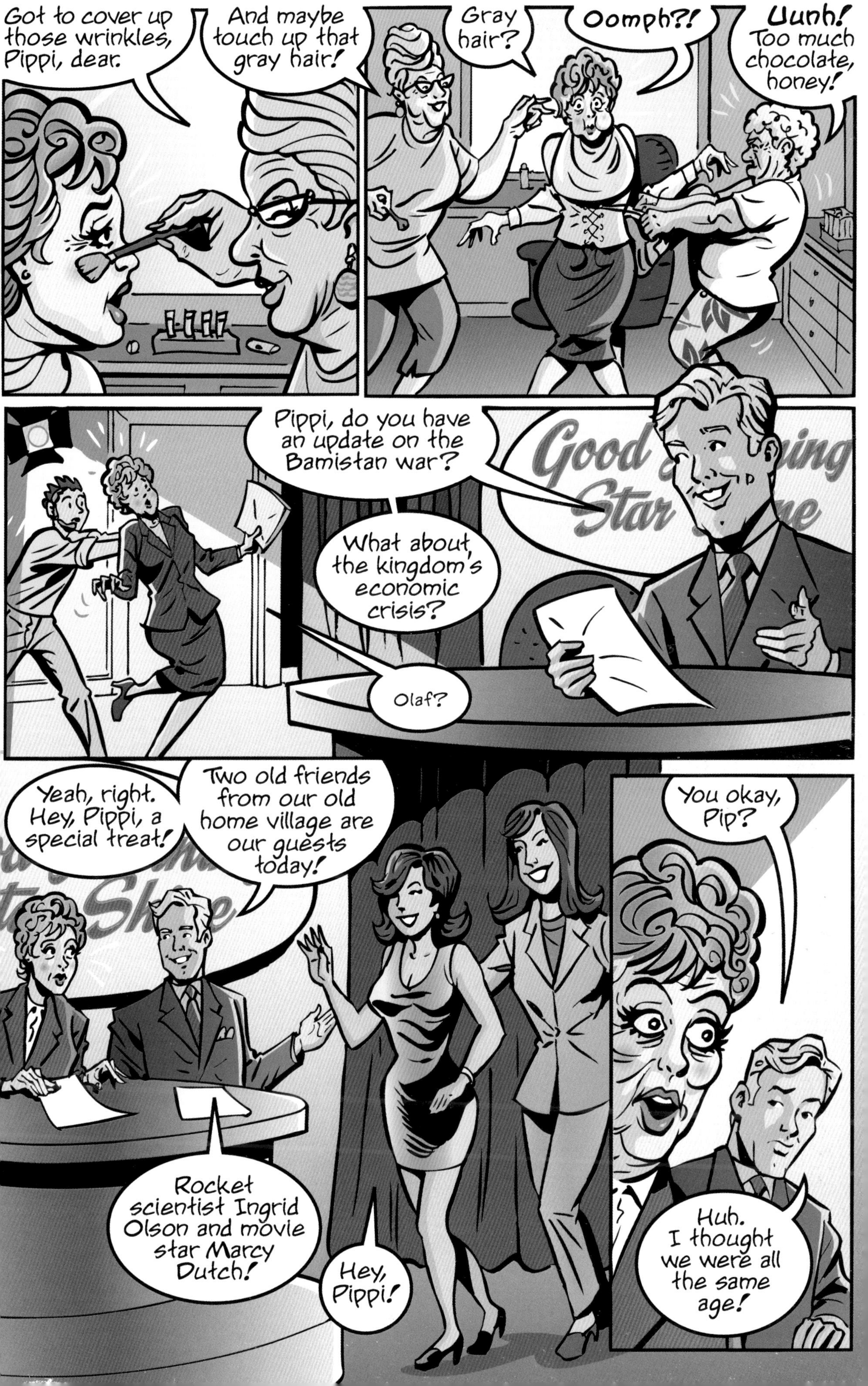
Got to cover up those wrinkles, Pippi, dear.
And maybe touch up that gray hair!
Gray hair?
Oomph?!
Uunh! Too much chocolate, honey!
Pippi, do you have an update on the Bamistan war?
What about, the kingdom's economic crisis?
Olaf?
Good Star
Yeah, right. Hey, Pippi, a special treat!
Two old friends from our old home village are our guests today!
Rocket scientist Ingrid Olson and movie star Marcy Dutch!
Hey, Pippi!
You okay, Pip?
Huh. I thought we were all the same age!

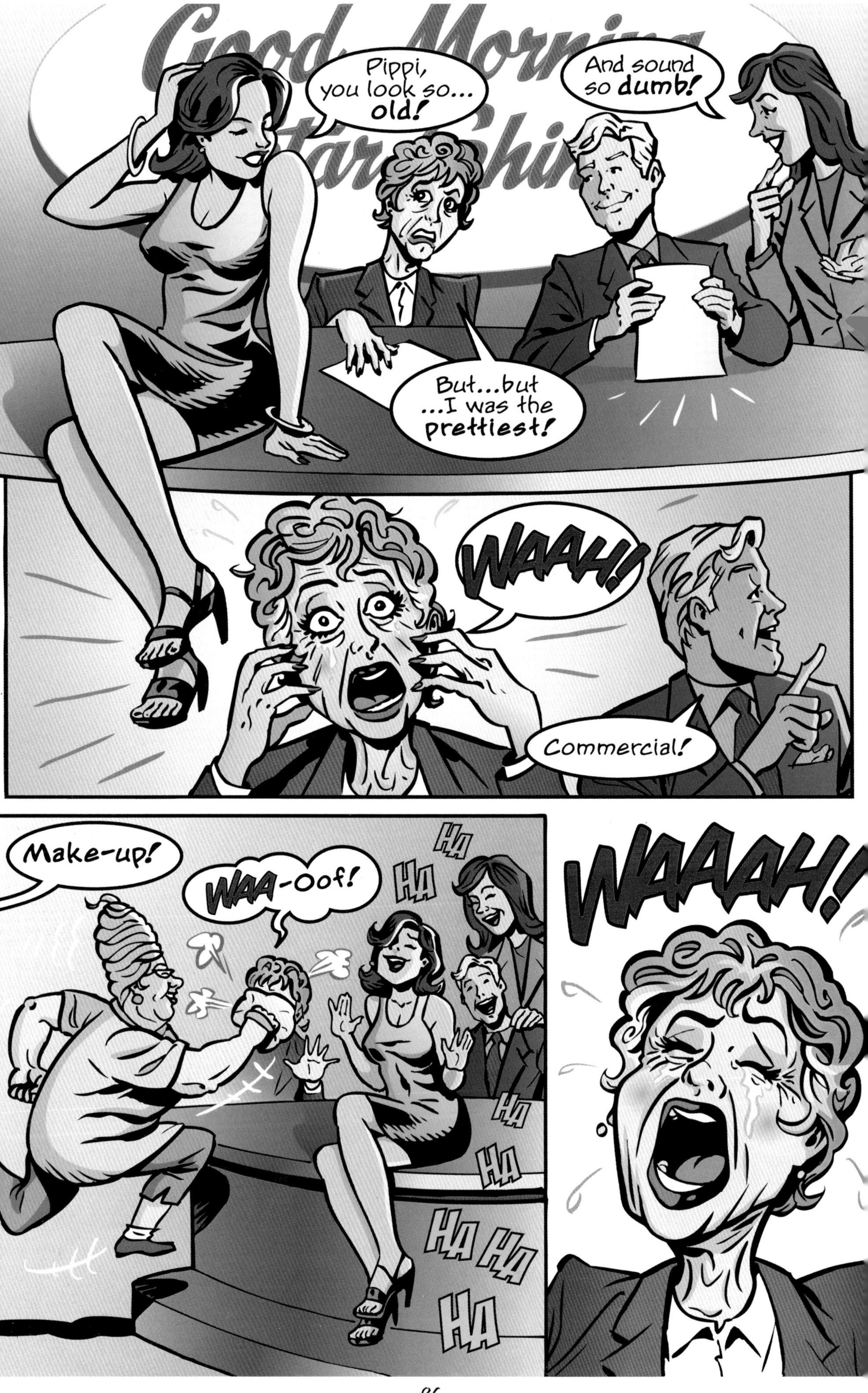
Good Morning Starshine
Pippi, you look so... old!
And sound so dumb!
But...but ...I was the prettiest!
WAAH!
Commercial!
Make-up!
WAA-Oof!
HA HA HA HA HA HA HA HA
WAAAH!!

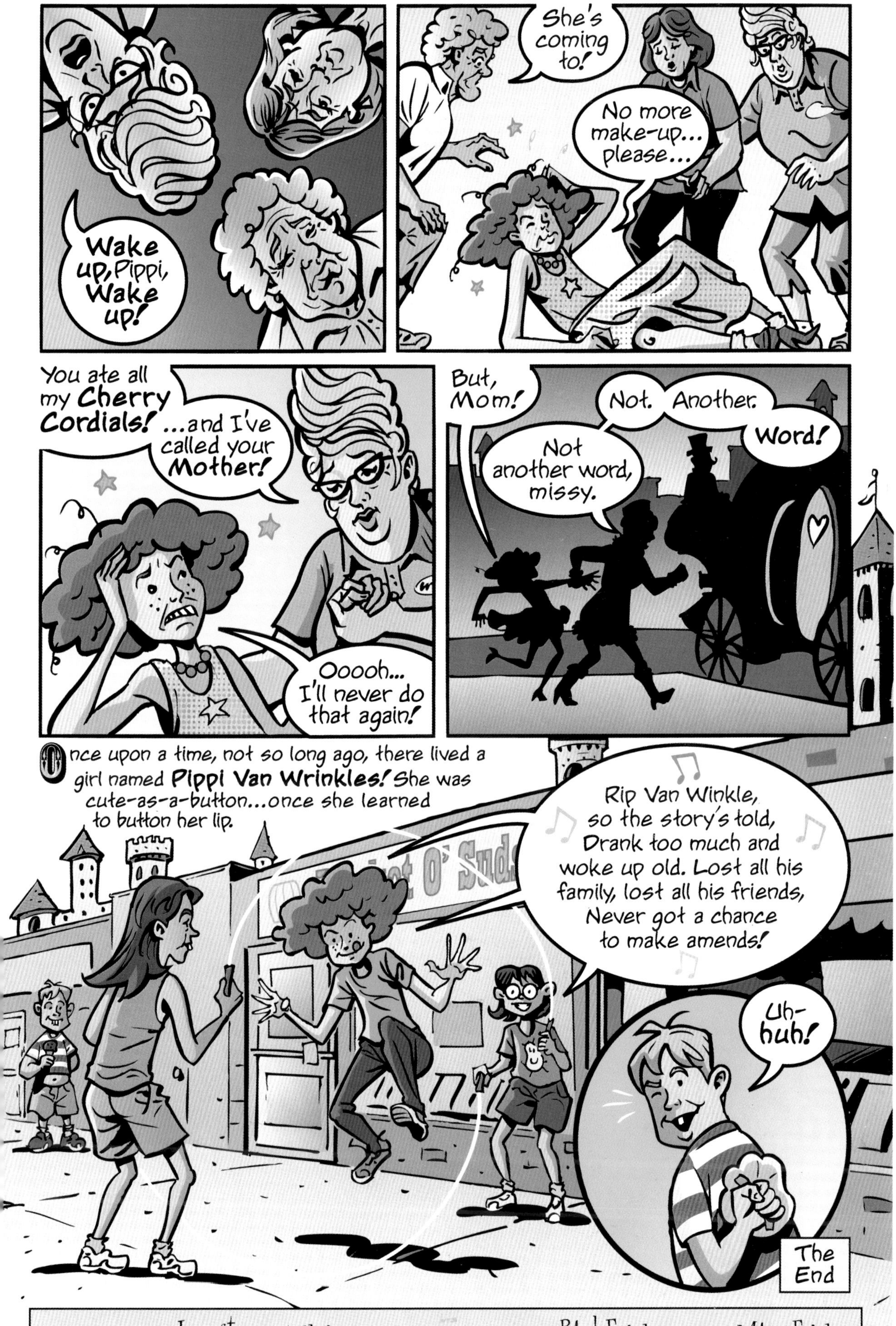
Wake up, Pippi, Wake up!
She's coming to!
No more make-up... please...
You ate all my Cherry Cordials!
...and I've called your Mother!
Ooooh... I'll never do that again!
But, Mom!
Not another word, missy.
Not.
Another.
Word!
Once upon a time, not so long ago, there lived a girl named Pippi Van Wrinkles! She was cute-as-a-button...once she learned to button her lip.
Rip Van Winkle, so the story's told, Drank too much and woke up old. Lost all his family, lost all his friends, Never got a chance to make amends!
Uh-huh!
The End

Story and script: Len Strazewski Story, art, letters & colors: Paul Fricke Colors: Mary Fricke

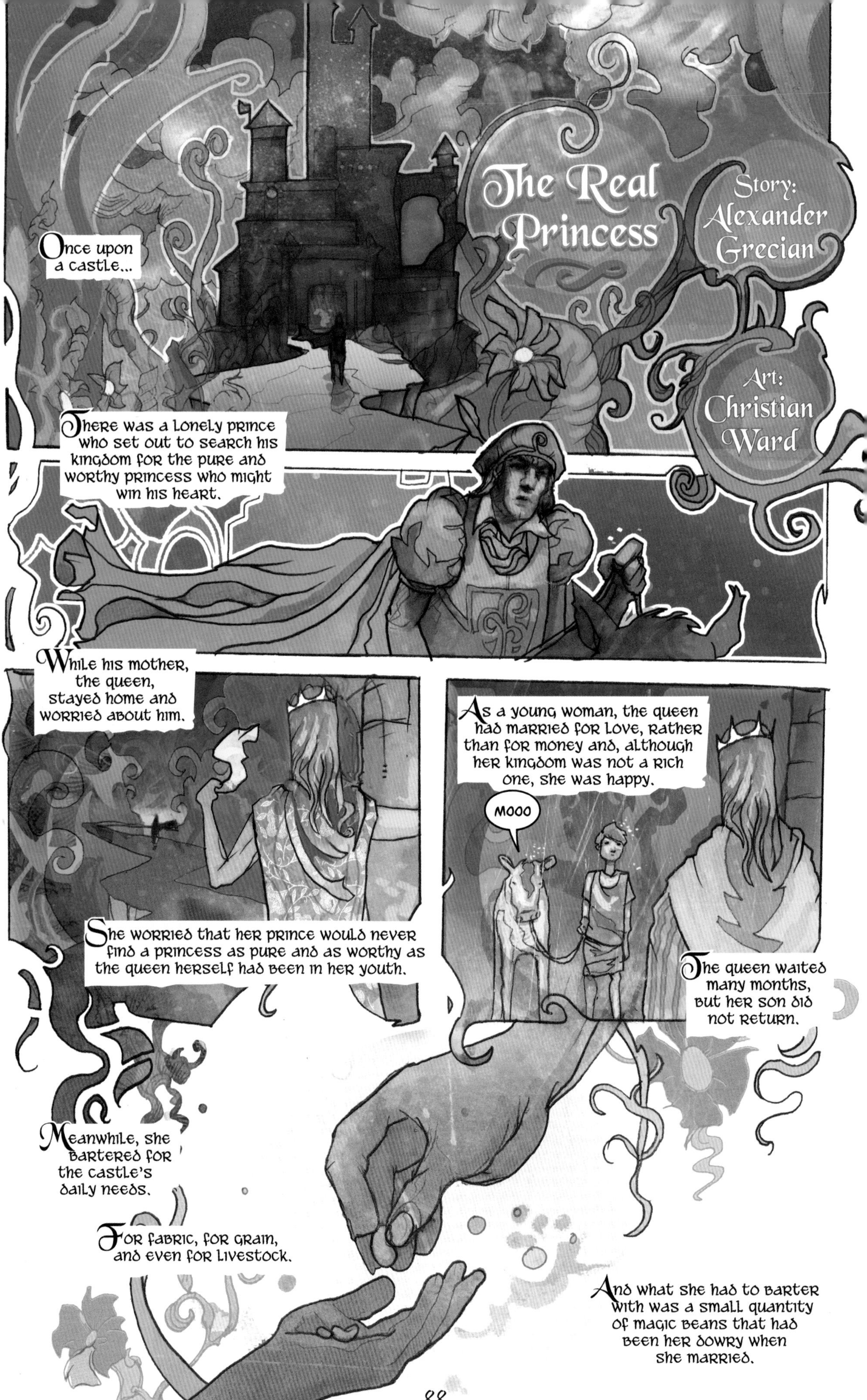
The Real Princess
Story: Alexander Grecian
Art: Christian Ward
Once upon a castle...
There was a lonely prince who set out to search his kingdom for the pure and worthy princess who might win his heart.
While his mother, the queen, stayed home and worried about him.
She worried that her prince would never find a princess as pure and as worthy as the queen herself had been in her youth.
As a young woman, the queen had married for love, rather than for money and, although her kingdom was not a rich one, she was happy.
MOOO
The queen waited many months, but her son did not return.
Meanwhile, she bartered for the castle's daily needs.
For fabric, for grain, and even for livestock.
And what she had to barter with was a small quantity of magic beans that had been her dowry when she married.

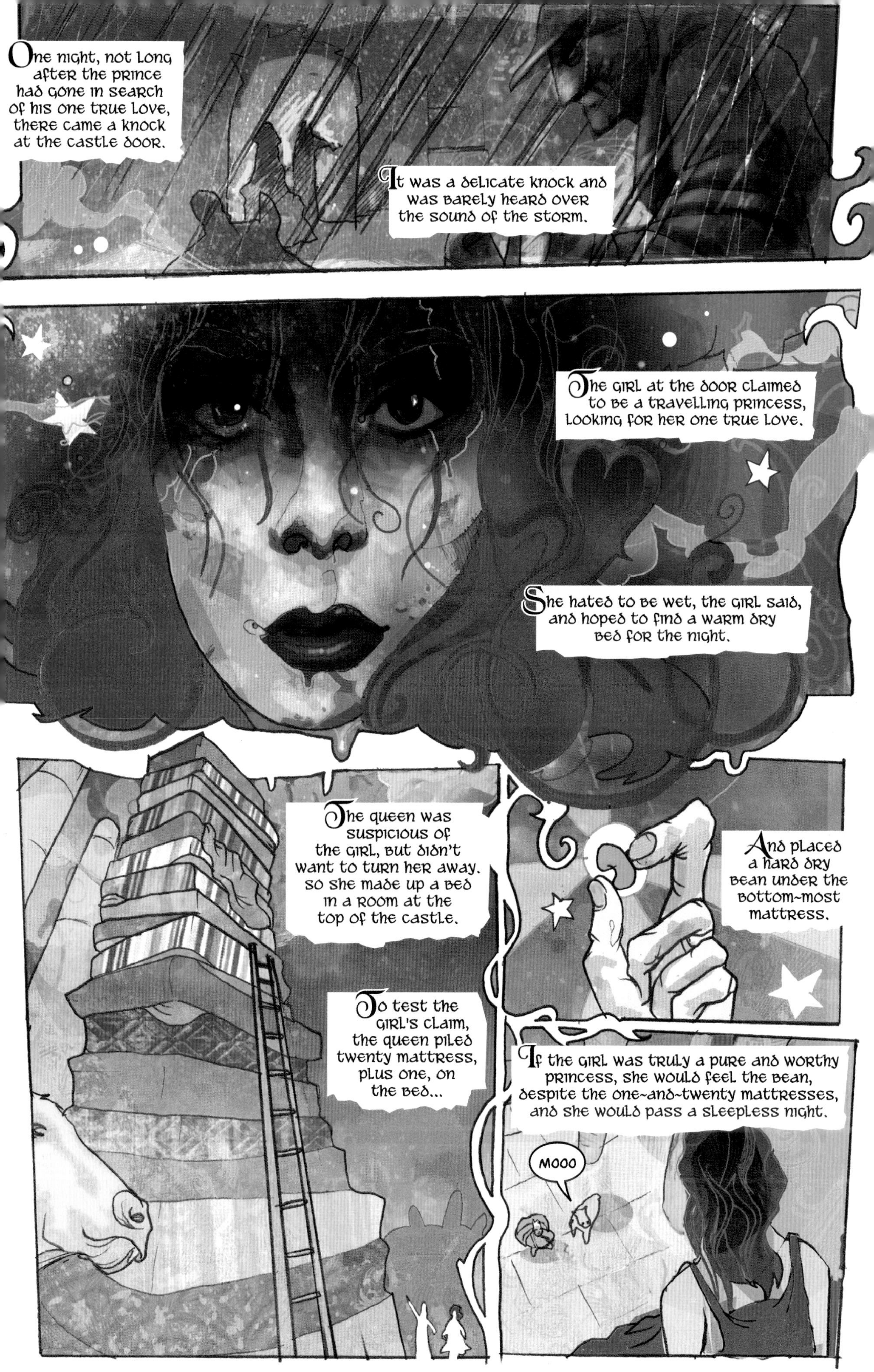
One night, not long after the prince had gone in search of his one true love, there came a knock at the castle door.
It was a delicate knock and was barely heard over the sound of the storm.
The girl at the door claimed to be a travelling princess, looking for her one true love.
She hated to be wet, the girl said, and hoped to find a warm dry bed for the night.
The queen was suspicious of the girl, but didn't want to turn her away, so she made up a bed in a room at the top of the castle.
To test the girl's claim, the queen piled twenty mattress, plus one, on the bed...
And placed a hard dry bean under the bottom~most mattress.
If the girl was truly a pure and worthy princess, she would feel the bean, despite the one~and~twenty mattresses, and she would pass a sleepless night.
MOOO

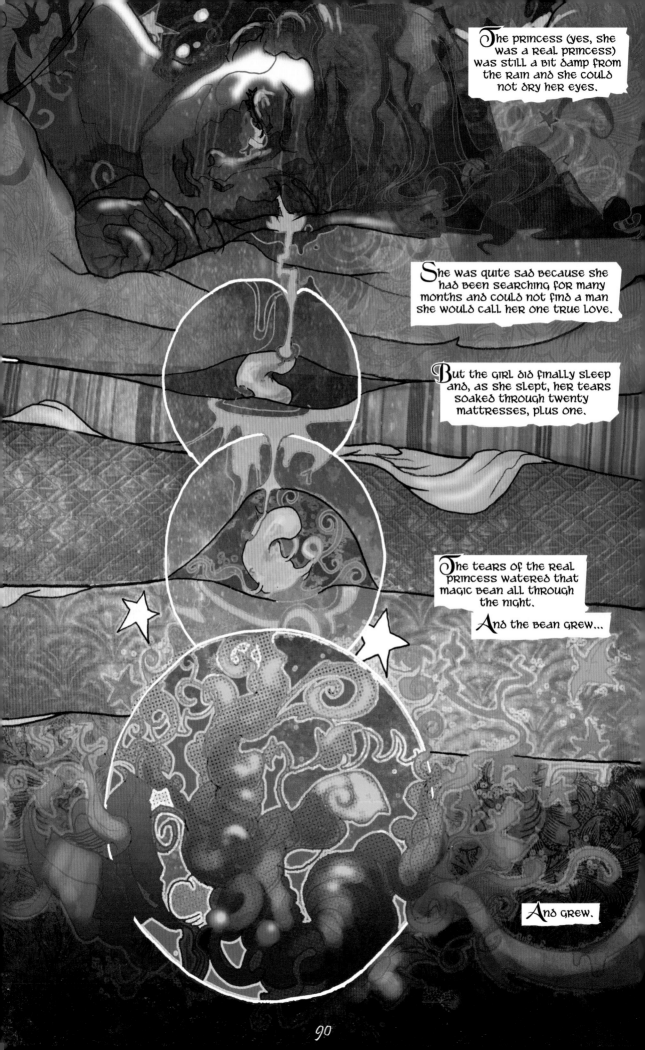

The princess (yes, she was a real princess) was still a bit damp from the rain and she could not dry her eyes.

She was quite sad because she had been searching for many months and could not find a man she would call her one true love.

But the girl did finally sleep and, as she slept, her tears soaked through twenty mattresses, plus one.

The tears of the real princess watered that magic bean all through the night.

And the bean grew...

And grew.

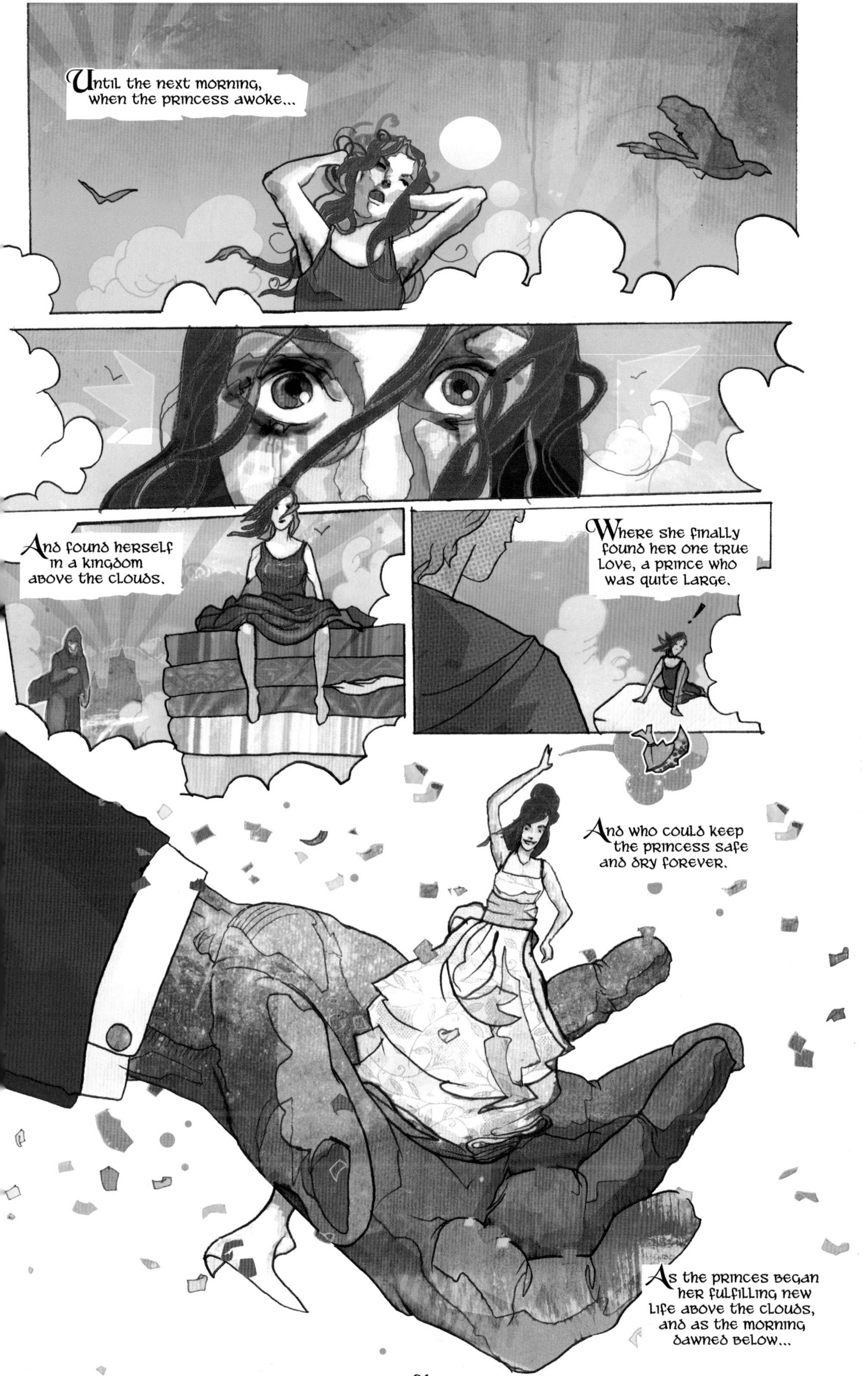
Until the next morning, when the princess awoke...
And found herself in a kingdom above the clouds.
Where she finally found her one true love, a prince who was quite large.
!
And who could keep the princess safe and dry forever.
As the princes began her fulfilling new life above the clouds, and as the morning dawned below...

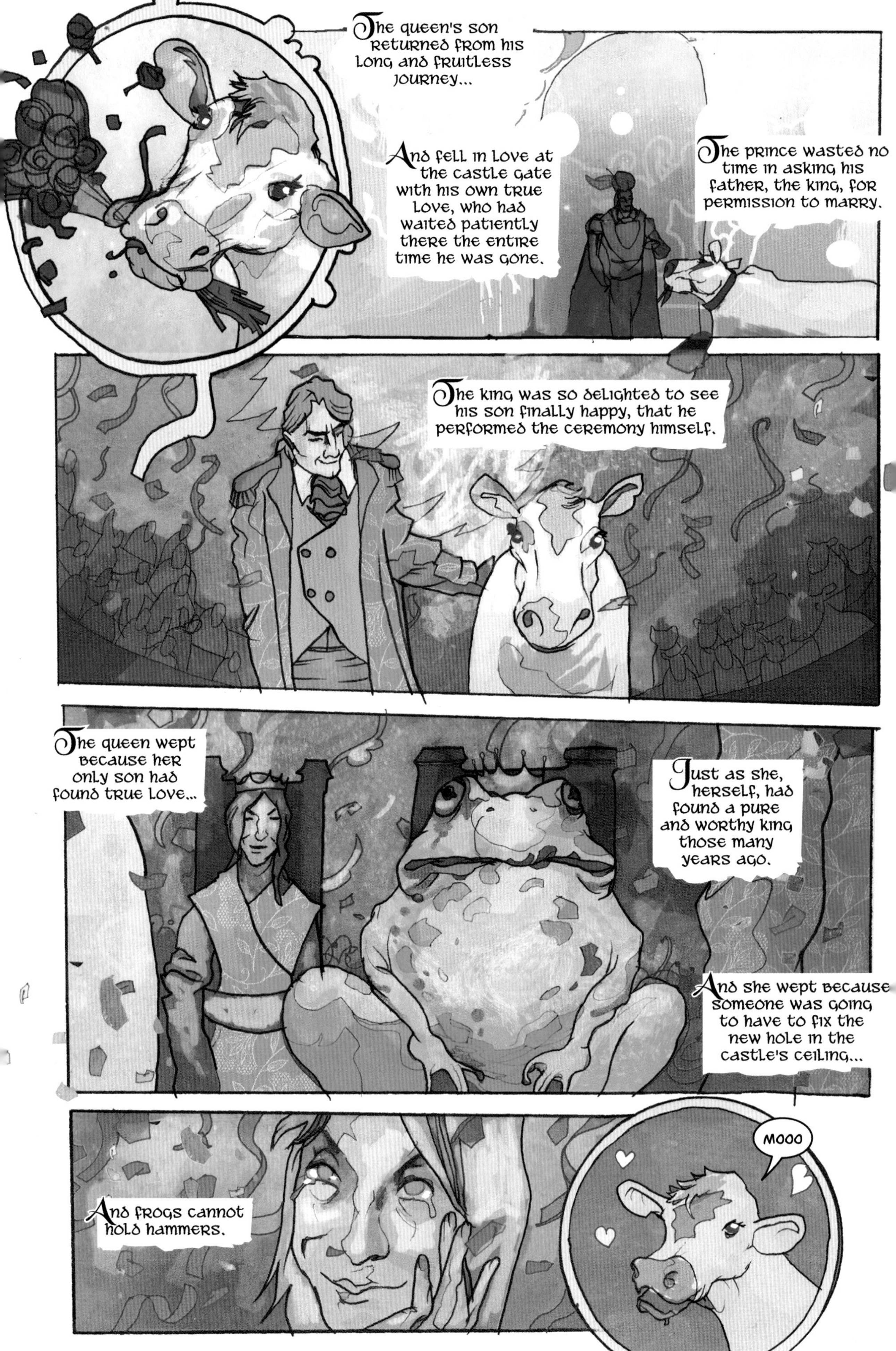
The queen's son returned from his long and fruitless journey...
And fell in love at the castle gate with his own true love, who had waited patiently there the entire time he was gone.
The prince wasted no time in asking his father, the king, for permission to marry.
The king was so delighted to see his son finally happy, that he performed the ceremony himself.
The queen wept because her only son had found true love...
Just as she, herself, had found a pure and worthy king those many years ago.
And she wept because someone was going to have to fix the new hole in the castle's ceiling...
And frogs cannot hold hammers.
MOOO

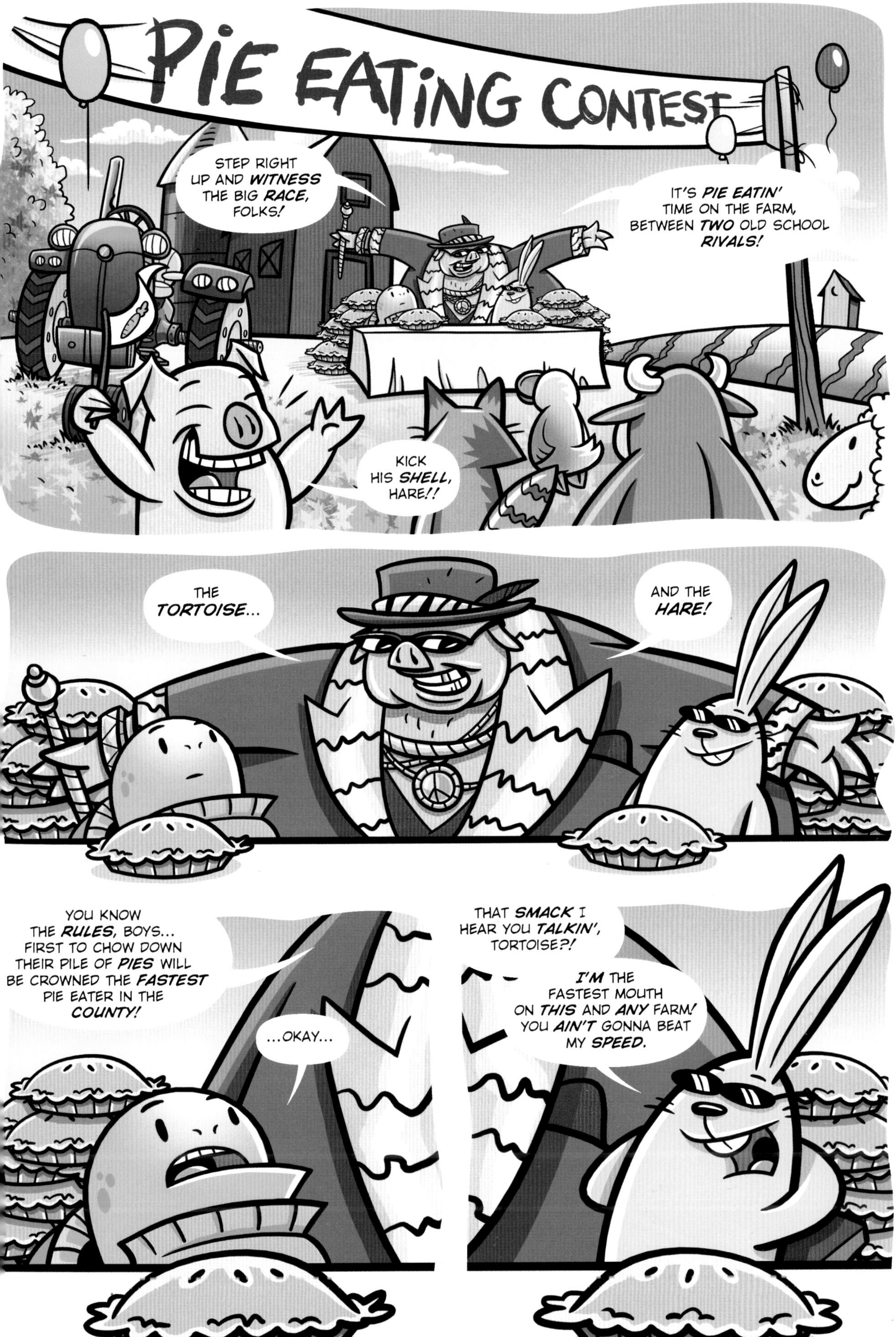
PIE EATING CONTEST
STEP RIGHT UP AND WITNESS THE BIG RACE, FOLKS!
IT'S PIE EATIN' TIME ON THE FARM, BETWEEN TWO OLD SCHOOL RIVALS!
KICK HIS SHELL, HARE!!
THE TORTOISE...
AND THE HARE!
YOU KNOW THE RULES, BOYS... FIRST TO CHOW DOWN THEIR PILE OF PIES WILL BE CROWNED THE FASTEST PIE EATER IN THE COUNTY!
...OKAY...
THAT SMACK I HEAR YOU TALKIN', TORTOISE?!
I'M THE FASTEST MOUTH ON THIS AND ANY FARM! YOU AIN'T GONNA BEAT MY SPEED.

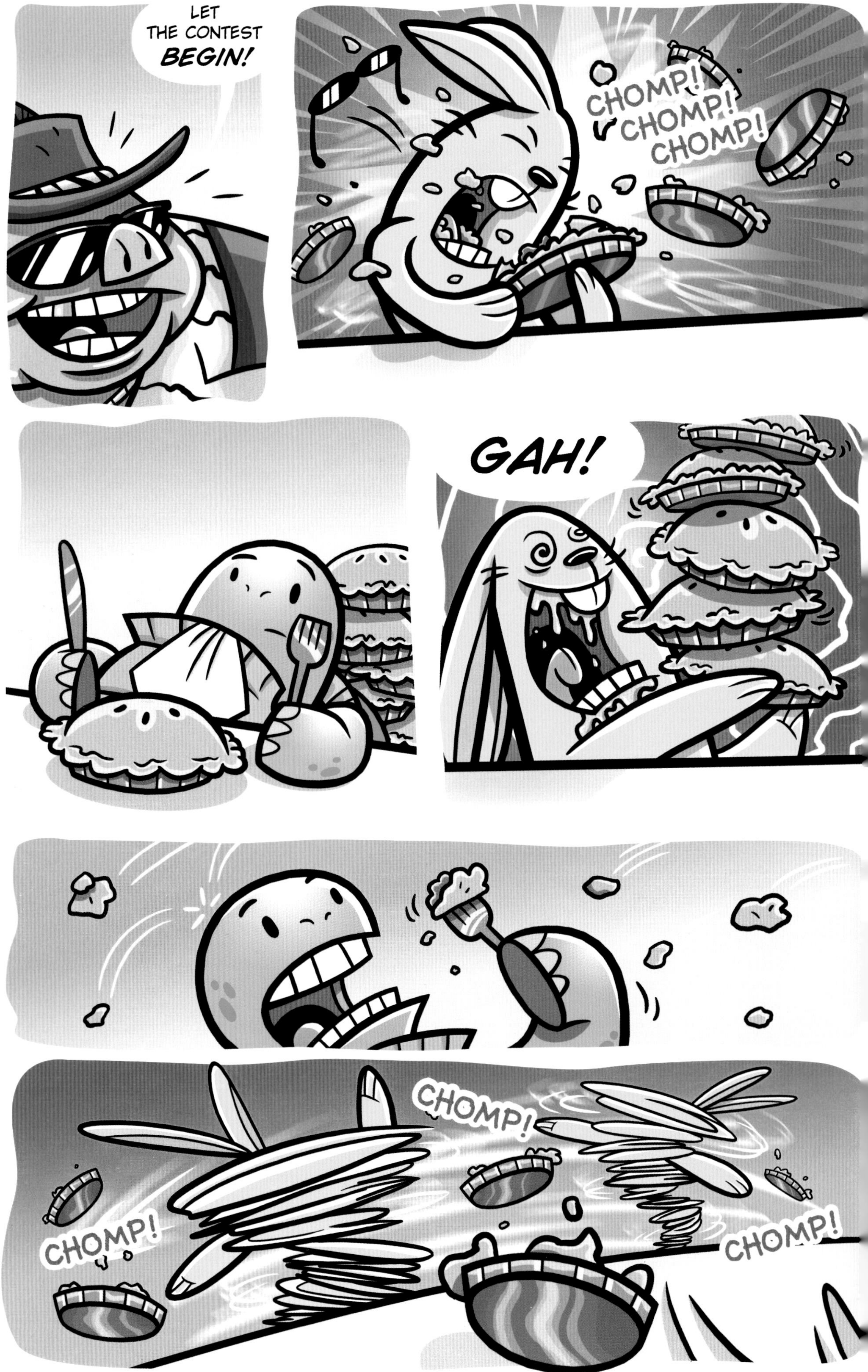
LET THE CONTEST BEGIN!
CHOMP! CHOMP! CHOMP!
GAH!
CHOMP!
CHOMP!
CHOMP!

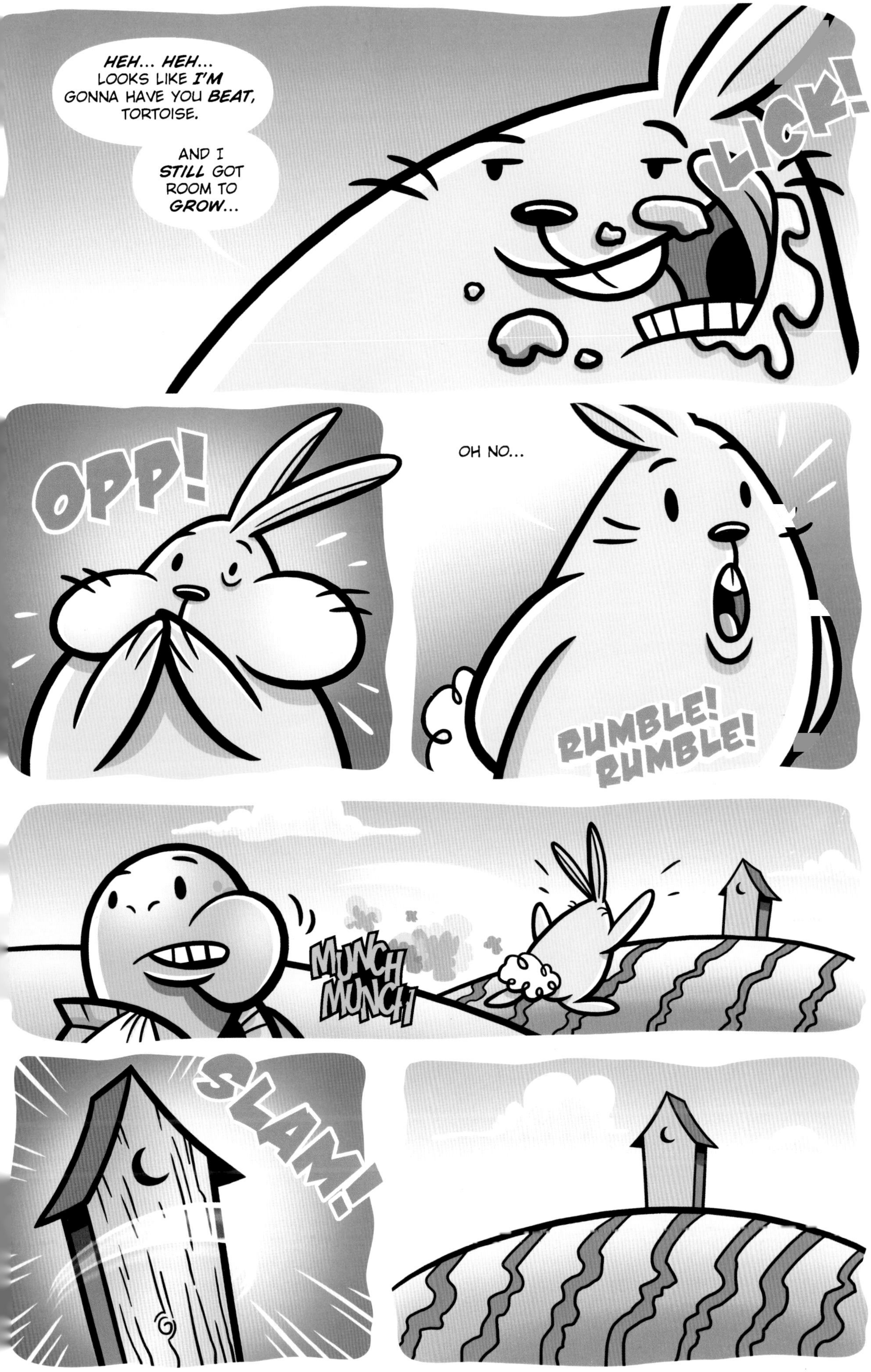
HEH... HEH... LOOKS LIKE I'M GONNA HAVE YOU BEAT, TORTOISE.
AND I STILL GOT ROOM TO GROW...
LICK!
OPP!
OH NO...
RUMBLE! RUMBLE!
MUNCH MUNCH
SLAM!

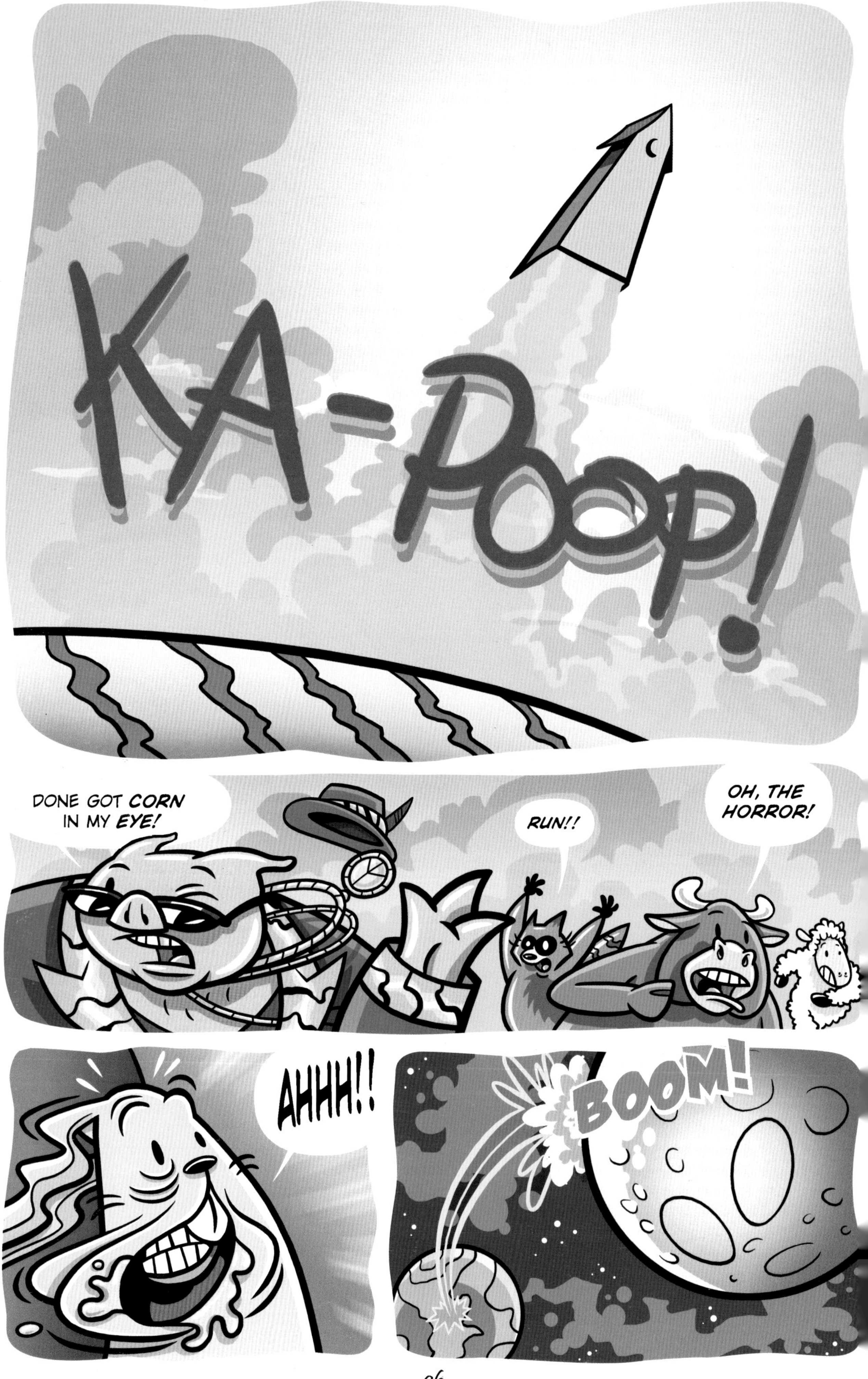
KA-POOP!
DONE GOT CORN IN MY EYE!
RUN!!
OH, THE HORROR!
AHHH!!
BOOM!

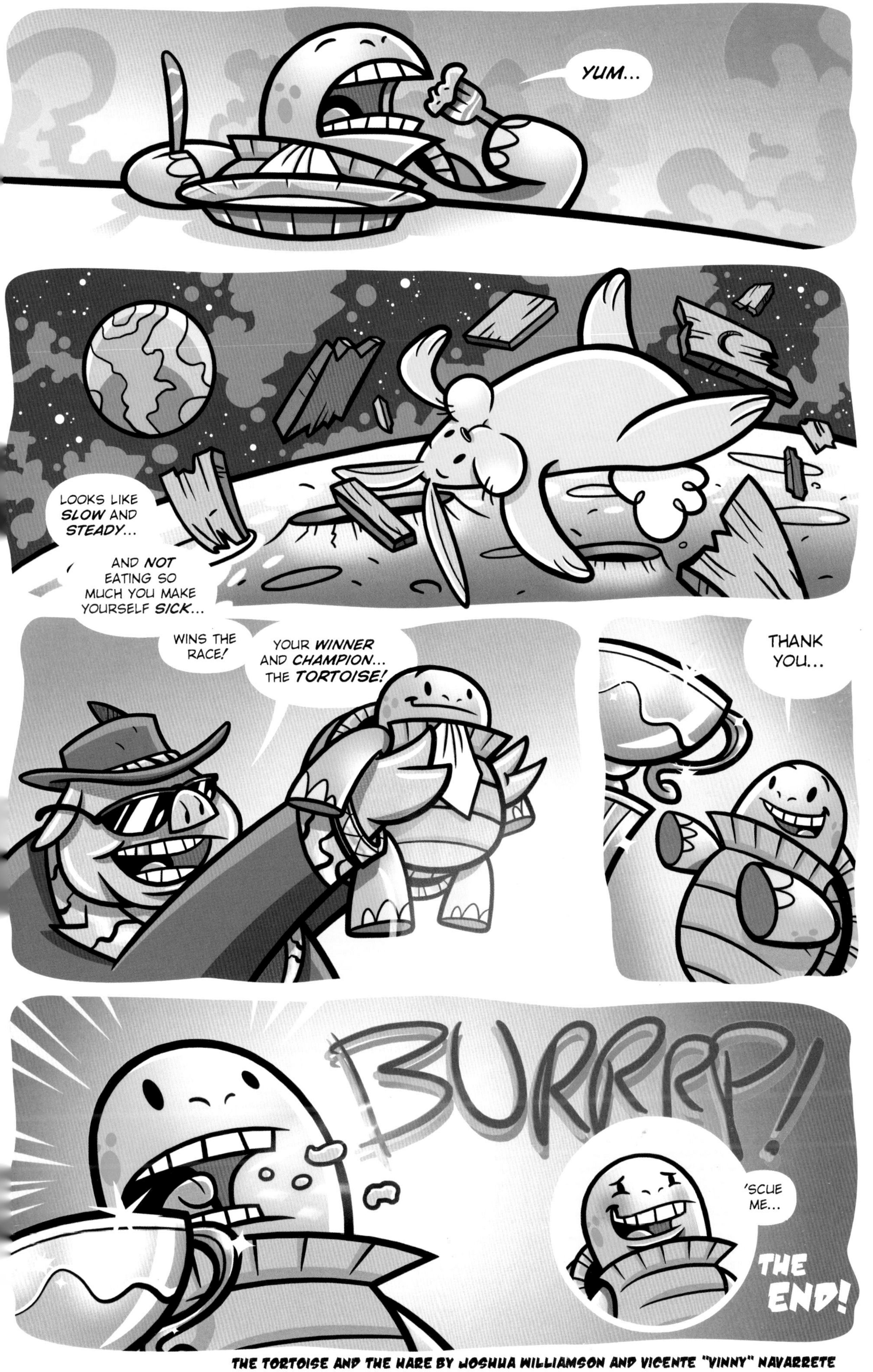
YUM...
LOOKS LIKE SLOW AND STEADY...
AND NOT EATING SO MUCH YOU MAKE YOURSELF SICK...
WINS THE RACE!
YOUR WINNER AND CHAMPION... THE TORTOISE!
THANK YOU...
BURRRP!
'SCUE ME...
THE END!

THE TORTOISE AND THE HARE BY JOSHUA WILLIAMSON AND VICENTE "VINNY" NAVARRETE

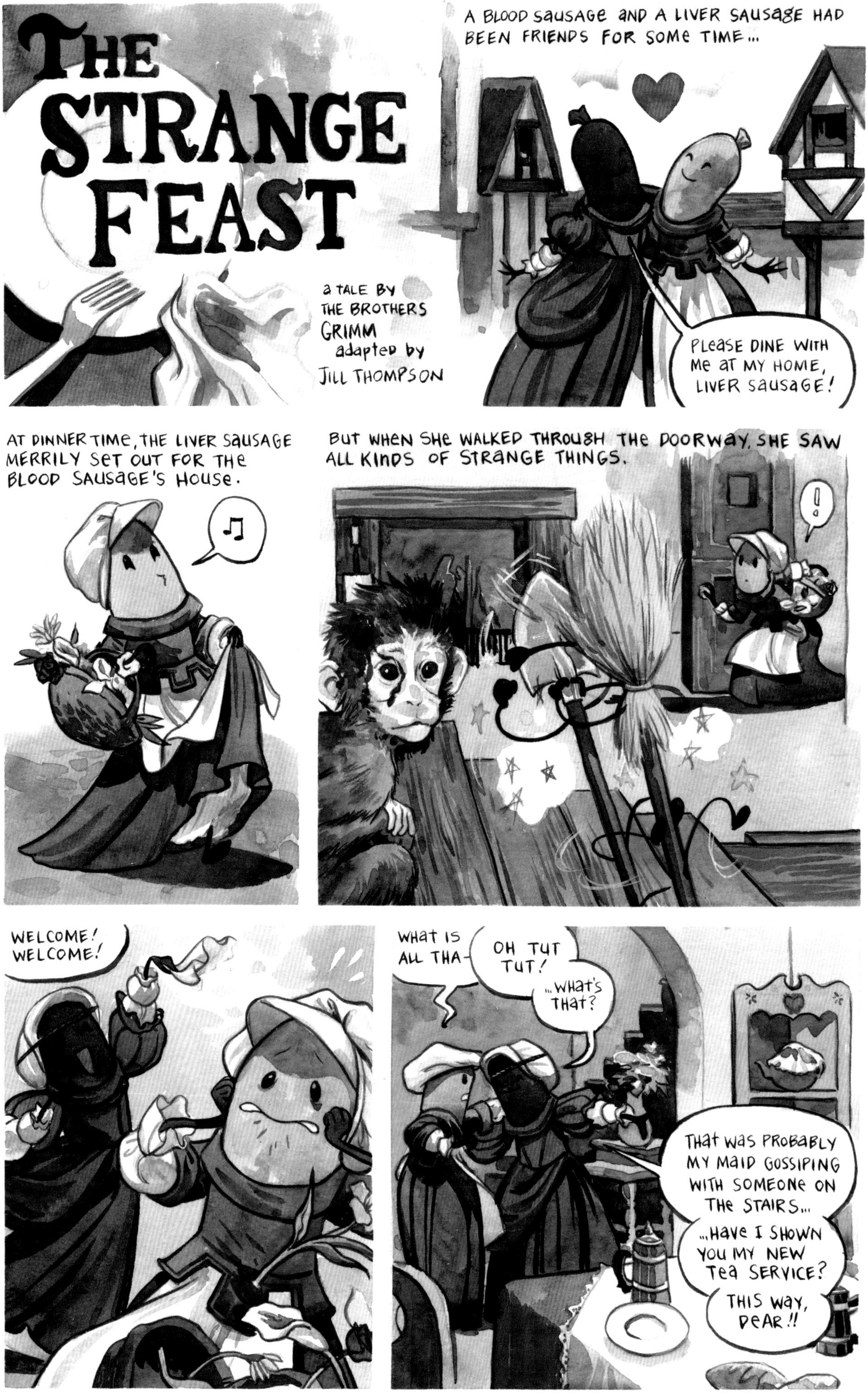
THE STRANGE FEAST
a TALE BY THE BROTHERS GRIMM
adapted by JILL THOMPSON
A BLOOD SAUSAGE AND A LIVER SAUSAGE HAD BEEN FRIENDS FOR SOME TIME...
PLEASE DINE WITH ME AT MY HOME, LIVER SAUSAGE!
AT DINNER TIME, THE LIVER SAUSAGE MERRILY SET OUT FOR THE BLOOD SAUSAGE'S HOUSE.
♫
BUT WHEN SHE WALKED THROUGH THE DOORWAY, SHE SAW ALL KINDS OF STRANGE THINGS.
!
WELCOME! WELCOME!
WHAT IS ALL THA-
OH TUT TUT!
...WHAT'S THAT?
THAT WAS PROBABLY MY MAID GOSSIPING WITH SOMEONE ON THE STAIRS...
...HAVE I SHOWN YOU MY NEW TEA SERVICE?
THIS WAY, DEAR!!

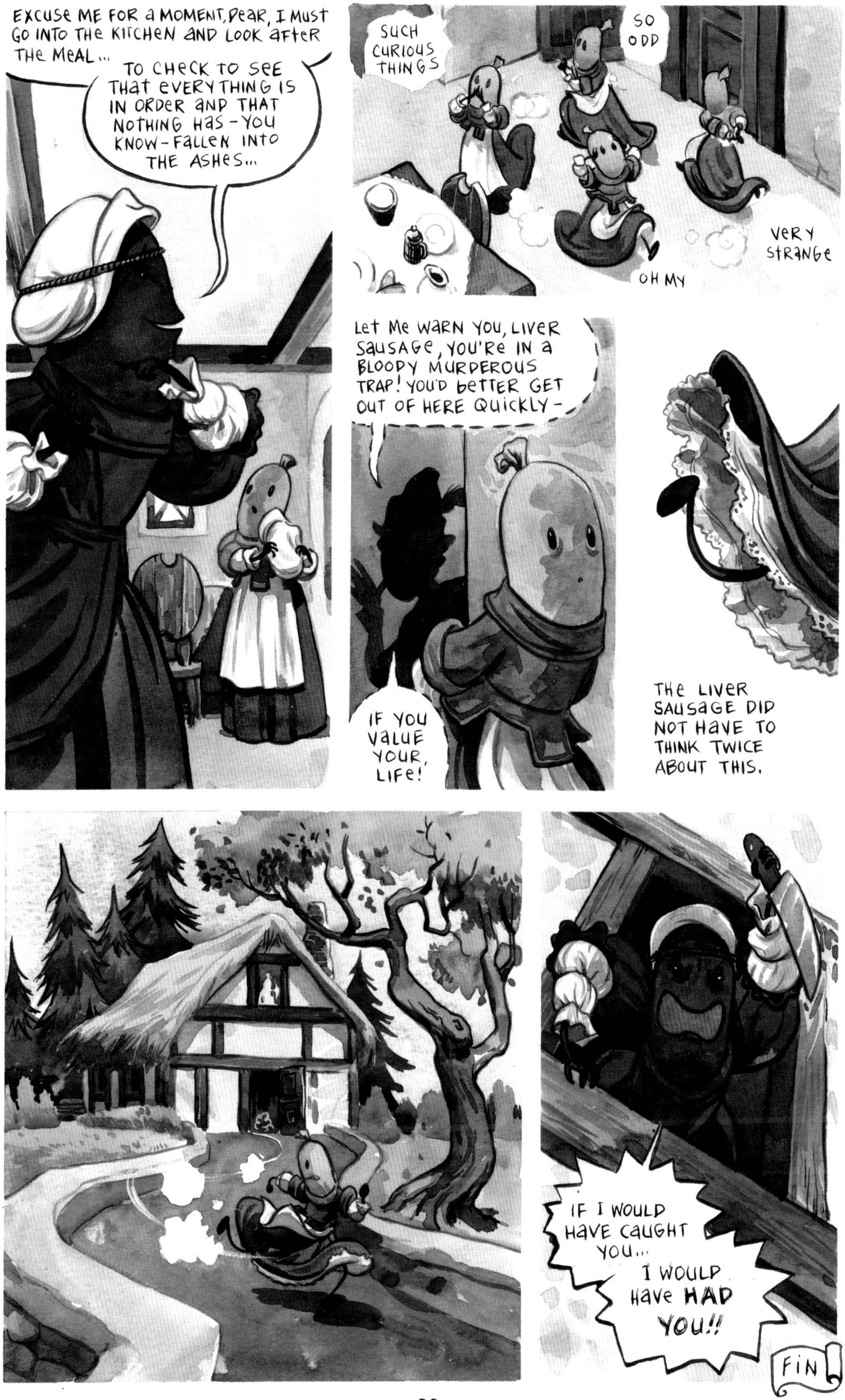
EXCUSE ME FOR A MOMENT, DEAR, I MUST GO INTO THE KITCHEN AND LOOK AFTER THE MEAL...
TO CHECK TO SEE THAT EVERYTHING IS IN ORDER AND THAT NOTHING HAS - YOU KNOW - FALLEN INTO THE ASHES...
SUCH CURIOUS THINGS
SO ODD
VERY STRANGE
OH MY
LET ME WARN YOU, LIVER SAUSAGE, YOU'RE IN A BLOODY MURDEROUS TRAP! YOU'D BETTER GET OUT OF HERE QUICKLY -
IF YOU VALUE YOUR LIFE!
THE LIVER SAUSAGE DID NOT HAVE TO THINK TWICE ABOUT THIS.
IF I WOULD HAVE CAUGHT YOU...
I WOULD HAVE HAD YOU!!
FIN

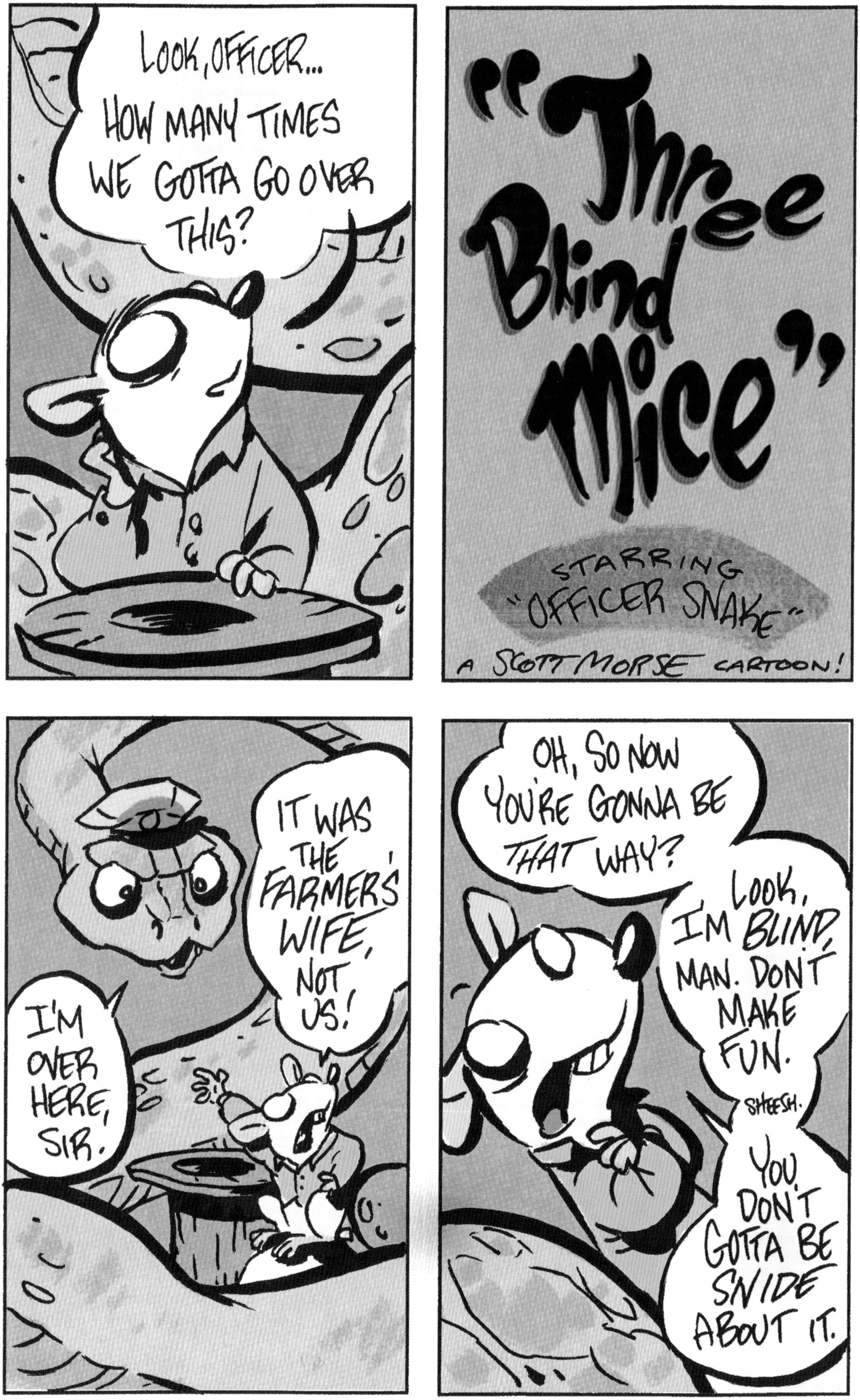
LOOK, OFFICER... HOW MANY TIMES WE GOTTA GO OVER THIS?
"Three Blind Mice"
STARRING "OFFICER SNAKE"
A SCOTT MORSE CARTOON!
IT WAS THE FARMER'S WIFE, NOT US!
I'M OVER HERE, SIR.
OH, SO NOW YOU'RE GONNA BE THAT WAY?
LOOK, I'M BLIND, MAN. DONT MAKE FUN.
SHEESH.
YOU DON'T GOTTA BE SNIDE ABOUT IT.

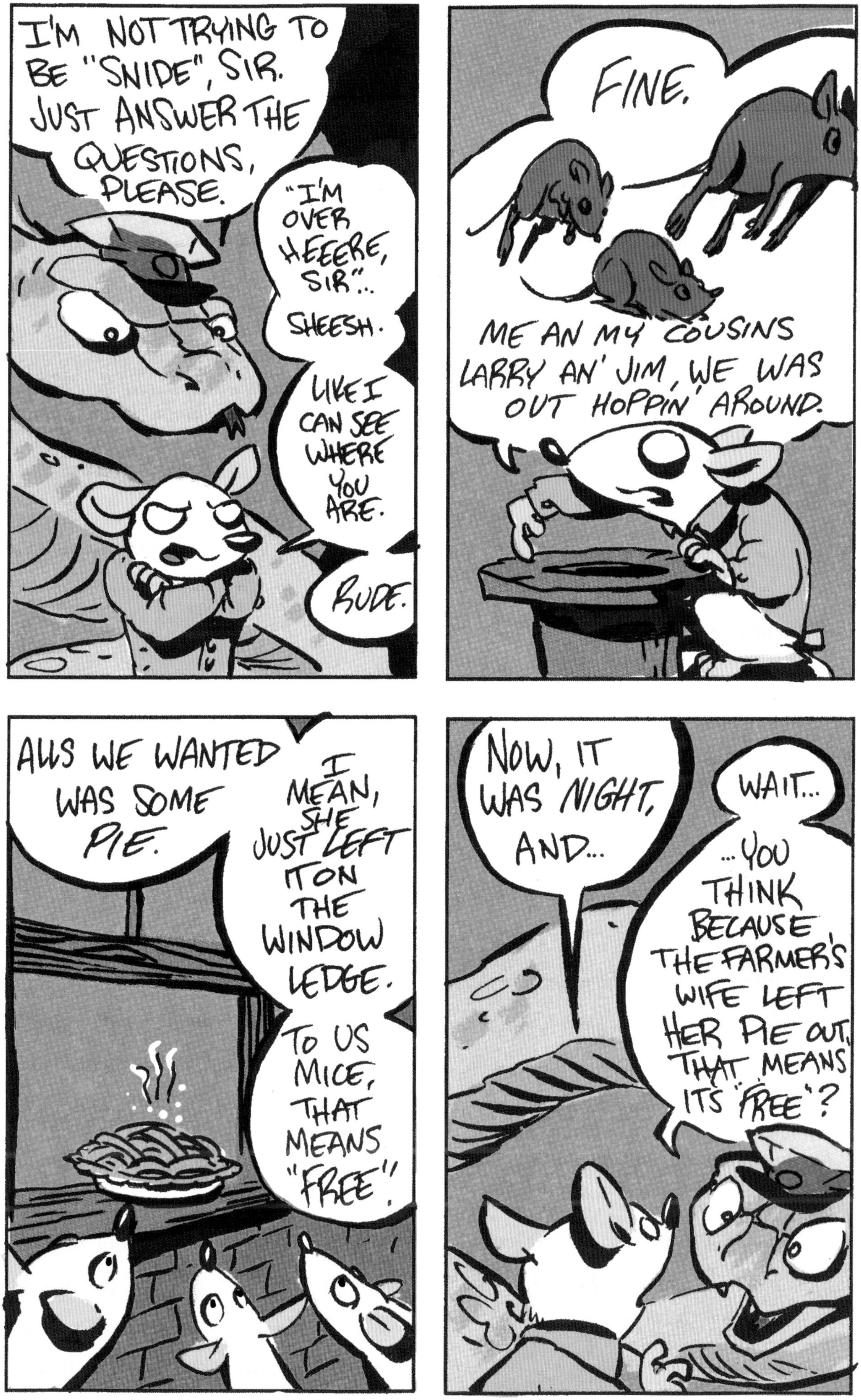
I'M NOT TRYING TO BE "SNIDE", SIR. JUST ANSWER THE QUESTIONS, PLEASE.
"I'M OVER HEEERE, SIR"... SHEESH.
LIKE I CAN SEE WHERE YOU ARE.
RUDE.
FINE.
ME AN MY COUSINS LARRY AN' JIM, WE WAS OUT HOPPIN' AROUND.
ALLS WE WANTED WAS SOME PIE.
I MEAN, SHE JUST LEFT IT ON THE WINDOW LEDGE.
TO US MICE, THAT MEANS "FREE".
NOW, IT WAS NIGHT, AND...
WAIT...
...YOU THINK BECAUSE THE FARMER'S WIFE LEFT HER PIE OUT, THAT MEANS ITS "FREE"?

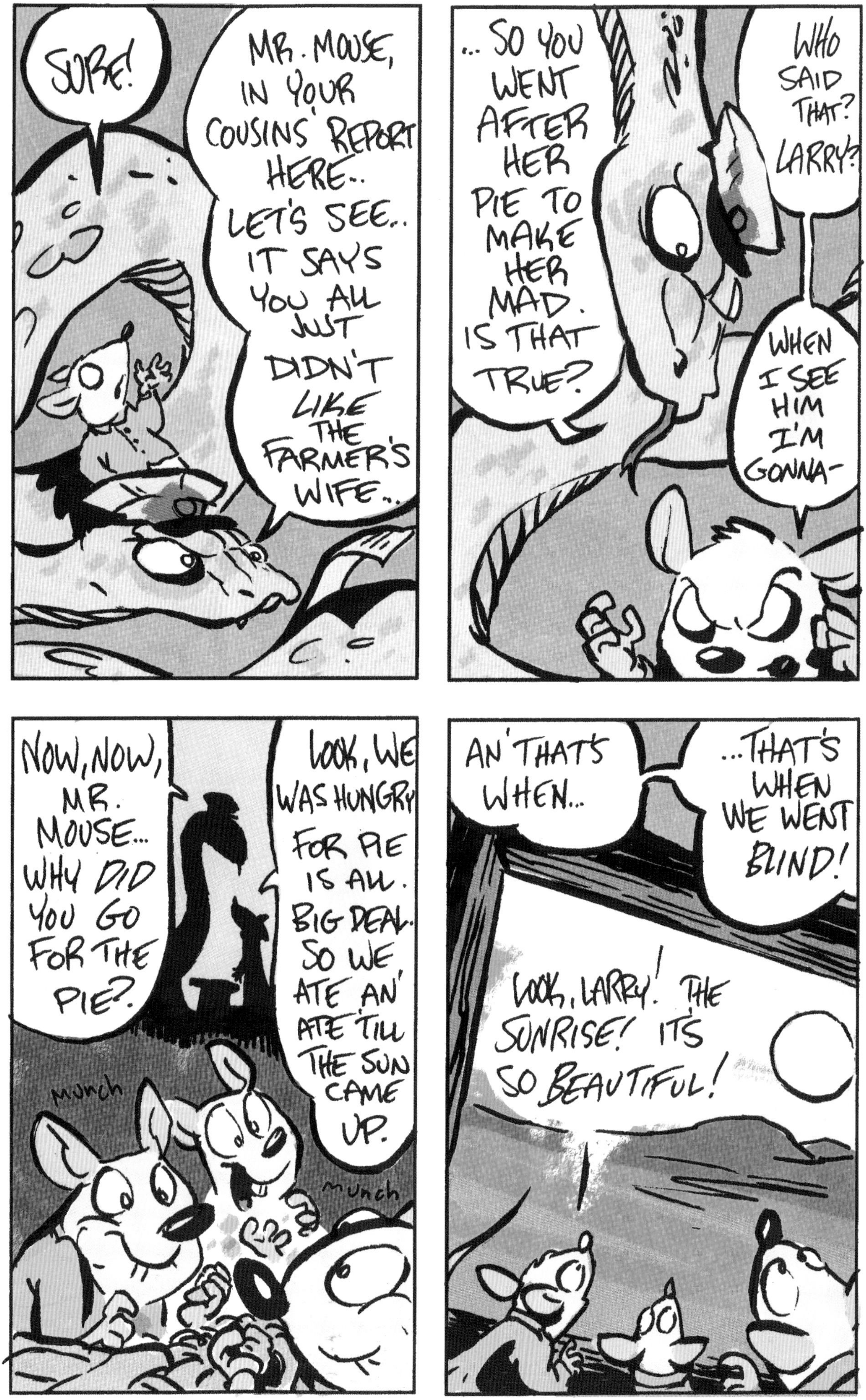
SURE!
MR. MOUSE, IN YOUR COUSINS' REPORT HERE.. LET'S SEE.. IT SAYS YOU ALL JUST DIDN'T *LIKE* THE FARMER'S WIFE..
...SO YOU WENT AFTER HER PIE TO MAKE HER MAD. IS THAT TRUE?
WHO SAID THAT? LARRY?
WHEN I SEE HIM I'M GONNA-
NOW, NOW, MR. MOUSE... WHY *DID* YOU GO FOR THE PIE?
LOOK, WE WAS HUNGRY FOR PIE IS ALL. BIG DEAL. SO WE ATE AN' ATE TILL THE SUN CAME UP.
munch
munch
AN' THAT'S WHEN...
...THAT'S WHEN WE WENT *BLIND*!
LOOK, LARRY! THE SUNRISE! IT'S SO *BEAUTIFUL*!

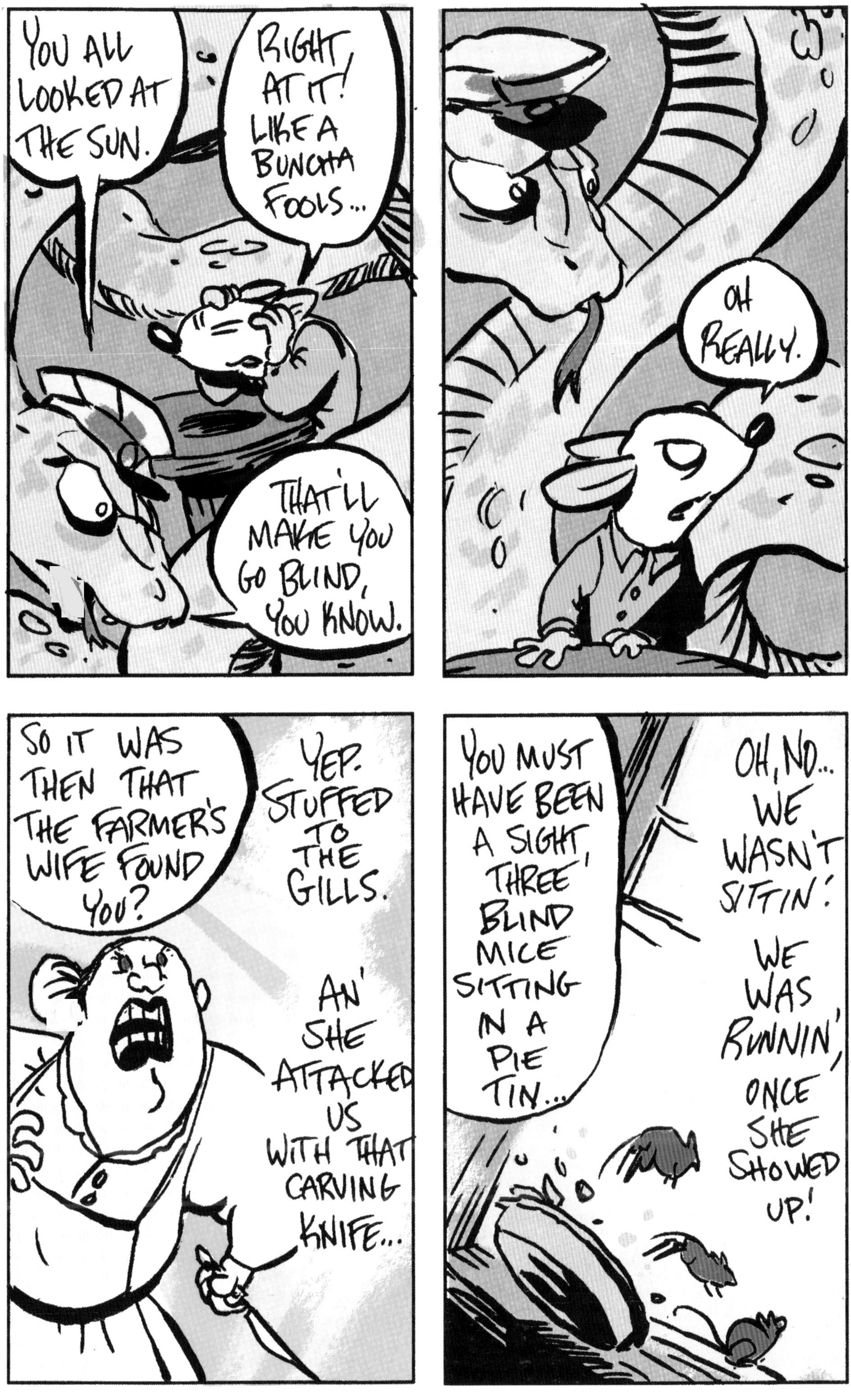
YOU ALL LOOKED AT THE SUN.
RIGHT AT IT! LIKE A BUNCHA FOOLS...
THAT'LL MAKE YOU GO BLIND, YOU KNOW.
OH REALLY.
SO IT WAS THEN THAT THE FARMER'S WIFE FOUND YOU?
YEP. STUFFED TO THE GILLS.
AN' SHE ATTACKED US WITH THAT CARVING KNIFE...
YOU MUST HAVE BEEN A SIGHT, THREE BLIND MICE SITTING IN A PIE TIN...
OH, NO... WE WASN'T SITTIN'!
WE WAS RUNNIN', ONCE SHE SHOWED UP!

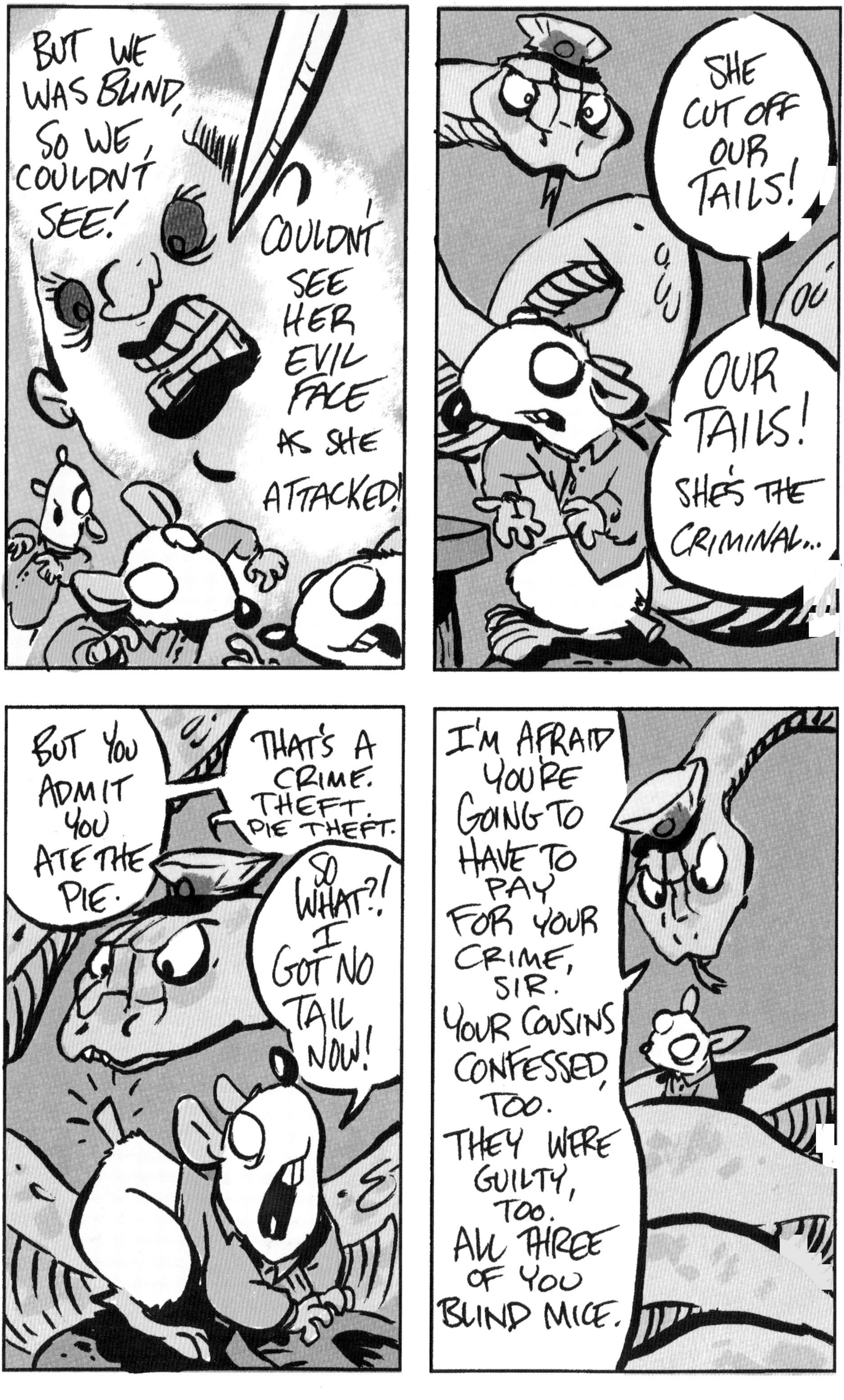
BUT WE WAS BLIND, SO WE COULDN'T SEE!
COULDN'T SEE HER EVIL FACE AS SHE ATTACKED!
SHE CUT OFF OUR TAILS!
OUR TAILS! SHE'S THE CRIMINAL...
BUT YOU ADMIT YOU ATE THE PIE.
THAT'S A CRIME. THEFT. PIE THEFT.
SO WHAT?! I GOT NO TAIL NOW!
I'M AFRAID YOU'RE GOING TO HAVE TO PAY FOR YOUR CRIME, SIR. YOUR COUSINS CONFESSED, TOO. THEY WERE GUILTY, TOO. ALL THREE OF YOU BLIND MICE.

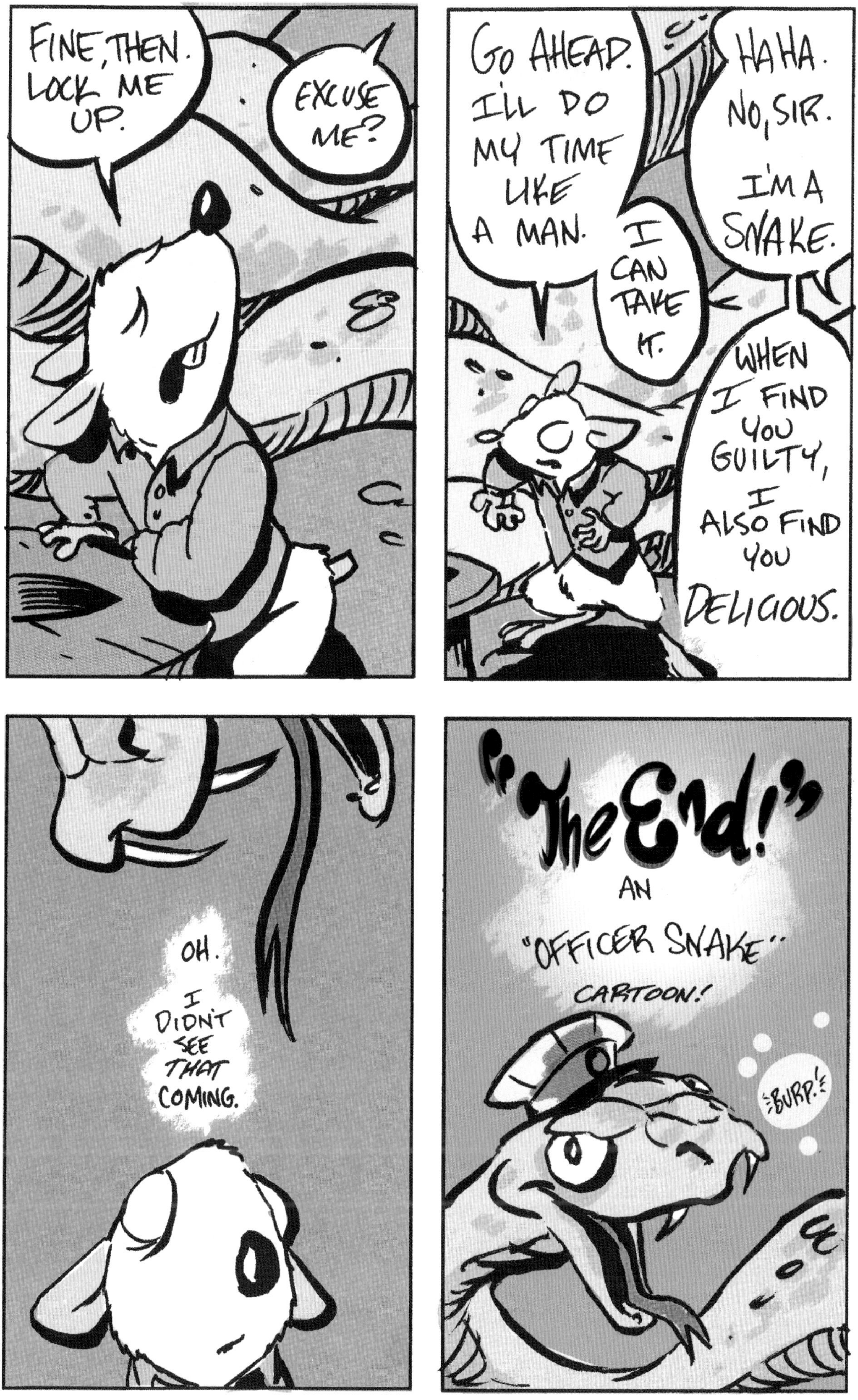
FINE, THEN. LOCK ME UP.
EXCUSE ME?
GO AHEAD. I'LL DO MY TIME LIKE A MAN.
I CAN TAKE IT.
HAHA. NO, SIR.
I'M A SNAKE.
WHEN I FIND YOU GUILTY, I ALSO FIND YOU DELICIOUS.
OH.
I DIDN'T SEE THAT COMING.
"The End!"
AN "OFFICER SNAKE" CARTOON!
BURP!

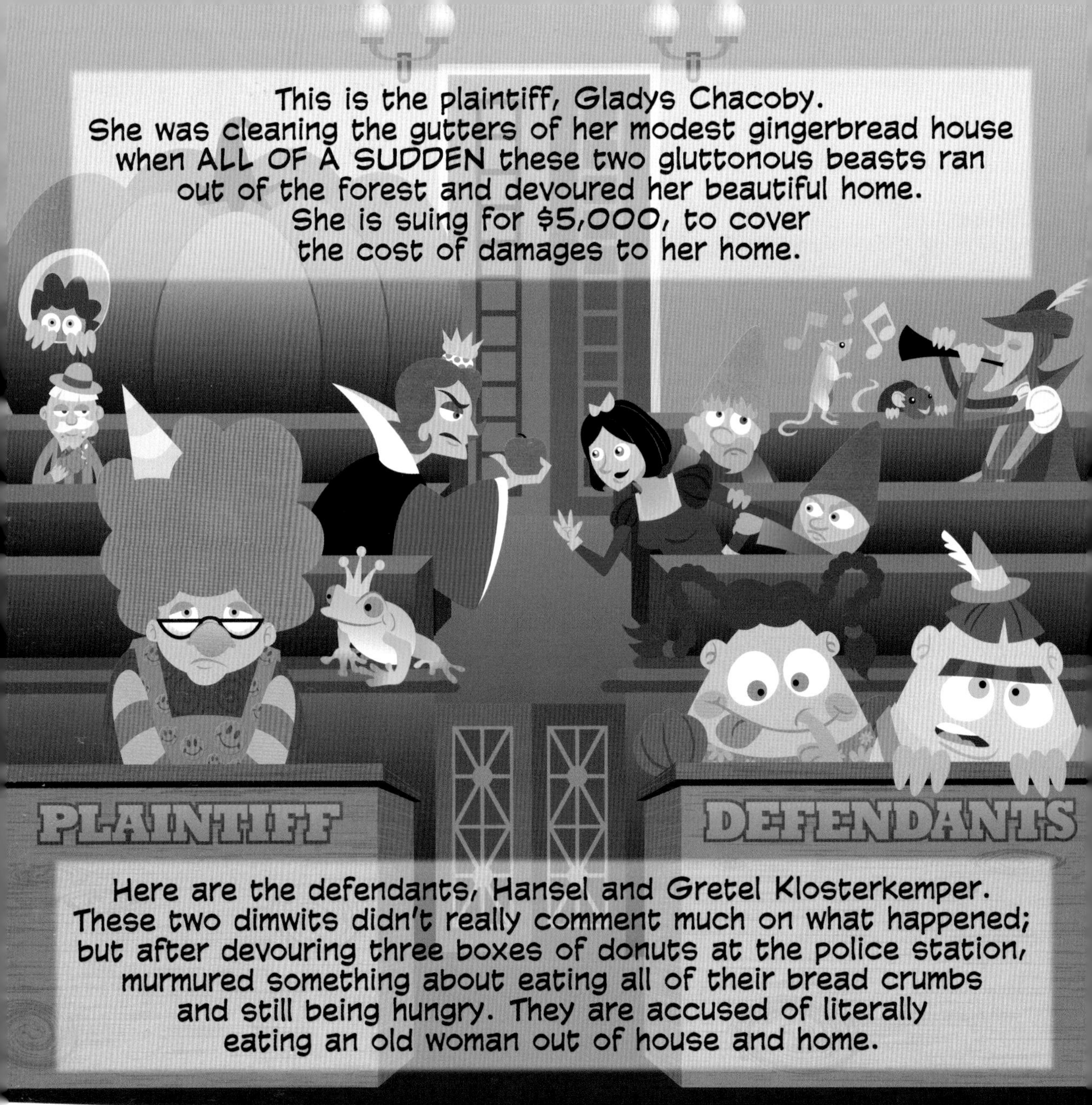
This is the plaintiff, Gladys Chacoby.
She was cleaning the gutters of her modest gingerbread house when ALL OF A SUDDEN these two gluttonous beasts ran out of the forest and devoured her beautiful home.
She is suing for $5,000, to cover the cost of damages to her home.
PLAINTIFF
DEFENDANTS
Here are the defendants, Hansel and Gretel Klosterkemper. These two dimwits didn't really comment much on what happened; but after devouring three boxes of donuts at the police station, murmured something about eating all of their bread crumbs and still being hungry. They are accused of literally eating an old woman out of house and home.

THE PEOPLE VS. HANSEL & GRETEL™

BY: JEREMY R. SCOTT

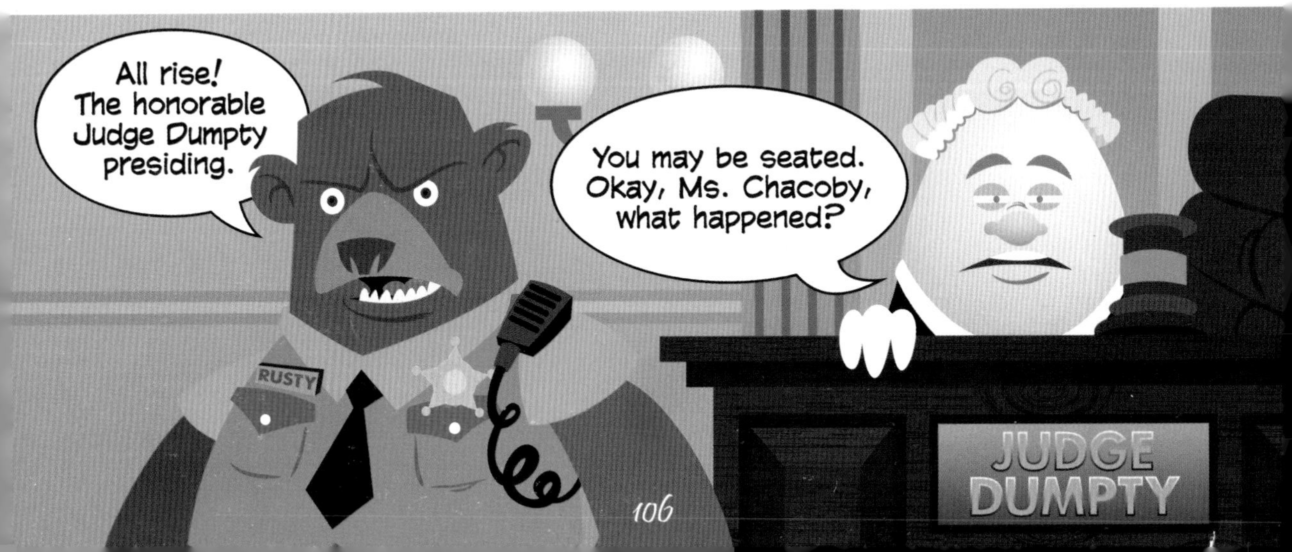
All rise! The honorable Judge Dumpty presiding.
You may be seated. Okay, Ms. Chacoby, what happened?
RUSTY
JUDGE DUMPTY

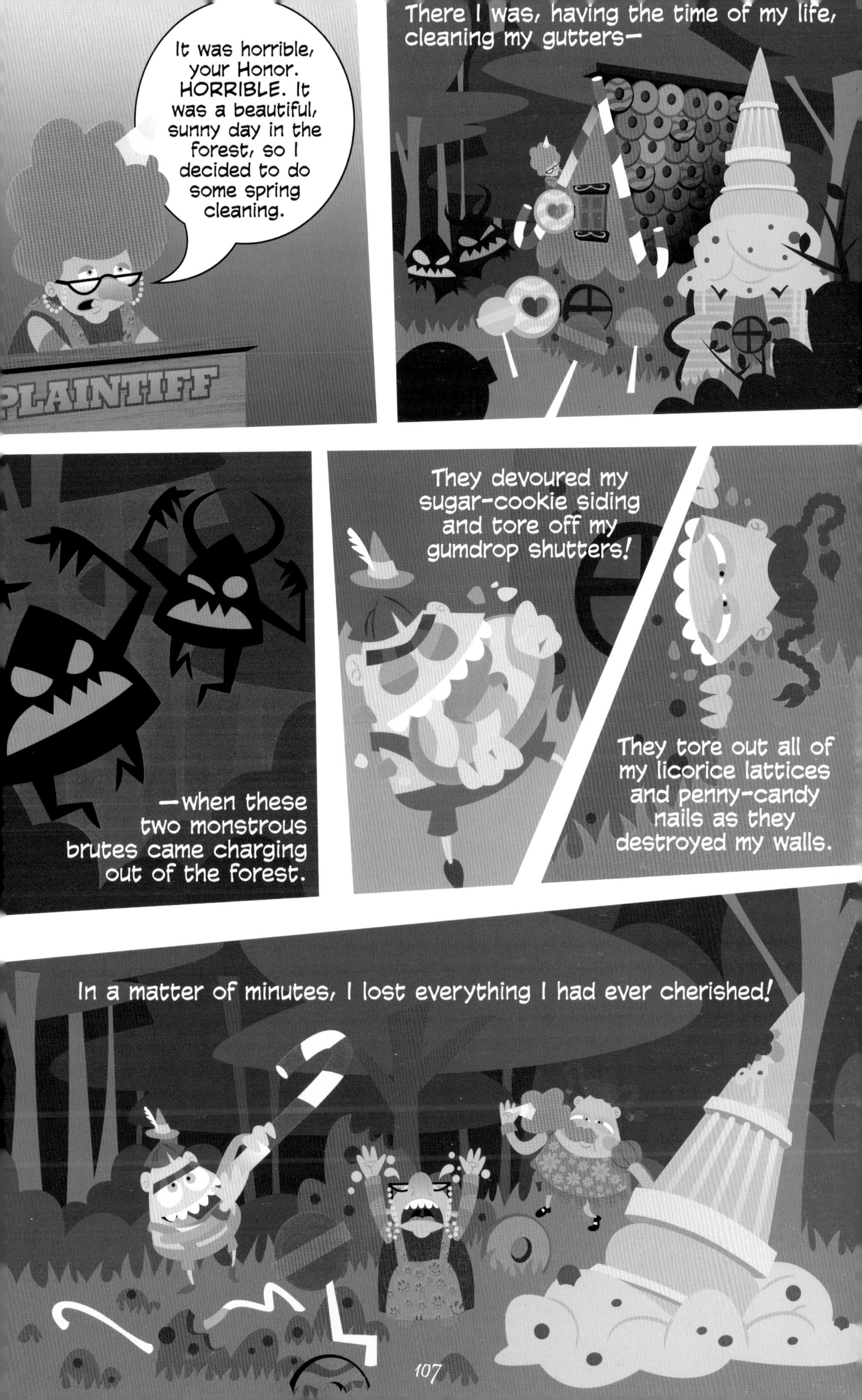
It was horrible, your Honor. HORRIBLE. It was a beautiful, sunny day in the forest, so I decided to do some spring cleaning.
PLAINTIFF
There I was, having the time of my life, cleaning my gutters—
—when these two monstrous brutes came charging out of the forest.
They devoured my sugar-cookie siding and tore off my gumdrop shutters!
They tore out all of my licorice lattices and penny-candy nails as they destroyed my walls.
In a matter of minutes, I lost everything I had ever cherished!

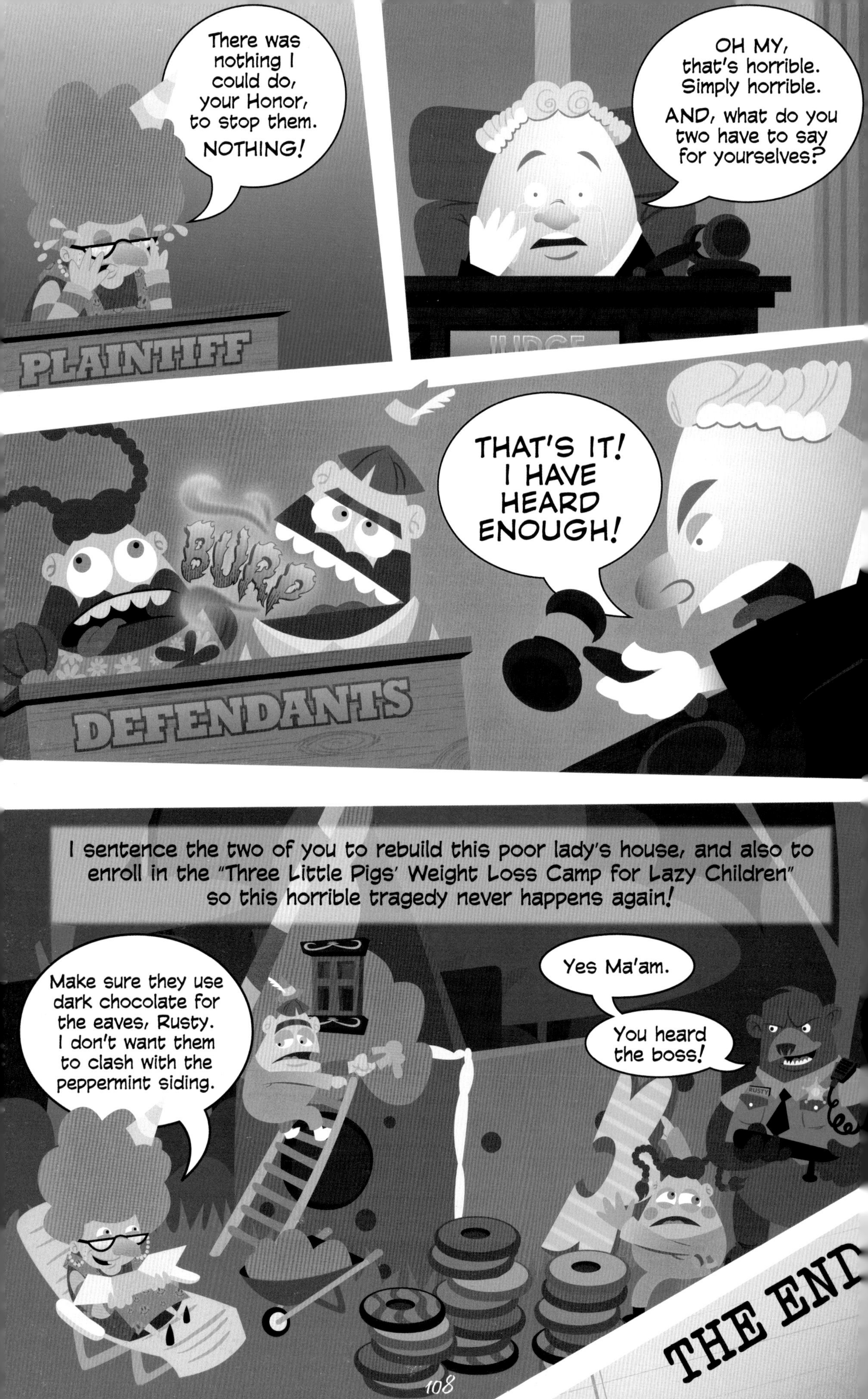
There was nothing I could do, your Honor, to stop them. NOTHING!
PLAINTIFF
OH MY, that's horrible. Simply horrible.
AND, what do you two have to say for yourselves?
BURP
THAT'S IT! I HAVE HEARD ENOUGH!
DEFENDANTS
I sentence the two of you to rebuild this poor lady's house, and also to enroll in the "Three Little Pigs' Weight Loss Camp for Lazy Children" so this horrible tragedy never happens again!
Make sure they use dark chocolate for the eaves, Rusty. I don't want them to clash with the peppermint siding.
Yes Ma'am.
You heard the boss!
RUSTY
THE END

Snoring Beauty

Once upon a time, there was a King and Queen who had at last been blessed with a beautiful daughter.

Kristen Simon
STORY

Seth Damoose
ART

Paul Little
COLORS

Ed Dukeshire
LETTERS

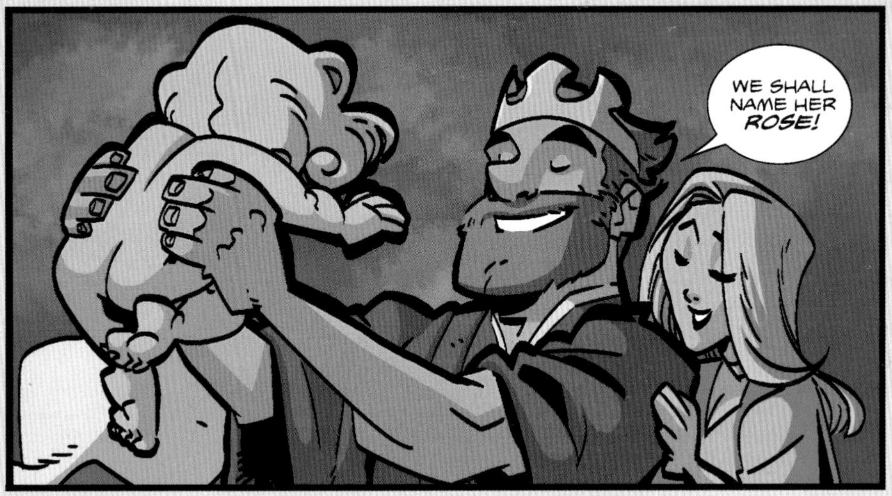

WE SHALL NAME HER *ROSE!*

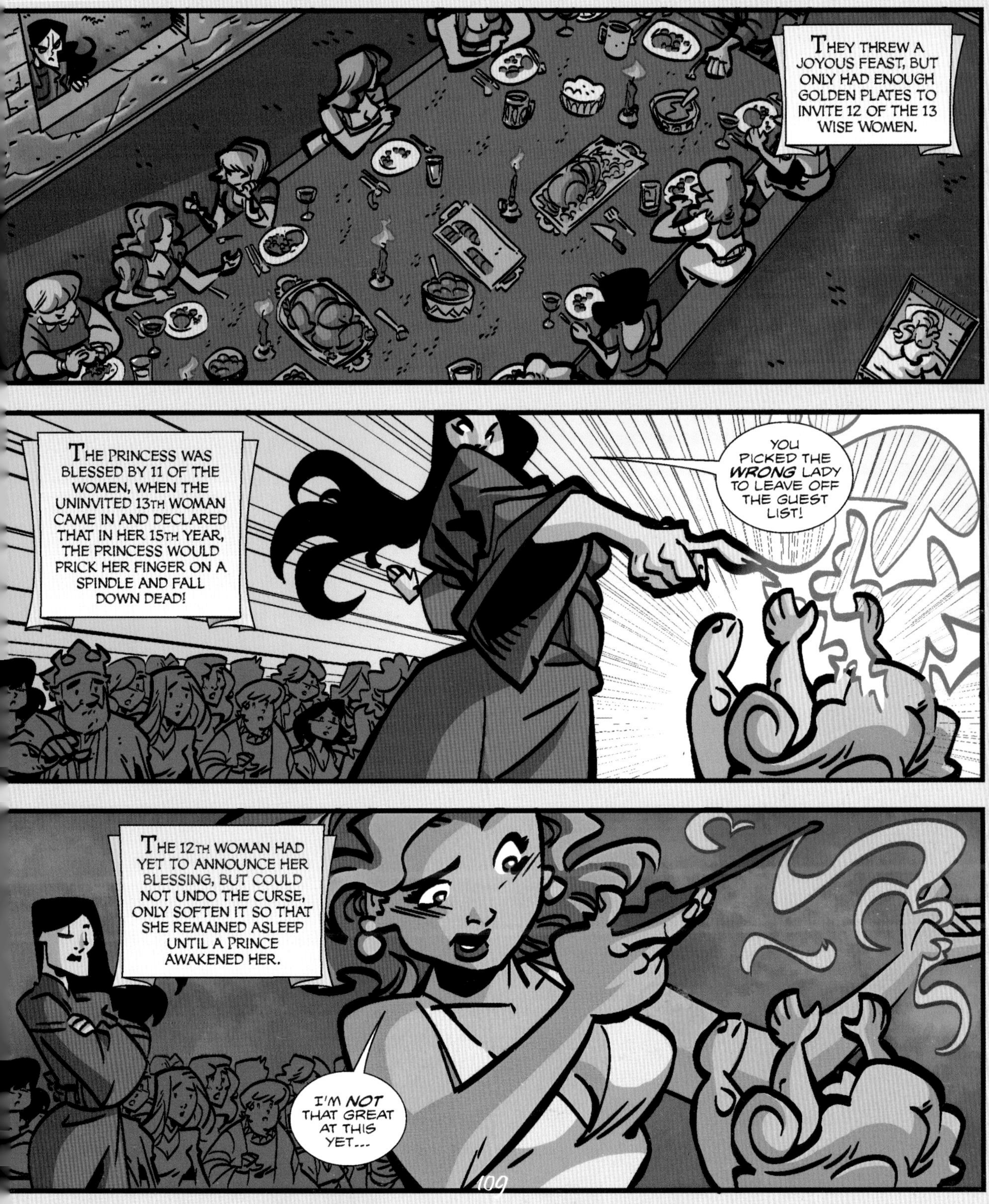

They threw a joyous feast, but only had enough golden plates to invite 12 of the 13 wise women.
The princess was blessed by 11 of the women, when the uninvited 13th woman came in and declared that in her 15th year, the princess would prick her finger on a spindle and fall down dead!
YOU PICKED THE ***WRONG*** LADY TO LEAVE OFF THE GUEST LIST!
The 12th woman had yet to announce her blessing, but could not undo the curse, only soften it so that she remained asleep until a prince awakened her.
I'M ***NOT*** THAT GREAT AT THIS YET...

THE PRINCESS TURNS 15, AND SURE ENOUGH, THE CURSE COMES TO PASS.

WHAT NO ONE HAD COUNTED ON WAS THE LOUD SNORING THAT CAME FROM THE TINY PRINCESS WHILE SHE SLEPT!

CAN YOU *ROLL HER OVER* OR SOMETHING?!

ZZZZZZZZZZZZZZZZZ

ZZZZZZZZZZZZZ

THE PRINCESS BECAME KNOWN AS *BRIAR ROSE* FOR THE THORNY ROSE BUSHES THAT GREW AROUND HER CASTLE, MAKING IT HARD FOR PRINCES TO COME AND RESCUE HER.

ZZZZZZZZZZZZZ

MAKE IT STOP! MAKE IT *STOP!!*

HOWEVER, THE PRINCESSES SNORING WAS SO LOUD, NO ONE COULD GET CLOSE TO HER FOR FEAR OF GOING DEAF!

110

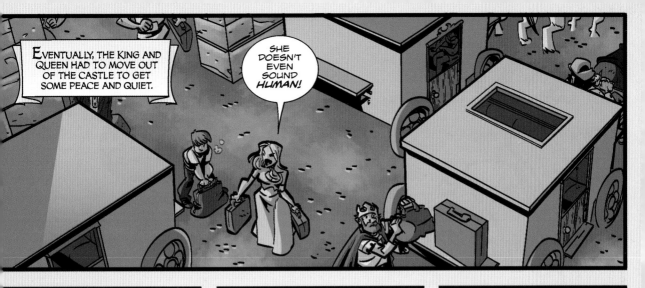

EVENTUALLY, THE KING AND QUEEN HAD TO MOVE OUT OF THE CASTLE TO GET SOME PEACE AND QUIET.

SHE DOESN'T EVEN SOUND *HUMAN!*

SNNRRRRKK!

BUT STRANGELY, THE EMPTIER THE CASTLE WAS, THE LOUDER THE SNORING BECAME!

SNOOORRKK

IT WAS SO LOUD, THAT EVENTUALLY THE TOWNSPEOPLE MOVED AWAY, LEAVING THE ENTIRE TOWN DESERTED, ASIDE FROM THE SNORING PRINCESS.

ALONE IN THE KINGDOM, THE PRINCESS SNORED ON, OBLIVIOUS TO THE TERRIBLE NOISE SHE WAS CREATING AND WITH LITTLE HOPE OF EVER BEING AWAKENED!

GRROOONNKK!

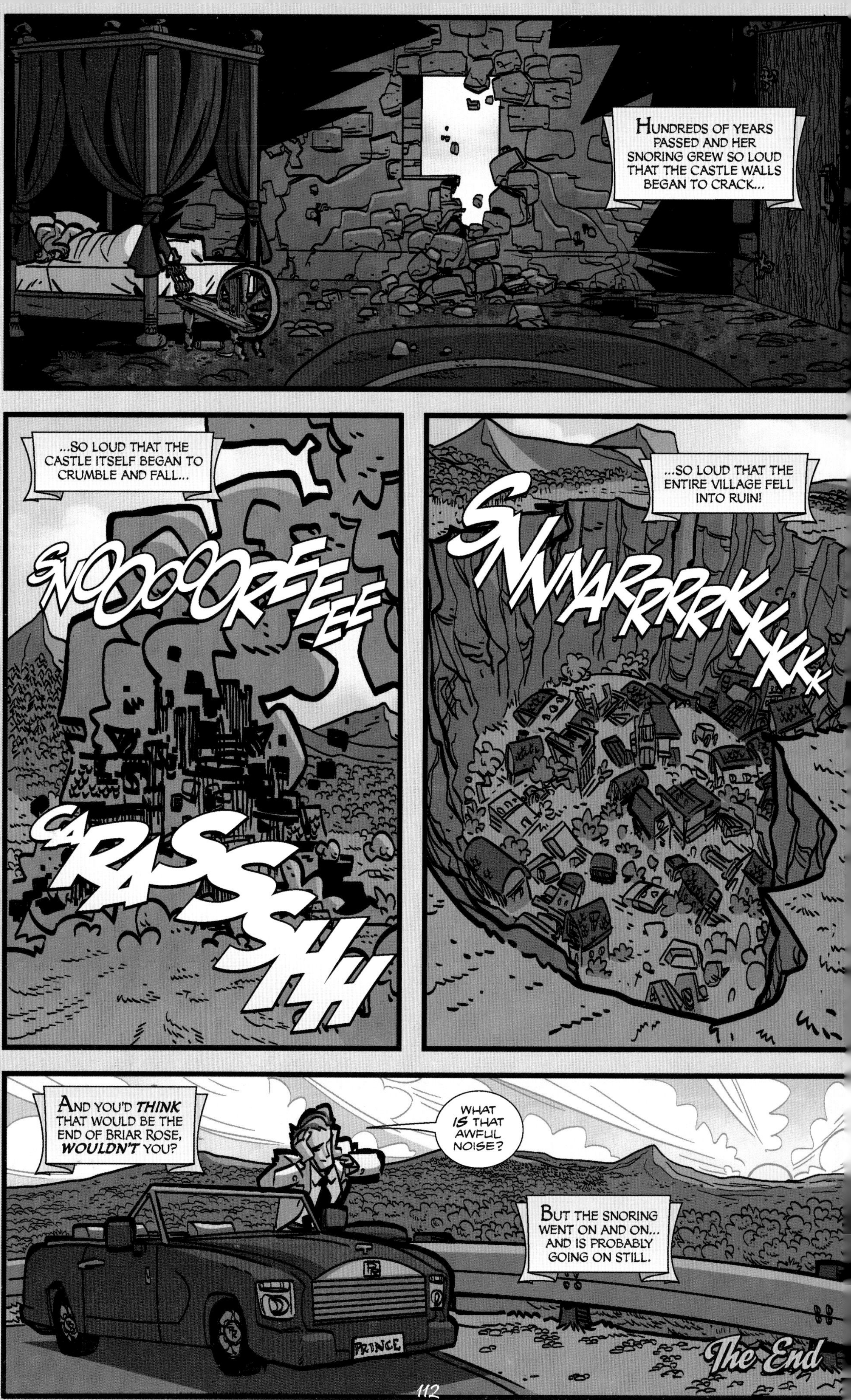
HUNDREDS OF YEARS PASSED AND HER SNORING GREW SO LOUD THAT THE CASTLE WALLS BEGAN TO CRACK...
...SO LOUD THAT THE CASTLE ITSELF BEGAN TO CRUMBLE AND FALL...
SNOOOOOREEEE
CRASSSHH
...SO LOUD THAT THE ENTIRE VILLAGE FELL INTO RUIN!
SNNNARRRRKKKKK
AND YOU'D THINK THAT WOULD BE THE END OF BRIAR ROSE, WOULDN'T YOU?
WHAT IS THAT AWFUL NOISE?
BUT THE SNORING WENT ON AND ON... AND IS PROBABLY GOING ON STILL.
PRINCE
The End

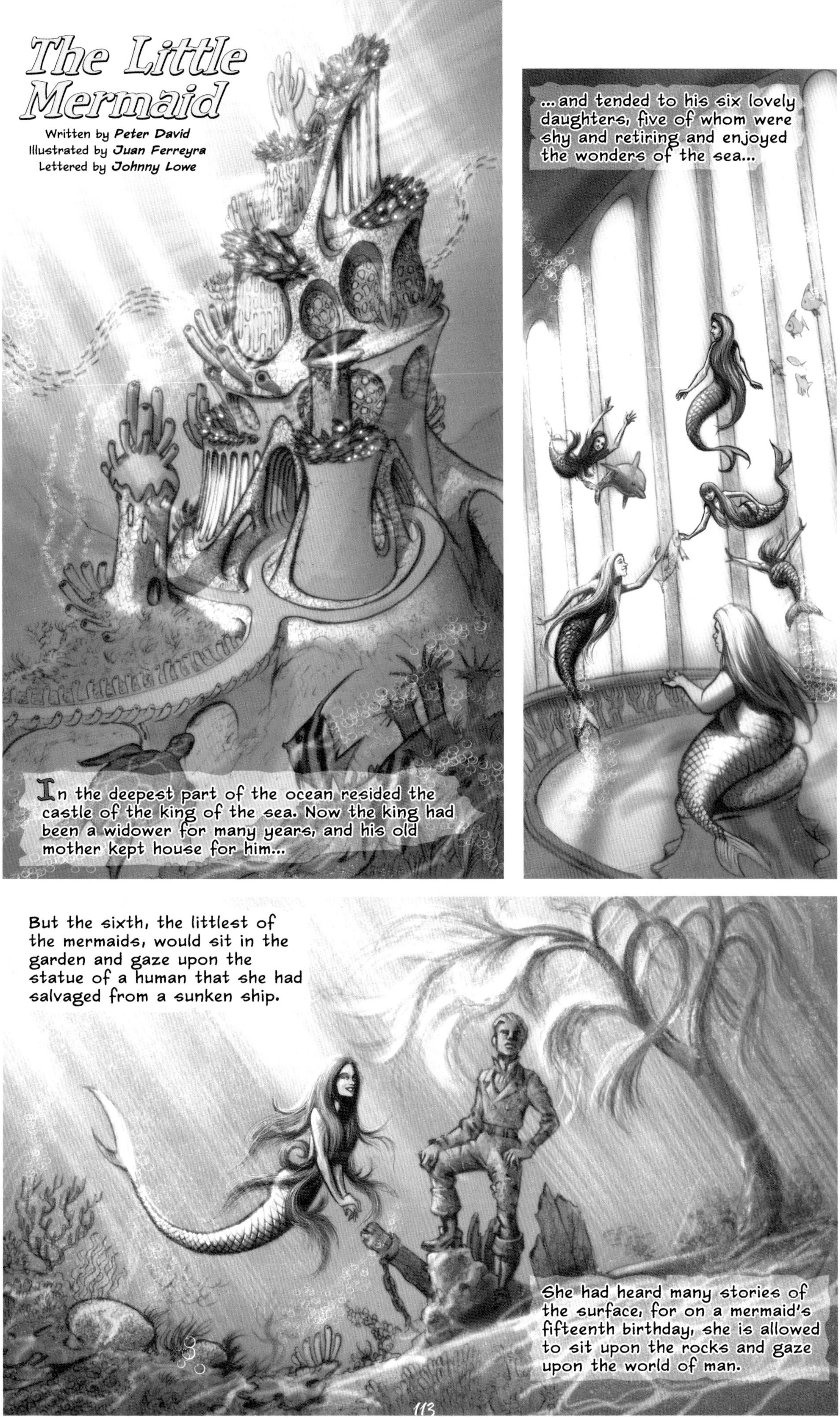
The Little Mermaid
Written by Peter David
Illustrated by Juan Ferreyra
Lettered by Johnny Lowe
In the deepest part of the ocean resided the castle of the king of the sea. Now the king had been a widower for many years, and his old mother kept house for him...
...and tended to his six lovely daughters, five of whom were shy and retiring and enjoyed the wonders of the sea...
But the sixth, the littlest of the mermaids, would sit in the garden and gaze upon the statue of a human that she had salvaged from a sunken ship.
She had heard many stories of the surface, for on a mermaid's fifteenth birthday, she is allowed to sit upon the rocks and gaze upon the world of man.

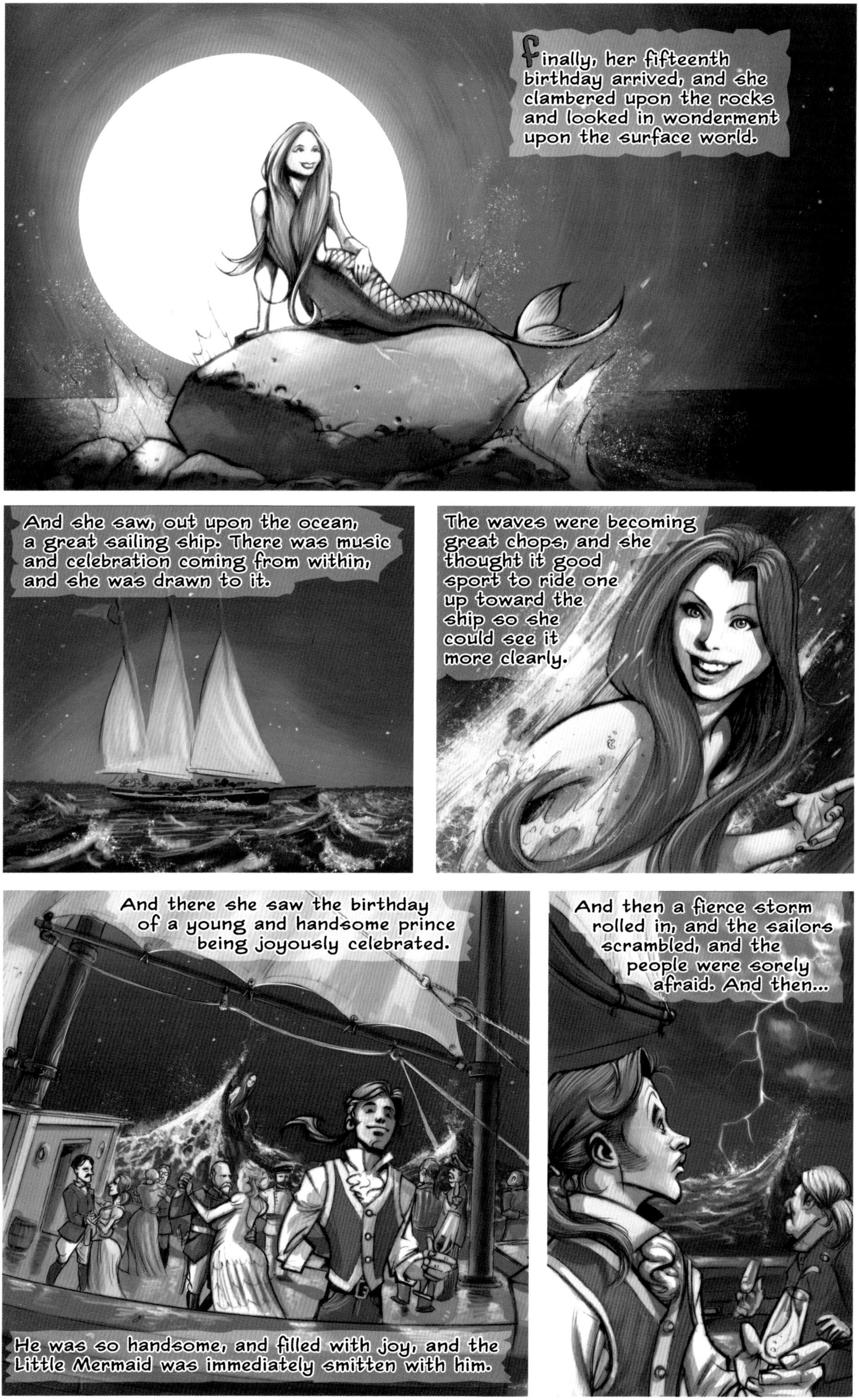
Finally, her fifteenth birthday arrived, and she clambered upon the rocks and looked in wonderment upon the surface world.
And she saw, out upon the ocean, a great sailing ship. There was music and celebration coming from within, and she was drawn to it.
The waves were becoming great chops, and she thought it good sport to ride one up toward the ship so she could see it more clearly.
And there she saw the birthday of a young and handsome prince being joyously celebrated.
He was so handsome, and filled with joy, and the Little Mermaid was immediately smitten with him.
And then a fierce storm rolled in, and the sailors scrambled, and the people were sorely afraid. And then...

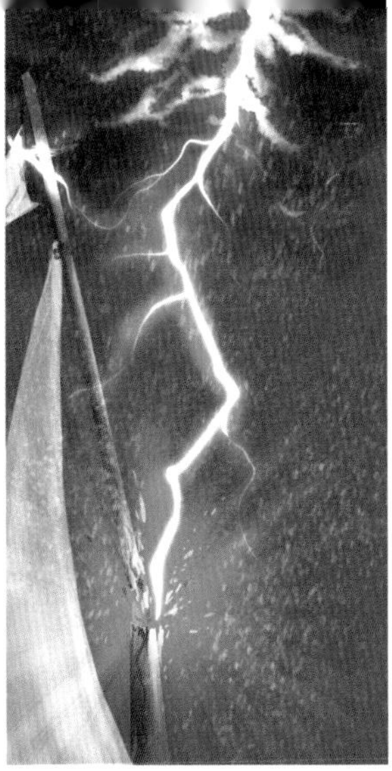

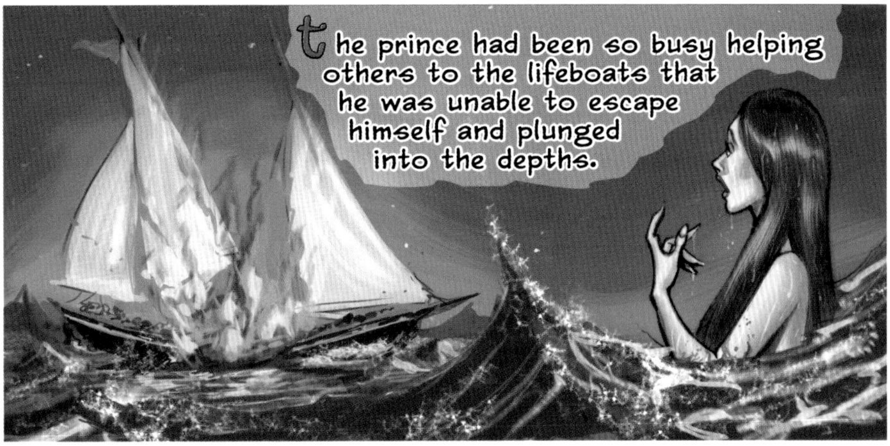
The prince had been so busy helping others to the lifeboats that he was unable to escape himself and plunged into the depths.

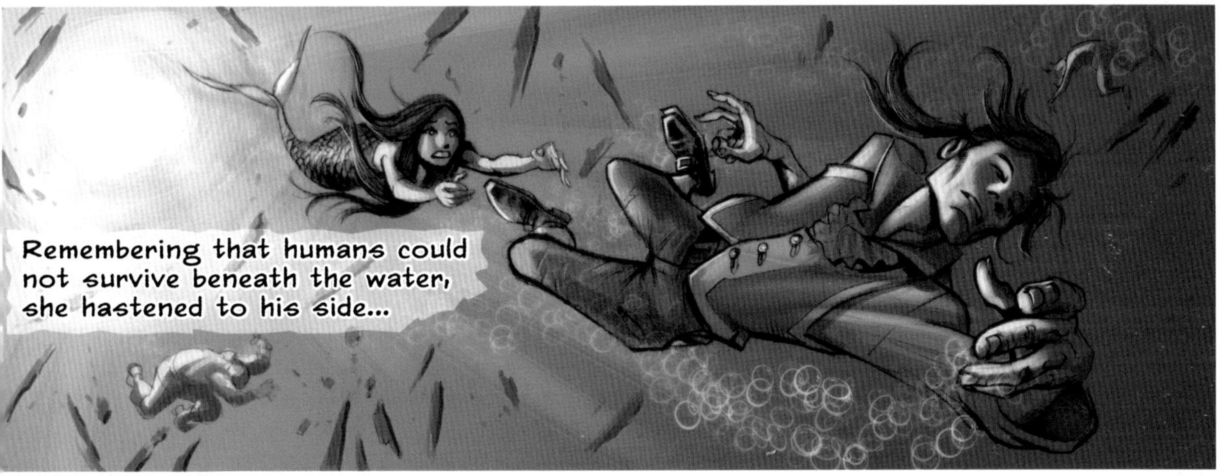
Remembering that humans could not survive beneath the water, she hastened to his side...

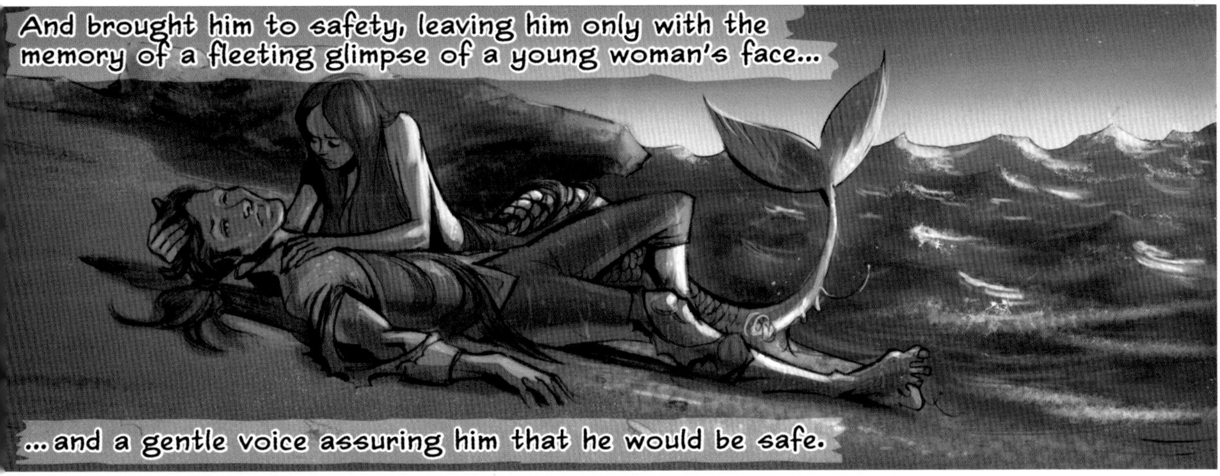
And brought him to safety, leaving him only with the memory of a fleeting glimpse of a young woman's face...
...and a gentle voice assuring him that he would be safe.

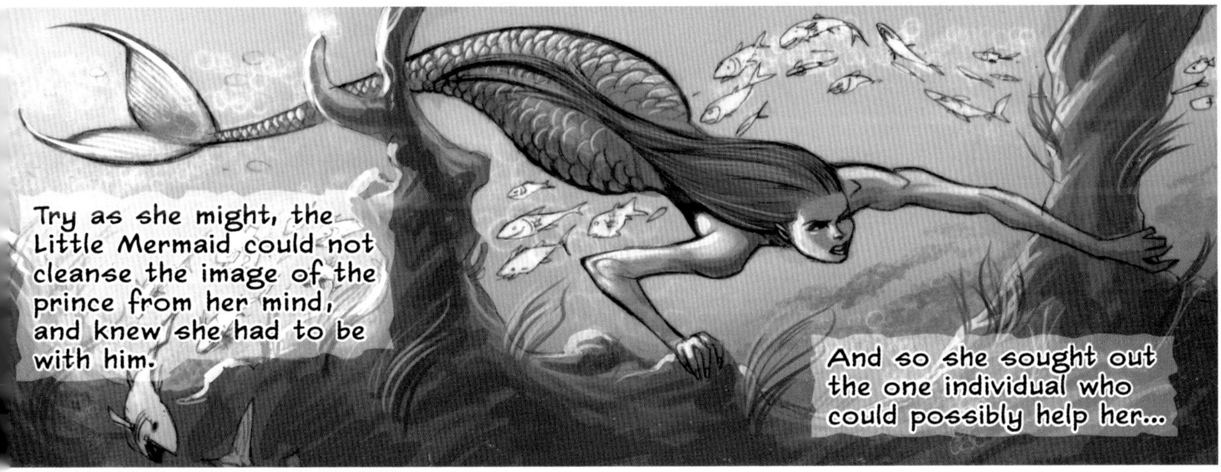
Try as she might, the Little Mermaid could not cleanse the image of the prince from her mind, and knew she had to be with him.
And so she sought out the one individual who could possibly help her...

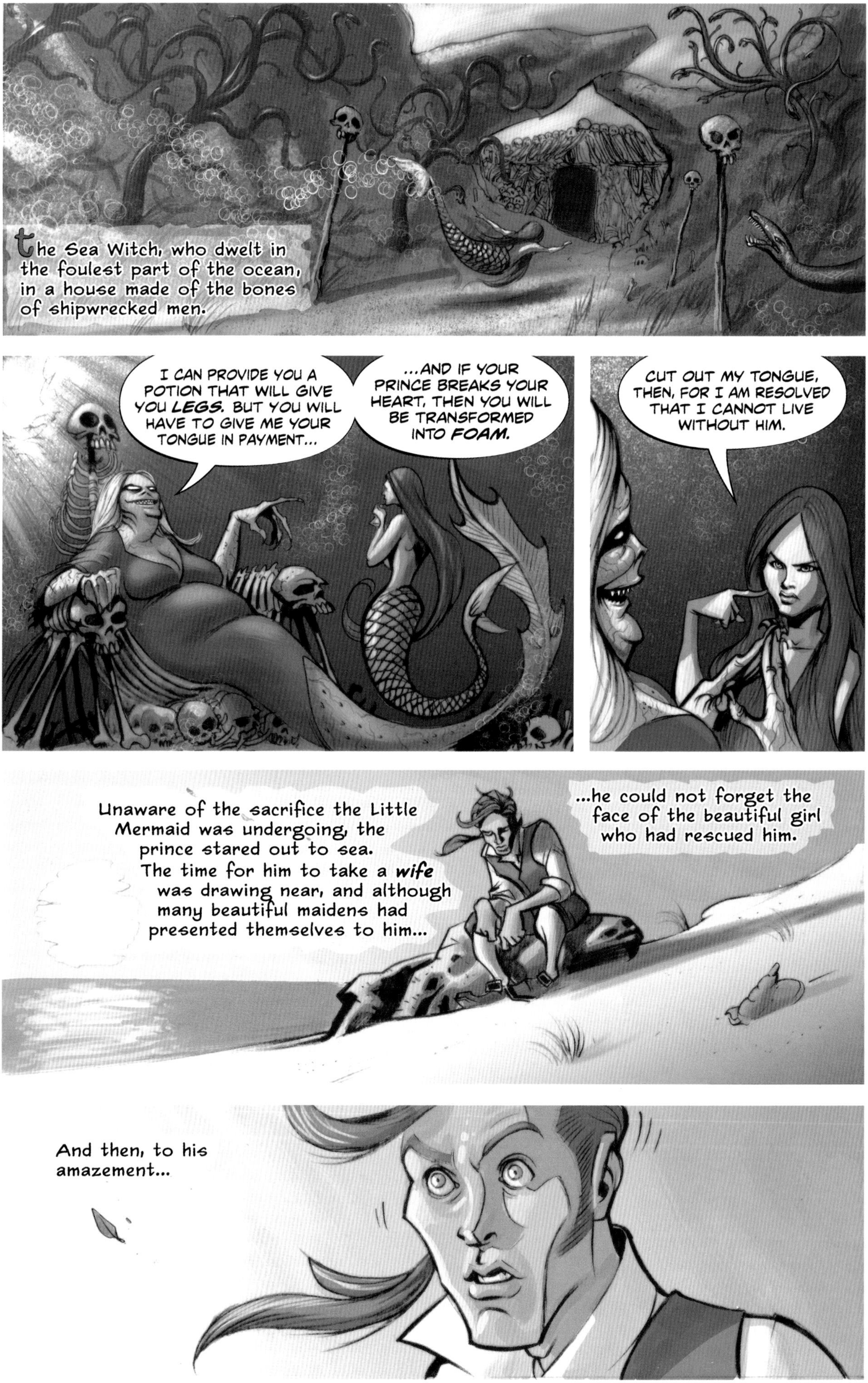
The Sea Witch, who dwelt in the foulest part of the ocean, in a house made of the bones of shipwrecked men.
I CAN PROVIDE YOU A POTION THAT WILL GIVE YOU LEGS. BUT YOU WILL HAVE TO GIVE ME YOUR TONGUE IN PAYMENT...
...AND IF YOUR PRINCE BREAKS YOUR HEART, THEN YOU WILL BE TRANSFORMED INTO FOAM.
CUT OUT MY TONGUE, THEN, FOR I AM RESOLVED THAT I CANNOT LIVE WITHOUT HIM.
Unaware of the sacrifice the Little Mermaid was undergoing, the prince stared out to sea. The time for him to take a wife was drawing near, and although many beautiful maidens had presented themselves to him...
...he could not forget the face of the beautiful girl who had rescued him.
And then, to his amazement...

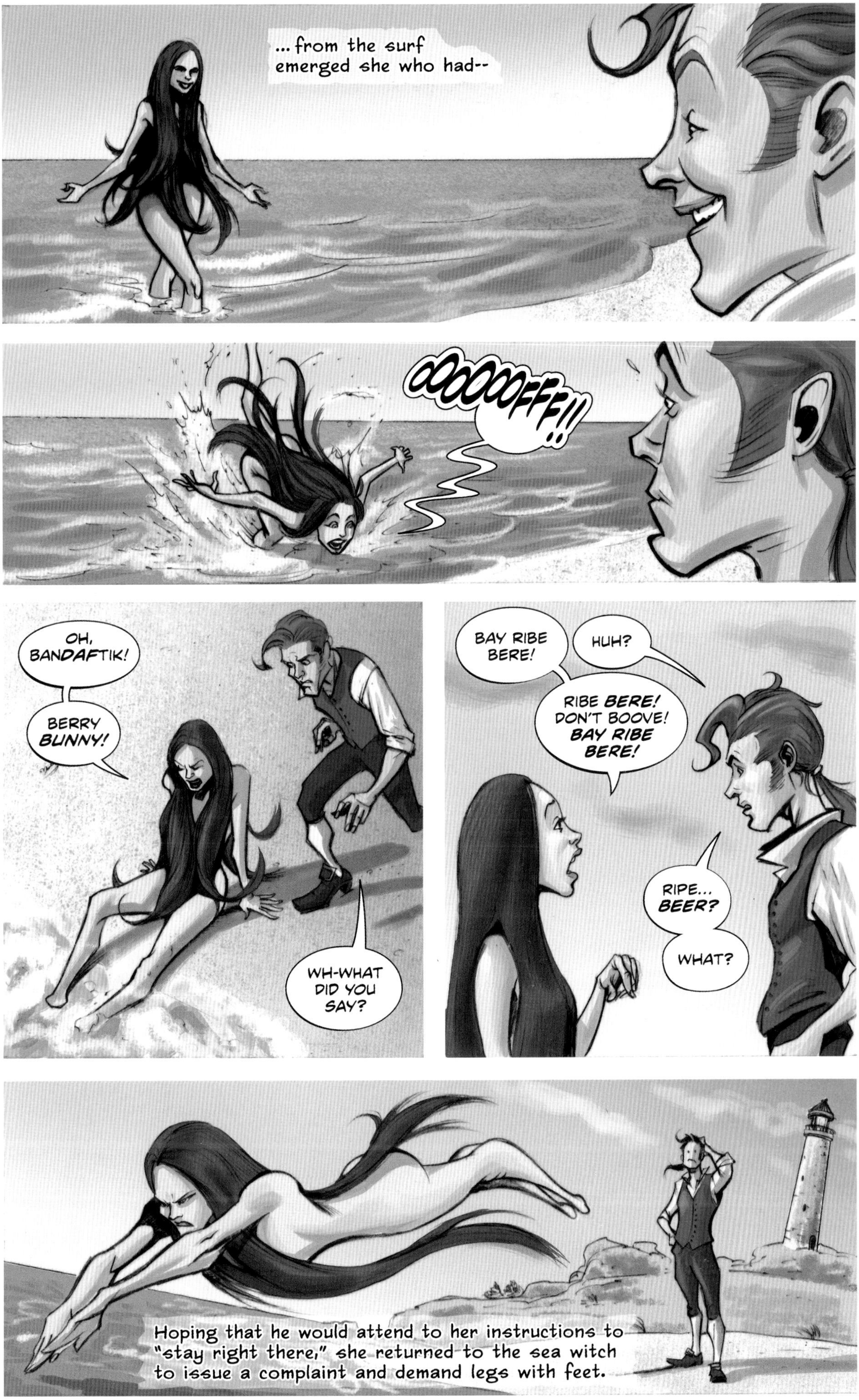
...from the surf emerged she who had--
OOOOOOFFF!!
OH, BANDAFTIK!
BERRY BUNNY!
WH-WHAT DID YOU SAY?
BAY RIBE BERE!
HUH?
RIBE BERE! DON'T BOOVE! BAY RIBE BERE!
RIPE... BEER?
WHAT?
Hoping that he would attend to her instructions to "stay right there," she returned to the sea witch to issue a complaint and demand legs with feet.

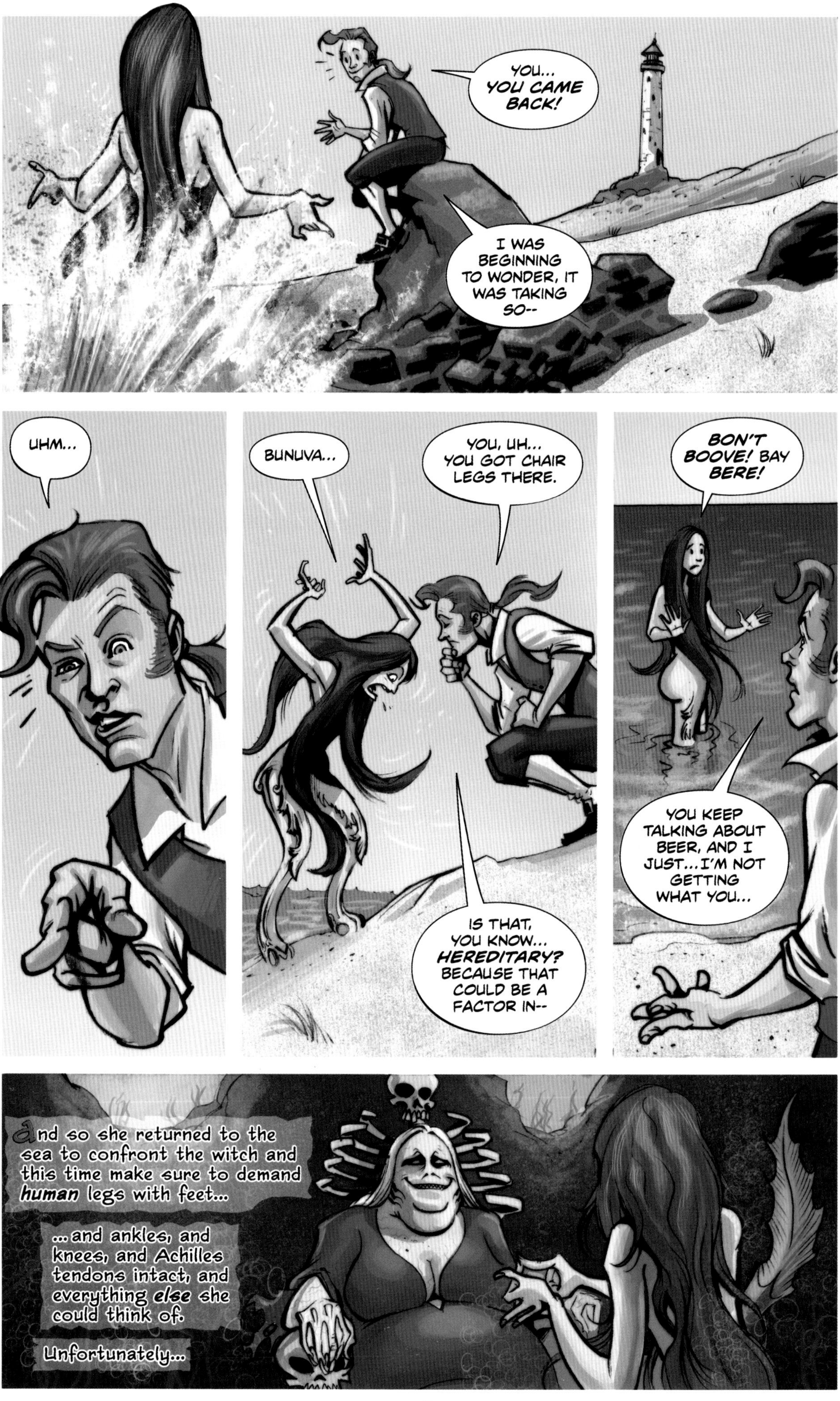
YOU... YOU CAME BACK!
I WAS BEGINNING TO WONDER, IT WAS TAKING SO--
UHM...
BUNUVA...
YOU, UH... YOU GOT CHAIR LEGS THERE.
IS THAT, YOU KNOW... HEREDITARY? BECAUSE THAT COULD BE A FACTOR IN--
BON'T BOOVE! BAY BERE!
YOU KEEP TALKING ABOUT BEER, AND I JUST... I'M NOT GETTING WHAT YOU...
And so she returned to the sea to confront the witch and this time make sure to demand human legs with feet...
...and ankles, and knees, and Achilles tendons intact, and everything else she could think of.
Unfortunately...

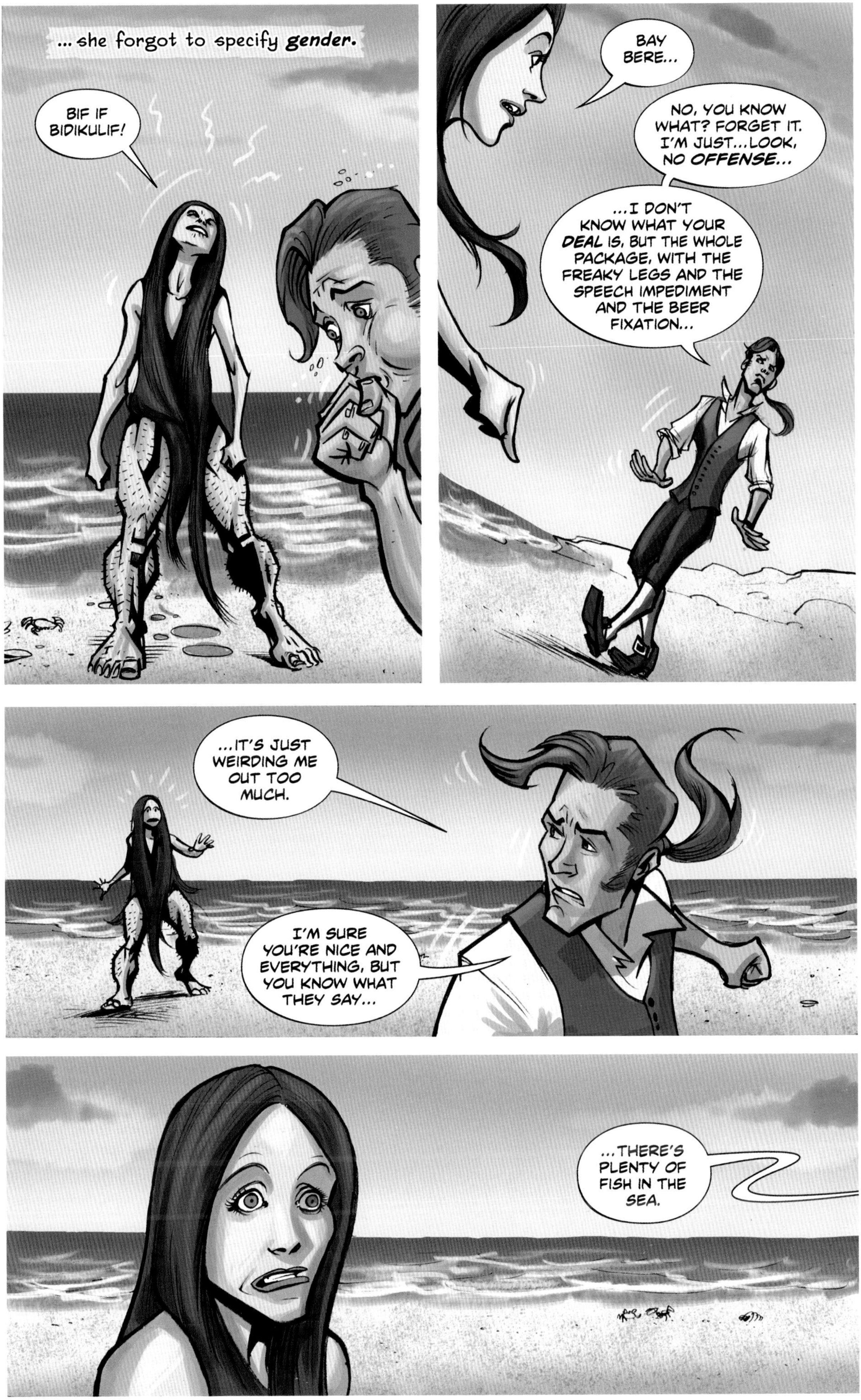
...she forgot to specify **gender.**
BIF IF BIDIKULIF!
BAY BERE...
NO, YOU KNOW WHAT? FORGET IT. I'M JUST...LOOK, NO OFFENSE...
...I DON'T KNOW WHAT YOUR DEAL IS, BUT THE WHOLE PACKAGE, WITH THE FREAKY LEGS AND THE SPEECH IMPEDIMENT AND THE BEER FIXATION...
...IT'S JUST WEIRDING ME OUT TOO MUCH.
I'M SURE YOU'RE NICE AND EVERYTHING, BUT YOU KNOW WHAT THEY SAY...
...THERE'S PLENTY OF FISH IN THE SEA.

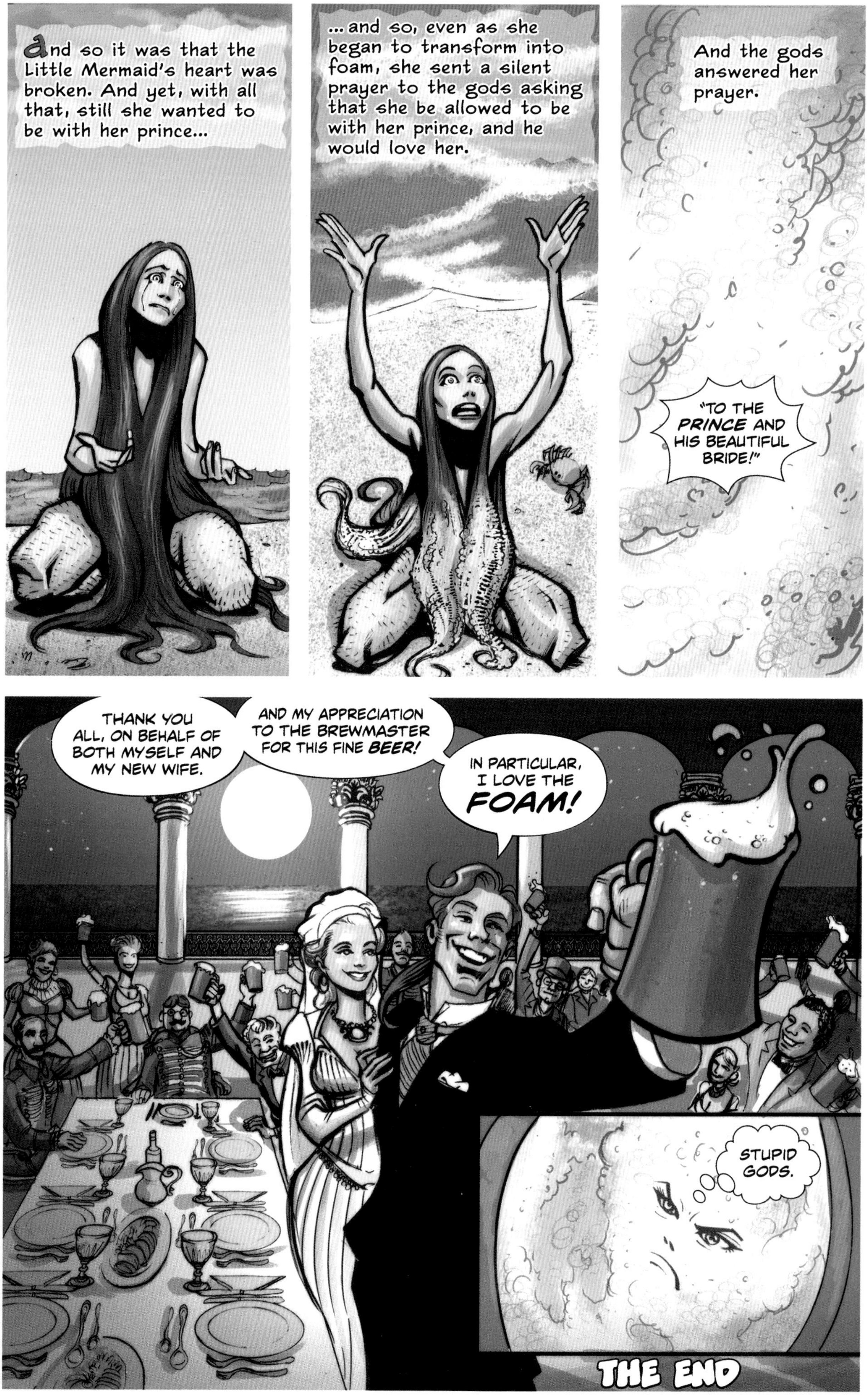
And so it was that the Little Mermaid's heart was broken. And yet, with all that, still she wanted to be with her prince...
...and so, even as she began to transform into foam, she sent a silent prayer to the gods asking that she be allowed to be with her prince, and he would love her.
And the gods answered her prayer.
"TO THE PRINCE AND HIS BEAUTIFUL BRIDE!"
THANK YOU ALL, ON BEHALF OF BOTH MYSELF AND MY NEW WIFE.
AND MY APPRECIATION TO THE BREWMASTER FOR THIS FINE BEER!
IN PARTICULAR, I LOVE THE FOAM!
STUPID GODS.
THE END

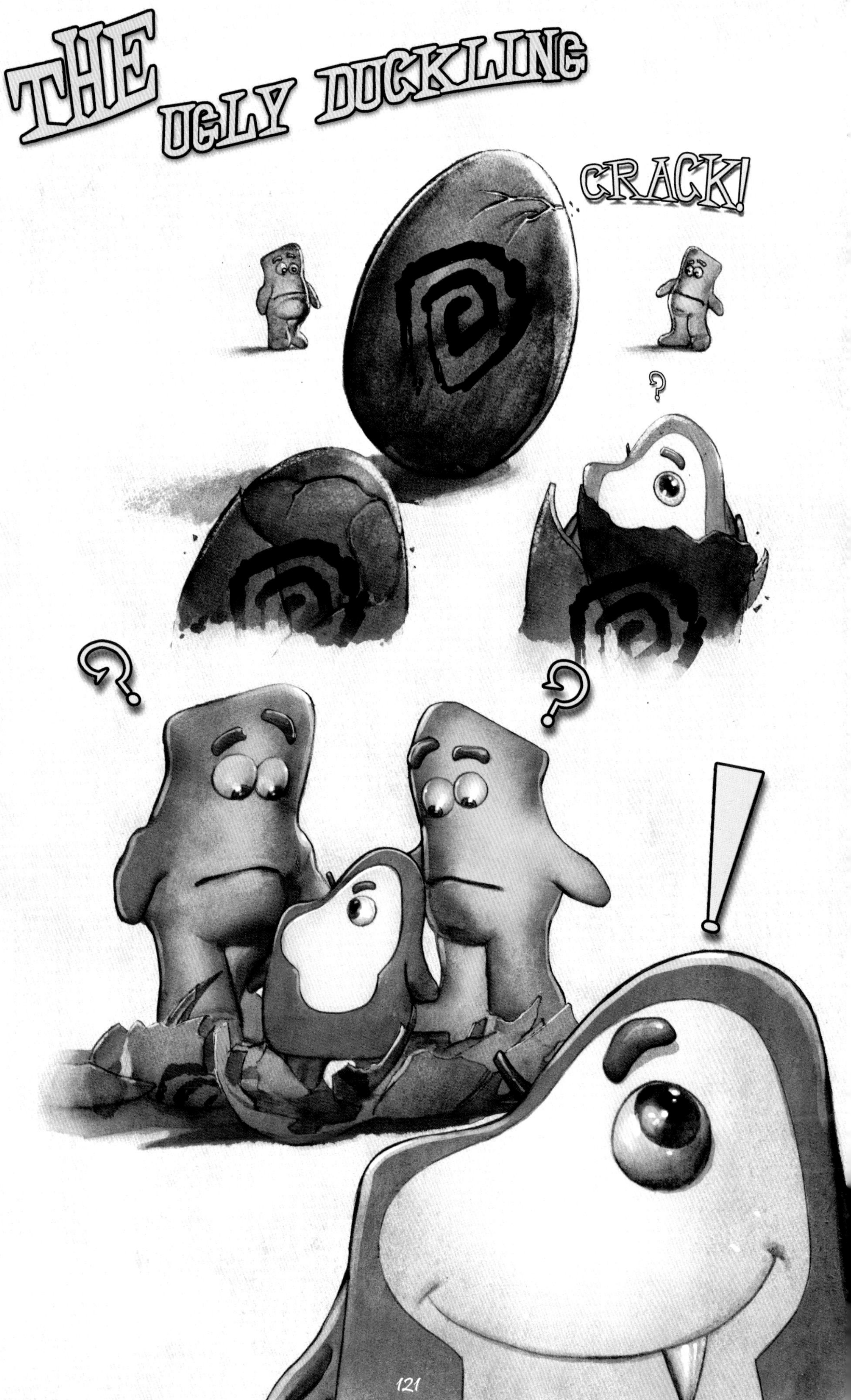
THE UGLY DUCKLING
CRACK!

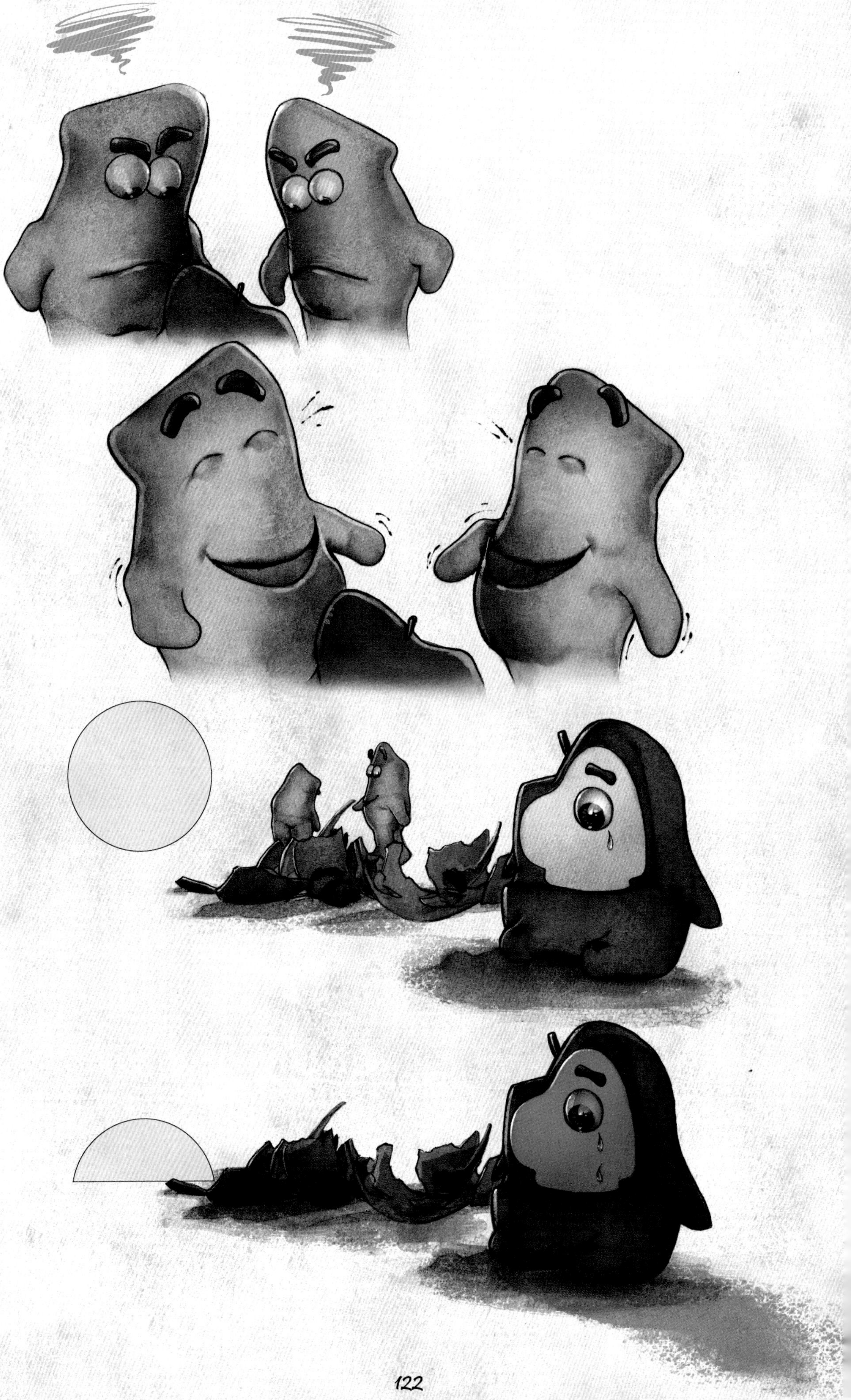

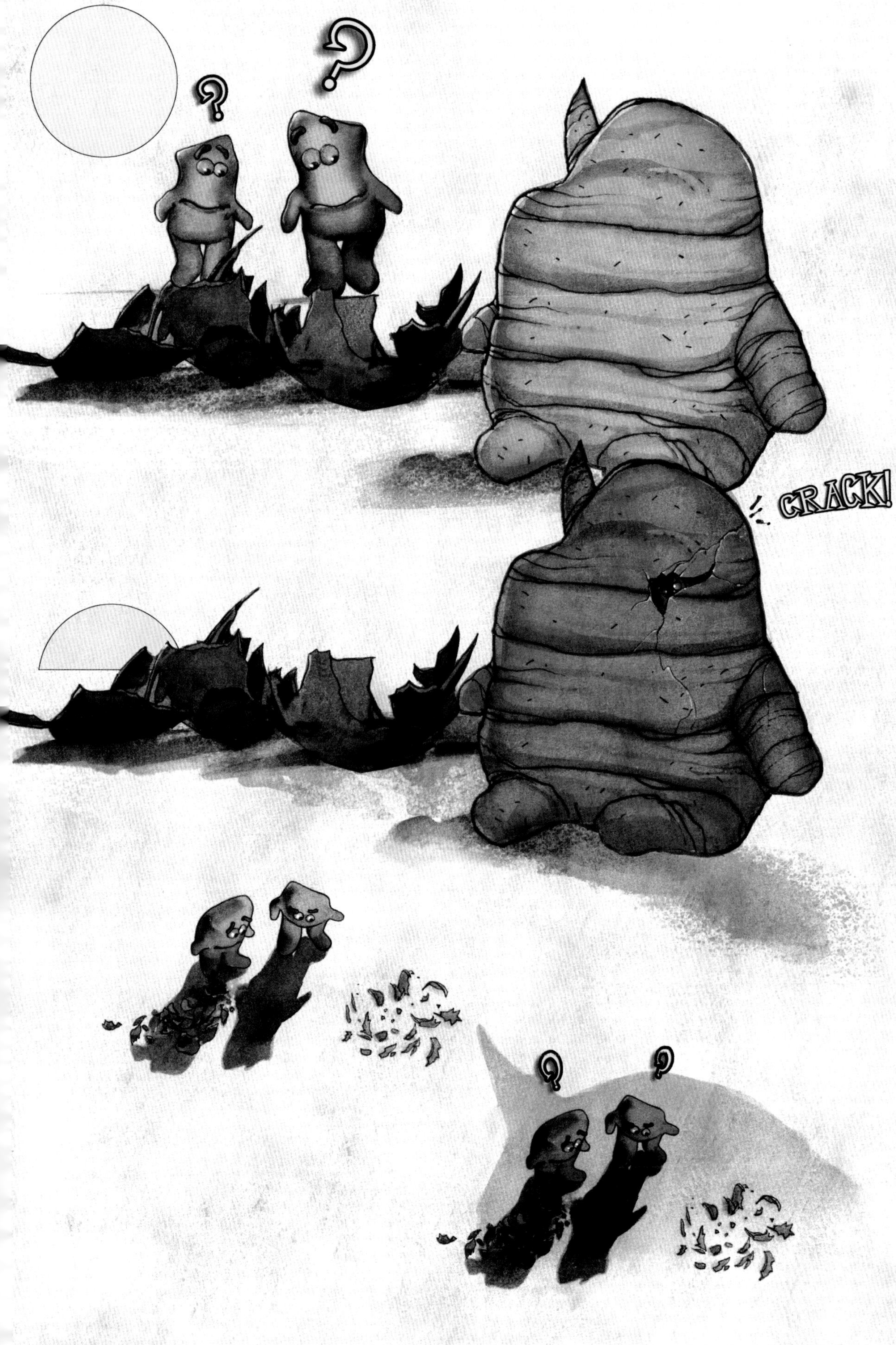
?
?
CRACK!
?
?

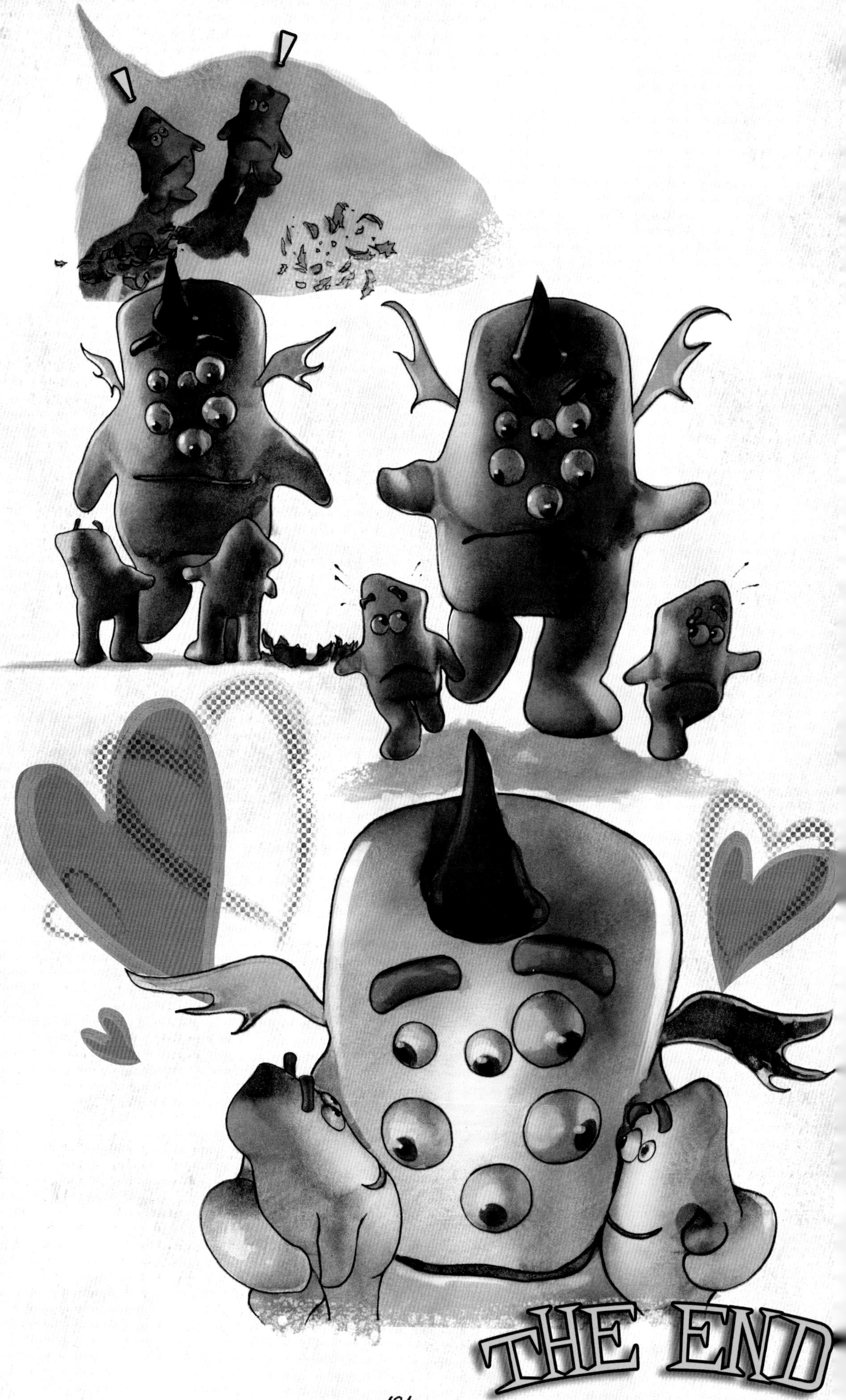
!
!
THE END

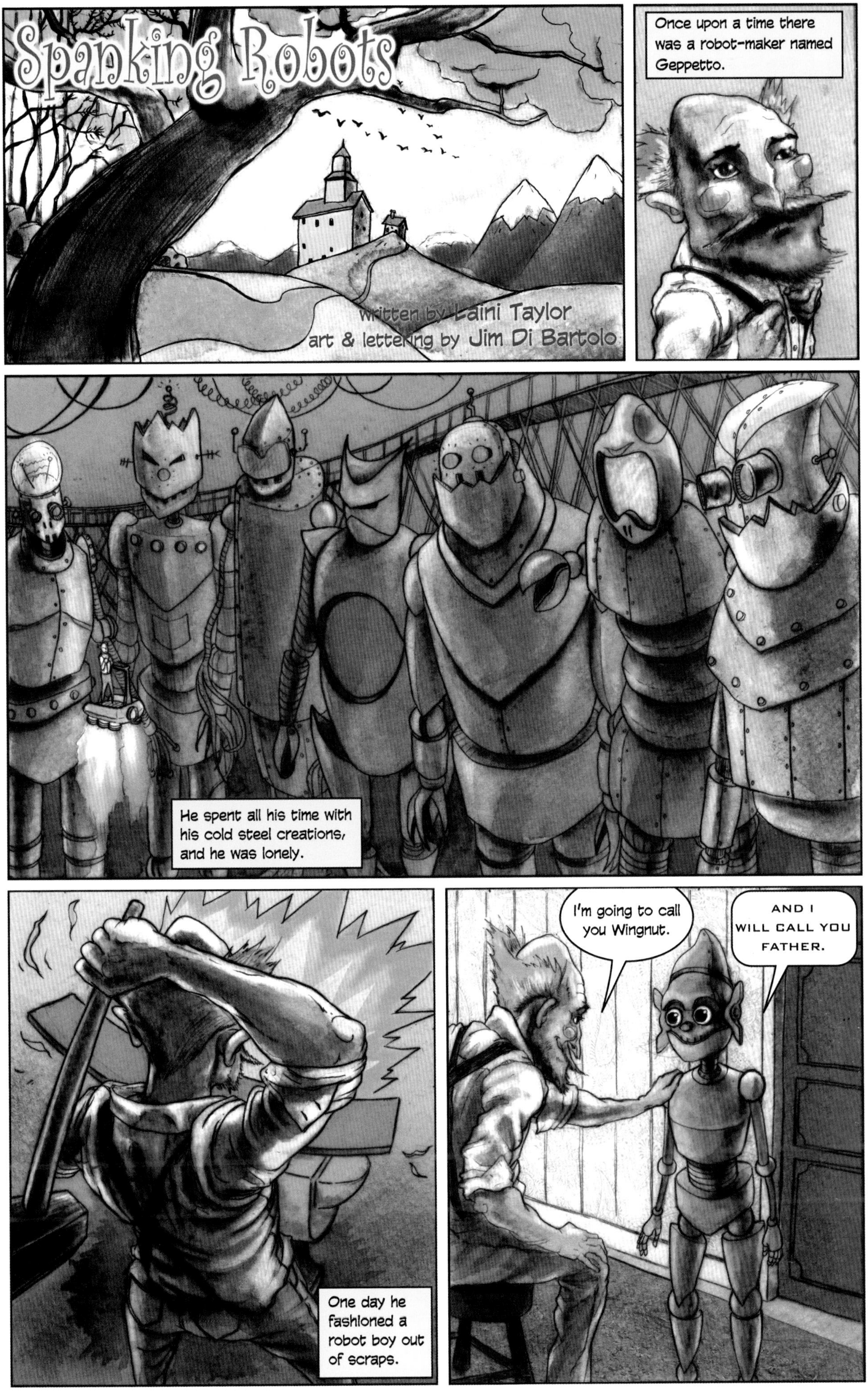
Spanking Robots
written by Laini Taylor
art & lettering by Jim Di Bartolo
Once upon a time there was a robot-maker named Geppetto.
He spent all his time with his cold steel creations, and he was lonely.
One day he fashioned a robot boy out of scraps.
I'm going to call you Wingnut.
AND I WILL CALL YOU FATHER.

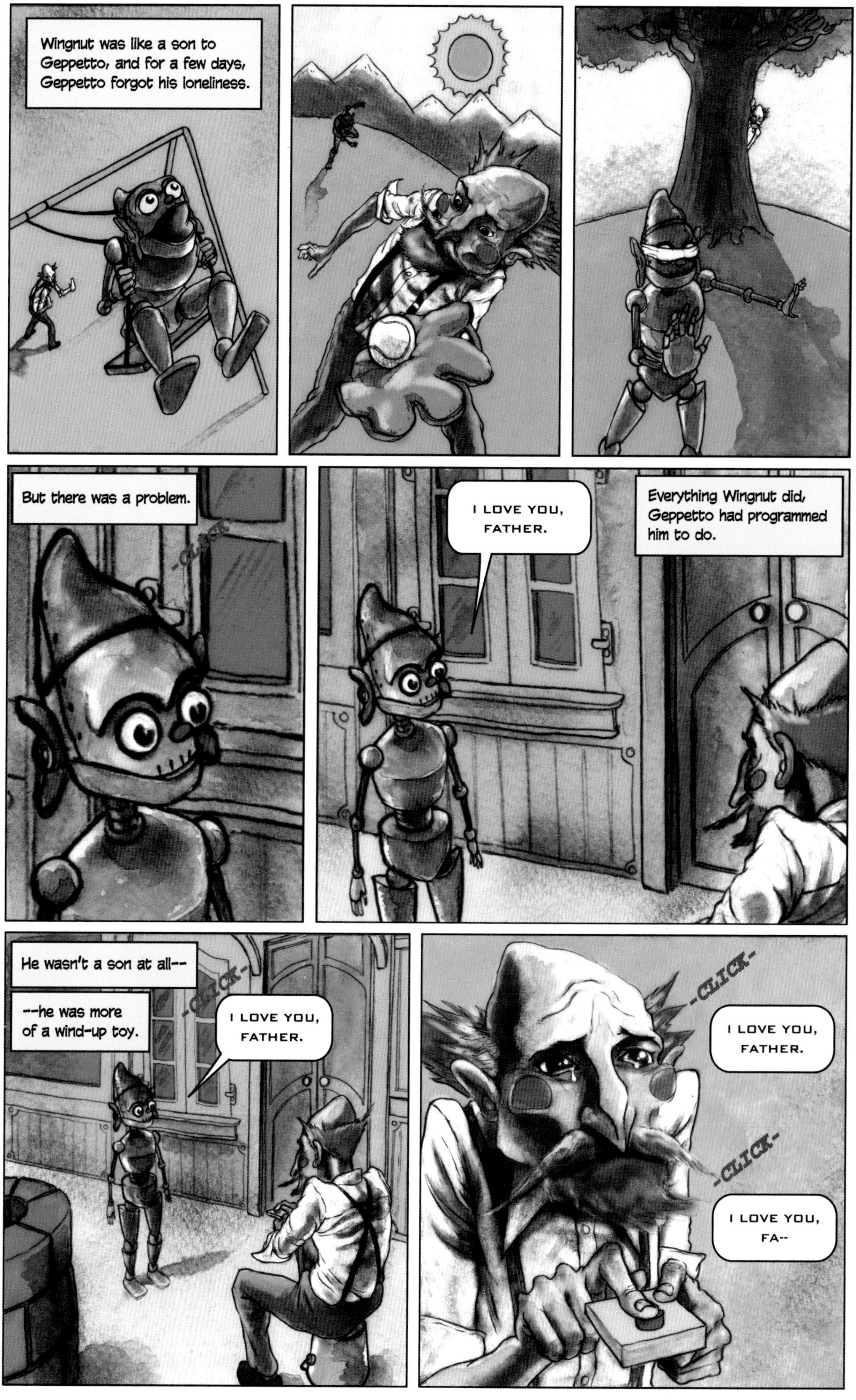
Wingnut was like a son to Geppetto, and for a few days, Geppetto forgot his loneliness.
But there was a problem.
-CLICK-
I LOVE YOU, FATHER.
Everything Wingnut did, Geppetto had programmed him to do.
He wasn't a son at all--
--he was more of a wind-up toy.
-CLICK-
I LOVE YOU, FATHER.
-CLICK-
I LOVE YOU, FATHER.
-CLICK-
I LOVE YOU, FA--

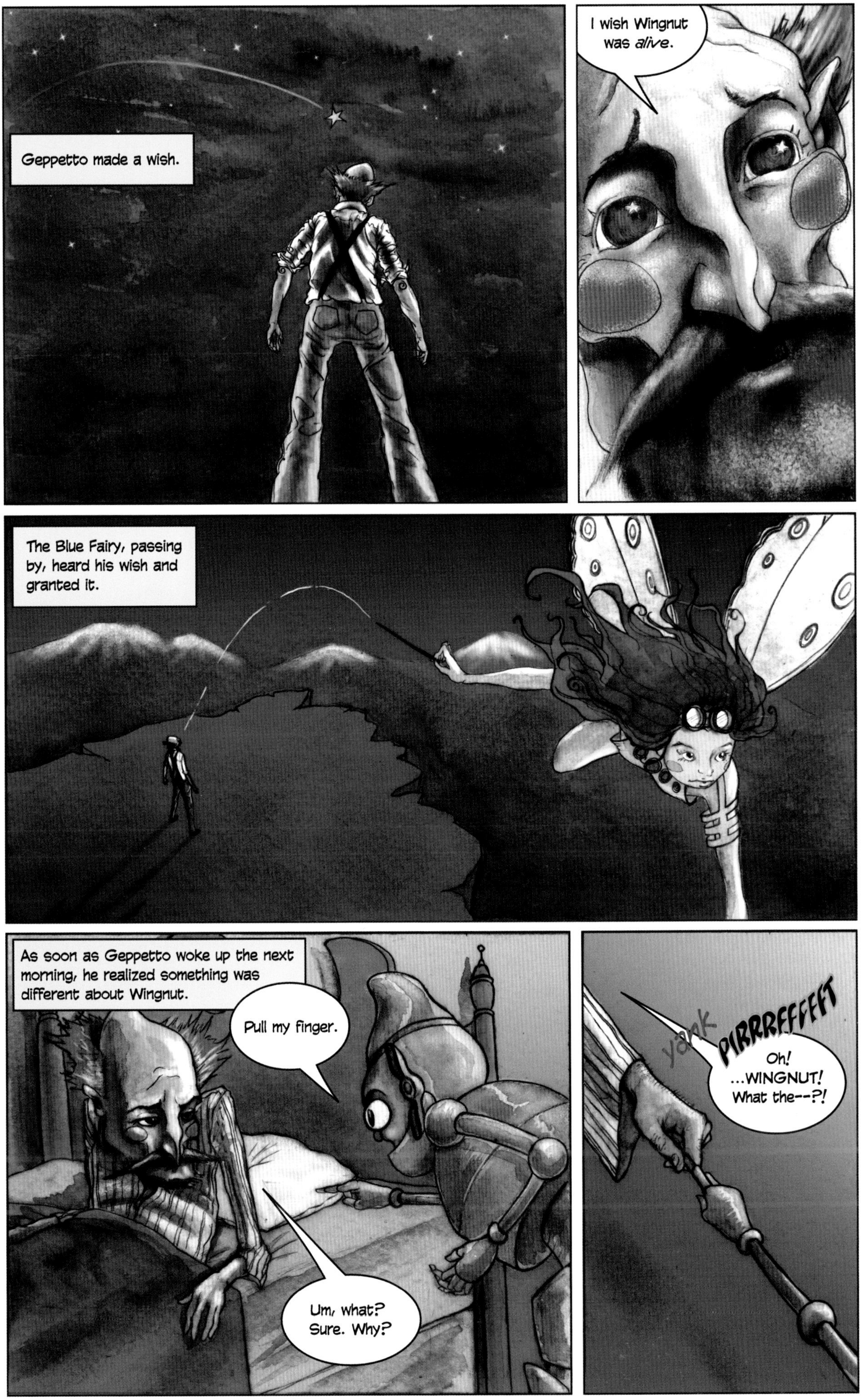
Geppetto made a wish.
I wish Wingnut was *alive*.
The Blue Fairy, passing by, heard his wish and granted it.
As soon as Geppetto woke up the next morning, he realized something was different about Wingnut.
Pull my finger.
Um, what? Sure. Why?
yank
PIRRRFFFFFT
Oh! ...WINGNUT! What the--?!

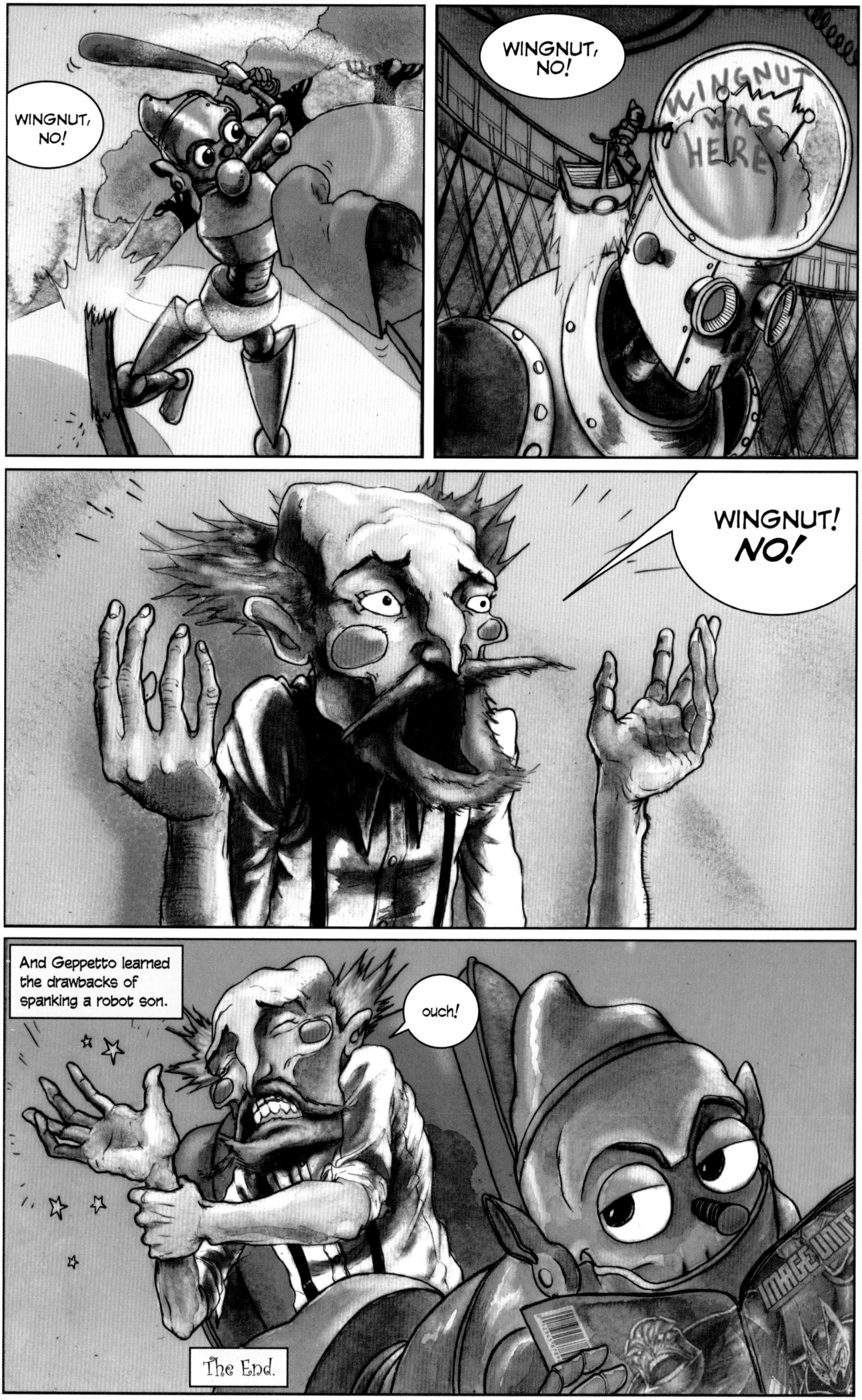
WINGNUT, NO!
WINGNUT, NO!
WINGNUT WAS HERE
WINGNUT! NO!
And Geppetto learned the drawbacks of spanking a robot son.
ouch!
The End.

The Little Matchstick Girl

by: Joel Valentino

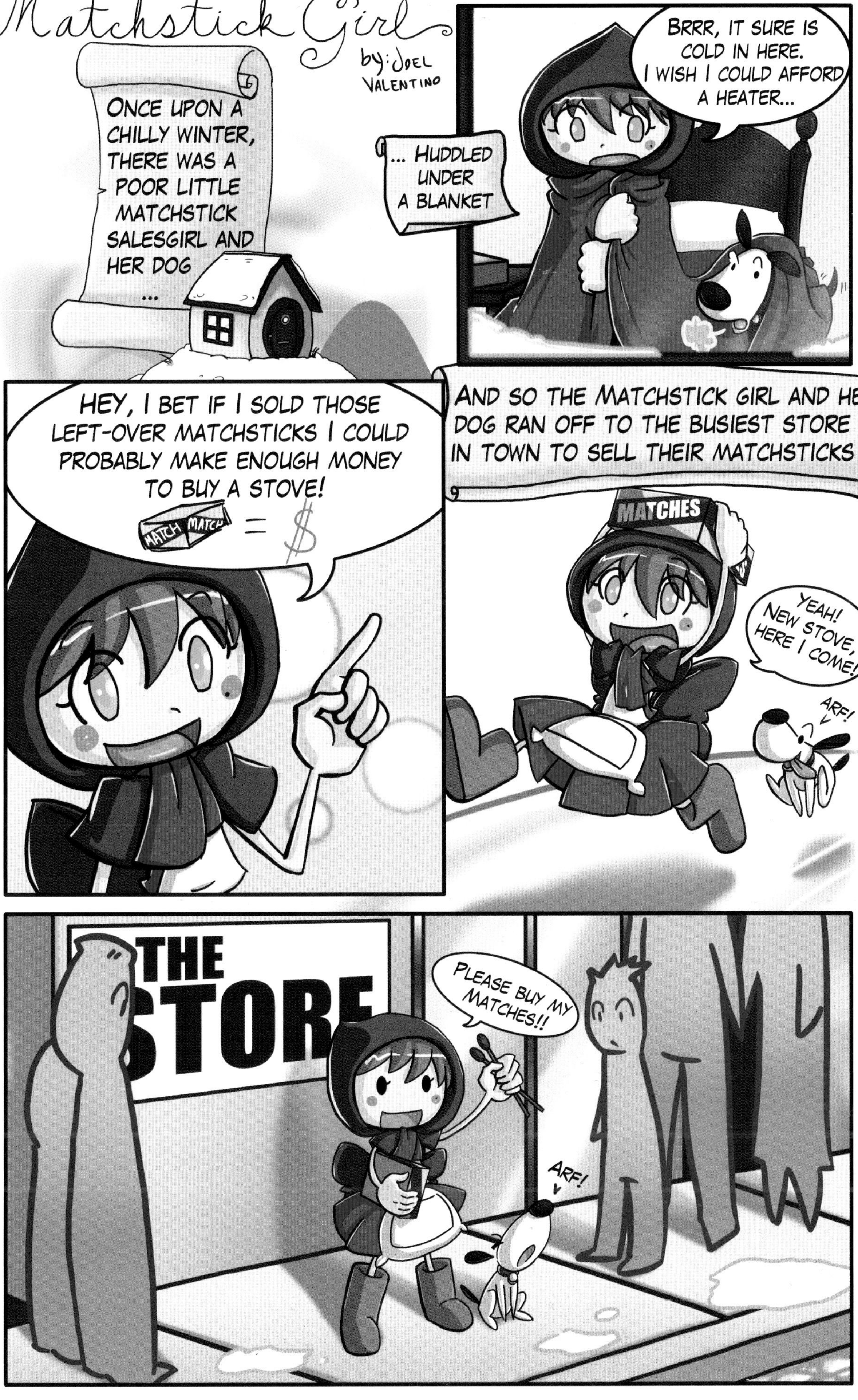

ONCE UPON A CHILLY WINTER, THERE WAS A POOR LITTLE MATCHSTICK SALESGIRL AND HER DOG ...
... HUDDLED UNDER A BLANKET
BRRR, IT SURE IS COLD IN HERE. I WISH I COULD AFFORD A HEATER...
HEY, I BET IF I SOLD THOSE LEFT-OVER MATCHSTICKS I COULD PROBABLY MAKE ENOUGH MONEY TO BUY A STOVE!
MATCH MATCH = $
AND SO THE MATCHSTICK GIRL AND HER DOG RAN OFF TO THE BUSIEST STORE IN TOWN TO SELL THEIR MATCHSTICKS
MATCHES
YEAH! NEW STOVE, HERE I COME!
ARF!
THE STORE
PLEASE BUY MY MATCHES!!
ARF!

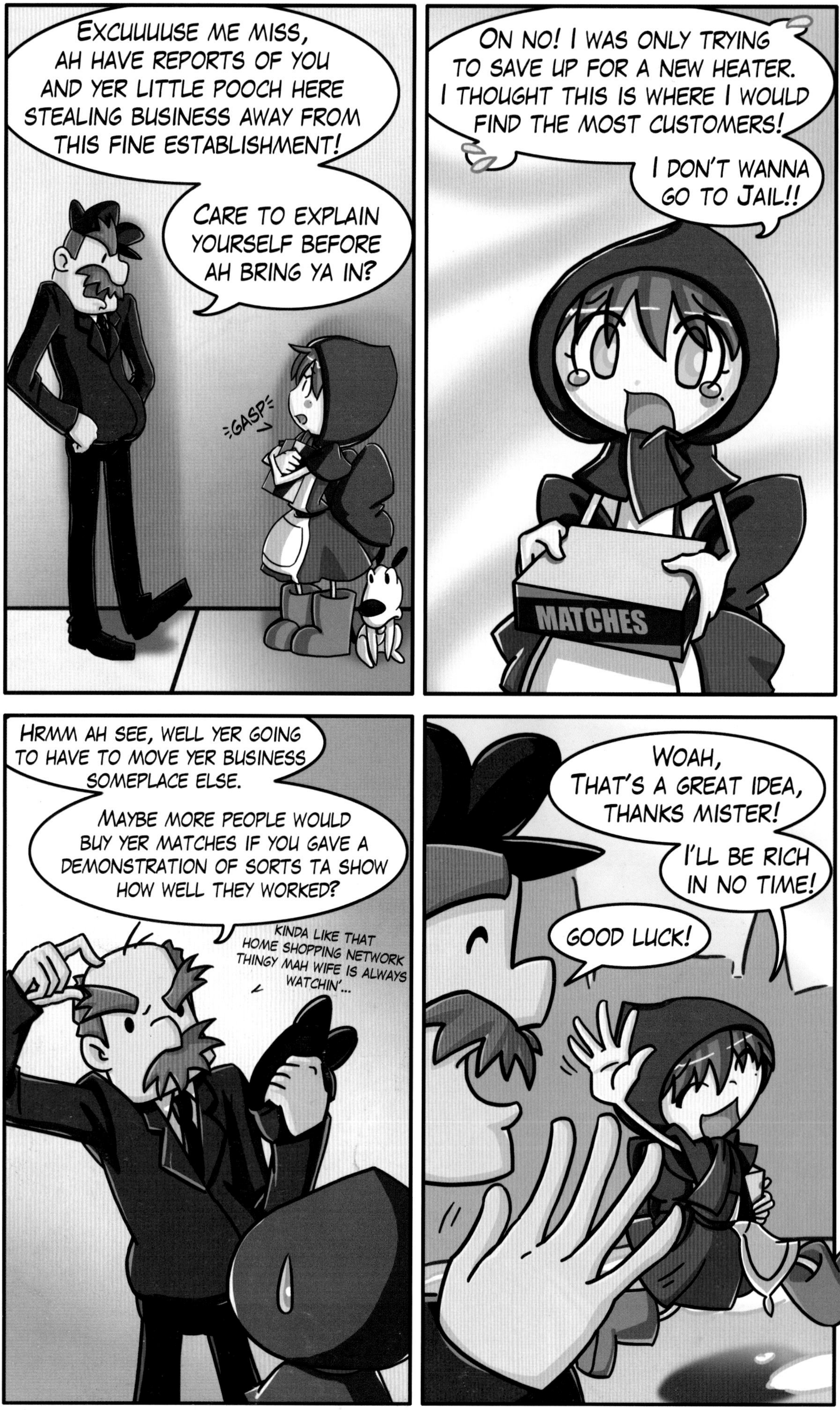
EXCUUUUSE ME MISS, AH HAVE REPORTS OF YOU AND YER LITTLE POOCH HERE STEALING BUSINESS AWAY FROM THIS FINE ESTABLISHMENT!
CARE TO EXPLAIN YOURSELF BEFORE AH BRING YA IN?
GASP
ON NO! I WAS ONLY TRYING TO SAVE UP FOR A NEW HEATER. I THOUGHT THIS IS WHERE I WOULD FIND THE MOST CUSTOMERS!
I DON'T WANNA GO TO JAIL!!
MATCHES
HRMM AH SEE, WELL YER GOING TO HAVE TO MOVE YER BUSINESS SOMEPLACE ELSE.
MAYBE MORE PEOPLE WOULD BUY YER MATCHES IF YOU GAVE A DEMONSTRATION OF SORTS TA SHOW HOW WELL THEY WORKED?
KINDA LIKE THAT HOME SHOPPING NETWORK THINGY MAH WIFE IS ALWAYS WATCHIN'...
WOAH, THAT'S A GREAT IDEA, THANKS MISTER!
I'LL BE RICH IN NO TIME!
GOOD LUCK!

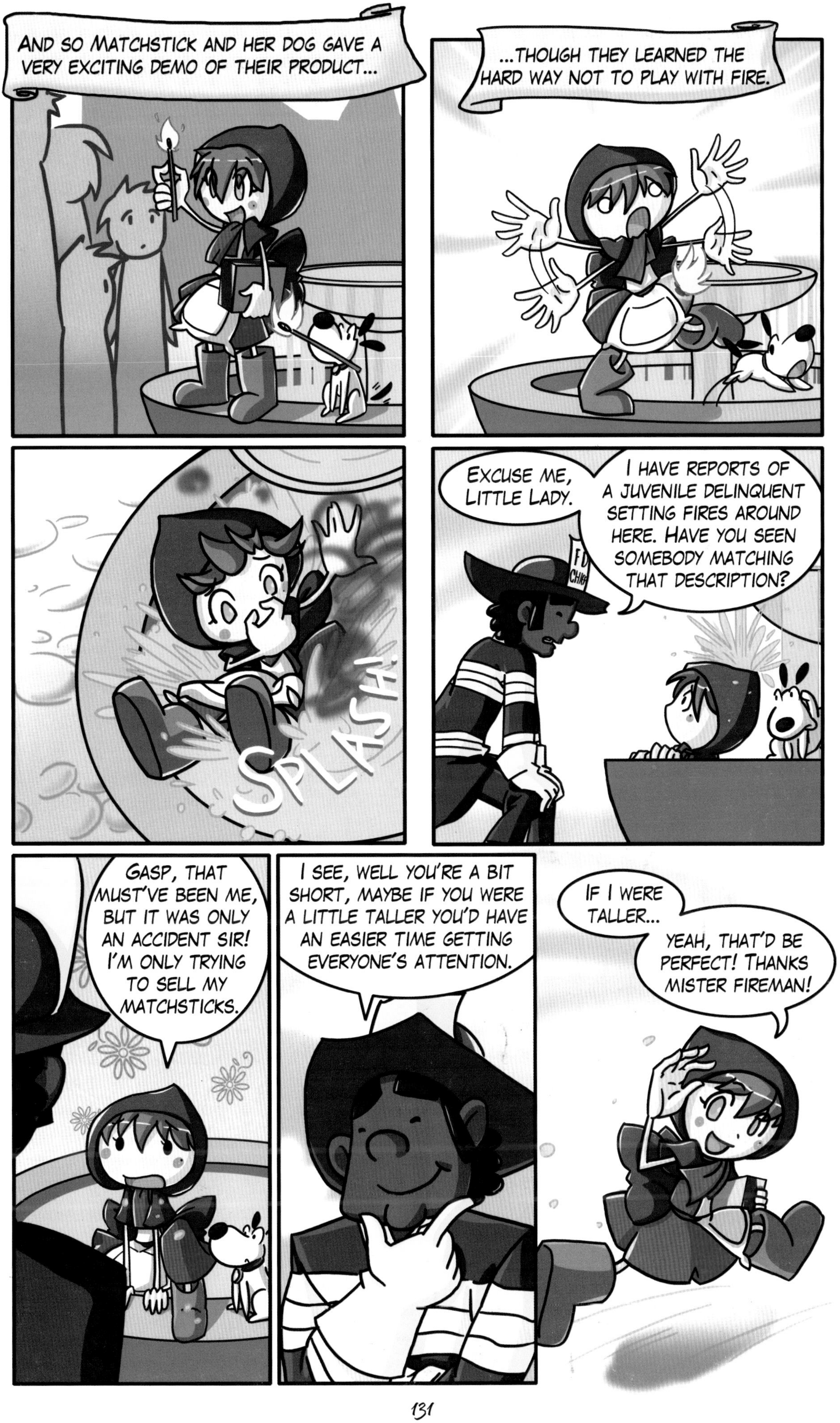
And so Matchstick and her dog gave a very exciting demo of their product...
...though they learned the hard way not to play with fire.
Splash!
Excuse me, little lady.
I have reports of a juvenile delinquent setting fires around here. Have you seen somebody matching that description?
FD CHIEF
Gasp, that must've been me, but it was only an accident sir! I'm only trying to sell my matchsticks.
I see, well you're a bit short, maybe if you were a little taller you'd have an easier time getting everyone's attention.
If I were taller...
Yeah, that'd be perfect! Thanks mister fireman!

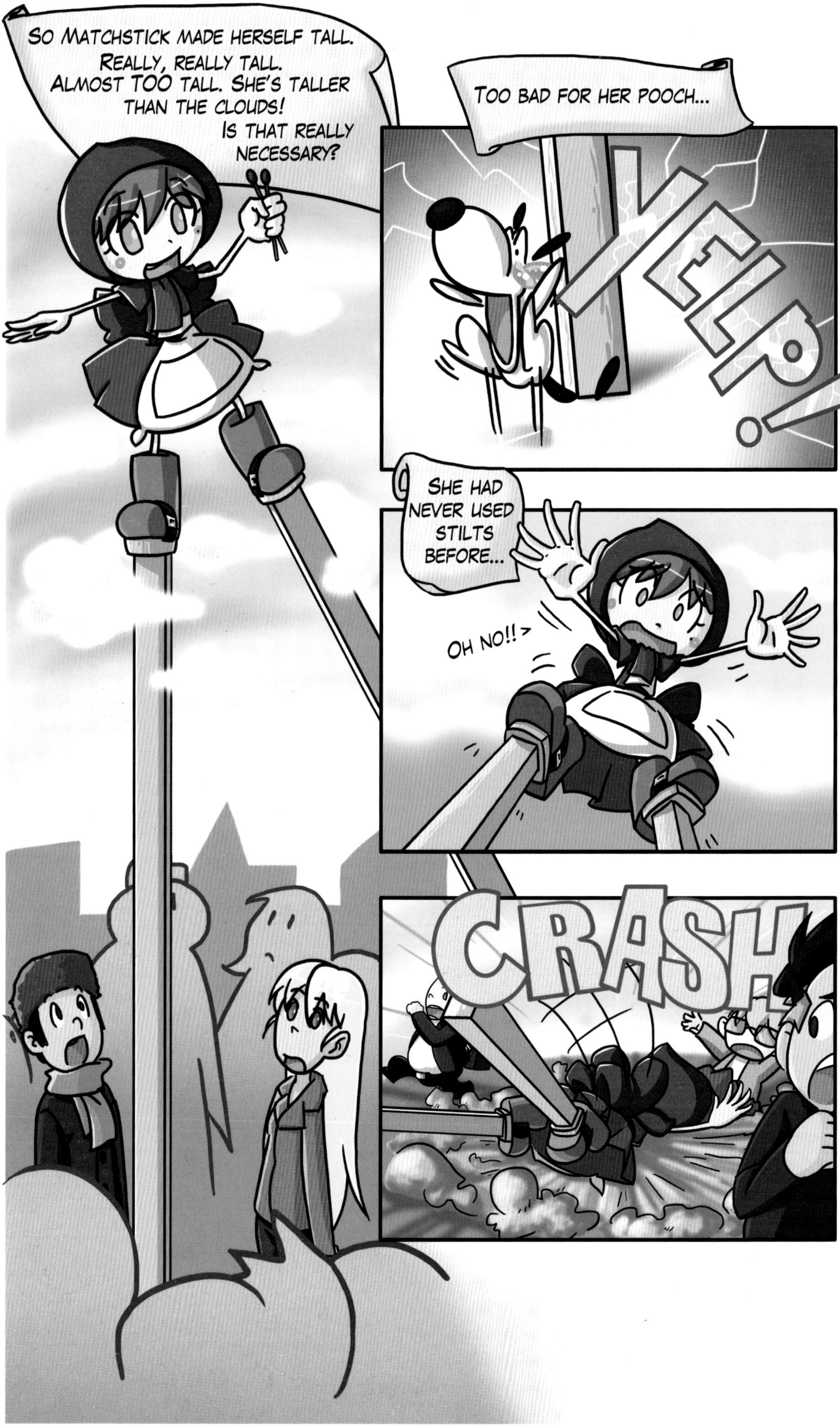
So Matchstick made herself tall.
Really, really tall.
Almost TOO tall. She's taller than the clouds!
Is that really necessary?
Too bad for her pooch...
YELP!
She had never used stilts before...
Oh no!!
CRASH

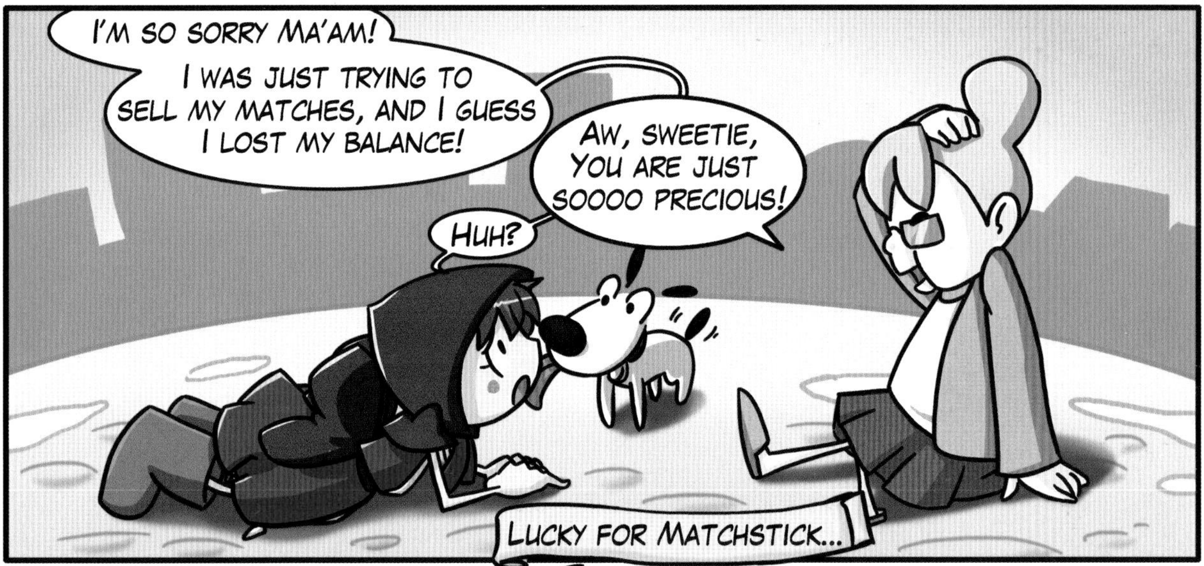
I'M SO SORRY MA'AM!
I WAS JUST TRYING TO SELL MY MATCHES, AND I GUESS I LOST MY BALANCE!
AW, SWEETIE, YOU ARE JUST SOOOO PRECIOUS!
HUH?
LUCKY FOR MATCHSTICK...

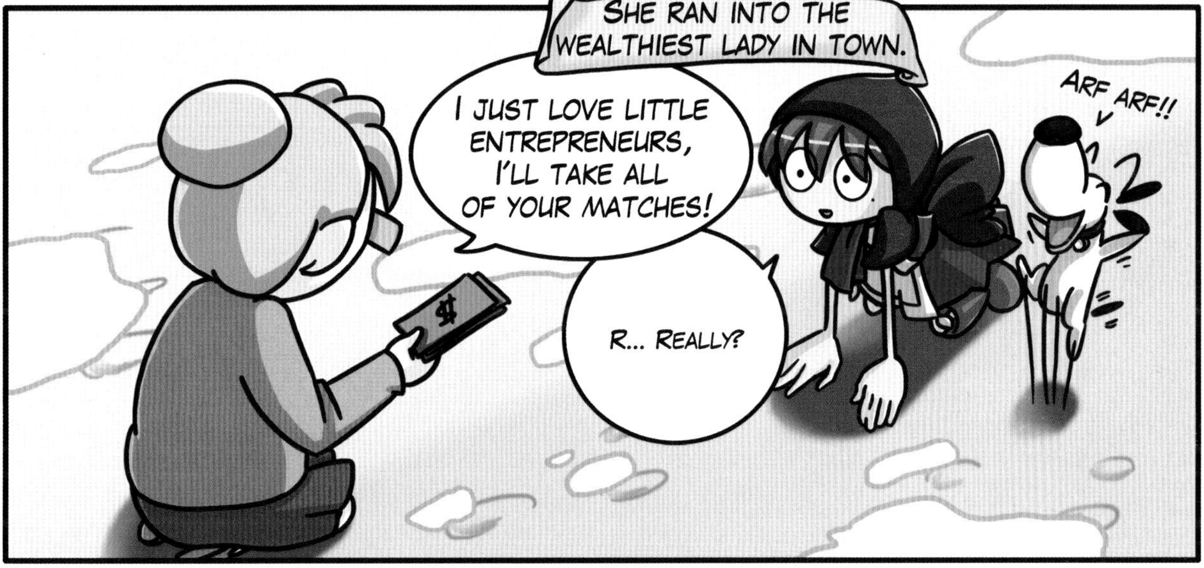
SHE RAN INTO THE WEALTHIEST LADY IN TOWN.
I JUST LOVE LITTLE ENTREPRENEURS, I'LL TAKE ALL OF YOUR MATCHES!
R... REALLY?
ARF ARF!!

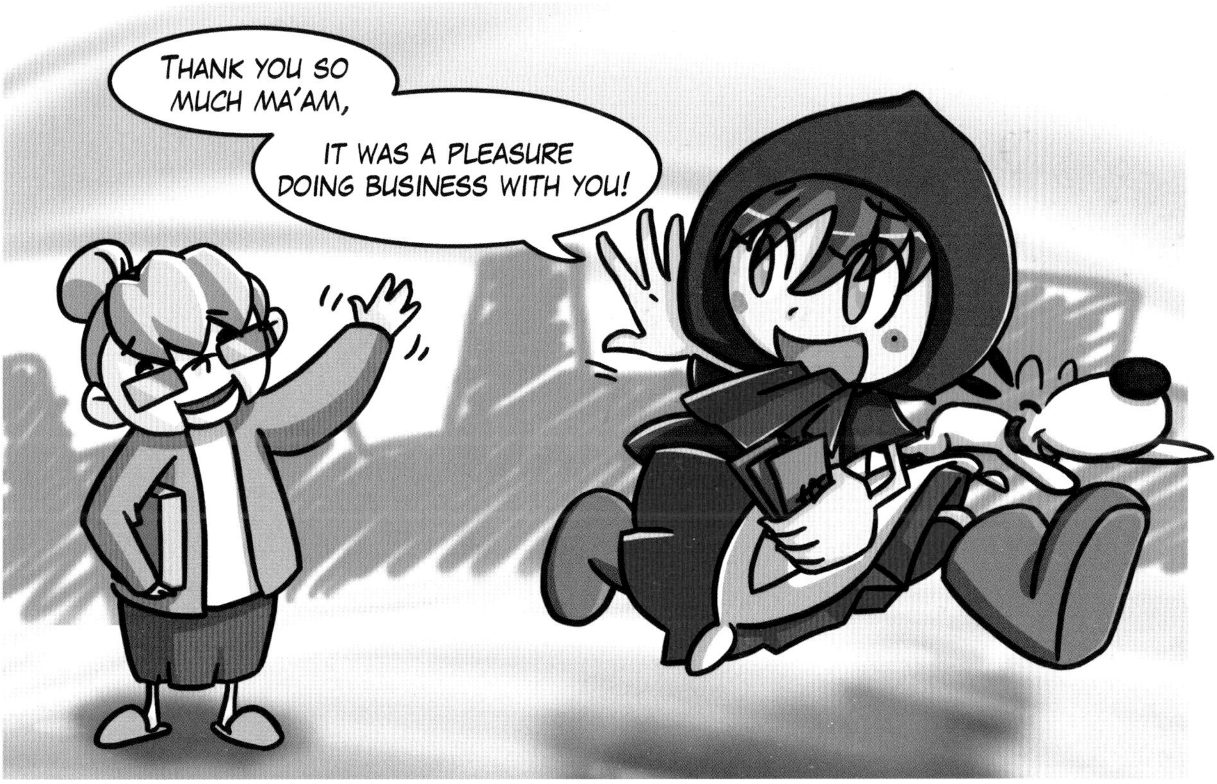
THANK YOU SO MUCH MA'AM,
IT WAS A PLEASURE DOING BUSINESS WITH YOU!

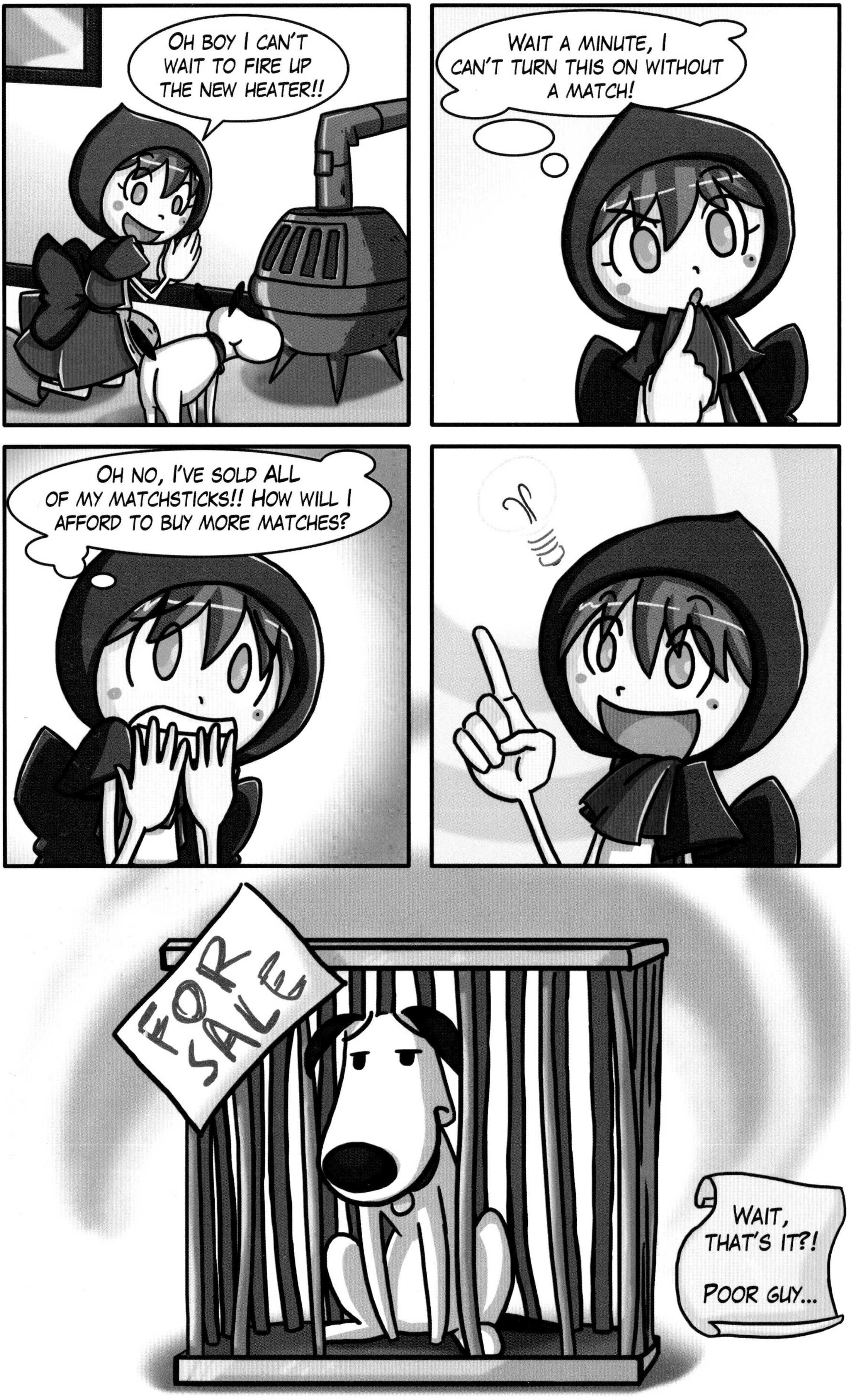
OH BOY I CAN'T WAIT TO FIRE UP THE NEW HEATER!!
WAIT A MINUTE, I CAN'T TURN THIS ON WITHOUT A MATCH!
OH NO, I'VE SOLD ALL OF MY MATCHSTICKS!! HOW WILL I AFFORD TO BUY MORE MATCHES?
FOR SALE
WAIT, THAT'S IT?!
POOR GUY...

-THE END-

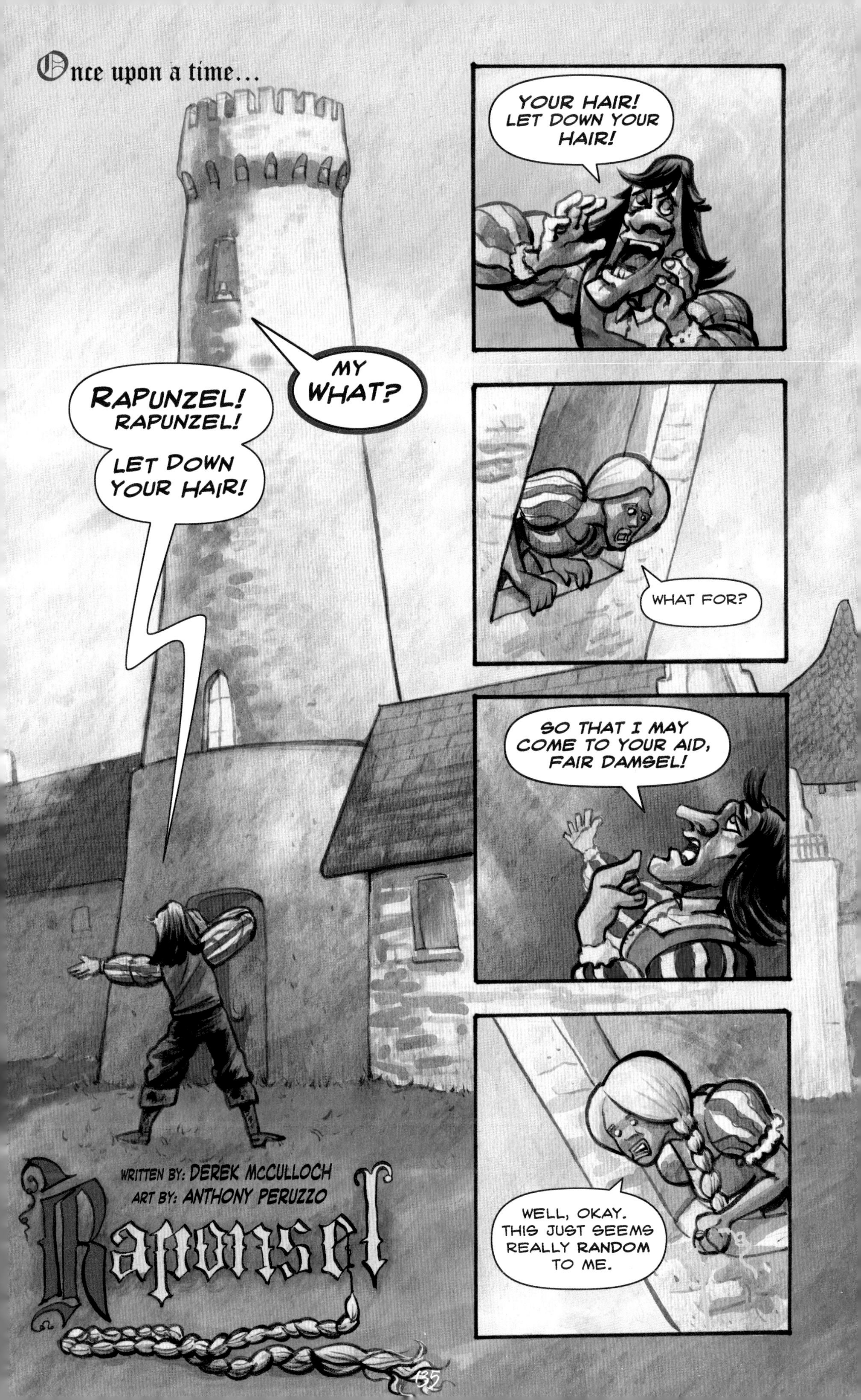
Once upon a time...
RAPUNZEL! RAPUNZEL!
LET DOWN YOUR HAIR!
MY WHAT?
YOUR HAIR! LET DOWN YOUR HAIR!
WHAT FOR?
SO THAT I MAY COME TO YOUR AID, FAIR DAMSEL!
WELL, OKAY. THIS JUST SEEMS REALLY RANDOM TO ME.
WRITTEN BY: DEREK McCULLOCH
ART BY: ANTHONY PERUZZO
Raponsel

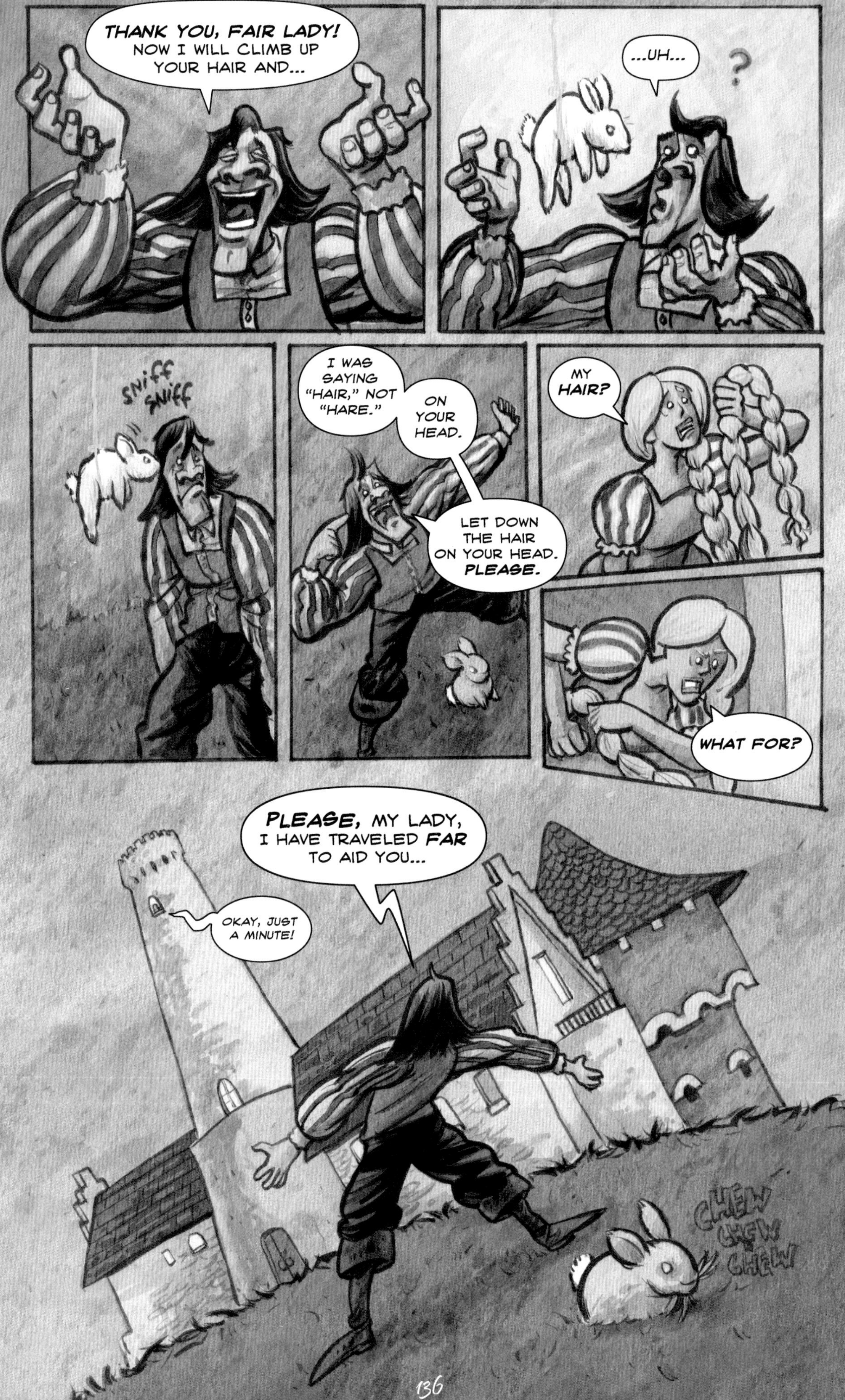
THANK YOU, FAIR LADY! NOW I WILL CLIMB UP YOUR HAIR AND...
...UH...
?
SNIFF SNIFF
I WAS SAYING "HAIR," NOT "HARE."
ON YOUR HEAD.
LET DOWN THE HAIR ON YOUR HEAD. PLEASE.
MY HAIR?
WHAT FOR?
PLEASE, MY LADY, I HAVE TRAVELED FAR TO AID YOU...
OKAY, JUST A MINUTE!
CHEW CHEW CHEW!

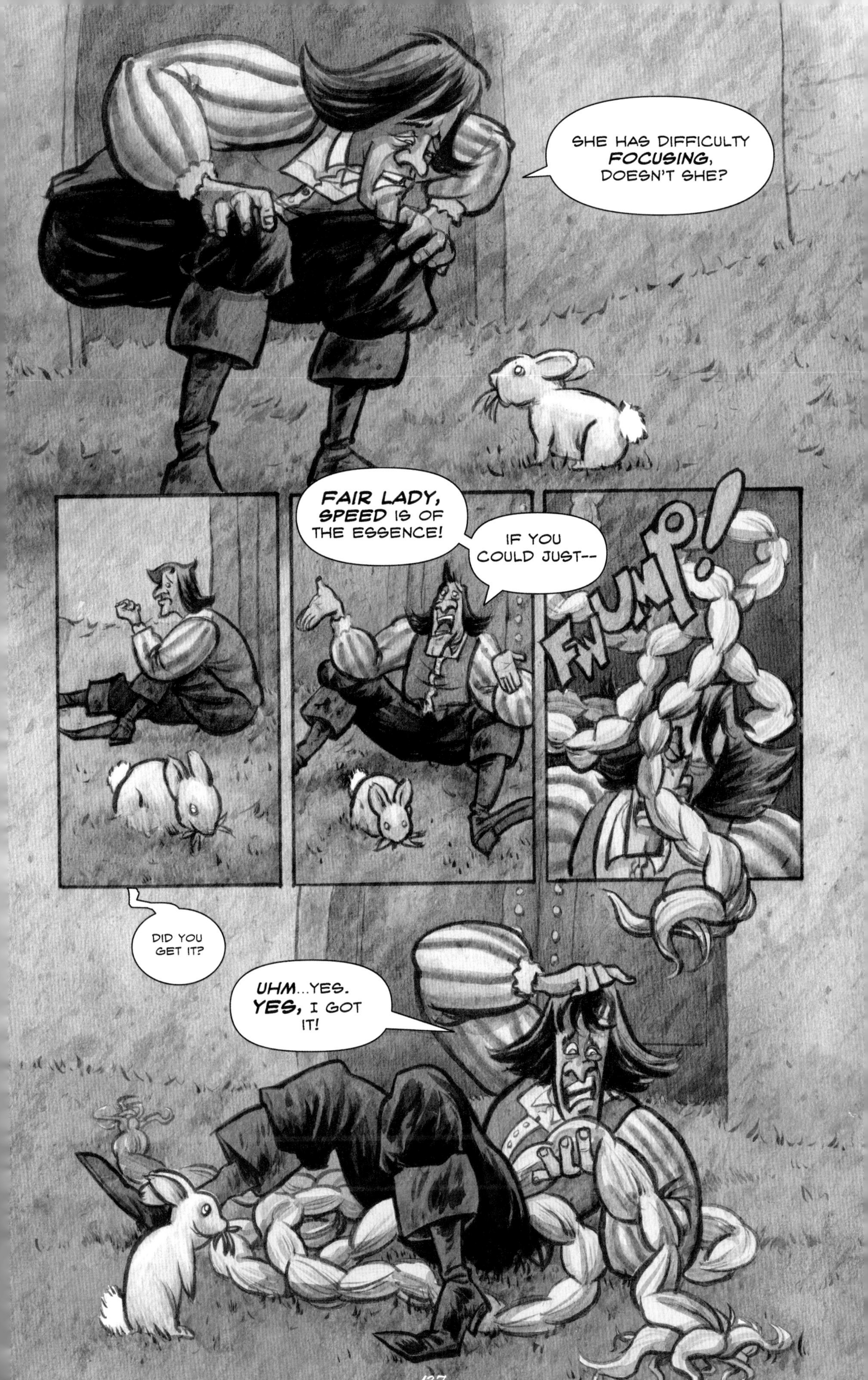
SHE HAS DIFFICULTY FOCUSING, DOESN'T SHE?
FAIR LADY, SPEED IS OF THE ESSENCE!
IF YOU COULD JUST--
FWUMP!
DID YOU GET IT?
UHM...YES. YES, I GOT IT!

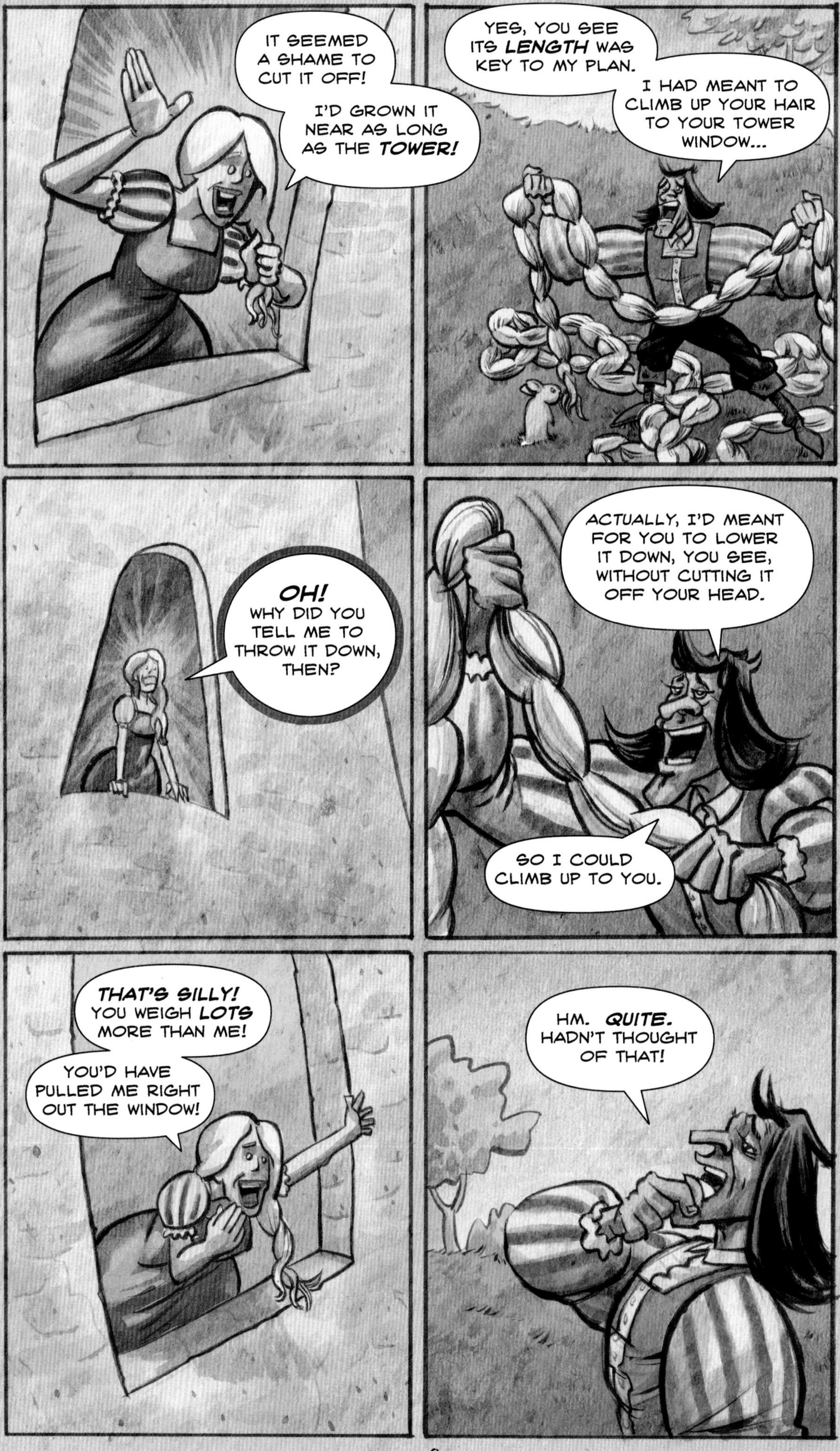
IT SEEMED A SHAME TO CUT IT OFF!
I'D GROWN IT NEAR AS LONG AS THE **TOWER!**
YES, YOU SEE ITS **LENGTH** WAS KEY TO MY PLAN.
I HAD MEANT TO CLIMB UP YOUR HAIR TO YOUR TOWER WINDOW...
OH! WHY DID YOU TELL ME TO THROW IT DOWN, THEN?
ACTUALLY, I'D MEANT FOR YOU TO LOWER IT DOWN, YOU SEE, WITHOUT CUTTING IT OFF YOUR HEAD.
SO I COULD CLIMB UP TO YOU.
THAT'S SILLY! YOU WEIGH **LOTS** MORE THAN ME!
YOU'D HAVE PULLED ME RIGHT OUT THE WINDOW!
HM. **QUITE.** HADN'T THOUGHT OF THAT!

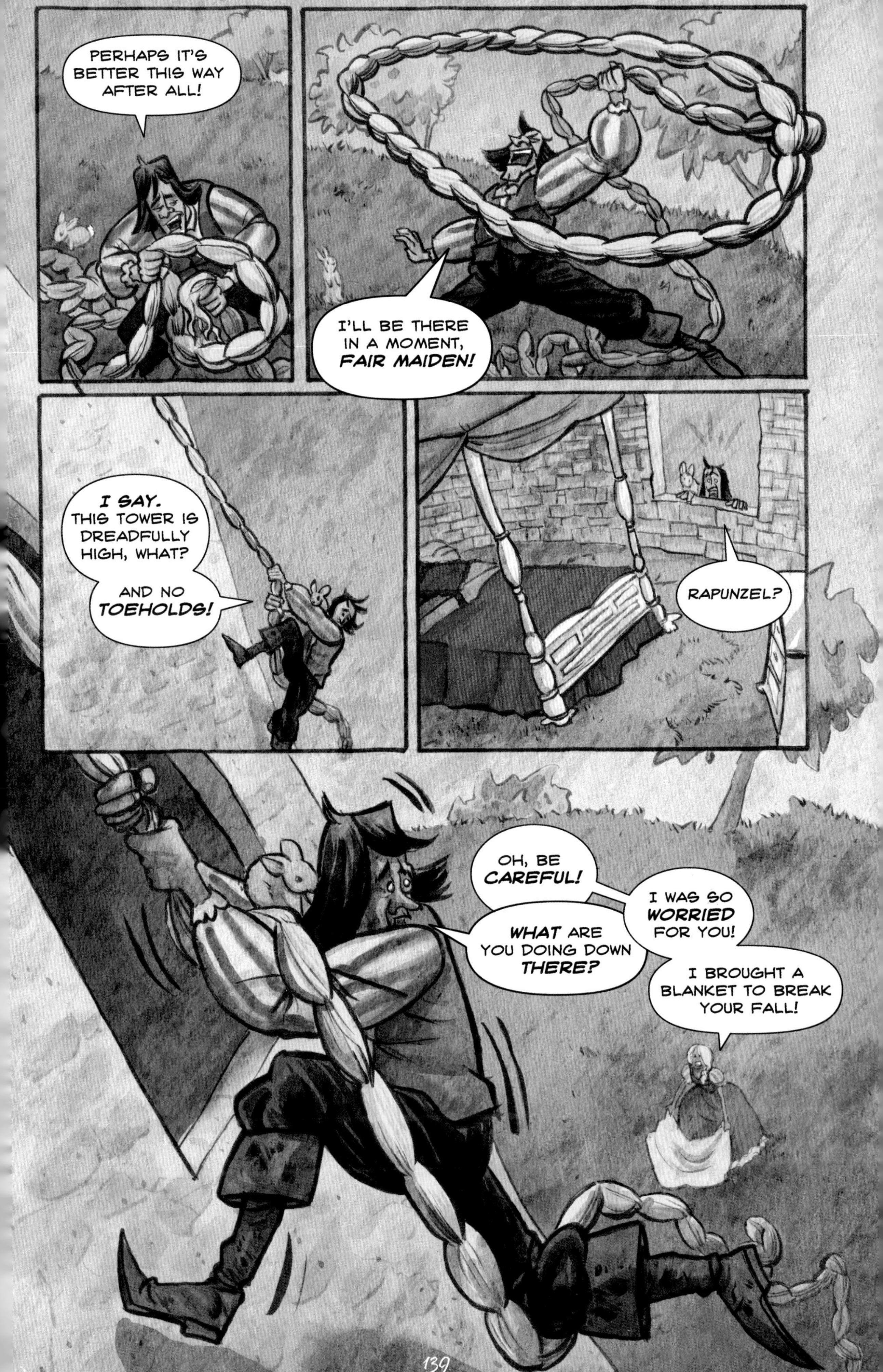

PERHAPS IT'S BETTER THIS WAY AFTER ALL!
I'LL BE THERE IN A MOMENT, FAIR MAIDEN!
I SAY. THIS TOWER IS DREADFULLY HIGH, WHAT?
AND NO TOEHOLDS!
RAPUNZEL?
OH, BE CAREFUL!
I WAS SO WORRIED FOR YOU!
WHAT ARE YOU DOING DOWN THERE?
I BROUGHT A BLANKET TO BREAK YOUR FALL!

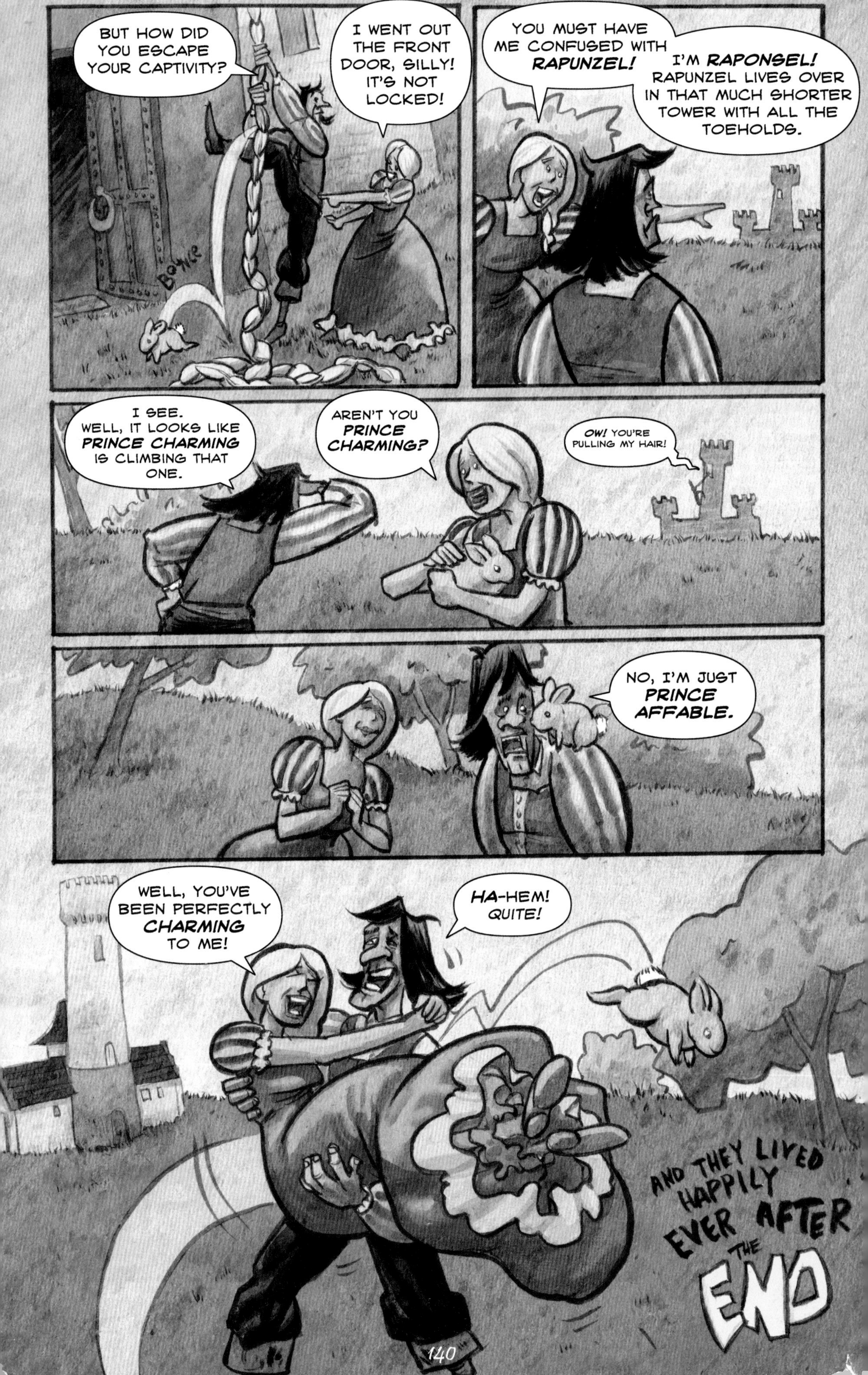
BUT HOW DID YOU ESCAPE YOUR CAPTIVITY?
BOING
I WENT OUT THE FRONT DOOR, SILLY! IT'S NOT LOCKED!
YOU MUST HAVE ME CONFUSED WITH RAPUNZEL!
I'M RAPONSEL! RAPUNZEL LIVES OVER IN THAT MUCH SHORTER TOWER WITH ALL THE TOEHOLDS.
I SEE. WELL, IT LOOKS LIKE PRINCE CHARMING IS CLIMBING THAT ONE.
AREN'T YOU PRINCE CHARMING?
OW! YOU'RE PULLING MY HAIR!
NO, I'M JUST PRINCE AFFABLE.
WELL, YOU'VE BEEN PERFECTLY CHARMING TO ME!
HA-HEM! QUITE!
AND THEY LIVED HAPPILY EVER AFTER
THE END

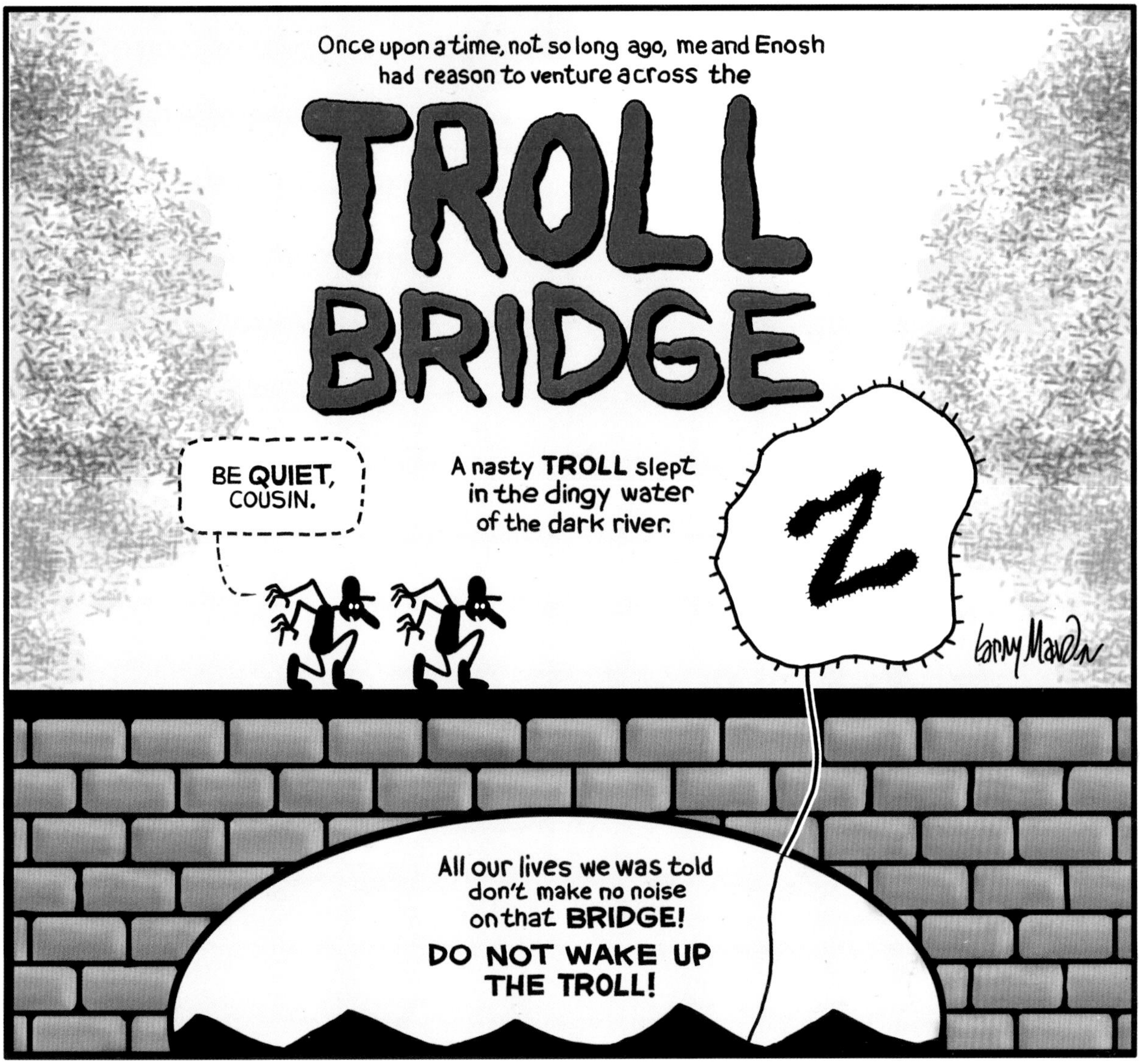
Once upon a time, not so long ago, me and Enosh had reason to venture across the
TROLL BRIDGE
BE QUIET, COUSIN.
A nasty TROLL slept in the dingy water of the dark river.
Z
Larry Marder
All our lives we was told don't make no noise on that BRIDGE!
DO NOT WAKE UP THE TROLL!

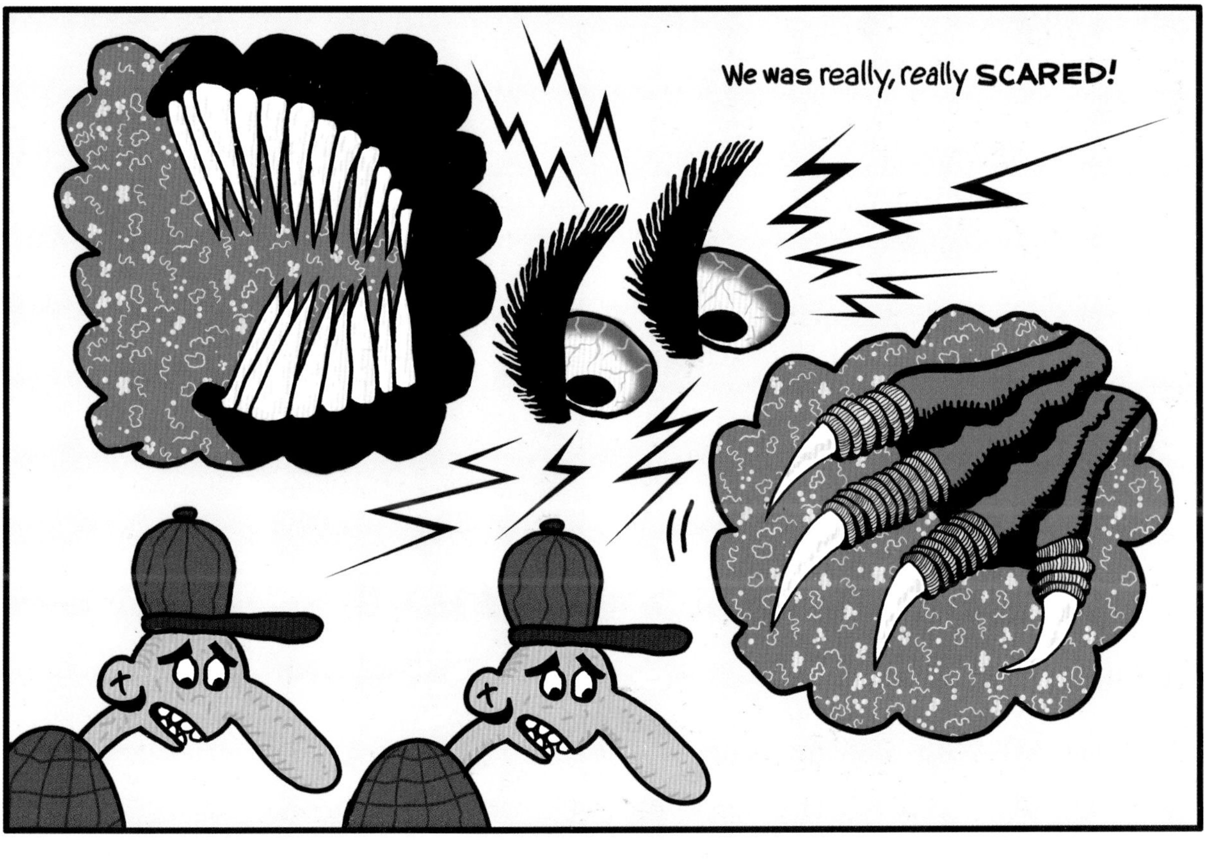
We was really, really SCARED!

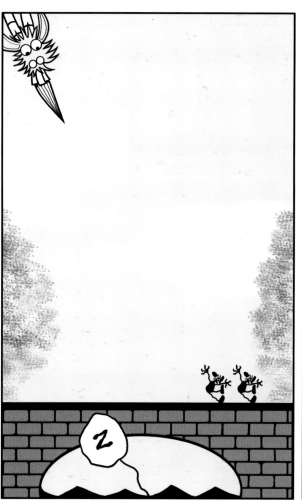

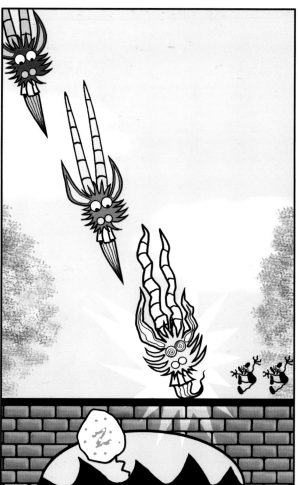

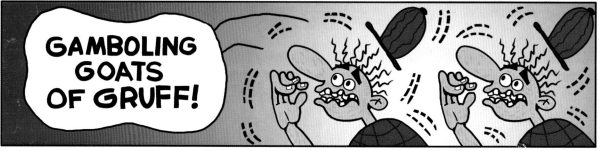

Z
GAMBOLING GOATS OF GRUFF!
Them crazy GAMBOLING GOATS...
HA! HA! HA! HA! HA! HA! HA! HA! HA! HA! HA! HA!
...was making a very loud rumpus!
HA! HA! HA! HA! HA! HA! HA! HA! HA! HA! HA! HA! HA! HA!

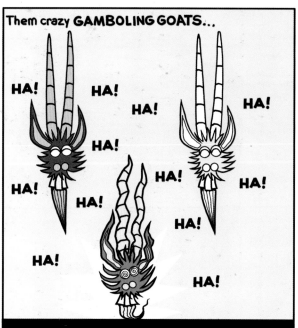

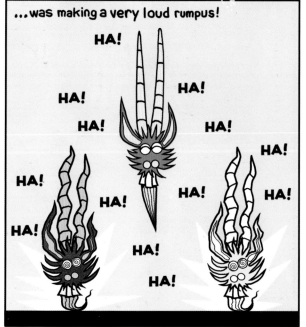

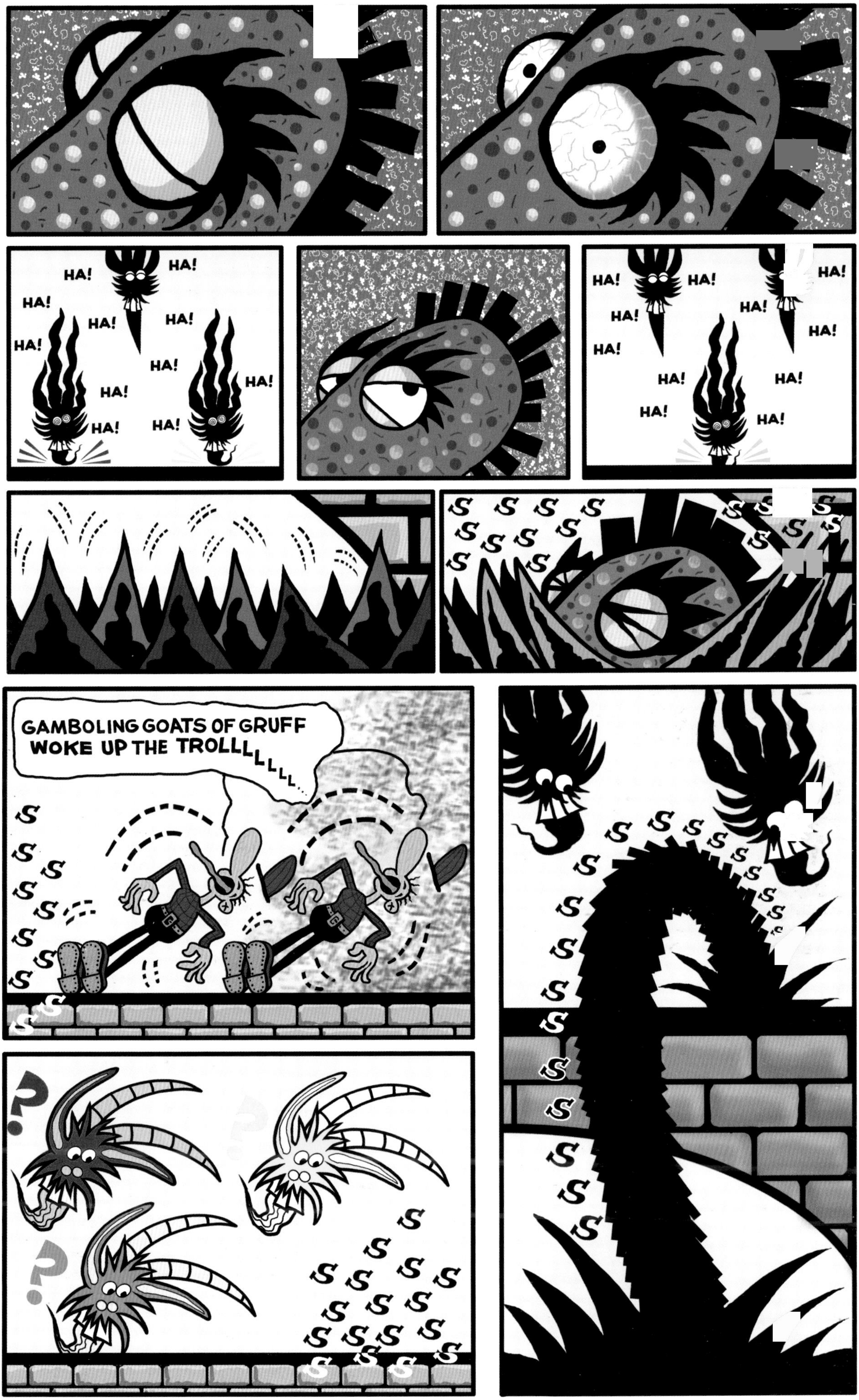
HA! HA! HA! HA! HA! HA! HA! HA! HA! HA! HA!
HA! HA! HA! HA! HA! HA! HA! HA! HA! HA! HA!
GAMBOLING GOATS OF GRUFF WOKE UP THE TROLLLLLLLL...

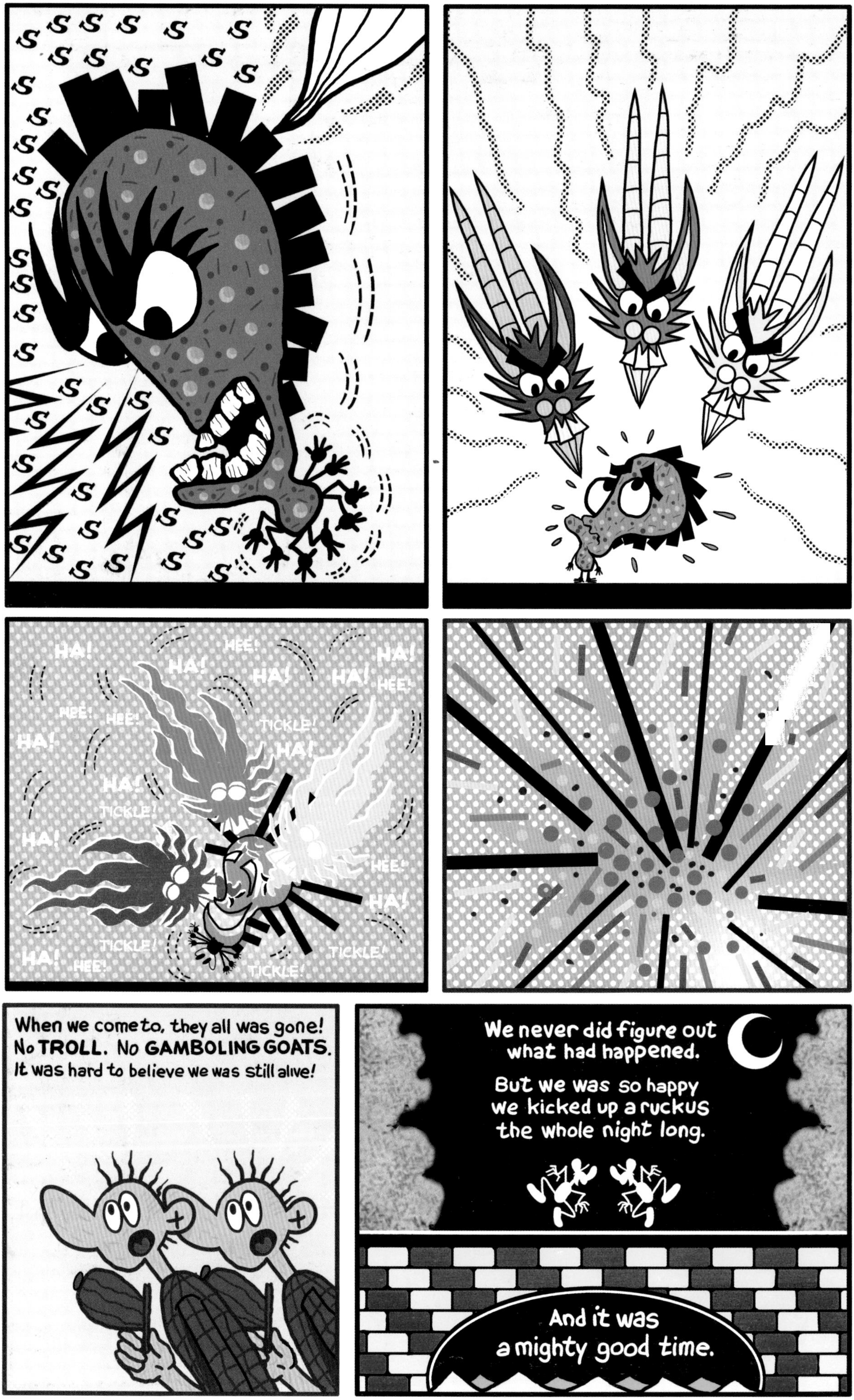
HA!
HEE!
HA!
HA!
HA!
HEE!
HEE!
HEE!
TICKLE!
HA!
HA!
HA!
TICKLE!
HA!
HEE!
HA!
TICKLE!
HA!
HEE!
TICKLE!
TICKLE!
When we come to, they all was gone!
No TROLL. No GAMBOLING GOATS.
It was hard to believe we was still alive!
We never did figure out what had happened.
But we was so happy we kicked up a ruckus the whole night long.
And it was a mighty good time.

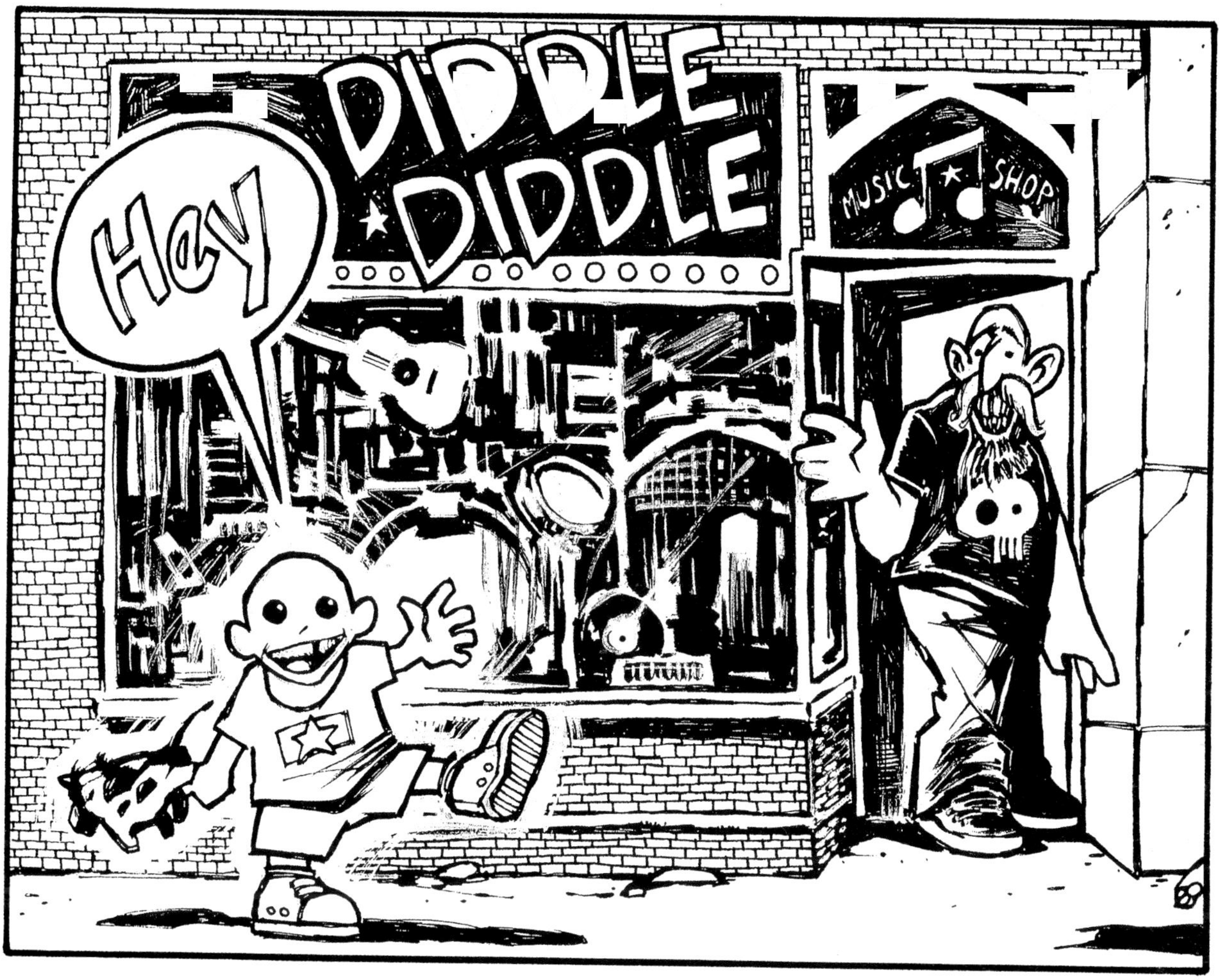
Hey
DIDDLE DIDDLE
MUSIC SHOP

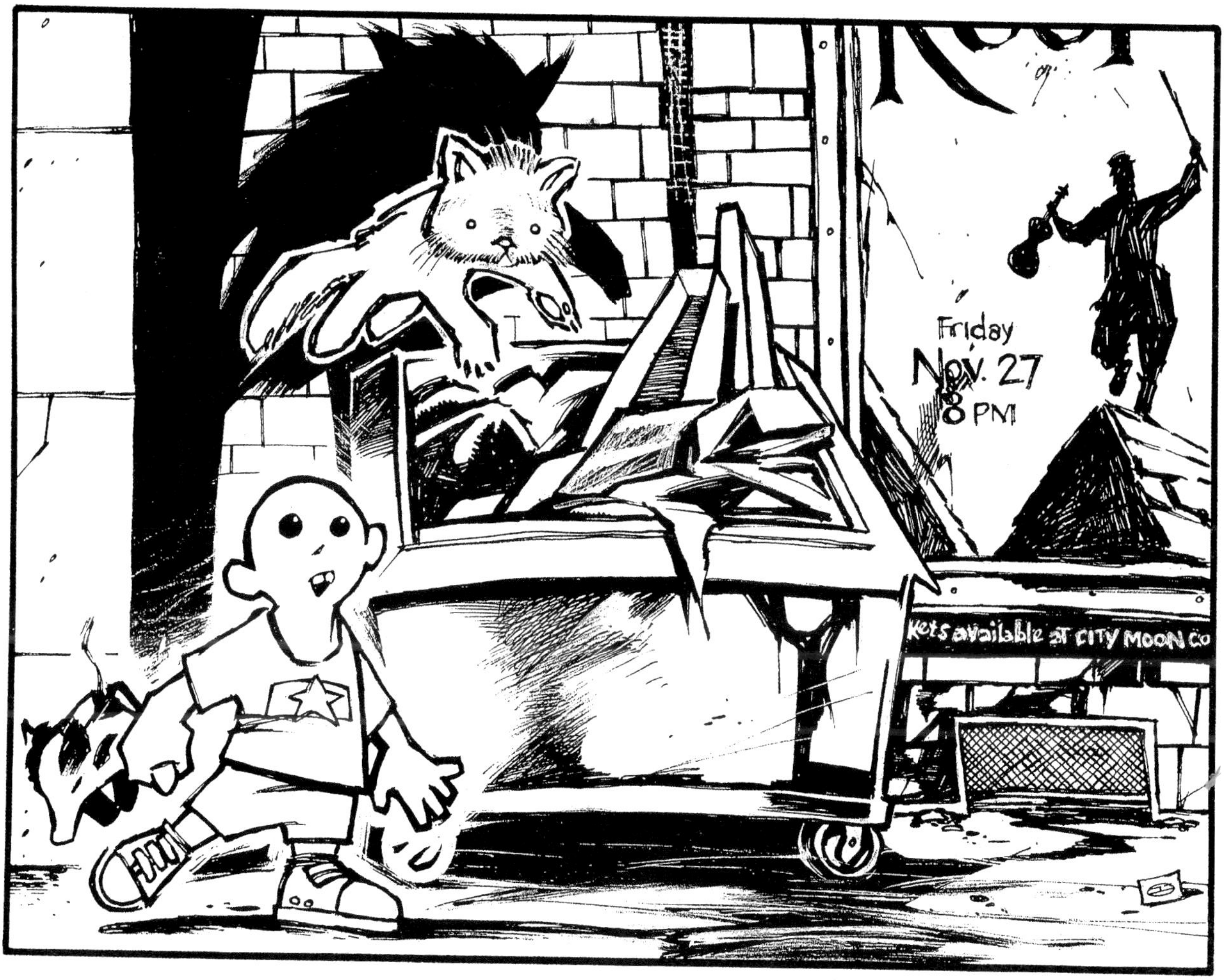
Friday
Nov. 27
8 PM
kets available at CITY MOON Co

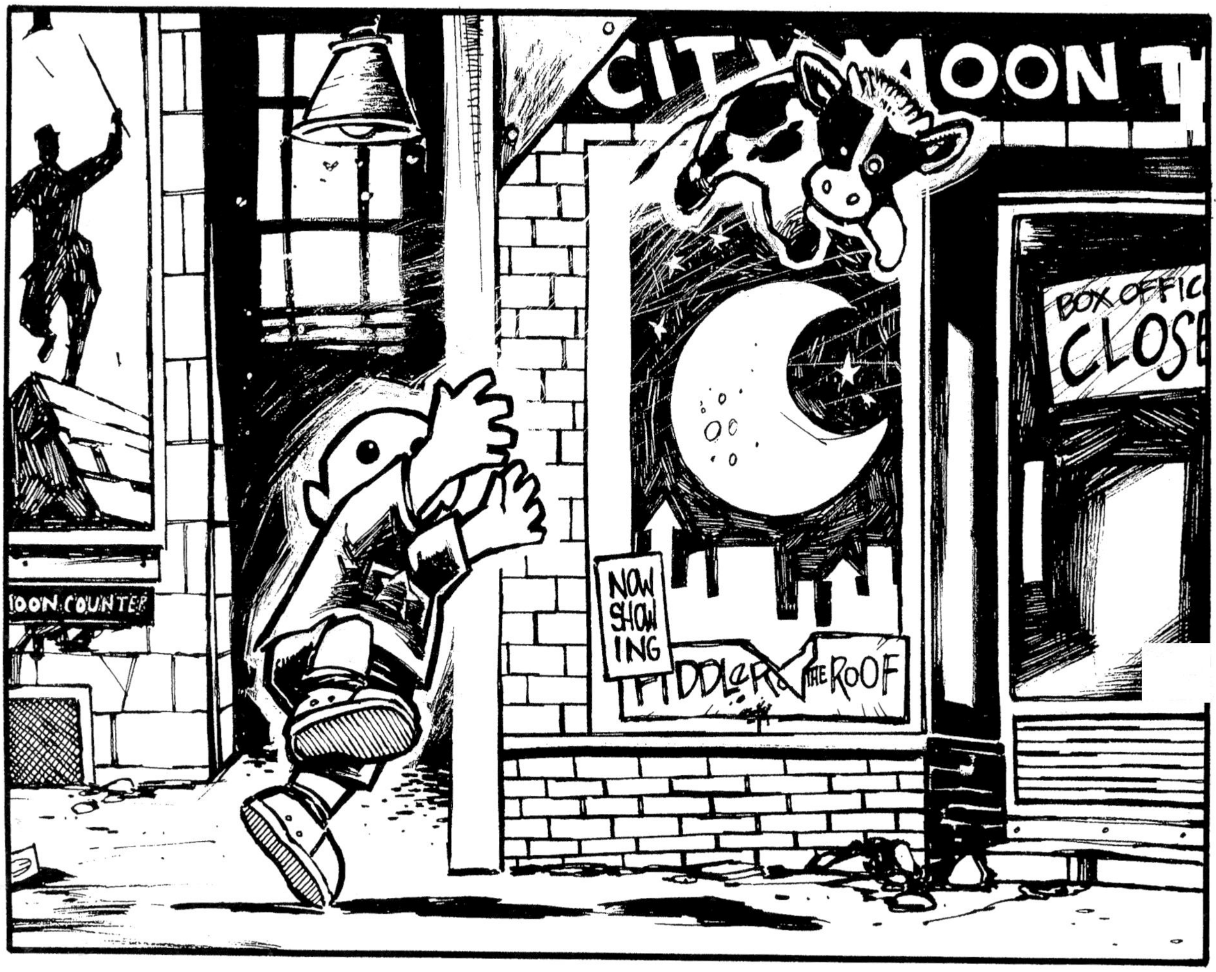
CITY MOON
NOW SHOWING
FIDDLER THE ROOF

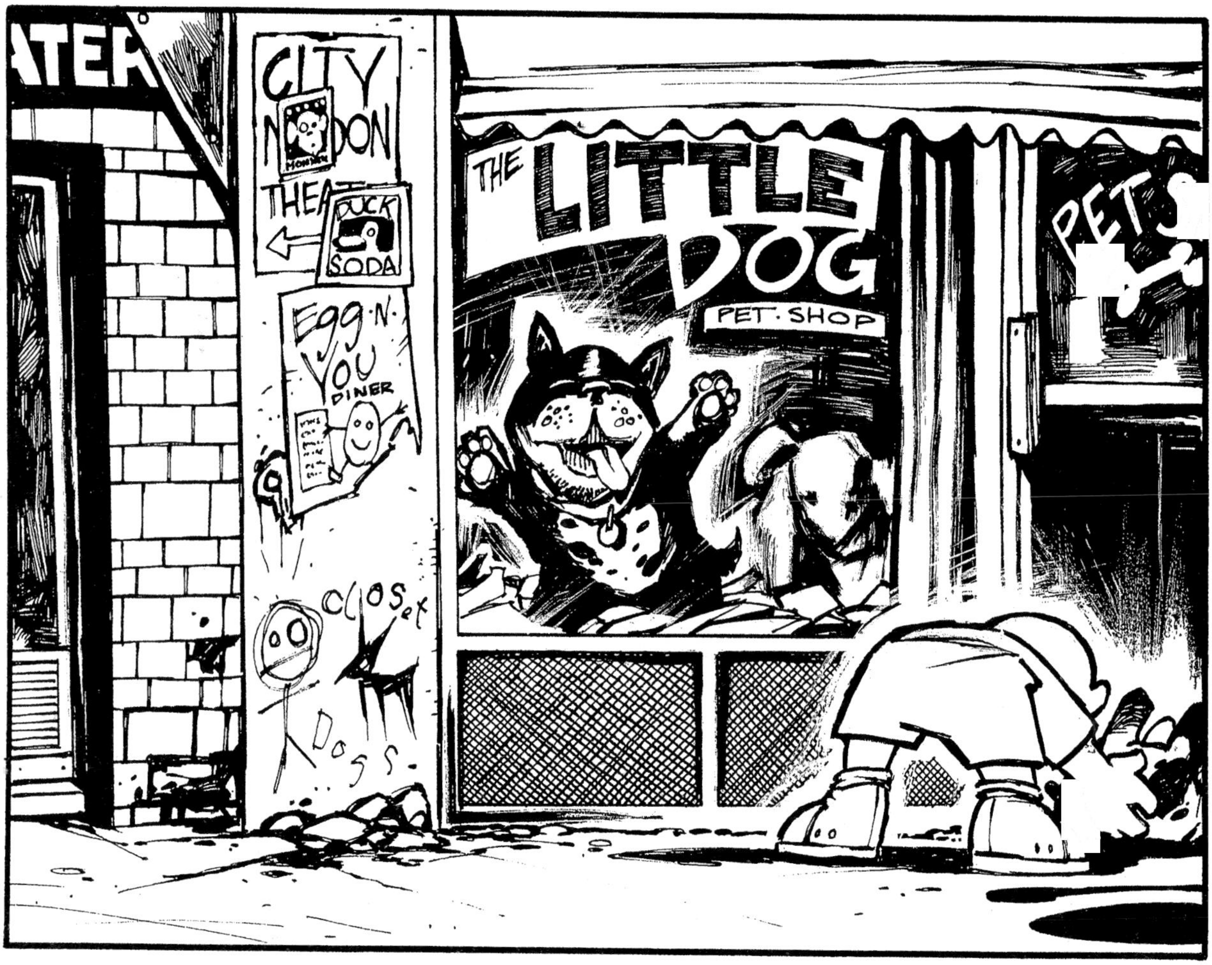
CITY
THEA
DUCK SODA
EGG N YOU DINER
THE LITTLE DOG
PET SHOP

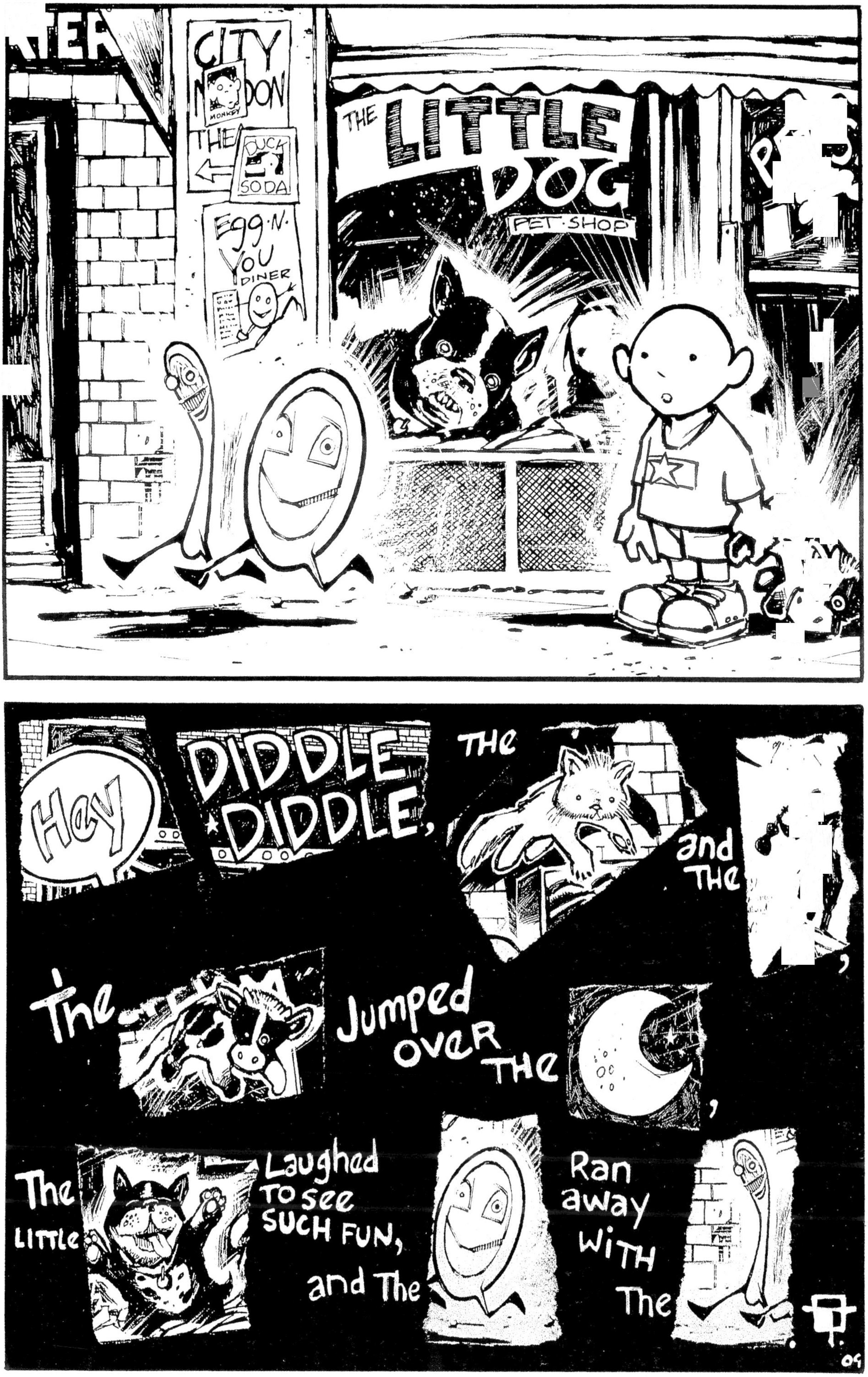
MONKEY
THE
DUCK
SODA
EGG·N·YOU DINER
THE LITTLE DOG
PET·SHOP
Hey
DIDDLE DIDDLE,
THE
and THE
The
Jumped over THE
The LITTLE
Laughed To see SUCH FUN,
and The
Ran away WITH The

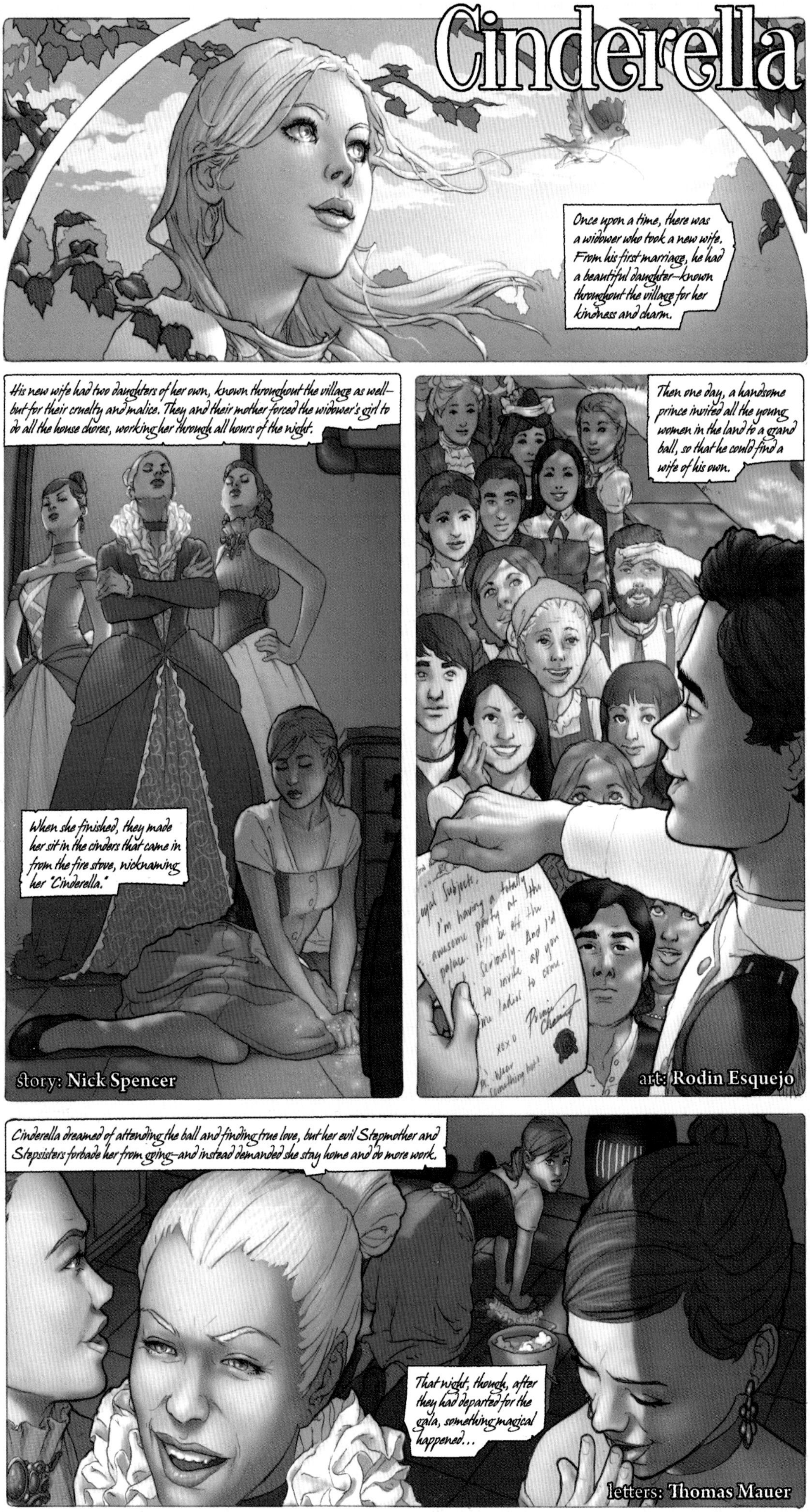
Cinderella
Once upon a time, there was a widower who took a new wife. From his first marriage, he had a beautiful daughter—known throughout the village for her kindness and charm.
His new wife had two daughters of her own, known throughout the village as well—but for their cruelty and malice. They and their mother forced the widower's girl to do all the house chores, working her through all hours of the night.
When she finished, they made her sit in the cinders that came in from the fire stove, nicknaming her "Cinderella."
story: Nick Spencer
Then one day, a handsome prince invited all the young women in the land to a grand ball, so that he could find a wife of his own.
art: Rodin Esquejo
Cinderella dreamed of attending the ball and finding true love, but her evil Stepmother and Stepsisters forbade her from going—and instead demanded she stay home and do more work.
That night, though, after they had departed for the gala, something magical happened...
letters: Thomas Mauer

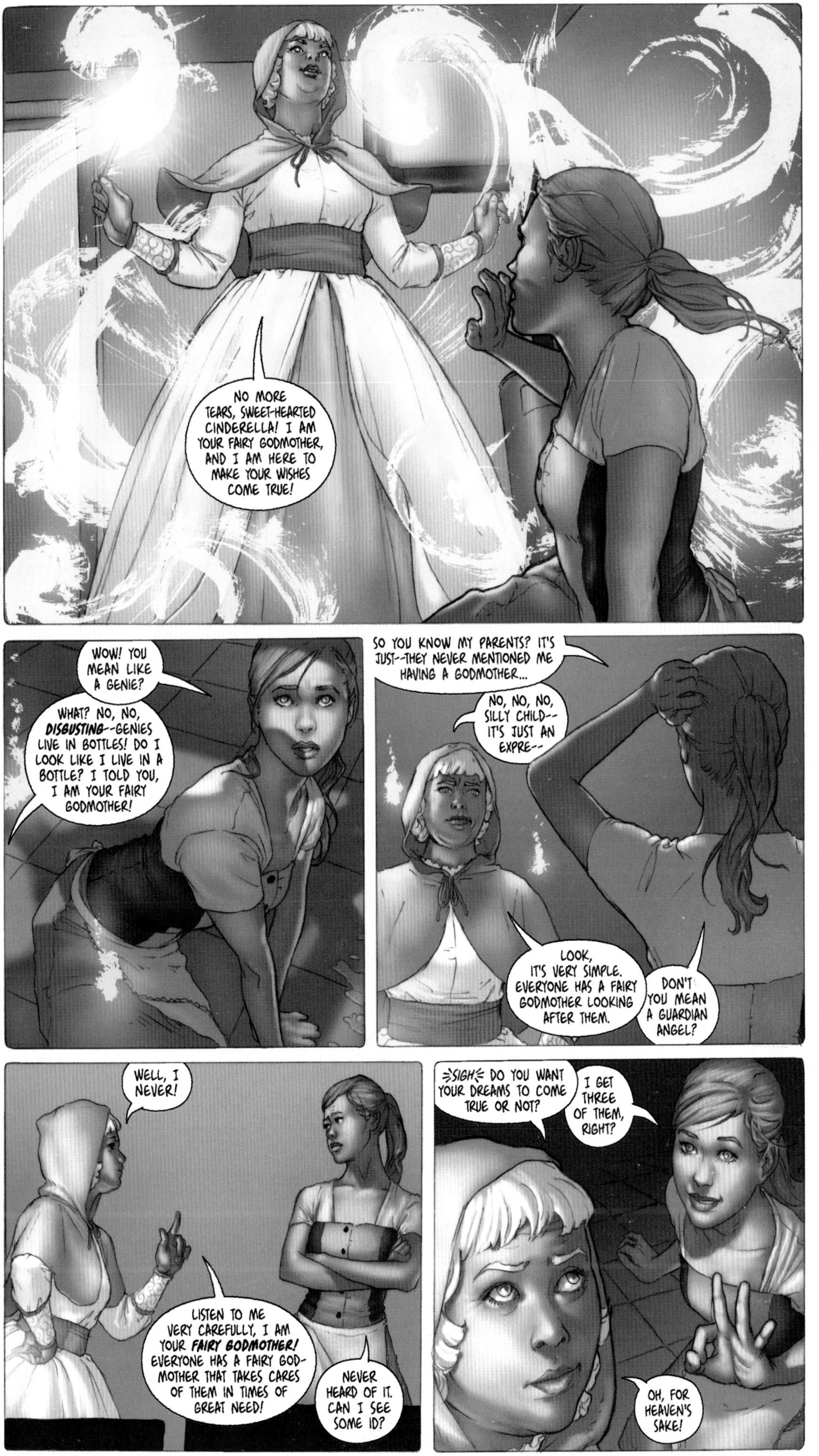
NO MORE TEARS, SWEET-HEARTED CINDERELLA! I AM YOUR FAIRY GODMOTHER, AND I AM HERE TO MAKE YOUR WISHES COME TRUE!
WOW! YOU MEAN LIKE A GENIE?
WHAT? NO, NO, DISGUSTING--GENIES LIVE IN BOTTLES! DO I LOOK LIKE I LIVE IN A BOTTLE? I TOLD YOU, I AM YOUR FAIRY GODMOTHER!
SO YOU KNOW MY PARENTS? IT'S JUST--THEY NEVER MENTIONED ME HAVING A GODMOTHER...
NO, NO, NO, SILLY CHILD--IT'S JUST AN EXPRE--
LOOK, IT'S VERY SIMPLE. EVERYONE HAS A FAIRY GODMOTHER LOOKING AFTER THEM.
DON'T YOU MEAN A GUARDIAN ANGEL?
WELL, I NEVER!
LISTEN TO ME VERY CAREFULLY, I AM YOUR FAIRY GODMOTHER! EVERYONE HAS A FAIRY GOD-MOTHER THAT TAKES CARES OF THEM IN TIMES OF GREAT NEED!
NEVER HEARD OF IT. CAN I SEE SOME ID?
SIGH DO YOU WANT YOUR DREAMS TO COME TRUE OR NOT?
I GET THREE OF THEM, RIGHT?
OH, FOR HEAVEN'S SAKE!

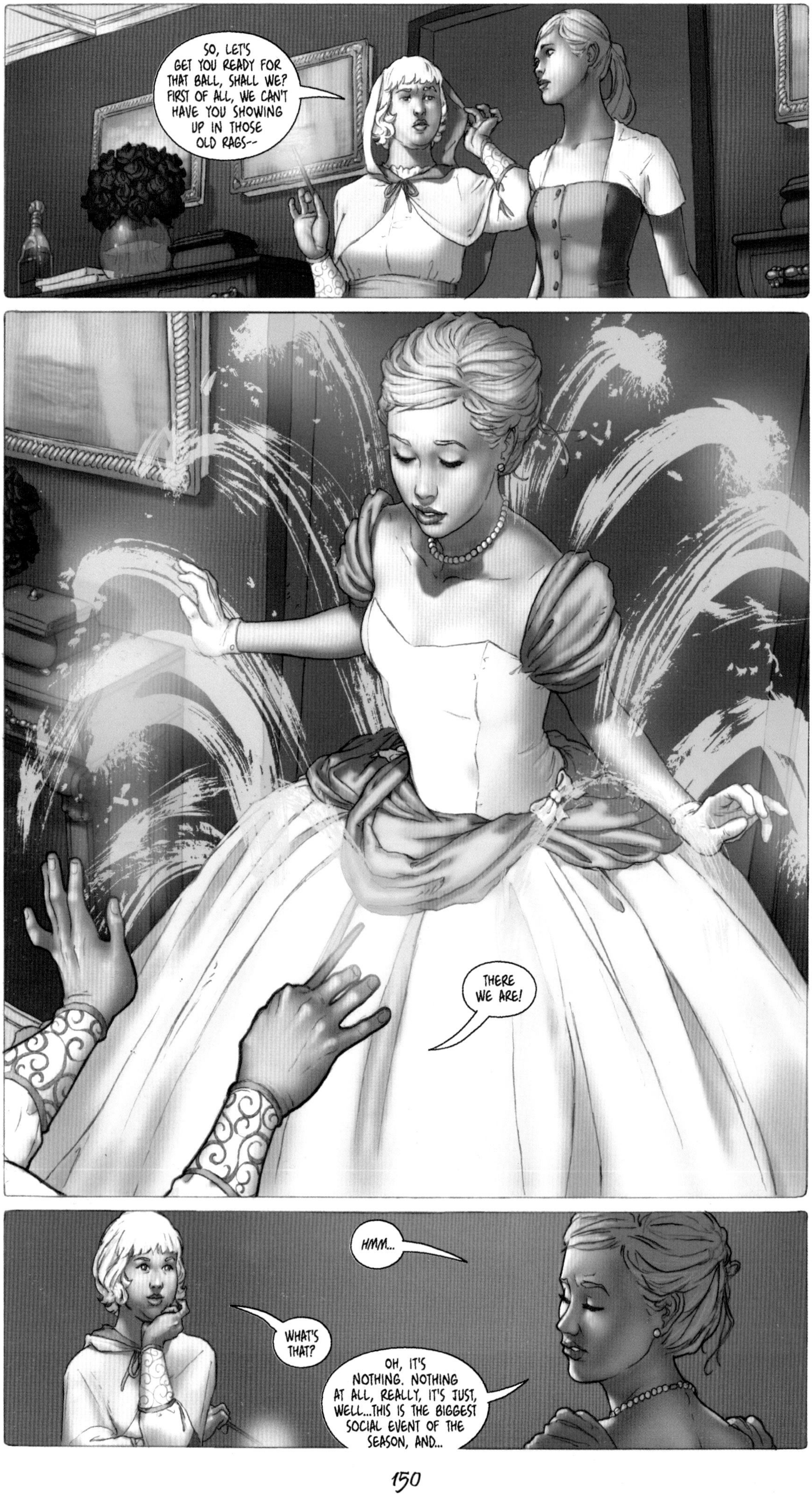
SO, LET'S GET YOU READY FOR THAT BALL, SHALL WE? FIRST OF ALL, WE CAN'T HAVE YOU SHOWING UP IN THOSE OLD RAGS--
THERE WE ARE!
HMM...
WHAT'S THAT?
OH, IT'S NOTHING. NOTHING AT ALL, REALLY, IT'S JUST, WELL...THIS IS THE BIGGEST SOCIAL EVENT OF THE SEASON, AND...

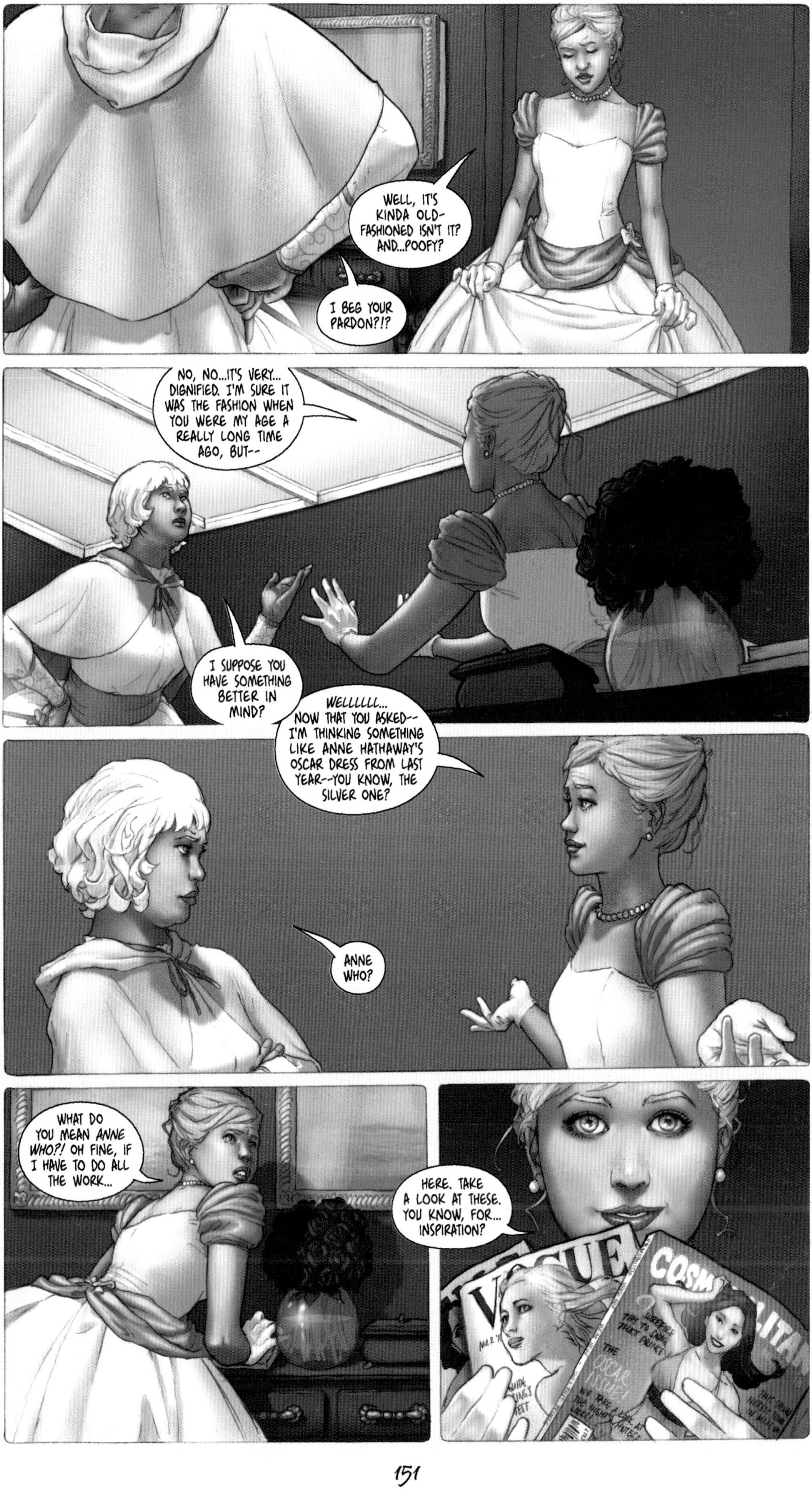
WELL, IT'S KINDA OLD-FASHIONED ISN'T IT? AND...POOFY?
I BEG YOUR PARDON?!?
NO, NO...IT'S VERY... DIGNIFIED. I'M SURE IT WAS THE FASHION WHEN YOU WERE MY AGE A REALLY LONG TIME AGO, BUT--
I SUPPOSE YOU HAVE SOMETHING BETTER IN MIND?
WELLLLLL... NOW THAT YOU ASKED-- I'M THINKING SOMETHING LIKE ANNE HATHAWAY'S OSCAR DRESS FROM LAST YEAR--YOU KNOW, THE SILVER ONE?
ANNE WHO?
WHAT DO YOU MEAN *ANNE WHO?!* OH FINE, IF I HAVE TO DO ALL THE WORK...
HERE. TAKE A LOOK AT THESE. YOU KNOW, FOR... INSPIRATION?
THE OSCAR ISSUE!

HMM...
TOO MILEY.
TOO
SELINA.
UGH--TOO
LINDSAY AFTER A
BREAKUP-EY.
THAT'S IT!
THAT'S IT!
PERFECT!

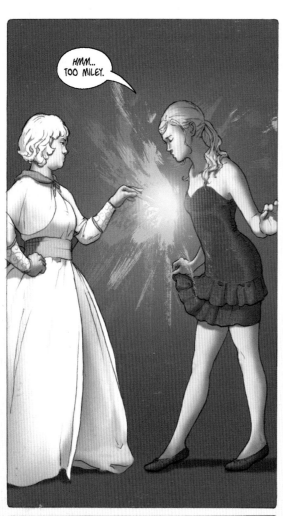

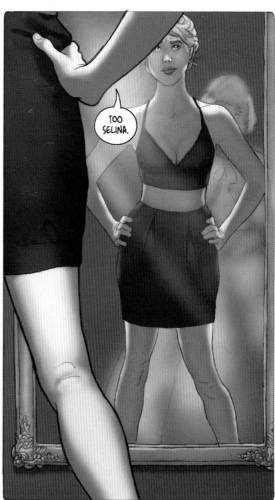

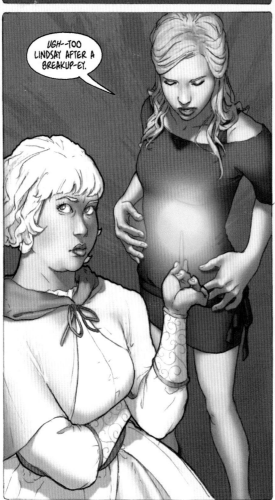

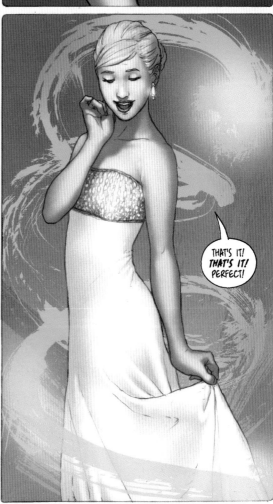

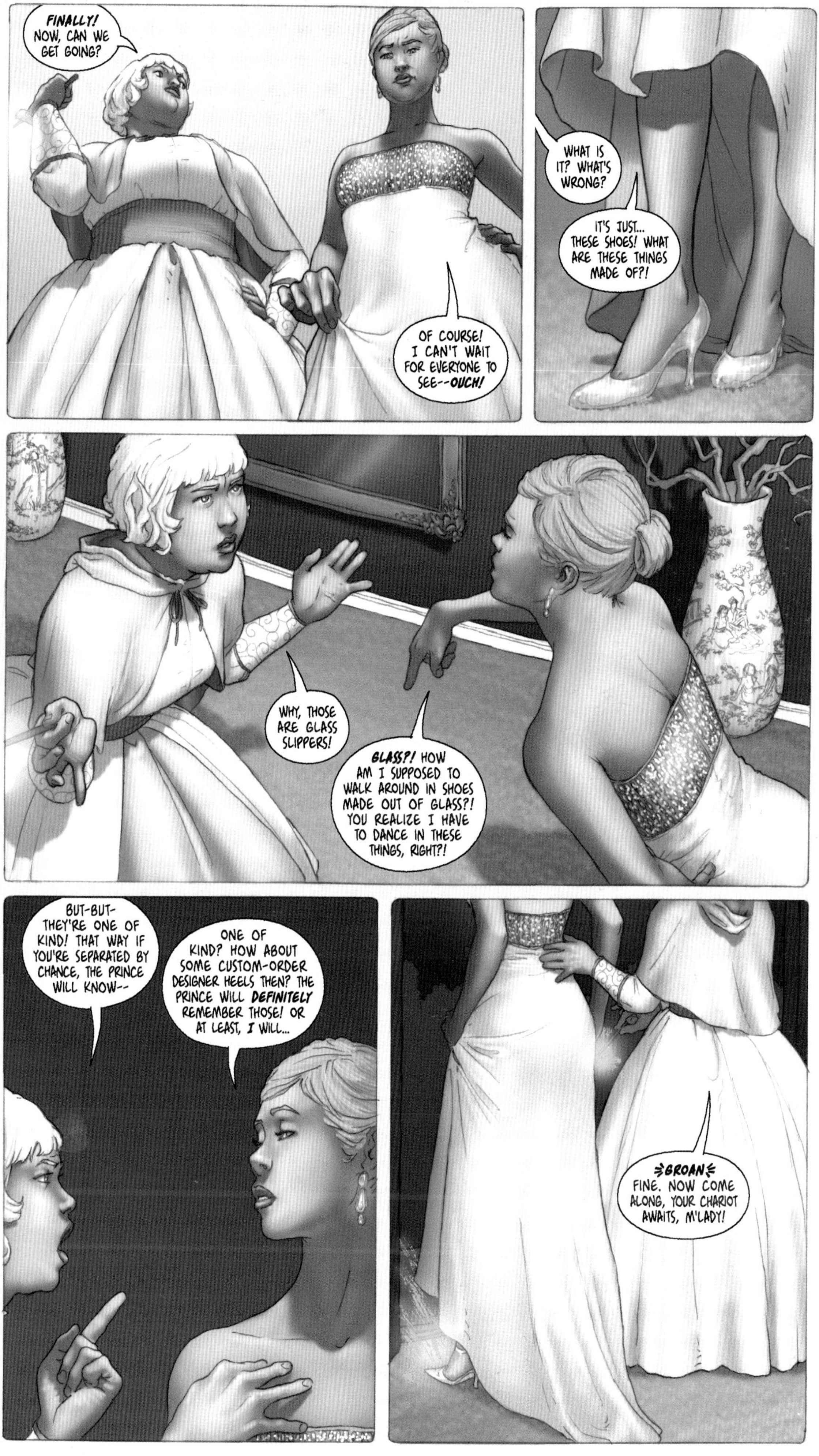
FINALLY! NOW, CAN WE GET GOING?
OF COURSE! I CAN'T WAIT FOR EVERYONE TO SEE--OUCH!
WHAT IS IT? WHAT'S WRONG?
IT'S JUST... THESE SHOES! WHAT ARE THESE THINGS MADE OF?!
WHY, THOSE ARE GLASS SLIPPERS!
GLASS?! HOW AM I SUPPOSED TO WALK AROUND IN SHOES MADE OUT OF GLASS?! YOU REALIZE I HAVE TO DANCE IN THESE THINGS, RIGHT?!
BUT-BUT- THEY'RE ONE OF KIND! THAT WAY IF YOU'RE SEPARATED BY CHANCE, THE PRINCE WILL KNOW--
ONE OF KIND? HOW ABOUT SOME CUSTOM-ORDER DESIGNER HEELS THEN? THE PRINCE WILL DEFINITELY REMEMBER THOSE! OR AT LEAST, I WILL...
GROAN
FINE. NOW COME ALONG, YOUR CHARIOT AWAITS, M'LADY!

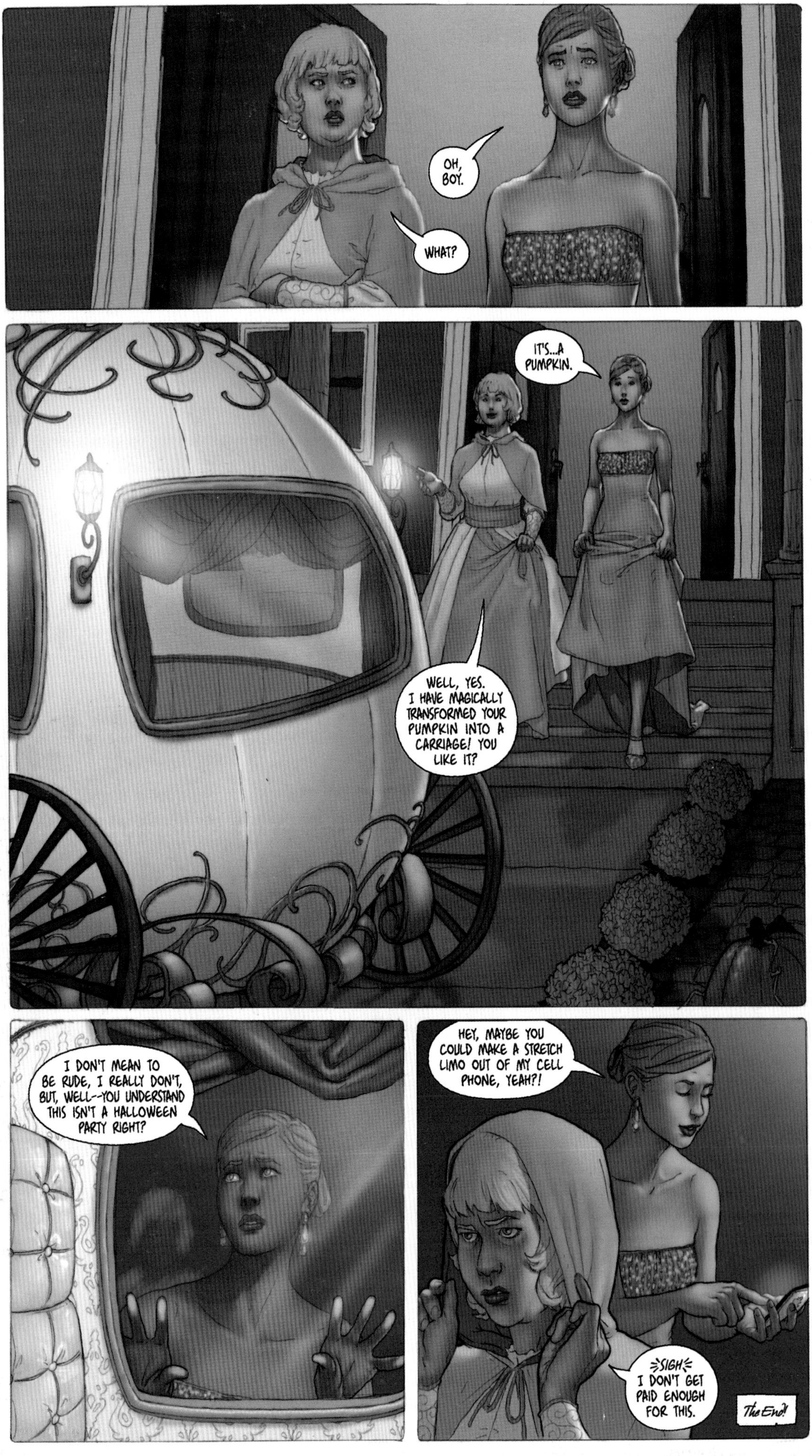
OH, BOY.
WHAT?
IT'S...A PUMPKIN.
WELL, YES. I HAVE MAGICALLY TRANSFORMED YOUR PUMPKIN INTO A CARRIAGE! YOU LIKE IT?
I DON'T MEAN TO BE RUDE, I REALLY DON'T, BUT, WELL--YOU UNDERSTAND THIS ISN'T A HALLOWEEN PARTY RIGHT?
HEY, MAYBE YOU COULD MAKE A STRETCH LIMO OUT OF MY CELL PHONE, YEAH?!
SIGH I DON'T GET PAID ENOUGH FOR THIS.
The End!

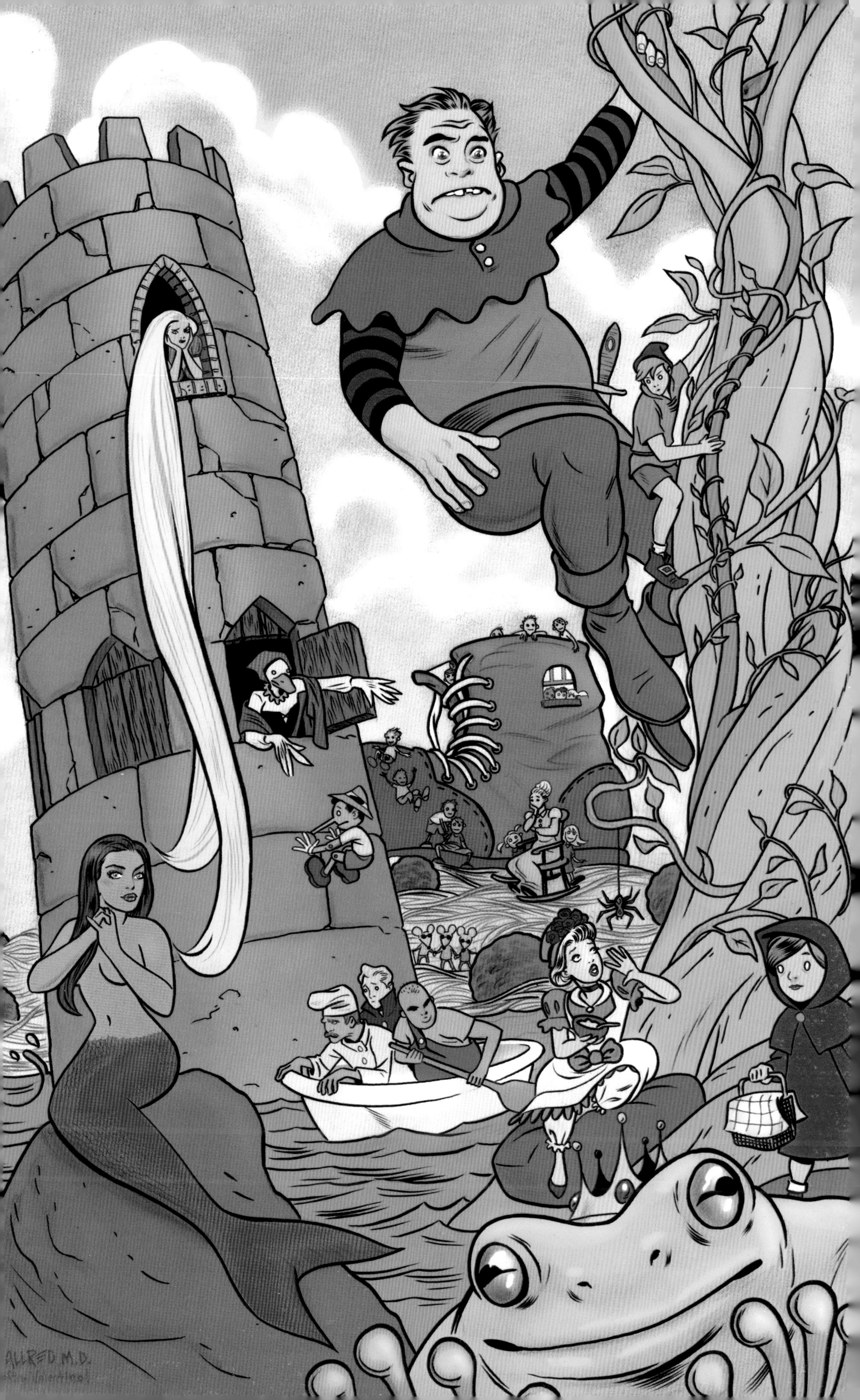
ALLRED M.D.

Bios

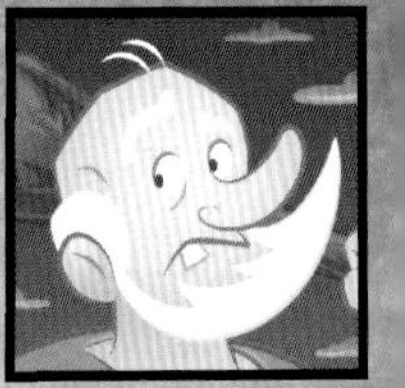

Bill Alger (page 49) is a Brooklyn-based artist who has illustrated titles including SCOOBY DOO, DEXTER'S LABORATORY, TONKA TOUGH TRUCKS and HAMTARO. He also wrote and illustrated JUNE COMICS.

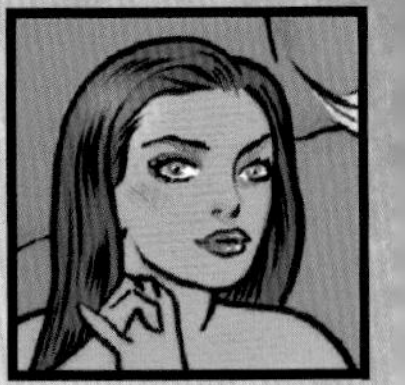

Laura Allred (Cover and page 155) is an award-winning artist in her own right. She works primarily with her husband, Mike, and is one of the most respected colorists in the field.

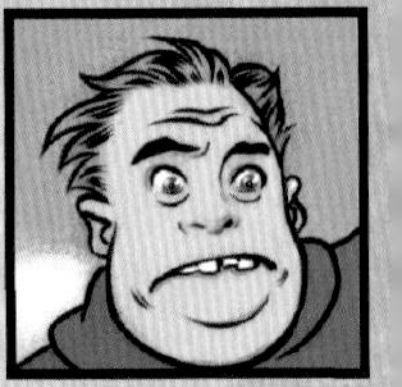

Mike Allred (Cover and page 155) first tasted success in the comics field with his wildly popular MADMAN series, which is currently being developed for a live action movie with filmmaker Robert Rodriguez. Mike has drawn SANDMAN, created X-MEN, and has worked on every major comic book character including BATMAN, SUPERMAN, SPIDER-MAN, IRON MAN, and the HULK.

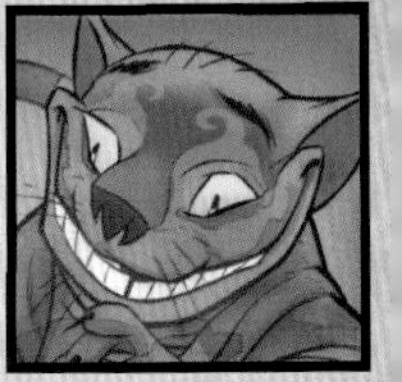

Grant Bond (page 9) is a cartoonist who created and illustrated THE ABSURD ADVENTURES OF ARCHIBALD AARDVARK series for Shadowline in 2009. He is best-known for REVERE: REVOLUTION IN SILVER, just in case your U.S. History teacher left out the part where Paul Revere mangled a werewolf.

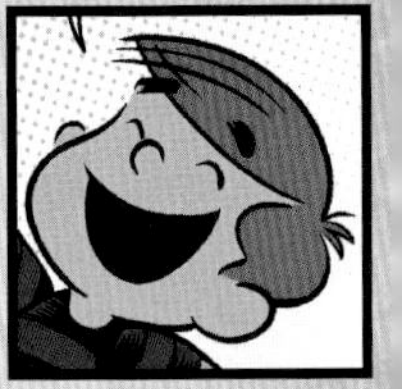

Serban Cristescu (page 55) is best known for his innovative contributions as Designer for Matt Groening's hit TV series, FUTURAMA, and for his design and coloring work for Bongo Entertainment's cornucopia of FUTURAMA and THE SIMPSONS books and calendars.

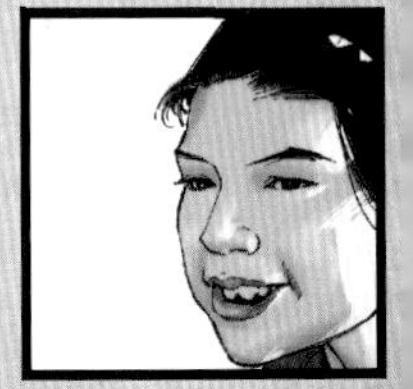

Marie Cruz (page 30) is a writer of young adult novels and picture books, a scientist, a proud mother of two teens and the wife of a Jedi knight (her husband's name is Obi!). Reading is one of her favorite things to do. She also loves to knit. It's a great remedy for writer's block.

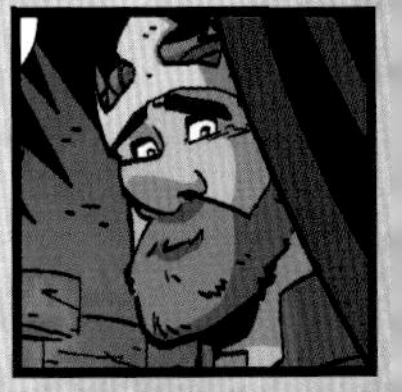

Seth Damoose (page 109) has worked on a variety of projects, such as BRAT-HALLA, STEAMPUNK FAERIES, and SPOOK'D. However, Seth is best known for the Shadowline series I HATE GALLANT GIRL, and BOMB QUEEN PRESENTS: ALL GIRL COMICS.

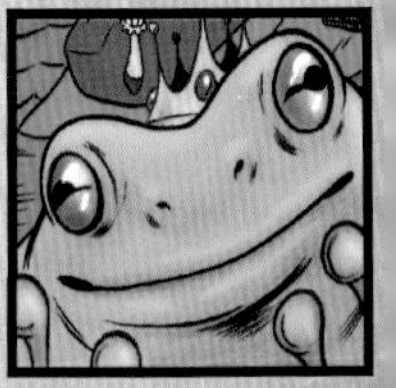

Tim Daniel (Cover graphics and logo) has been contributing logos and production designs to the covers and interiors of many comics over the last several years including, EXISTENCE 2.0/3.0, FORGETLESS, POWERS, SKY PIRATES OF NEO TERRA, SHUDDERTOWN and SCARLET. He lives in Montana with his wife and daughter.

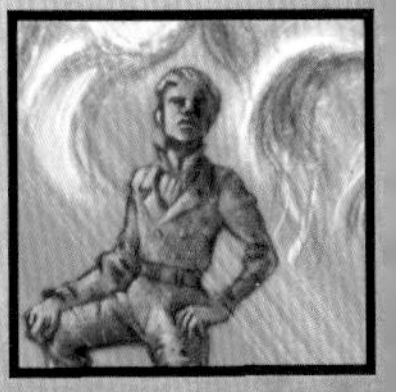

Peter David (page 113), writer of stuff, has produced over a thousand comic books and seventy novels. He currently writes X-FACTOR and STEPHEN KING'S DARK TOWER for Marvel Comics, and FALLEN ANGEL for IDW. He named his third daughter "Ariel" after the Little Mermaid and apologizes profusely to both of them.

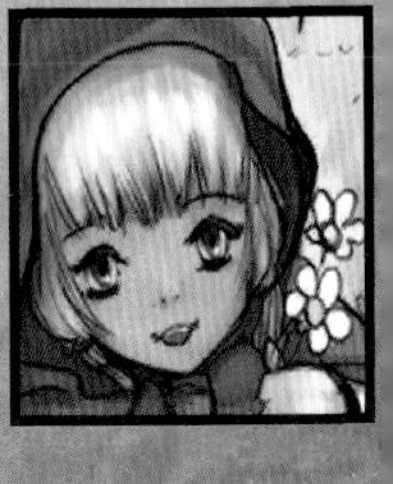

Camilla d'Errico (page 16) lives the double life of character creator and comic artist/painter. She has expanded her style into designer toys, fashion, merchandise, and videogames. She has distinguished herself through her ability to seamlessly weave comic art and manga. One of her most recent works is SKY PIRATES OF NEO TERRA for Image Comics.

Jim Di Bartolo *(page 125)* is an illustrator that has collaborated on three novels and one graphic novel (THE DROWNED, through Image Comics) with his wife, writer Laini Taylor. Their most recent collaboration (LIPS TOUCH: THREE TIMES) was a finalist for the National Book Award. He lives in Portland, Oregon with his wife and baby daughter.

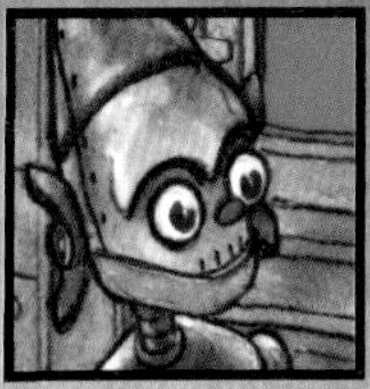

Nikki Dy-Liacco *(page 73)* is a marketing professional from the Philippines and currently lives in Singapore. She has authored three children's books since 2005 including THE YELLOW PAPERCLIP WITH BRIGHT PURPLE SPOTS, her first book with May Ann Licudine and wishes she had more time to daydream, watch clouds and write stories.

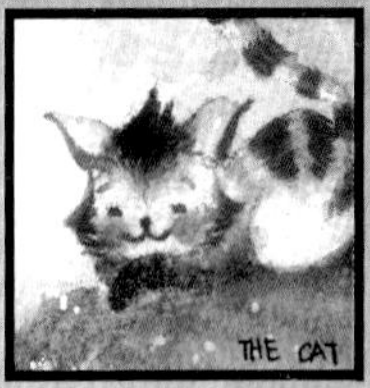
THE CAT

Rodin Esquejo *(page 148)* is a freelance artist based out of the Bay Area, California. Since receiving his B.A. in Graphic Design, he has been working steadily on projects for Hasbro, com.X, Vineyard Press, as well as private commissions.

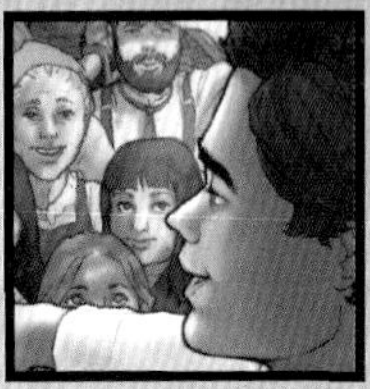

Juan Ferreyra *(page 113)* is an Argentinean illustrator whose work includes Shadowline's LAZARUS, EMISSARY and SMALL GODS and Dark Horse's REX MUNDI. He was also featured in JIM VALENTINO'S SHADOWHAWK #13: PAST LIVES, drawing the first female ShadowHawk.

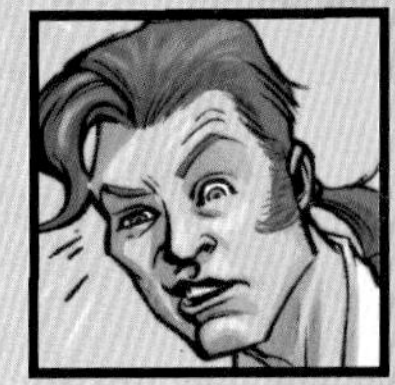

Paul Fricke *(page 81)* is a freelance cartoonist of twenty-five years, working in comics and illustration for various applications. His first childrens book, NIGHT OF THE BEDBUGS is now available from Image/Silverline Books. He lives in Minnesota with his wife and two daughters; a family of artists.

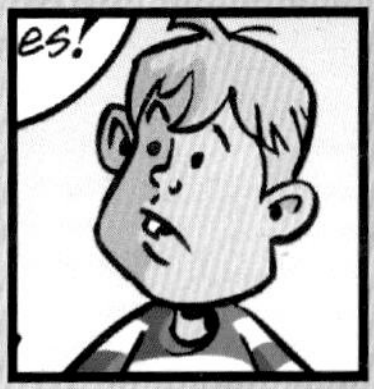

Alexander Grecian *(page 88)* wrote the graphic novels SEVEN SONS and SQUEAK! and continues to write the critically-acclaimed PROOF series. He sleeps reasonably well near Kansas City with his one true love and their son.

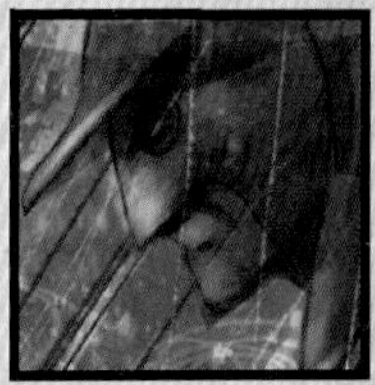

Brian Haberlin *(page 121)* and his studio do work for Image, Marvel and DC Comics. Brian is known as a WITCHBLADE co-creator, and also for his Avalon Studios titles such as ARIA and HELLCOP and his recent run on SPAWN with David Hine. He is currently working on a new 250 page graphic novel called ANOMALY to come out later this year, he writes for 3DWorld Magazine, and teaches at Minneapolis College of Art and Design.

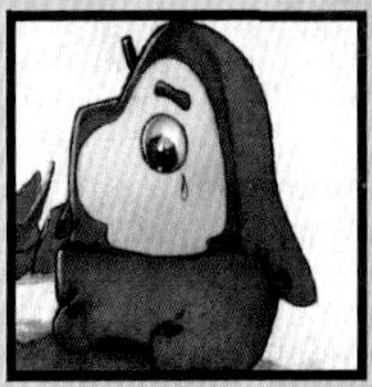

Phil Hester's *(page 58)* work has been featured in: SWAMP THING, GREEN ARROW, NIGHTWING, ANT-MAN, THE COFFIN, DEEP SLEEPER, and the Eisner-nominated THE WRETCH. Current work includes: FIREBREATHER for Image Comics, and THE DARKNESS for Top Cow. Phil lives in small town Iowa with his wife and two children.

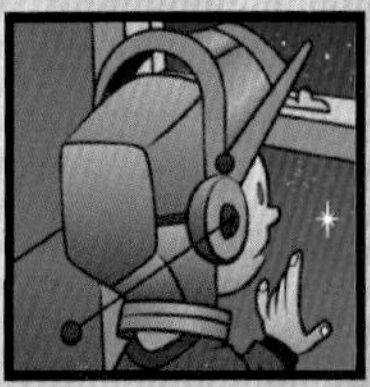

Neil Kleid *(page 67)* is a Xeric Award winning cartoonist who authored NINETY CANDLES, a graphic novella about life, death, legacy and comics; Neil also wrote the series THE INTIMIDATORS for Shadowline, and has been featured in the award-winning Image anthologies COMIC BOOK TATTOO and POPGUN. He also writes the webcomic ACTION, OHIO on the Shadowline webcomics hub.

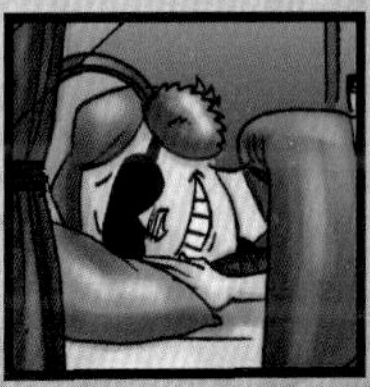

Keaton Kohl *(page 58)* has a B.F.A. from the Kansas City Art Institute. He loves writing, inking, coloring, lettering and prop building. Currently he is the Head of Make-up for the four largest haunted houses in the country. In his free time he inks pencils for artists Mike Laughead and Jake Schmidt.

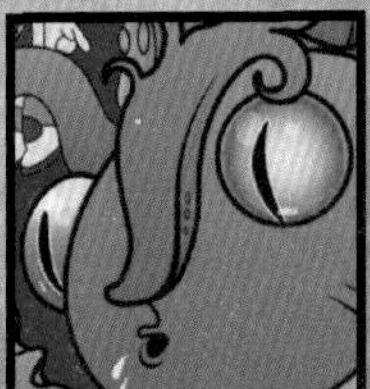

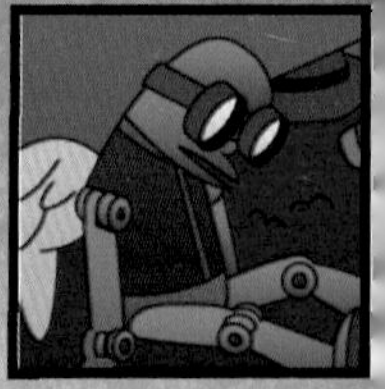

Mike Laughead *(page 58)* sits in a small room and draws pictures. Some of those pictures entertain his 2 young daughters. When not entertaining, Mike also does freelance illustration and comics. He is currently drawing a children's picture book and trying to be a good husband.

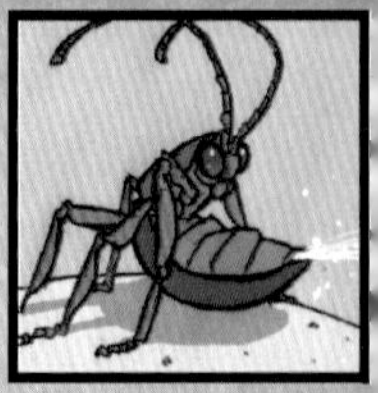

Royden Lepp *(page 60)* was born at a very young age in Brandon, Manitoba Canada. He grew up in British Columbia and was trained in 2d animation at the Vancouver Film School. Royden currently lives with his wife in the Seattle area, working in games and drinking coffee. His other works include the DAVID: THE SHEPHERD'S SONG, and the BARNABAS BEAR series.

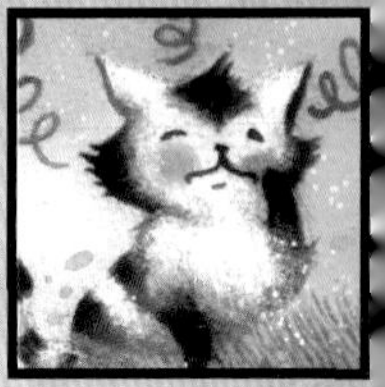

May Ann Licudine *(page 73)* is a Filipino freelance illustrator and visual artist that lives in La Union, Philippines. She is a graduate in Certificate of Fine Arts at the University of the Philippines, Baguio City. She has competed and won in some prestigious art competitions both locally and internationally. Her illustrations have been exhibited in various galleries in Europe and the USA.

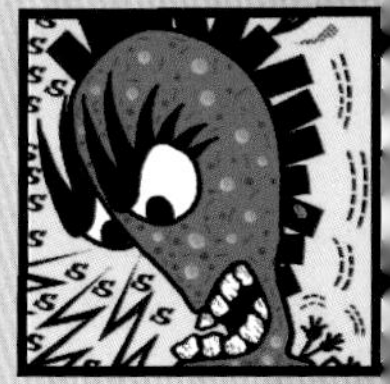

Larry Marder *(page 141)* released the first issue of BEANWORLD in 1985. He later joined the comic book circus full-time as the Executive Director of Image Comics and later President of McFarlane Toys. In 2007, he retired from business and returned to creating BEANWORLD full-time. He lives in Orange County, California, with his wife, Cory, and their two cats, Olive and Chipper.

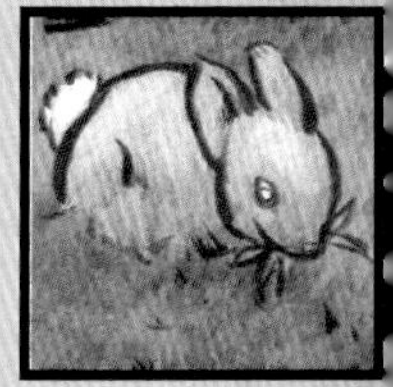

Derek McCulloch *(page 135)* collaborated with artist Jimmie Robinson on the children's book T. RUNT! for Shadowline's younger readers imprint Silverline Books. His graphic novels for adults include STAGGER LEE, with Shepherd Hendrix; PUG, with Greg Espinoza; and GONE TO AMERIKAY, with Colleen Doran (coming from Vertigo in 2011).

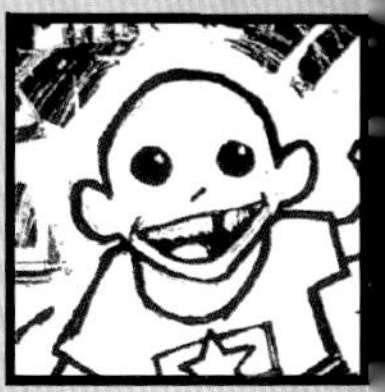

Ted McKeever *(page 145)* is the Eisner-nominated creator behind such prominent works as TRANSIT, EDDY CURRENT, METROPOL and PLASTIC FORKS. More recently, he has worked on various DC and IDW titles, and contributed to Image's Tori Amos anthology, COMIC BOOK TATTOO. Currently, he is working on a brand new series called META 4, to be released through Shadowline in 2010.

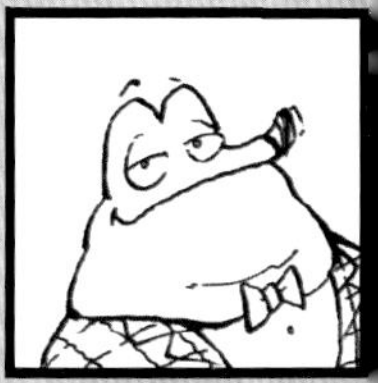

Terry Moore *(page 21)* is an Eisner and Harvey Award winning cartoonist, best known for his self-published series, ECHO and STRANGERS IN PARADISE. In addition to his own books, Moore has worked with every major comic book publisher, writing and/or drawing for titles such as STAR WARS, RUNAWAYS, SPIDER-MAN LOVES MARY JANE, BUFFY THE VAMPIRE SLAYER and GEN 13.

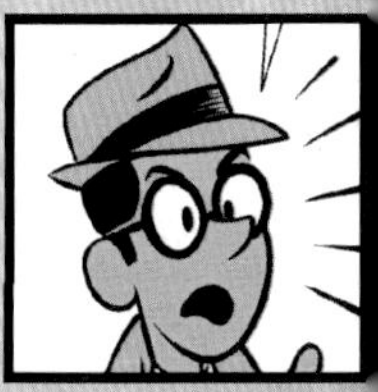

Bill Morrison *(page 55)* has worked as an automotive illustrator, a Disney movie poster artist, a photo-realistic airbrush illustrator, and a merchandise artist for THE SIMPSONS. Since 1994, he has been creating comics and books for Matt Groening's Bongo Entertainment. Bill's current extracurricular project is LADY ROBOTIKA, which he co-created with Jane Wiedlin and is being released through Shadowline.

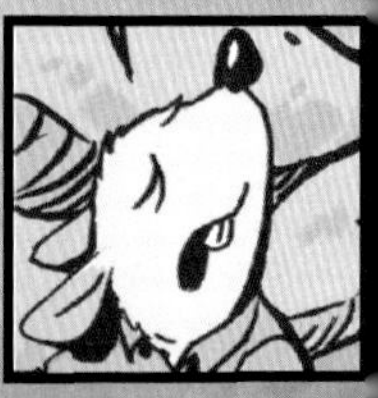

Scott Morse *(page 100)* is the creator of the Eisner and Ignatz Award nominated SOULWIND, as well as the graphic novels VISITATIONS, VOLCANIC REVOLVER, and MAGIC PICKLE for Oni Press and ANCIENT JOE for Dark Horse. In animation, Morse has worked as a character designer, storyboard artist, and art director for studios including Disney, Universal and Cartoon Network.

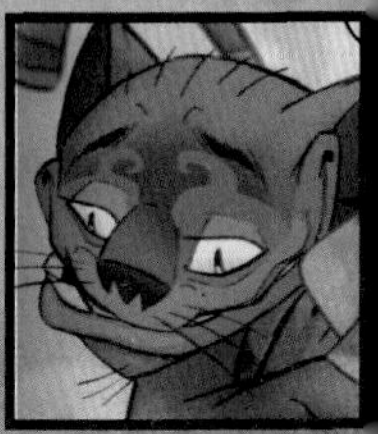

Dara Naraghi *(page 9)* lives in Columbus, Ohio and has written comics for kids and grown ups, including THE ABSURD ADVENTURES OF ARCHIBALD AARDVARK (Image), IGOR, and GHOSTBUSTERS. His favorite color is green, he has a hound dog named Duncan, and believe it or not, he likes brussel sprouts!

Vicente Navarrete (page 93), or 'Vinny' to his friends, illustrated DEAR DRACULA for
Silverline Books, Shadowline's imprint for younger readers. He's also the writer and
llustrator for his creator-owned book called KITE DAY.

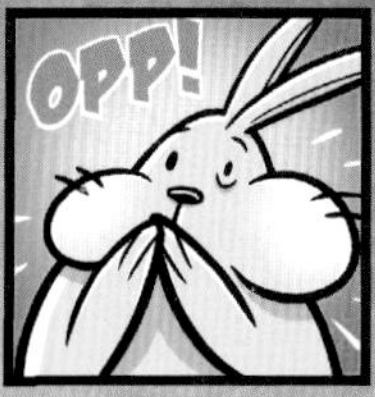
OPP!

Anthony Peruzzo (page 135) is an artist living in Minnesota. His work has been
published by Image comics, Desperado Publishing and DC Comics' online division, Zuda
comics.

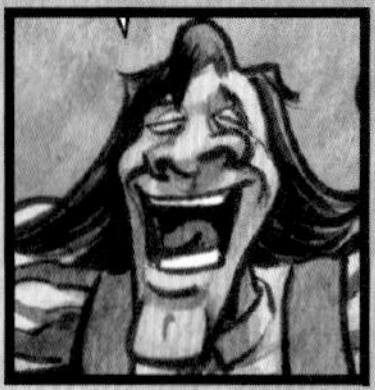

Fernando Pinto (page 67) has worked on TALES OF THE TMNT, HACK/SLASH,
POPGUN and URSA MINORS. You can find him nowadays working on his online
graphic novel called WARPED! at warpedcomic.wordpress.com and at his website
ernandopintoart.com. He'll like you if you're nice.

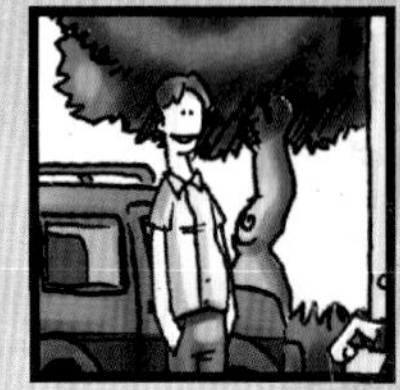

Whilce Portacio (page 30) became noted for his work on such Marvel titles as THE
PUNISHER, X-FACTOR, and THE UNCANNY X-MEN. In 1992, Portacio left Marvel to
co-found Image Comics with six other high-profile artists. Currently, he just wrapped up
a run on SPAWN and is working on IMAGE UNITED with those same high profile artists
rom 1992 and will be launching his own Image series from it called FORTRESS.

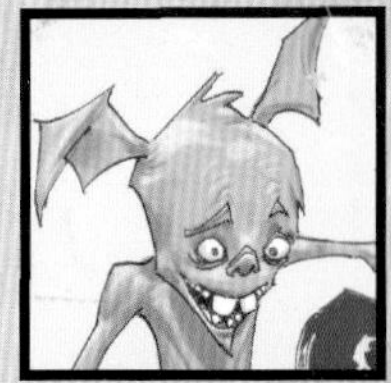

Jeremy R. Scott (page 106) is the graphic artist on THE LAVA IS A FLOOR from
Silverline Books, and also Silverline Books' first wordless picture book entitled PTA
NIGHT.

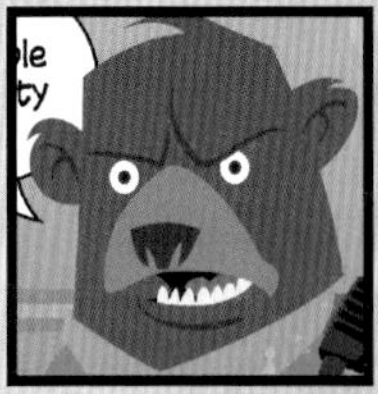

Kristen K. Simon (pages 24 and 109) has been the Editor for Shadowline and
Silverline Books since 2004, and has also authored two Silverline Books titles called
BRUCE THE LITTLE BLUE SPRUCE and TIFFANY'S EPIPHANY. She is also the
creator of ALL GIRL COMICS, and is the inspiration for the character "Editor Girl," who
appears frequently in Shadowline comics.

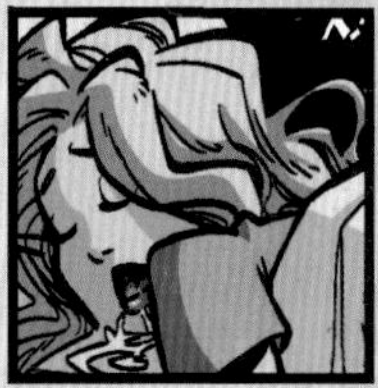

Nick Spencer (page148) is the writer of no less than four titles from Shadowline: The
critically acclaimed EXISTENCE 2.0 and EXISTENCE 3.0, FORGETLESS,
SHUDDERTOWN and the upcoming MORNING GLORIES.

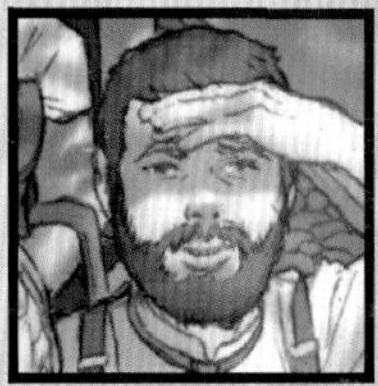

Len Strazewski (page 81) has been writing comics for more than 20 years and is best
known for JUSTICE SOCIETY OF AMERICA by DC Comics, PRIME by Malibu
Ultraverse/Marvel Comics and TERROR TOTS by Caliber Comics. He is presently
associate professor and acting chair of the Journalism Department at Columbia College
Chicago.

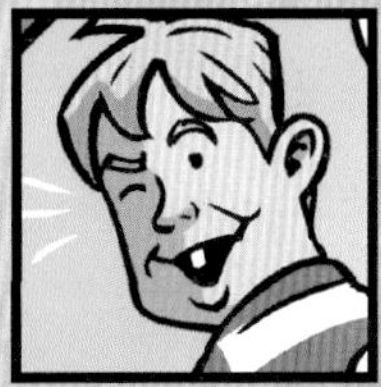

Bryan Talbot (page 16) has worked on stories for JUDGE DREDD, BATMAN,
HELLBLAZER, SANDMAN and FABLES and has written and drawn the graphic novels
THE ADVENTURES OF LUTHER ARKWRIGHT, HEART OF EMPIRE, THE TALE OF
ONE BAD RAT and ALICE IN SUNDERLAND. In 2009 he was awarded a Doctorate in
Arts. His new book is GRANDVILLE, a steampunk detective thriller.

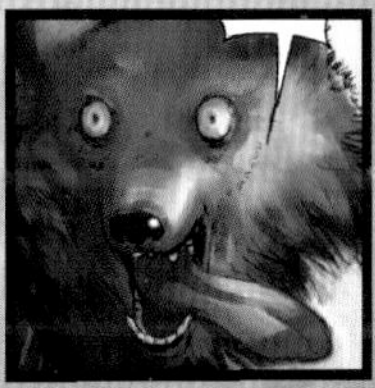

Laini Taylor (page 125) was a finalist for the National Book Award. She lives in
Portland, Oregon with husband, Jim DiBartolo and new daughter Clementine Pie. Her
novels for young people, DREAMDARK: BLACKBRINGER, DREAMDARK:
SILKSINGER, and LIPS TOUCH: THREE TIMES have garnered starred reviews from
Kirkus, Booklist and Publisher's Weekly.

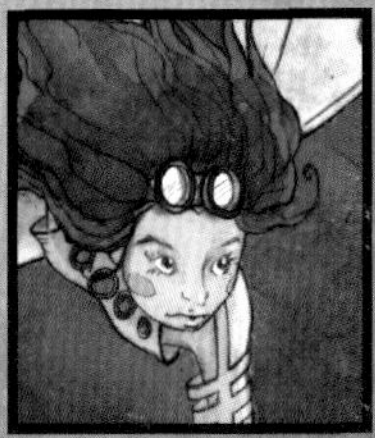

Ben Templesmith *(page 13)* is a New York Times best-selling artist and writer most widely known for his work in the American comic book industry where he has received multiple nominations for the International Horror Guild Awards as well as the industry's top prize, the Eisner Award. As a creator, his most notable works have been 30 DAYS OF NIGHT (which has now spawned a major motion picture) and FELL. Currently Ben is working on his creator-owned title CHOKER through Image Comics.

Doug TenNapel *(page 41)* In addition to creating EARTHWORM JIM, Doug is also known for his work on graphic novels such as FLINK, MONSTER ZOO, and POWER UP. TenNapel is also the lead singer of an independent band called Truck and is currently working on a Cartoon Network Original called PHIBIAN MIKE.

Jill Thompson *(page 98)* is the creator of the critically acclaimed and Eisner Award-winning children's book SCARY GODMOTHER and as a comic book artist has garnered acclaim and multiple awards for her work on WONDER WOMAN, SWAMP THING, BLACK ORCHID and the award-winning title SANDMAN with Neil Gaiman.

Aaron Valentino *(page 24)* has been telling stories all his life, creating his first character at age 5 for Marvel's GUARDIANS OF THE GALAXY. His contribution here marks his first collaboration with his father. He is currently writing and illustrating his first graphic novel, LOGINIS.

Jim Valentino *(page 24)* In his 30 year career, Jim has worked for nearly every comic company as a writer, artist or both. He has won several awards, is a co-founder of Image Comics and the President/founder of Silverline Books. Jim is best known for such diverse creations as normalman, SHADOWHAWK, and A TOUCH OF SILVER among others.

Joel Valentino *(page 129)* Heavily influenced by manga and Anime, Joel is a college student in Southern California where he studies Japanese. An artist since childhood, his contribution here represents his first professionally published work.

Christian Ward *(page 88)* is currently found in London, often sports a beard and partakes in drawing of mysterious femme fatales, psychedelic mind clouds and men in capes. He co-created OLYMPUS from Image Comics and enjoys splashing pixels and paint around liberally.

Shannon Wheeler *(page 26)* is the creator of TOO MUCH COFFEE MAN. He won an Eisner and wrote an opera. He produces a weekly cartoon ironically titled "HOW TO BE HAPPY." He's cartooned for the print version of the Onion and the New Yorker. One can find his most recent cartoons on www.tmcm.com and www.act-i-vate.com. He lives in Portland, OR on a volcano with his kids, cats and chickens.

Shane White *(page 38)* at heart is a storyteller who exists on the comic fringe meandering in and out of styles and subjects that both challenge and suit his eclectic tastes. Some of his works include: NORTH COUNTRY, THE OVERMAN, COMIC BOOK TATTOO and THINGS UNDONE.

Joshua Williamson *(page 93)* writes comics, kids books and lives in Portland, home of big trees, rain, Oni Press, Dark Horse and Shadowline. He has been published by Shadowline; his credits include OVERLOOK, JOHNNY MONSTER and the children's book DEAR DRACULA, published by Shadowline's younger readers imprint Silverline Books.